THE COLVINS AND
THEIR FRIENDS

OTHER WORKS BY E. V. LUCAS

ESSAYS

A Rover I Would Be
A Fronded Isle
Events and Embroideries
Zigzags in France
Encounters and Diversions
Luck of the Year
Giving and Receiving
A Boswell of Baghdad
'Twixt Eagle and Dove
The Phantom Journal
Loiterer's Harvest
Cloud and Silver
One Day and Another
Fireside and Sunshine
Character and Comedy
Old Lamps for New
Urbanities
Specially Selected
'The More I See of Men . . .'
Out of a Clear Sky

ANTHOLOGIES

The Joy of Life
The Open Road
The Friendly Town
Her Infinite Variety
Good Company
The Gentlest Art
The Second Post
The Charles Lamb Day-Book
Three Hundred and Sixty-five Days and One More

BIOGRAPHY AND ART CRITICISM

The Life of Charles Lamb
The Life and Work of E. A. Abbey
Vermeer the Magical
The British School
John Constable, the Painter
A Wanderer among Pictures

STORIES

Advisory Ben
Genevra's Money
Rose and Rose
Verena in the Midst
The Vermilion Box
Landmarks
Listener's Lure
Mr. Ingleside
London Lavender
Over Bemerton's

VERSE

'Mr. Punch's' County Songs

TRAVEL

E. V. Lucas's London
A Wanderer in London
London Revisited
A Wanderer in Paris
A Wanderer in Venice
A Wanderer in Holland
A Wanderer in Florence
A Wanderer in Rome
Highways and Byways in Sussex
Roving East and Roving West
Introducing London
Introducing Paris

EDITIONS

Masterful Wilhelmine
The Hambledon Men
The Book of the Queen's Dolls' House Library
The Pocket Edition of the Works of Charles Lamb: I. Miscellaneous Prose; II. Elia; III. Children's Books; IV. Poems and Plays; V. and VI. Letters

DRAMA

The Same Star

FOR CHILDREN

Playtime & Company
A Book of Verses for Children
Another Book of Verses for Children
Three Hundred Games and Pastimes
Anne's Terrible Good Nature
The Slowcoach

Sir Sidney Colvin, 1921

THE COLVINS AND THEIR FRIENDS

BY

E. V. LUCAS

WITH A FRONTISPIECE IN PHOTOGRAVURE
AND TWENTY-FIVE OTHER ILLUSTRATIONS

SECOND EDITION

METHUEN & CO. LTD.
36 ESSEX STREET W.C.
LONDON

First Published . . October 18th 1928
Second Edition . . ` 1928

PRINTED IN GREAT BRITAIN

PREFACE

THIS book is the outcome of a wish expressed by the late Sir Sidney Colvin, both in conversation and in written words in his Will, that, if I thought the material warranted it, a record of his own and Lady Colvin's friendships should be published. To this end he had preserved and carefully arranged a large number of letters, and it is my choice among that correspondence which forms the principal part of the following pages. With these I have merged, by kind permission of Mr. Edward Arnold, many autobiographical passages from Colvin's *Memories and Notes*, 1921, together with other material gathered from his many miscellaneous articles and prefaces.

As my own knowledge of the Colvins covered a period of little more than twenty years, in only half of which can I claim to have been on terms of intimacy, I have had to lean much upon the testimony of others, chiefly Mrs. W. K. Clifford, Sir Martin Conway, Mr. Basil Champneys, and Mr. Laurence Binyon, to each of whom I am deeply indebted. I have also to thank Mr. Hugh Walpole for the character sketch which he wrote for this book; the literary executors of Joseph Conrad, Thomas Hardy, W. E. Henley, Henry James, Andrew Lang, and others, and all the writers of letters, who have allowed me to print from their correspondence; in particular naming Mr. Lloyd Osbourne, but for whose ready and generous acquiescence the book would be a much less living thing. For Commander Oliver

Locker-Lampson, M.P.'s permission to use articles in the *Empire Review* I am also grateful, and to the trustees of the Advocates' Library in Edinburgh, now the owners of the early Stevenson letters to Mrs. Sitwell.

In addition to the letters which Colvin preserved with the idea that they might some day be published wholly or in part, he had from time to time given examples to the collection of autographs in the Fitzwilliam Museum at Cambridge, of which he was for some years Director. From such of these as have not already been published, either in Colvin's *Memories and Notes* or in the biographies of their writers, I have, by kind permission of the present Director, Mr. Sydney Cockerell, taken extracts, while several are printed in full.

E. V. L.

June, 1928

CONTENTS

LIST OF ILLUSTRATIONS

THE COLVINS AND
THEIR FRIENDS

CHAPTER I

BOYHOOD AND CAMBRIDGE

1845–1866

SIDNEY COLVIN was born at Norwood on June 18, 1845. His father was Bassett David Colvin of The Grove, Little Bealings, in Suffolk. Since I have no first-hand knowledge of those distant days and there are no surviving contemporaries, I quote Colvin's own account of his family, boyhood and surroundings from *Memories and Notes*.

' The older one grows—I believe the observation is trite, and in my case it is certainly true—the more vividly does the mind become haunted by its earliest experiences, by memories of what one suffered and enjoyed and imagined and did or longed to do as a child and boy. My mother had a horror of schools for her sons, partly founded, I think, for she was a good deal of a reader, on the notions she had gathered from Cowper's *Tirocinium*. My dear lovable compliant father tenderly humoured her in all things ; and so the three of us, of whom I was by several years the youngest, were brought up under tutors at home. By all that I could ever learn, there was nothing much likeable or promising about me whether as boy or hobbledehoy ; certainly nothing in the eyes of the girl-cousins (we had no sisters), who tried with little success to teach me dancing and generally put a polish on me. But at least I was dead keen always on whatever I was about, although extremely shy and secret in regard to the things I most cared for. The home was a country-house three miles from Woodbridge in East Suffolk, with five hundred acres of land and more of shooting attached. My father loved the place. Most of

A

his days were spent in the conduct of his business as partner in a leading London firm of East India merchants, but in the intervals he could spare for home his chief refreshment was to stroll in his gardens or over his acres, or ride on his big bay gelding, Prince, about the country lanes or in and out of Woodbridge on his duties as a magistrate.

'Either as merchants or civil servants my people on both sides of the house had been connected with India for several generations.   My mother's father, William Butterworth Bayley, whom I remember as a commanding and withal humorous grand gentleman of the old school, wearing a high black stock and swallow-tail coat, had been acting governor-general in the interval between Lord Amherst and Lord William Bentinck, and for many years after his return was chairman of the board of directors of the old East India Company.   My father's next younger brother, John, was in my boyish days lieutenant-governor of the North-West Provinces.   When the Mutiny came and threatened ruin to our *ràj* and all connected with it, I well remember how my father's home and country interests were the sole things which enabled the dear man at moments to forget his cares—" my most cruel cares," as I can still after these sixty and odd years hear his agonized voice one day calling them.   Cruel indeed they were, including besides the prospect of public calamity and private ruin the intensest personal anxieties for beloved kinsfolk exposed to the horrors of the time.   Sometimes the strain would end in relief, as in the case of my cousin James Colvin, cooped up almost without stores in a hurriedly half-fortified bungalow at Arrah, with seven or eight English and fifty-odd faithful Sikhs, by a whole horde of Sepoy mutineers well armed and provided.   "There is much in common," writes Sir George Trevelyan, "between Leonidas dressing his hair before he went forth to his last fight, and young Colvin laughing over his rice and salt, while the bullets spattered on the wall like hail."   Relief came to this small garrison almost at the last gasp ; but more often the issue was tragic. A brilliant young sister of my mother's, being with child at the time, was forced to ride for her life the fifty miles from Shahjehanpore to Bareilly, and never got over it. Most harrowing of all, my aforesaid uncle John Colvin, in his seat of government at Agra, had to bear more than almost any other among the great civil servants of the stress and burden of the time, and died of his task before the final issue was made sure. He and my father had been brought up at St. Andrews together and were devotedly attached; John was the younger but much the stronger of the two, and again I can hear my father calling to mind aloud in his grief, how if any other youngster was bad to him, "John would always knock him down—always knock him down."

' My father's love of our country home was not shared by my mother. She had imbibed from the writings of Ruskin, whom she knew and idolized, an idea that hill or mountain majesty was a necessary feature of landscape beauty, and a consequent contempt for such quiet lowland scenery as that about our home. To make up for what she held its poverty, she lavished care and money on the beautifying of the grounds and gardens, matters which appealed also to my father, so that for their relatively small scale they came to be among the most admired in that country-side. She insisted also on a three or four months' annual change for the whole household, generally to some hired house in London or its outskirts, occasionally to Devonshire. I do not think either of my parents at all realized, readers though they were, the literary interests and associations which attached to our neighbouring country and coast. Certainly I was in youth never made to realize them. To my mother I cannot be grateful enough for one thing: she set me reading *Rob Roy* aloud to her when I was eight years old; the other Waverleys followed; and subsequent years have only deepened and confirmed my delight in the imaginary world of which I was thus early made free. It used to be a foolish habit among superfine and ultra-modern critics, during part of my life, to pooh-pooh Walter Scott as no artist, and admiration of him as an obsolete fashion. It is a joy in my old age to see him coming, among the wiser even of the youngest, to be fully acknowledged for what he was, that is, easily the second greatest creator in our language since Shakespeare, and for all his careless ways and long-winded openings an instinctive artist, in crucial scenes and moments unsurpassed.

' Going back upon my own boyish cares and pre-occupations, I recall in them an odd mixture of the civilized and the barbarous. To the passion for Scott there presently, before I was fifteen, succeeded a passion for Spenser. Entirely for myself and without direction, I had discovered the *Faery Queene* in my father's library, and insatiably devoured and set about doing my best to imitate it. Not for the world would I have let any one into the secret of my absurd attempts and ambitions, but on summer mornings not long after dawn, must needs clamber down from my bedroom window, and go off to the stable-shed beyond the home paddocks, where a beloved little Arab mare was housed, the gift to me of an old East-Indian general, my godfather, and in her company alone, nursing her muzzle the while, sit and spin out of my head the stanzas of my poem. The theme, if I remember aright, was one of mythical ancient British history taken from Spenser himself. But other and, for aught I can remember, alternate mornings were spent not less eagerly in visiting, long before the dew was off the grass, the night-lines I had laid the evening before in the pools of one or the other of our two near brooks to catch the big silver-bellied eels : lines barbarously baited, for the prey would take no other lure, with the unfledged young of hedgerow birds stolen from the nest. A certain bandy-legged stable-help, I remember, was my confidant and instigator in these and divers baser kinds of sport, among them rat-hunting with a thorough-bred little Dandie Dinmont terrier bitch who shared her affections equally between him and me. In other and more avowable pastimes

THE GROVE, BEALINGS

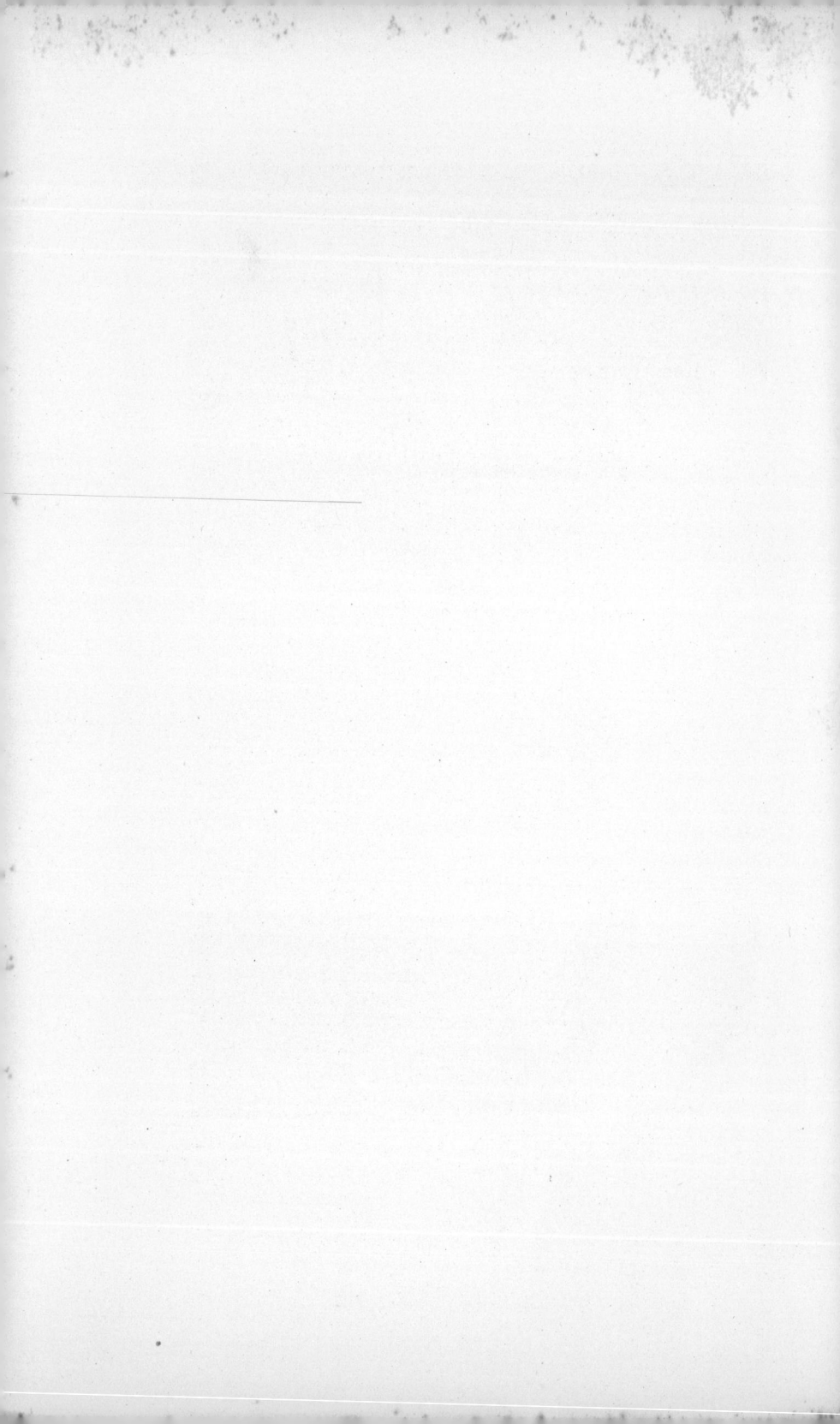

I suppose a little later, I was equally keen, as in captaining
a village team of cricketers, or tramping the turnips after
partridges, or standing waiting for rocketing pheasants kept
by a neighbouring captain of militia, who, fine sportsman
as he was and looked on his gallant roan Silverlocks, had a
somewhat ungrateful task in what was essentially not a
hunting but a shooting country. A clumsy horseman and
an indifferent shot, nothing could exceed the zest with
which I pursued these commonplace country sports, unless
it were that with which in the same years (say from twelve
to seventeen) I used to devour my Scott and Shakespeare,
and *Faery Queene* and *Modern Painters* and *Stones of Venice*
. . . and learn long screeds of them, both verse and prose,
by heart. These relatively high-flown literary tastes did
not at all debar me from delighting in Marryat and Mayne
Reid and Fenimore Cooper, and planning for myself under
their inspiration futures of the wildest adventure.

'In the same years I was getting some formal education
under an elderly tutor, who neither by age nor disposition
was any sort of friend or companion. But he must have
been as capable as he was remarkable for his dyed whiskers
and corpulent figure and choleric temper ; seeing that when
the time came for going to Cambridge I found to my surprise
that I was as well on almost in the classics as picked lads
from the public schools, and in modern languages much
better.'

In due course Colvin passed on to Cambridge, to Trinity,
taking with him not only a considerable store of classical
learning, but a passion for the writings and personality of
Ruskin. 'From very tender years,' he writes in *Memories
and Notes*, 'I used to be taken from time to time to visit
the Ruskins in their family abode on Denmark Hill. But
from these earliest days I retain less recollection of the great
man himself than of his mother. Stern old Calvinist as she
was, and more than Spartan as had been her upbringing of
her own son, she chose to make something of a pet of me. I
have now before me a copy, with its shiny yellow boards all

rubbed and dingy, of her son's tale for children, *The King of the Golden River*, with Richard Doyle's illustrations, which she gave me in 1852, when I was just short of seven years old, and which my governess helped me to adorn on the back of the frontispiece with a grateful inscription, set in an ornamental border of crimson lake and cobalt. A little later, I remember—at least I hope it was a little later —she used to regale me on each visit with a glass of fine sherry (the house of Ruskin, Telfer and Domecq were great sherry merchants) and a slice of plum cake. It was not until my ninth year that I was taken with my two elder brothers expressly to see the great man himself and be admitted to his own room.

' He received us raw boys with extraordinary kindness, and one thing, I remember, instantaneously delighted us. This was a scene between him and his white Spitz terrier Wisie (I think there is mention of Wisie somewhere in *Praeterita*). The dog burst into the drawing-room just after we had arrived, and not having seen his master for some time leapt and capered and yelped and fumed about and over him as he sat, with a passion, almost a frenzy, of pent-up affection, and was caressed with little less eagerness in return. Ruskin then took us up to his working-room, and by way of giving us a practical drawing-lesson, made before our eyes a sketch in body-colours of one corner of the room, with its curtain, wall-paper and furniture—all of them of a type which to the altered taste of the next generation would have seemed too Philistine and early Victorian to be endured. For very many years I had that sketch by me, but fear that in one or another of my various changes of domicile it has now got lost beyond recovery. During the next few years such visits and lessons were several times repeated. But the Turners on the walls and their owner's kind endeavours to interest me in them used still, I fear, to make less impression upon me than the slice of cake and glass of sherry with which the old lady never failed to regale me.

'This for the first four or five years; but before I was
fifteen I had become intensely sensitive both to the magnet-
ism of Ruskin's personality and to the power and beauty
of his writings. No man had about him more—few can
ever have had so much—of the atmosphere and effluence of
genius, and when he came into the room I used consciously
to thrill to his presence. In those years, a little before and
after the fortieth of his age, he was elegant after the fashion
of his time, as well as impressive in a fashion all his own.
There remains with me quite unfaded the image of his
slender, slightly stooping figure clad in the invariable dark
blue frock coat and bright blue neck-tie; of his small head
with its strongly marked features, its sweep of thick brown
hair and closely trimmed side-whiskers; above all, of the
singular bitter-sweet expression of his mouth (due partly,
as I have always understood, to the vestiges of a scar left
on the upper lip by a dog's bite in boyhood) and of the
intense weight and penetration of his glance as he fixed his
deep blue eyes upon yours from under the thick bushy
prominence of his eyebrows (these were an inheritance from
his father, who had them shaggier and longer than I have
seen on any other man). The warmth and almost caressing courtesy of his welcome were as captivating as its
manner was personal : in shaking hands he would raise the
forearm from the elbow, which he kept close to his side,
and bringing the hand down with a full sweep upon yours
would hold you firmly clasped until greetings were over
and talk, which generally turned immediately to teaching,
began.

'To such teaching, when it was addressed to myself, I
could naturally, at my age, only listen in adoring acquiescence. But what I loved better still was to be allowed, as
occasionally happened, to sit by while he let himself go in
the company of some friend who could meet and draw him
out on equal terms. It was not very often that I saw him,
since my people spent the greater part of each year in our
country home in Suffolk; but for two or three years he was

hardly ever out of my thoughts, except during the hours when they were quite engrossed by those rough outdoor sports of hare-hunting, pheasant-shooting, village cricket and the like, of which I have already spoken. The fifth volume of *Modern Painters*, which appeared when I was in my sixteenth year, was a gospel which for a while I pored over incessantly, and held incomparable for insight and wisdom and eloquence ; and by it I was led to an equally passionate study of the *Seven Lamps*, the *Stones of Venice*, and the rest of the early works on art.'

'I believe,' said Colvin, in his speech at the banquet given to him on his retirement from the British Museum in 1912, ' I believe I cherished about this time the swollen idea that I might become something like a Ruskin and a Matthew Arnold rolled into one—Ruskin, the idol of my boyhood, Arnold, a great stimulus of my undergraduate days : only a Ruskin, so I fondly thought, without his extravagances and lack of balance and an Arnold without his superior airs and graces : as though the twists or flaws of genius were not ever vitally inwoven with its strength, or as though a balanced Ruskin or an unsuperior Arnold were a thinkable being.'

In the tripos Colvin was placed next to Sir Frederick Pollock. He won the Chancellor's Gold Medal for a poem on Florence, which I have not seen ; nor among all his papers do I find a line of verse—with one exception, to which we shall come later.

To Mr. Basil Champneys, now [1928] in his eighty-seventh year, I am indebted for some reminiscences of Colvin as an undergraduate and in his early London days. ' My acquaintance with Sidney Colvin,' Mr. Champneys writes, ' dates from 1861, and as I was with him shortly before his death in 1927, I can reckon sixty-six years of friendship. An elder brother of his was my contemporary at Trinity, Cambridge, and introduced me to his family circle. They invited me to Little Bealings, Sidney Colvin's early home, about which I have pleasant recollections—of a quiet

SIR SIDNEY COLVIN'S MOTHER

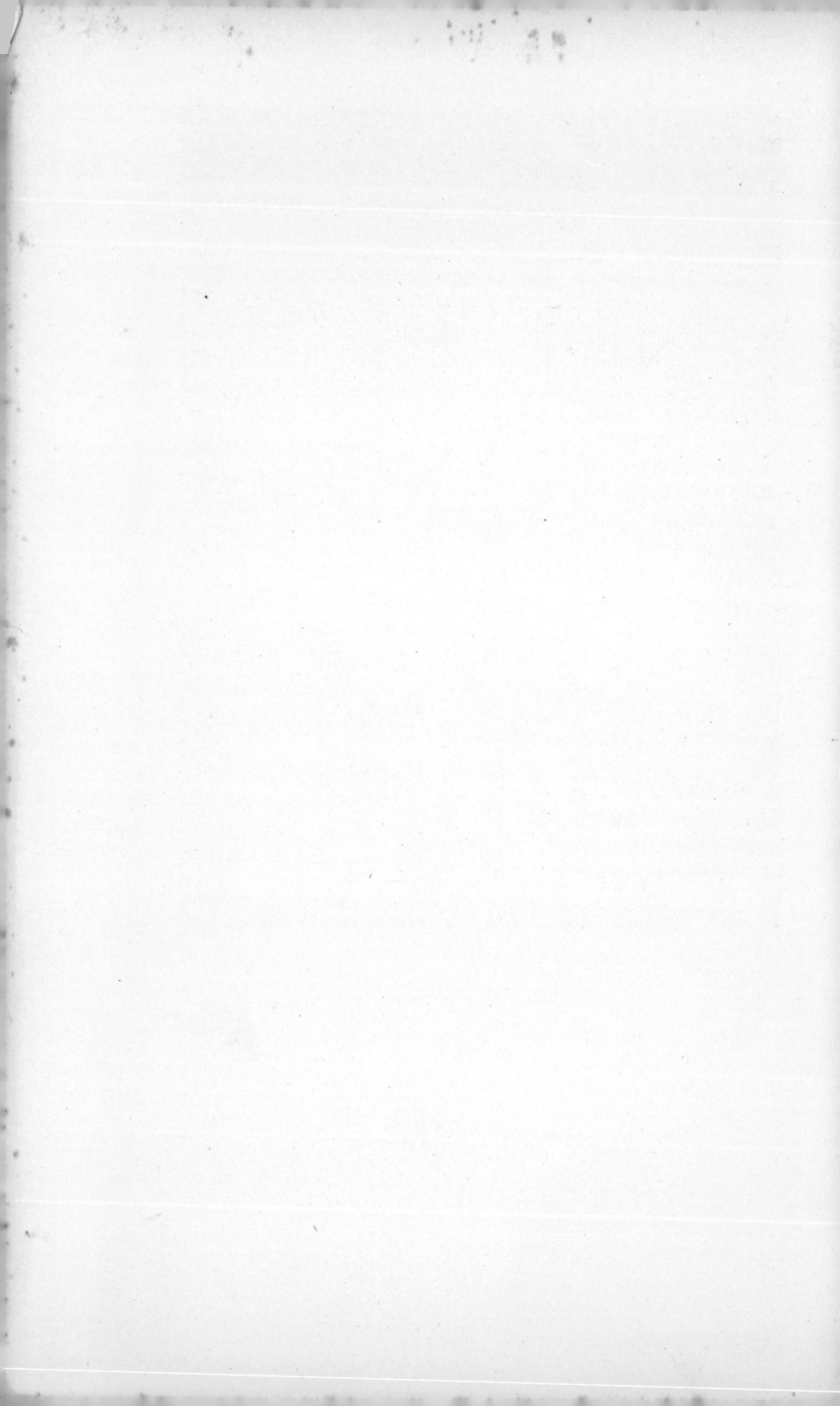

country life, diversified by long drives to interesting scenes
and places, and occasional runs with the local harriers. (It
is worth noting by those who knew Sidney Colvin only as a
sedentary student that he was an accomplished rider.) I
was a frequent guest at Little Bealings for the next year
or two, and in 1863 Sidney Colvin came up to Trinity, where
I was entering on my fourth year. I was able, during the
few months for which we were together, to introduce him
to some of my seniors and contemporaries, and specially
recall a dinner in my rooms at which he was present, with
H. Sidgwick, already a Fellow, J. H. Swainson, afterwards
a Fellow, and John Burnell Pain, who later was a fellow-
contributor with Sidney Colvin to the *Pall Mall Gazette*,
then edited by John Morley; and doubtless there were
others whose names I have forgotten.'

Later in the same speech from which I have already
quoted, Colvin spoke thus felicitously of some of the great
Cambridge luminaries of his time : ' Of Henry Sidgwick
the philosopher, with his almost over-subtly posed im-
partiality of wisdom, his helpfulness, his smile, exquisitely
kind even in irony, his hesitating speech that was happier
than eloquence : of Jebb, the incomparable Hellenist, in
whose character firm authority and sagacity, and the most
engaging vein of playfulness among his intimates, were
interwoven with a strain of sensitiveness almost too acute
for the uses of life : of that gracious, capricious, provoking,
but to some of us infinitely attaching and attractive lover
of art, Italy, and beauty, George Howard, with whose death
last year [1911] a great piece of my own early life seems to
have been broken away : of Felix Cobbold, scholar, banker,
humorist, sentimentalist, politician, and prince of country-
house hosts, whose guests we shall never be again in that
ideal library and garden of his on the Suffolk shore : of
Henry Butcher, Jebb's all but equal in scholarship, the
ablest of teachers and administrators, the most charming
and most chivalrous of Irish gentlemen : of Verrall, the
flame of whose intellect, unextinguishable by bodily pain

and disablement, cast to the end so vivid, so wayward, so
stimulating an illumination on so many matters of literature and learning.'

Colvin returned to early Cambridge names in the
dedication of *Memories and Notes* to his wife in 1921. He
would have liked, he says, to have written about other personalities no longer living : ' such as those two successive
masters and stately figure-heads of my own college in my
early days, Whewell and Thompson ; such as the famous
classical coach Shilleto, whom I can still see in my mind's
eye, at his table littered with snuff-boxes and bandana
handkerchiefs—still hear while he pounds into my sense
the stiffest meanings of Thucydides ; or such again as
J. W. Clark, equally keen and accomplished in the pursuits
of natural history and architectural history and amateur
stage-craft ; or those two fine contrasted types of classical
scholar and public orator, W. G. Clark, the most frankly
urbane and straightforwardly courteous of men, and Jebb,
probably the most faultless Grecian of them all, . . . whose
tensely strung nature and ever-tingling nerves did not
prevent him from being a successful man of the world and
fine representative of his university in Parliament.'

It is odd that neither in the speech nor the dedication was
there any mention of Aldis Wright, who to many visitors
to Cambridge, myself included, stood for Trinity, even more
than the urbane Master himself. When however Aldis Wright
died, full of years, in 1914, Colvin wrote for the *Journal of
Philology* a little ' Personal Appreciation,' which ran thus :
' It is just half a century since, as an undergraduate of
Trinity, I began to take in the successive volumes of the
great Cambridge Shakespeare edited by W. G. Clark in
association (after the first volume) with the vigorous scholar
whose loss we have had lately to deplore, William Aldis
Wright. Clark was then a tutor of the College, the most
accomplished and urbane of dons and men, whose word of
encouragement or admonition to an undergraduate of a
literary turn was a thing prized beyond gold. With him,

though I was not his pupil, I had had before my degree the good luck to come more than once into admiring contact. But his colleague in the Shakespeare work (and afterwards in the editorship of this Journal), Aldis Wright, was in those days a much more secluded personage, and to the average undergraduate even unknown. Once on the foundation, indeed, one could scarcely fail to come in contact with him in his capacity of College librarian ; and to consult him was to learn how much zeal in labour and promptness in help could go together with how strict a reserve and brevity in manner and accost.

'From that day until all but yesterday, Aldis Wright stood in my mind, as in the minds of so many of us, as a typical, established, abiding personality in the college life, a personality that was in itself an institution. Probably this impression may have been strongest on those who, like myself, have held a variable relation to that life, for considerable periods intimate, and then, through pressure of circumstance, for longer periods much more detached and casual than we should have wished. For whatever stay, prolonged or fleeting, we might come back, there for a certainty would be Aldis Wright ; physically, after he once turned iron-grey, more unchanging than almost any man, filling with exact diligence for a quarter of a century the office of senior bursar, for twenty-six years exercising a courteous hospitality as Vice-Master, and working all the while, we knew, with unshakable tenacity of toil at a surprising diversity of subjects. There was something about his bodily presence that accurately bespoke and corresponded to the character of his mind ; something set, austerely square-cut and vigorously compact, with a manner plain and self-sufficing which invited no intimacy. But his austerity was largely on the surface, and even on the surface was largely tempered with humour : humour grim and sardonic enough, no doubt, in dealing with anything that struck him as cant or flummery or affectation, but very kindly towards those who moved him to liking or respect. The square and

solid sense of fun that was in him was seen at its best, I have
been told and can well believe, in contrast with and enjoyment of the whimsicality and charm of a humorist of a
much airier type, the late Canon Ainger.

' Of whole fields of Wright's work in criticism and research
I have no capacity to speak. But all of us who love letters
can in some measure discern and appreciate the qualities of
rigid exactness and common sense, the steadfastness of
true zeal and scorn of gush or pretension, which mark and
render invaluable his work on the text of Shakespeare and
Milton, on Bacon, and in the preparation of the great
edition of Burton which he did not live to complete. Grateful, too, we can and should all be for the sympathy which
attached this man of few intimacies in bonds of almost
filial affection to a spirit of a stamp most dissimilar to his
own—a brother East-Anglian, it is true, but an East-
Anglian of Irish blood and name—I mean of course Edward
FitzGerald. As a Suffolk-bred boy myself, I was used constantly to encounter and, I fear, unknowing all he was,
inwardly to deride that eccentric, ineffectual recluse of
genius (remember his own name for himself, Ballyblunder),
as he strolled or rather vaguely drifted, an odd, rumpled,
melancholy-looking figure in grey plaid, green eye-shade,
and shabby back-tilted hat, along the lanes and highways
of the Woodbridge neighbourhood. Certainly no greater
apparent contrast could have been found than between him
and that model of purposeful and business-like efficiency in
life and learning, Aldis Wright, in whom he found so serviceable a friend and so faithful an editor.'

CHAPTER II

LONDON, ART CRITICISM AND ART TEACHING

1869–1873

On leaving Cambridge Colvin settled in London to devote himself to the study of the Fine Arts, ancient and modern, theoretical and practical. He also did whatever art criticisms and reviewing came his way, for the *Pall Mall Gazette* and the *Globe*, and quickly carried enough weight to be allowed by John Morley, in 1867, to sum up the state of English painting in that year for the readers of the *Fortnightly Review*. This is the earliest article that I can find, and it is interesting in reading it to see how true to his youthful creed the writer remained to the end. He had not changed his gods sixty years later. His belief, which his own special poet, Keats, had more than once enunciated, was always that beauty is truth and that the artist's only concern is to pursue and capture it. The most promising hope for English painting in 1867 he found in the work of Albert Moore, Rossetti, Burne Jones, Watts, Arthur Hughes, and George Mason.

I quote a passage on Whistler : ' Mr. Whistler is another artist who aims at beauty without realism. No artist's works more completely mystify the average spectator than his. Everyone can perceive his neglect of form, his contempt of executive finish, the apparently slurring method by which he achieves exactly as much as he wishes, and attempts no more ; but not everyone can perceive in what his real strength lies, his perfect mastery of the *rapports* of tone, and of what Mr. Rossetti calls the " delicate aberrances and intricate haphazards of colour." These, and these

13

alone, are what he attempts to seize, whether in his grey and brown studies of shore and harbour or his brilliant and harmonious compositions of Japanese decorative colour.   That these are artistic successes after their kind is undeniable ; but it may fairly be urged that as pictures, as idealisations of fact, they lose value by their exclusiveness of aim and one-sidedness of treatment.'

Colvin's first publication appeared in 1869 through the house of Macmillan, which in 1917 was to issue his large book on Keats.   The publication was only a pamphlet containing Colvin's notes, printed first in the *Globe*, on the chief exhibitors at the Royal Academy and the old Water-Colour Society, and now extended.   His favourite painters at Burlington House were Millais, George Mason, Frederick Walker, Albert Moore, and Legros.   Among the artists in water-colour only one really fired him : Edward Burne-Jones, or Mr. E. B. Jones, as he figured in the catalogue.

Among the exhibitors at the Royal Academy Colvin was best pleased by Albert Moore, and wrote thus : ' *The Quartett : a Painter's Tribute to the Art of Music.* " Le goût des anciens," wrote M. Villemain, " est une sympathie, une disposition de l'âme, bien plus qu'il n'est une érudition, une doctrine."   Mr. A. Moore, I think, possesses, above any other artist of our time, an inborn Greekness ; he possesses this sympathy, this disposition of the soul, this affinity with the ancients that comes by nature and not by learning.   His work does really breathe some of the spirit of the great Greek times.   In the drawing of the human body he can rise through the subtlest accuracy into the most ideal beauty.   He can design his figures with a large grace and a pure nobility, and can group them on his canvas in lovely and harmonious relations with one another.'

When some years later Colvin gave W. E. Henley an introduction to Albert Moore, for an interview, ' You will find,' he wrote, ' a person resembling in looks and manner a dissipated beau of the working classes ; but a very interesting artist.'

I quote also the *Globe* note on Frederick Walker : ' *The Old Gate*. Mr. Walker shares with Mr. Mason the gift of making every-day modern folks look artistically beautiful. We said that Mr. Mason's girls were beautiful in the same sense as any Oread or Bacchant might be beautiful ; and similarly this navvy with the pipe might be likened to an athlete or an Apollo. This sounds like hyperbole, but the true test of artistic affinities is the quality of the emotion produced in the spectator ; and, judged by this test, a scrap of a boy or girl by Mr. Walker comes nearer, in its humble way, to the ideal of Pheidias or Raphael than many an academic piece in the great style by painters bent upon the sublime. To have effected this is to have solved perhaps the chief problem of modern art.'

Later in 1869 Colvin seems to have gone over to the *Pall Mall Gazette*, then edited by Frederick Greenwood, his first considerable task being to pass in review the Old Masters assembled at Burlington House in January of 1870. These critical notes he again revised for private circulation. I am tempted, as illustrating the precision and distinction of his style even at that time, and the catholicity of his interests, to quote certain of his remarks on the Dutch painters, on Velasquez, and on Reynolds and Gainsborough.

Here are the Dutch : ' The Marquis of *Bute* contributes a large and admirable *Cuyp*, showing us a scene upon the *Maas*—of course a scene of diffused summer light and calm water.   In speaking of *Rembrandt*, I alluded to his vehement Landscape as being of the generalized and pre-scientific kind ; and, in speaking of this other and serene class of *Dutch* Landscape, we must bear the same epithets in mind. There were plenty of things even in the monotonous Nature about them which these *Dutchmen* did not, could not, or would not see.   They had not a fine eye for the geological conformation of the ground, nor for the botanical character of trees and plants, nor for the fine distinctions of things in general ; they were not very keenly alive to any beauty of form, to any impression of Dignity or Grandeur.   But they could take in the effect of warm and sleepy summer afternoons full of faint mist and steeped in quiet light; they could abstract from the Nature in which they lived all phænomena disturbing to this effect, and reproduce the effect so left quite honestly and almost perfectly both to the eye and the imagination. Thus, in making truly an appeal (such as it is) to the imagination, in recalling and reviving a certain class of Landscape pleasures, imperfect Pictures like these still properly fulfil the proper end of Pictures. . . . A modern *English* Artist might see much more beauty in a cow than *Paul Potter* has seen, and much more also in sunlighted grass and willows; he might draw them more accurately and paint them more truthfully; but he would not succeed in subduing and fusing them so simply into this pleasant musical unity, that makes its humble appeal to the imagination quite successfully, and, in so far as it goes, is a true Picture, having in it that which is the essence of Fine Art.'

Of the Spaniard : ' To describe or analyse the excellence of *Velasquez'* work is in truth impossible. What is it except an indescribable and indecipherable instinct obeyed, as we have said, by the hand of a technical Magician, that can make such an amazing effect of air, life, and colour with the red walls and buildings of this court-yard, the black-dressed attendants, the horse, and the Boy with his hat and feather? So again, in the case of the well-known sketch "Las Meniñas," lent by *Mrs. Bankes*. Here we have an almost absolute truth of interior colour, light, space, and an equally striking truth and naturalness of portrait suggestion, attained by means that defy detection or imitation. Could any Realist, no matter how laborious, approach the utter reality of the large canvas and easel, as seen from behind in this sketch; or could any Portrait-painter get more of character and dignity into his most finished work than *Velasquez* has got into this rough indication of himself ? '

And finally Sir Joshua and his great rival: ' Beside the inexhaustible variety and never-swerving *franchise* of

Reynolds, Gainsborough seems to me a little artificial, a little monotonous in his habit of reducing the faces of all his sitters towards a certain type—a certain refined convention, as I have said, in expression and character. There are certain dimplings about the corners of the mouth, expressive of urbane vivacity and arch sweetness, which all *Gainsborough's* subjects possess with remarkable uniformity—delicate tricks and artifices of a Master of Genius, which seem to have prepared the way for the coarser artifices of a Master without Genius, to have been the first step towards that mechanical, fictitious, and afflicting character of " honeyed blandness mingled with alert intelligence," which *George Eliot* has somewhere so justly signalized in the Portraits most popular with the generation next after *Gainsborough*—the Portraits of Sir *Thomas Lawrence.*'— There is some very good writing here, when the author was only twenty-four ; nor did he better it : he began almost fully armed. Indeed, he seems always to have had all the requirements of what Matthew Arnold called a ' serviceable prose style,' and never failed to add to them dignity and a sense of responsibility for every word.

To this chapter it is convenient to add a few further examples of Colvin's early art criticism, although they are not strictly chronological. In 1871 he was a contributor to a miscellany entitled *English Painters of the Present Day*, published by Seeley, Jackson and Halliday. Colvin wrote upon Poynter (who in 1897 was to paint his portrait), Burne-Jones, Simeon Solomon, Frederick Walker and Ford Madox Brown. A second series appeared in 1872, when Colvin dealt with Millais, George Mason, Thomas Armstrong and G. H. Boughton, the American. I quote a little : ' And so Mr. Millais goes on, and will go on—a strong, insular, independent genius, working by the light of his nature ; alternately, and with unaccountable vicissitudes, delighting or dismaying us, but always exciting and arousing ; with his manual power confirmed into a gift more unapproachable than ever, but put forth, it seems, only

B

with caprice, and as he chooses ; when and where he chooses
achieving no less than miracles ; and only falling short,
as to the material part of his art, in that last gift by which
the matter of painting, over and above all miracle of imitation, is refined, modified, modulated, into the rhythmic
and sonorous harmony by which art at its highest can
soothe and exalt the innermost places of the imagination.'

In 1871 Colvin was contributing regularly and with
weight to the *Portfolio*, a new artistic periodical founded by
Philip Gilbert Hamerton, and it was no doubt the position
which he was taking as an arbiter of taste which procured
him, in that year, his election to the Society of Dilettanti,
of which from 1891 to 1896 he was to be honorary secretary.
His friend George Howard, afterwards Earl of Carlisle,
was elected in the same year. When the *History of the
Society of Dilettanti* came to be prepared for private circulation in 1914, it was compiled by Mr. Lionel Cust and edited
by Colvin. The society can trace its existence informally
as far back as 1732 and formally to 1736, when its member-
ship was forty-six. Its ruling spirit at that time was Sir
Francis Dashwood, afterwards Lord le Despencer. In
Colvin's words, ' the history to be narrated in the following
chapters is that of a small private society of gentlemen
which for more than a century and a half has exercised an
active influence in matters connected with public taste
and the fine arts in this country, and whose enterprise in the
special field of classical excavation and research has earned
the grateful recognition of scholars and the cultivated
public throughout Europe. There may be persons, outside
the limited circle of its members, who will feel some surprise
on learning that such a society exists ; that it was founded
in the early years of the reign of George II. ; and has
maintained its existence with an unbroken record up to
the present day. This fact is the more remarkable, since,
although the Royal Society and the Society of Antiquaries
are actually older in point of date, the Society of Dilettanti
was not formed, as these were, with any definite intention

BASSETT DAVID COLVIN
FATHER OF SIR SIDNEY COLVIN

of promoting the cause of either science or art, but simply, in the first instance, for the purposes of social and convivial intercourse.'

The presiding Dilettante when Colvin was elected was Charles Newton, afterwards Sir Charles, of the British Museum, of whom we are to see more as this record advances. Colvin resigned in 1896, and in 1897 his portrait by Poynter was added to the Society's collection, now preserved in the St. James's Club. It is not good.

In November 1871 Colvin's father died, and was buried in Little Bealings churchyard. I find Lady Carlisle writing thus, after the bereavement : ' I feel sure that your father's death will have harrowed you fearfully, and I know what it is to watch the long agonizing approach of death. . . . It is very awful to watch this—and I am sure you are much worn out—but you have the gift from your great tenderness of heart of being able to soothe and comfort—and I know you must have been everything to your father and very very much now to all those whom you love and to whom you know so well how to give sympathy and thoughtful tenderness.

' I am glad dear Mrs. Sitwell [the earliest reference to this lady] is well—It will seem strange to you that the look and mood of her's I like best to recall is her merry and *loving* laugh—She does not seem one of those persons made to be sad or morbid—and there is a rare charm about her joyousness which must make it all the more terrible for those who love her to see her clouded life—Ramsgate must be very odious—but if she only keeps well I suppose you will be satisfied—I cannot tell you how sorry I am you are not coming to us, nor how eagerly we have looked for a letter from you saying " I am coming "—everything is beautiful as ever in this glorious Italy.'

From Lady Carlisle, to Colvin, in August 1872 : ' I cannot bear to think of your losing that lovely home of your's—for one clings so passionately to one's country home and you and yr. father had cared for it so much—I know it must have been a heavy pang to let it go and to look yr. last at its beautiful flowers. In this I feel very much for you. But heavier troubles have no doubt made this one seem almost slight. . . . What a very dear and delightful letter you wrote to me. You don't know how glad I was to get it—Of course I knew you had not forgotten us, any more than we had forgotten you. You are so often in my thoughts and I wish so very much to see you here and renew old memories of pleasant days spent here with you. . . . I have read yr. article on V. Hugo and cannot express how much I enjoyed it. Surely it is admirable in every way, excellent in style, perfectly clear tho' profound in matter and absorbingly interesting—I was delighted—How beautiful are those extracts f. the poem. I should like to read more of the fine chapters without going through the declamation against the Germans. . . .'

After his father's death The Grove had to be given up, chiefly for financial reasons but also because Mrs. Colvin preferred moving about to keeping a stationary home. The Victor Hugo article was the review of *L'Année terrible*, reprinted in part in *Memories and Notes*.

In another article in the *Pall Mall Gazette* in 1872 we find Colvin catholic enough to embrace Degas : ' The danger of the sort of work, as it appears to us, as it was the danger of the partly kindred work of Mr. Mason among ourselves, is that of failing to get dignity and pathos free from affectation. We think M. Millet is generally clear enough of that danger. But there is a school of young French painters so determined, both on instinct and principle, to keep absolutely clear of it, that they will not allow themselves the least attempt at ideal pathos or dignity. And then, if they are to avoid commonness, it must be by extraordinary alertness of their perceptions as to common and unideal fact. That is just what M. Degas exhibits, and in a really amazing degree. It is impossible to exaggerate the subtlety of exact perception, and the felicitous touch in expressing it, which reveal themselves in his little picture of ballet-girls training beneath the eye of the ballet-master, and his other picture of a bourgeois family in an open carriage at the races—the father on the box, within the mother watching her baby in the arms of its wet-nurse. Without the slightest pretension, these are both of them real masterpieces, and especially the former. It is a scheme of various whites, gauzes and muslins, fluttering round the apartment, and the ballet-master in white ducks and jacket in the middle ; and all the little shifts of indoor light and colour, all the movements of the girls in rest and strained exercise, expressed with the most perfect precision of drawing and delicacy of colour, and without a shadow of a shade of that sentiment which is ordinarily implied by a picture having the ballet for its subject.'

In 1872 Colvin collected in book form for Seeley, Jackson and Halliday his *Portfolio* papers on *Children in Italian and English Design.* I never heard either Colvin or Lady Colvin refer to this book, nor was there, to my knowledge, a copy of it on their shelves ; but it is charming work, comparing with much felicity the bambini of Lucca della Robbia, Marc Antonio and Correggio with the infants depicted in the drawings of Blake, Stothard and Flaxman. The essay on Blake is particularly happy ; and at that time, it must be borne in mind, every one had not ' the seed.'

The following letter from Edward Burne-Jones refers to this work :

' Lest I should be counted cold and brutal by you for not acknowledging that sweet baby book, you must know that I heard you were in Paris and that I must wait till you came back for congratulating you on it. I wish so you would make two fat books—a fat one on Florence and one, a few pages fatter, on Athens, and gladden one's heart— isn't it possible ? The baby book is perfectly delightful and the book of the little woodcuts—which I think excellent, has set me pining for more. Let us some day talk ourselves crazy about the other book.'

I cannot say what the second book was.

Other *Portfolio* articles, together with some from the *Fortnightly Review*, were collected and issued in 1873 under the title *A Selection from Occasional Writings on Fine Art*. The book was made up in this way : ' The Mausoleum of Halikarnassos,' from the *Fortnightly* ; ' The Virgins of Raphael,' a review of a French book, ' The History of Painting in Northern Italy,' a review of Crowe and Cavalcaselle, and ' The Dream of Poliphilus,' a review of a German book, all in the *Academy* ; ' A Nativity,' by Sandro Botticelli, from the *Portfolio* ; ' Old Masters at the Royal Academy,' and ' Italian Masters at the Royal Academy,' both from the *Pall Mall Gazette* ; ' The Bethnal Green Museum,' from the *Fortnightly* ; and a series of ten urbane and polished critical notices, entitled ' From Rigaud to Reynolds,' from the *Portfolio*. The series comprises Rigaud, Watteau, Boucher, the predecessors of Hogarth ; Hogarth, Chardin, Greuze, Vernet, Wilson and Gainsborough. I cite as a good example of the critic's sympathies and style an extract from the article on Chardin :

' But Chardin was very unlike a Dutchman, and completely original in his manner of treating subjects that may have been partly analogous to theirs. He does not draw and paint a dead rabbit or bird sedulously, mechanically, microscopically, hair by hair and feather by feather ; he lays together a few rich and cunning strokes of the brush that seem to have hardly a meaning when the eye is close to them, but grow, as you retire a little, into a faultless and living representation of the natural object. That is the proper magic of the brush, that is the true epic manner in painting, which raises the commonest subject to a level with the highest, and gives a butcher's joint by Chardin a truer pictorial dignity than may belong to a demigod by Lebrun. It is the one magic and the one manner whereby mere dead nature becomes worth painting by itself. For fruits and mugs and glasses, napkins and table-gear, objects and implements, Chardin is without a peer. His painting of them, over and above the satisfaction you get from its

perfect forcible likeness to the thing, has its own charm
of marrowy preciousness and melting succulence, gives its
own delight the luscious taste of which you can express
not by words, but by relishing noises in the mouth rather.
He is a consummate master of pictorial harmony ; and
without any special arrangement of his objects, which may
be merely taken straight from the parlour-table, or the
larder or scullery, makes perfect pictures of them by seeing
and rendering all their subtler, and what one can only call
their nobler, relations of substance, shadow, reflection, and
colour. It may be only a tumbler or a board between two
chestnuts and three walnuts ; or it may be a scarlet cloth
covered with the instruments of a band of music ; or it
may be a handsome set-out of grapes, plums, pears, pome-
granates, Sèvres china, and bottles and flasks of wine ;
or a snipe lying near a sprig of sweet-pea flower ; but there
will always be the same dignified magic of representation ;
a perfect expression of form, figure, and texture, a lovely
colour where nature is lovely, jewelled lights, and caressing
shadows, in which, as in nature, are mixed broken rays and
harmonious reverberations from all the colours that make
up the group of things before us. Read Mr. Ruskin's
account of the way in which Veronese paints a jewel ;
look at the way in which Chardin paints a peach or grape or
plum, and (to compare small things with great) you will
see that the Frenchman has found out for himself something
like that large manner of the immortals. And, strangely
for a Frenchman, he does it all without the faintest suspicion
of swagger ; he never says to himself or us how clever he
is, but is as modest in his art as in life. Never more than
one picture on his easel at a time ; everything done directly
and laboriously from nature ; each little inanimate study
the ill-paid work of almost months ; the essence of the
magic an uncompromising industry and sincerity.

' But for the majority and the untechnical, perpetual
representations of dead objects, however beautifully done,
will pall at last ; and it is to his second class of pictures

that the great contemporary popularity of Chardin was due. These represent the honest, modest, uncorrupted, straitened, but not unrefined household life of the petty French population—that lower *bourgeoisie* among whom the simpler virtues flourished, and in whom lay the strength and heart of the coming revolution.　The homely women go about their household work, or look after the children at their meals, or teach them their prayers or graces or lessons ; they wash or draw water from the pump, and cook and spin and knit and scour, in neat petticoats and great white caps, with perhaps a quiet daintiness of blue or rose-colour in some single bow or ribbon on cap or girdle or shoe.　An engraver's draughtsman sharpens his pencil ; a druggist arranges his gallipots ; a tavern waiter cleans his clothes ; a nurse brings slops and medicine to the bedside ; or again a boy builds a card house or blows bubbles, or a little girl in tidy cap and apron plays with a doll or a battledore and shuttlecock, or a toy windmill, or eats bread and butter.　It is a world not of sensual ideals and high-dressed indolence, but of quiet matter of fact and decent toil for the elder folks, of innocent reverent behaviour and simple quiet play for the children. It is not at all brutal, ugly, or besotted, like that grovelling world of the familiar Dutchmen, but has a pleasant unluxurious grace and natural goodness which are its own.'

The reward of Colvin's untiring activity as an art critic and the ardour with which he proclaimed his loyalties may be said to have come when in 1873 he was elected Slade Professor of Fine Arts at Cambridge.　It is amusing to find that Ruskin, who held the corresponding post at Oxford, was not in favour of his devotee's appointment.　Colvin seems to have asked his aid in the matter, for on November 13, 1872, we find Ruskin very decidedly expressing the opinion that a Slade Professor should be able to draw :—

'MY DEAR SIDNEY,—I have just got your letter.　I do not suppose I should have the slightest influence, if I wished to forward your views—but I would not use any I had in favour of any person not a draughtsman—You may very probably think I cannot draw myself—but I most assuredly should never have accepted this professorship if I had not supposed myself a good draughtsman. If you could send me a fair copy of any of my finished etchings in *Modern Painters*, I would give you what voice I had at once—though even then, not without doubt. For I saw a very clever critique of yours the other day on twelve different books—all on abstruse subjects. When I was your age, I believe I was quite impudent enough to have done such a thing, had I been asked—but in that very presumption, was as unfit as I think you will be for ten years at least to come, to be a teacher of art in any general sense.

' I had been at my wits' end in the confusion of setting up two new houses and had not seen the book on children yet, but I hear much good of it and am always very *truly* (as you may see), however rudely, yours,

'J. RUSKIN

' My sincere remembrances to your mother.'

Ruskin's insistence upon the Slade Professor being also an artist is intelligible enough. As a matter of fact, Colvin could draw a little ; the essay on Finisterre in *Memories and Notes* was, on its appearance in *Cornhill*, illustrated by quite capable woodcuts after sketches from his hand.

Some little while after Colvin was definitely in the Professor's chair Ruskin wrote, in March 1873 : ' Many thanks for the kind terms of your letter. May I hope that without clashing with any conviction which you have at heart—or in any wise cramping your plan of teaching at Cambridge or impertinently desiring to interfere with it, I may yet be permitted to speak to you on the points respecting which it seems to me deeply desirable that our teachings should be in consent with one another.'

It is probable that the appeal was too late, for we find Colvin writing, in *Memories and Notes* : ' During my

Cambridge years and afterwards, I seemed unwillingly to find, in those parts of his writings which I was able to check by my own studies, much misinterpretation of history, a habit of headlong and unquestioning but often quite unwarranted inference from the creations of art to the social conditions lying behind them, with much impassioned misreading of the relations of art in general to nature and to human life ; everywhere the fire of genius, everywhere the same lovingly, piercingly intense observation of natural fact ; everywhere the same nobleness of purpose and burning zeal for human welfare, the same beautiful felicity and persuasiveness of expression, the same almost unparalleled combination of utter sincerity with infinite rhetorical and dialectical adroitness and resource ; but everywhere also the same dogmatic and prophetic conviction of being able to set the world right by his own individual insight and judgment on whatever matters might occupy his mind and heart, the same intolerant blindness to all facts and considerations that might tell against his theories, the same liability to intermingle passages of illuminating vision and wisdom with others of petulant, inconsistent, self-contradictory error and misjudgment. In short, this demigod of my later boyhood, though still remaining an object of admiring affection and an inestimable source of stimulation and suggestion, came to count for me no longer as a leader and teacher to be followed except with reserve and critical afterthought.

' Our terms of intercourse, when intercourse occurred, continued nevertheless to be those of old family friendship, and I never found that his personal presence, whether at public gatherings or in private intercourse, had lost its power to charm and thrill. One of the instances, I remember, when its effect was strongest upon me was at a lecture of his at the Royal Institution in which he had occasion to recite Scott's ballad of *Rosabelle*. The whole genius of the man, as all those who remember him will agree—his whole intensity of spiritual and imaginative being—used to throw itself into and enkindle his recitation of poetry. His voice had a rare plangent and penetrating quality of its own, not shrill or effeminate and yet not wholly virile, which singularly enhanced the effect ; that evening he was at his very best, and for those who heard him the " wondrous blaze " never, I am sure, gleamed on Roslin's castled rock and the groves of caverned Hawthornden so magically before or since.'

Among his more eminent pupils as Slade Professor, Colvin mentioned, in the speech at the banquet in his honour in 1912, Sir Martin Conway, Mr. Lionel Cust, Mr. H. J. Ford, Mr. Charles Whibley, and Sir Harry Wilson. Sir Martin Conway has very kindly provided these pages with an account of Colvin on the Slade platform. ' A Slade Professor at Cambridge in the seventies,' he writes, ' can hardly be said to have had any students. There was no school, no organised routine. Art-history was not a University subject ; it led to no tripos ; it did not even form the subordinate part of one. If you were fool enough to take it up as a serious subject of study you shut yourself off to that extent from University honours. That was how it looked to an undergraduate. How did it look to the Professor ? He had no apparatus, not even a rudimentary collection of photographs. He had no lecture-room which could be darkened for the showing of lantern slides. He had no serious place in the scheme of University things. He was a luxury and was intended to be such. His business was not to teach anybody any definite set of things. He was there to stimulate, if he could, the taste of the rising generation, and it did not matter how he did it. Such was Colvin's problem when he became Slade Professor at Cambridge.

' Away off at Oxford there was Ruskin laying down æsthetic laws and fulminating against the spirit of the time. He knew nothing really about art-history, but took the current attributions for true and the old traditions about bygone artists for well founded. What did it matter to him whether such a work was by Carpaccio or not ? he could draw from it the moral he needed, and that sufficed. As he himself said to me the last time I saw him, " I don't believe I ever really cared about Art. What I have always loved was nature."

' Colvin at Cambridge, thoroughly impregnated as he was with the Cambridge horror of sentiment and love for fact, reacted against the method of his Oxford colleague. There was an anti-Ruskin undercurrent in his lectures. If he could not teach us the history of art systematically, the fact being that he did not know it himself, whatever he did undertake to tell should be the plain facts about things as discovered or surmised by the latest authorities.

' His audiences, which he liked to call " classes," though there was nothing of a lecturer's class about them, consisted for the most part of adult residents of the place, the wives and daughters of professors, a lot of junior dons, girls from Newnham and Girton, and a sprinkling of high-brow undergraduates. It was rather a large audience, two or three hundred in number. They were ignorant but they were eager after " taste." It was the time of the aesthetic craze. Instead of playing up to that, Colvin gave them solid stuff. One set of a dozen lectures did not lead on to another. He chose any subject that he could make interesting, and especially that he could illustrate. We each of us paid a guinea, in return for which we received an envelope full of photographic reproductions at each lecture. These illustrations were the catch. He gave us wonderfully good stuff, for the most part quite off the ordinary lines. This he managed with great ingenuity. He would write a set of articles on early engravings for the *Portfolio*, illustrated with photogravures, and he would have the plates reprinted for us, so that we took away in all forty large-paper prints admirably selected. Only the other day I saw the staircase of a house in Newcastle hung with these same Colvin prints suitably framed. I have no doubt they might be found to-day scattered all over the world.

Another time it would be Raphael's drawings, or again the recent excavations and discoveries at Olympia.

' There was nothing slipshod about these lectures. He worked hard at them and read them from his manuscript. I think the first set of lectures I heard him deliver were on all sorts of mediaeval " Sevens "—the Seven Virtues, Seven Vices, Seven Liberal Arts, and so forth. The subject enabled him to link together manuscript illuminations, Florentine pictures, early Italian prints, and the like. He opened the mediaeval world to many of us thereby along a previously unsuspected route. He made no attempt at eloquence ; he had no impassioned perorations ; he did not try to move our emotions. He just gave us facts and left it at that.

' He often said to me that Art was not his chief interest ; that was literature. Art provided his bread and butter, first at Cambridge, afterward at the British Museum, but all the time he was looking forward to the day when he could lay it aside and write the life of Keats. Within the category of the formative arts he would have preferred to devote himself to the sculpture and archæology of ancient Greece, but he had no opportunity of laying a thorough foundation of that kind of knowledge which was not taught in Cambridge in his youth. His lectures on the work of the Germans at Olympia were the nearest he ever came to this subject. He looked forward to the day when Greek archæology would find a place in the Classical Tripos, and, in his capacity as Director of the Fitzwilliam Museum, he prepared the way by forming the nucleus of the collection of casts of Greek sculpture which has since assumed considerable proportions.

' Whether he would actually have set himself to fulfil the functions of a teacher of Greek archæology when this Museum was opened I cannot say, for just then he was called to the Keepership of the British Museum Print-room, and Waldstein arrived in Cambridge as Reader in that subject.

' Such undergraduates as attended Colvin's lectures in
any serious spirit were more than kindly treated by him.
He entertained them to periodic breakfasts in his rooms,
and it was even pathetically evident that he desired to
enter into friendly relations with them. Any opportunity
he could find of helping them was eagerly seized. He
commended them in their foreign wanderings to the kindness of the learned heads of Museums, and his letters of
introduction were always of more than merely formal
utility.

' I am told that he used to say that I was his most serious
pupil. That is probably true. I did not follow the line
of any of his leading interests, but I learnt a great deal
from him, and I owe to his unassuming help many a com-
forting push over an impediment and the opening of many
a door in the way of my hesitating youthful enterprises.
His friendship remained a valued possession to the end of
his life, and is a happy memory which will not fade.'

Sir Martin Conway's remark about Colvin's preference
for literature is supported by the walls of the residence in
the Museum and the house in Palace Gardens Terrace,
which were those of a platonic lover of painting rather
than a passionate one. During the eighteen years of my
acquaintance with him I can remember him buying only
one work of art—a drawing of a woman's head by Augustus
John. His other pictures, dating from an earlier period,
did not number more than a dozen. Conspicuous among
them were two water-colour sketches by Randolph Caldecott,
a water-colour sketch of a Greek island by Leighton, a
typical Alfred Parsons garden, a typical figure by George
Boughton, a little pencil cherub by Burne-Jones, and a
drawing of an Italian piazza by Muirhead Bone : all, I
imagine, votive offerings. This last he bequeathed to the
Fitzwilliam Museum, where it now hangs. In addition
were portraits of Lady Colvin and Joseph Conrad by
Percy Anderson, which Colvin had commissioned. All
these were in the drawing-room. In the two downstairs

rooms were a miniature of Bassett David Colvin and photographs of R. L. Stevenson and J. L. Garvin. Among the very few drawings which Colvin kept in a portfolio were original pencil portraits of Mrs. Sitwell by W. B. Richmond and Burne-Jones: neither, he used to say, sufficiently like. The only work of art to which he ever drew one's attention was a terra-cotta group by Dalou, which also was left to the Fitzwilliam.

So much for possessions and the possessive instinct. When it came to visual and emotional pleasure in painting or sculpture, Colvin could be intensely moved and was far from the academic expositor.

CHAPTER III

EDWARD BURNE-JONES AND D. G. ROSSETTI

1867 AND ON

MR. CHAMPNEYS tells me that Colvin, although as a Fellow of Trinity—elected in 1868—occupying rooms at Cambridge, lived now much in London : for a while in Arlington Street, Piccadilly, for a while with Mr. Champneys at Hampstead, and for a while at Norwood.   It was in the Arlington Street rooms that Mr. Champneys remembers Rossetti reading from his poems ; and this brings us to two of the principal objects of Colvin's adoration at that time—Dante Gabriel Rossetti and Edward Burne-Jones.

Returning again to the notes on the Summer Exhibitions of 1869, I find Colvin rising to his greatest heights of enthusiasm before a set of allegorical water-colours by Mr. E. B.-Jones.   These are his words : ' Among lovers of the rarer kinds of imaginative art, Mr. Jones's reputation has long been above cavil.   His present work ought to set it above cavil also among the critics and the public.   The sentiment which informs it, from having been somewhat tender and exotic, is becoming hardier and more robust. If any spectator finds these things strange, startling, unaccountable, it is simply because they differ from the paltry, unbeautiful, every-day art, the art of mere incident, whether jocose or pathetic, to which he has been accustomed. Let him go to the National Gallery, or to the Elgin room of the British Museum, and learn from his heart to appreciate what he sees there, and he will no longer find Mr. Jones's work strange or uncomfortable.   Its secret is that it does, more than anything else produced among us, touch the

32

same chords and appeal to the same emotions as the great art, not of any particular time or manner, but of all times and all manners. That is why some wise folks find it " archaic." And we may this year see that Mr. Jones is labouring not in vain to add complete technical efficiency to that intense poetic charm which his work has always had, and which, although it does not make his work " archaic," does constitute for him a genuine title to " kindred with the great of old." '

This criticism brings us naturally to the painter himself ; to Colvin's reminiscences of him and to extracts from the many letters from E. B.-J. to Colvin and to Mrs. Sitwell. The two men first met in 1866 or 1867, when Burne-Jones was thirty-three or so, twelve years Colvin's senior.

' In my own early life,' Colvin writes, in *Memories and Notes*, ' both the zest of public battle on his behalf, and the pleasure of being often with him in such spare hours as he could afford his friends of an evening or on Sunday, counted for very much. . . . It was Rossetti who had ordered Burne-Jones (his advice to his friends was always virtually an order) to attack at twenty-two the practice of imaginative and poetic painting without any of the usual preliminary training of hand and eye. From this first impulsion, or compulsion, and from study of the earlier painters of Italy, together, Burne-Jones drew the impetus which, working in his own intense and intensely personal artistic temperament, carried him on, after a few trying years of derision and neglect, through a full career of passionately strenuous labour to ultimate recognized success.

' Of course—and it should need no saying—the primary and essential appeal of every picture must needs be to the eye, by its harmonies and rhythms of line and colour, its balancings and massings and proportions and contrasts of light and shade, and by their direct effect upon the visual emotions. If such appeal and such effect are not forthcoming, or if they fail, the picture is naught ; but if they succeed and the picture is a picture indeed, then the more

c

of mind that can be felt behind it, the richer the associations and suggestions it conveys, surely the better. Full
as are the gifts of mind to be discerned behind Burne-
Jones's work, rich as are the imaginative associations it
calls up, it represents only a part of the wealth and colour
of his being. For one thing, notwithstanding all its beauty,
its felicity and inexhaustible original invention in colour
and linear design, as far as concerns the human types it
depicts it is in the main of a melancholy cast. . . . Yet in
company he charmed no less by a rich laughter-loving
gaiety than by his surprising range of knowledge and
attainment and the ease and beauty and simplicity
of language with which he brought them to bear in
conversation.

' Modern imaginative literature of the best kind Burne-
Jones possessed in a scarcely less degree than ancient, at
least so much of it as is to be read in English ; his two
chief favourites being (as they are the favourites of every
wise reader) Walter Scott and Dickens. As the books of
Louis Stevenson came out successively he gave them a
place in his affection next almost to these. In Dickens
what Burne-Jones loved especially were the parts most
riotously comic. I can see and hear him now shouting
with laughter as he echoed the choicer utterances of Sam
Weller or Micawber or Mrs. Gamp, his head flung back
and beard in the air (in early days it was the fine forked
and flowing red-brown beard depicted in Watts' well-
known portrait, but later, one grizzled or grizzling and
shorter trimmed). And he was very capable of original
Dickens-like observations and inventions of his own. No
one had a quicker or more healthy amused sense, without
sting or ill-nature, of the grotesque and the absurd in ordinary
life. No one loved better to make or had a better gift for
making, by speech or pencil, happy fun and laughter with
his children and grandchildren.'

One or two of Burne-Jones's letters to Colvin are printed
in *Memories and Notes*. From a large number of others

EDWARD BURNE-JONES
AT THE AGE OF 41

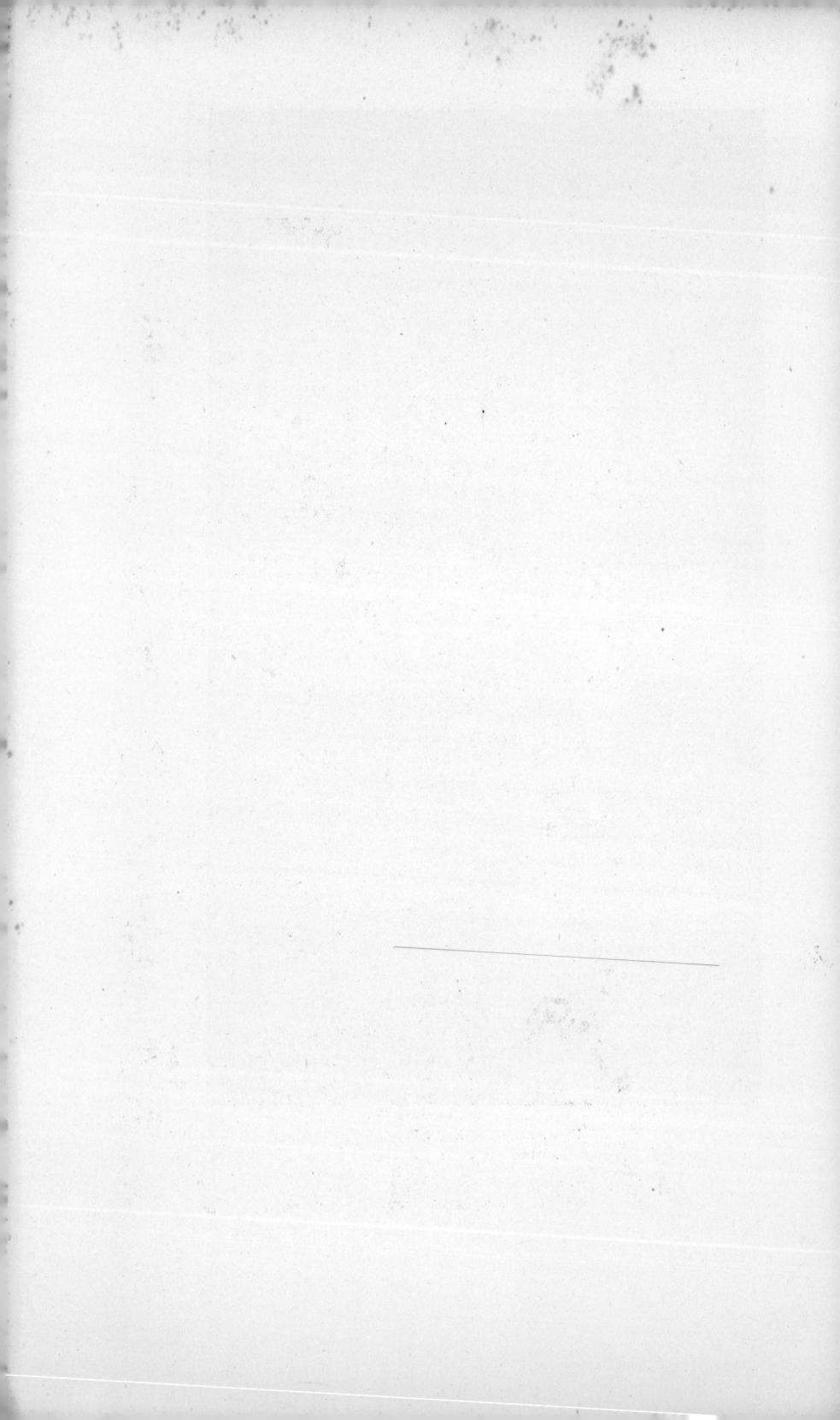

that lie before me I make extracts. Few of them have dates, and, as in the reminiscences that have just been quoted, we advance by degrees far beyond the year 1869.

This is the first : ' Morris seemed very pleased with the Gudrun article, so it must have been a tremendous puff (by this time you have found out the poet's soul, and how easily it is vexed and how you cannot fathom it)—he said he should write to you at once and express the same—but as it is easier for him to write Gudruns than letters you will not wonder at the delay.'

Colvin had reviewed Morris's *Earthly Paradise*, Part III., in the *Pall Mall Gazette*. ' The Lovers of Gudrun ' will be found there.

Of William Morris, I might remark here, Colvin has left no personal record, although he must often have met him ; but I find a friend both of Burne-Jones and Colvin—Lady Carlisle—writing thus of the poet in 1870 : ' Morris arrived early this morning—with such a diminutive carpet-bag— He was rather shy—and so was I—I felt that he was taking an experimental plunge amongst " barbarians," and I was not sure what would be the resulting opinion in his mind. However, he has grown more urbane—and even 3 hours has worked off much of our mutual shyness—A walk in the glen made me know him better and like him more than I fancied I should. He talks so clearly and seems to think so clearly that what seems paradox in Webb's mouth, in his seems convincing sense. He lacks sympathy and humanity tho'—and this is a fearful lack to me—only his character is so fine and massive that one must admire—He is agreeable also—and does not snub me—This I imagine may be attributed to Georgy having said some things in my favour—Not that I think he will like me—but if he puts up with me we shall jog along all right. . . .

' The little Morris girls are delightful, and I could tell you amusing things about the little May who is such a materialist that she says " the soul is nothing but the imaginary part of her body "—that there is nothing left but bones after death—that it is the brain that lives—She has not been taught these things, simply brought up without theology.'

Webb would be Philip Webb, the architect and Morris's partner.   Georgy was Mrs. Burne-Jones.

I now resume the extracts from the E. B.-J. letters :

' I hated putting you off—but I never have and never can and never shall remember about engagements—That comes of not trusting to memory and depending on an engagement book.'

' I will send on your article on Rembrandt to Miss Graham when I know she is back—I read it with real delight and much was new to me—though you know I have to be taken by the hair of my head to be made to look at him.   Still I want to be just.'

' I saw yesterday at Hallé's (11 Mansfield Street), 4 little volumes of the earliest drawings of Doyle.   The earliest and to my thinking the best—they are miracles of skill— I think he never excelled them, and often fell below them— and I came away amazed.   Now the Museum ought to have them—1 vol. is a drawing of a journey to London— the three others are nondescript fancies—all are highly finished in pen and ink and miracles in their way.'

Doyle is Richard — or Dicky — Doyle, the humorous artist whose most famous work is the cover of *Punch*.   Many of his most fanciful drawings are preserved in the Irish National Gallery in Dublin.

' I wish it [the summer exodus] were all over and everyone at work again—there ought not to be such a place as London that we have to run away from in disgust and horror—a nice city ought to be better than the country in summer, with cool arcades, a fountain and little sheltered gardens— When I build a city it shall be like that.'

' I do wish the lecture was 2 hours later—I would go to every one of them—not that I should [not] read them and know what you say just as well as if I went—but that you might have the cheery comfort of a friendly mug—'

'I'm back in town—need I add with a brutal cold—the worst of colds—one that won't be hurried—that takes 3 days to think about it—and 3 days to get worse, and 3 days to stand still, and 3 to go away—leaving one at the end utterly dilapidated and doubting the thirty-nine articles,—that's my case at present and this is the fourth day only—'

'I've been seedy but am getting all right as usual in a day—the doctor came yesterday and I'm to grow fat at once—I think it was dissipation, dining out 3 times last week—so I'm not to—but to stop at home and lie on a sofa instead—which is nice—and gives a pretty prospect of the coming winter—damn—'

'Photo came—thanks—fat fat fat little back in a boat—I shall show it George and it will make him young again and his eyes will flash—alas for me, the days when fat backs could have satisfied I spent in thinking of St. Jerome.'

George would be Lord Carlisle.

'My long holiday is over—I took a thorough holiday this time—no running off and back the next day—but I stayed away like a man—like two men. But now I'm back I'm very stupid and always falling asleep, and gaping and being deaf and as silly as can be.'

To Mrs. Sitwell: 'I wasn't tired—at least not very tired—and I left very early—felt a bit shy and screwed myself into a little corner and it was fun—for some people I liked and some I loathed and that is always fun and is life—I am off this almost very minute to Rottingdean to see the tenantry and remit 98¾ per cent. of rent—Young Rottingdean left early this morn^g. for the seat of learning, having had a most brilliant season. I had a little talk of the serious kind but at the first tear I fled. . . .

'To think after all I have preached and said and painted about love that I should come at last to marry a hot bottle—she burst the other night and I divorced her at once and got another.'

Young Rottingdean was his son Philip.

To Mrs. Sitwell : ' I cannot tomorrow—for I must be in—
I think that every day and every hour someone has made
appointments with me—and sometimes I feel half wild :
and I wish more people would go out of London or make
themselves happy without enslaving me—to-day I do feel
half-wild—there came 3 yankees at lunch time suddenly
and killed me—and this isn't me that 's writing but the
ghost of me.'

To Mrs. Sitwell : ' Excuse this pencil. I have no ink
anywhere except on the floor where it has just gone—. . . .
—how kind you all were to Phil—he came back looking
happy and [as] if he had a warm heart for you.   He looks
improved for his civilizing visit and it was very good for
him.   I hope he will listen when you tell him things.'

' [Sidney] told me you were reading *John Inglesant*
abroad—I am afraid the beginning is the best—the story
is venerable criticism everywhere but there is a sort of
genius somewhere to the book—I regret I praised it so
unreservedly for you will be disappointed and when one
reads a story it isn't unfair to want it to be a story—and
the characters are nil—but some atmosphere of tormented
Christendom is in it, pleasant to scholars.—It is written for
Oxford ears, that home of lost causes.'

John Inglesant by J. H. Shorthouse was published in
1881.

In this same year, 1881, I find a delightful letter, illustrated
by comic drawings, from Philip Burne-Jones.   I give some
of it for its own sake and also to show that not a little of his
father's fun was also his.   The boy—as he was then—had
been staying with Mrs. Sitwell, with whose son he had been
at school : ' I wonder whether you would care to hear
about how I am spending the time here ?   I don't think
it would amuse you.   In mornings I work and in afternoons go expeditions—that is briefly what happens.
Rottingdean is a little village 2½ miles from Brighton—

and so deep down in a valley that as you drive from
the hideous metropolis hard by you never see it until,
so to speak, you are really in it.   There is a winding
street—we 're not proud and so we don't call it High
Street—which runs from the sea at one end of the village
to the church at the other end—*our* end, where is our
cottage.   As to shops, they are so arranged as to bewilder
the metropolitan mind.   To begin with there is the post
office which sells sweets—yellow ones which I can buy now
without being dependent on the whims and caprice of
Kathey—and eggs and vegetables—and stationery—There
is another shop which astounds the passer-by by declaring
itself to be a Tailor's—but on close acquaintance the
window proves to be filled with clocks and watches—and to
answer in every respect to the description of a working
jeweller's—were it not that behind the said watches is a
screen on which is emblazoned " Trowbridge, Tailor "—So
that we know that our eyes deceive us, and must never
again suggest the watch trade in connection with " Mr.
Trowbridge."—And so the shops go on—each one adding to
the surprise and dismay of the traveller—It is not unusual
to speak of buying potatoes at the draper's or again of purchasing mushrooms and fireirons at the Baker's—or at all
events that is the impression left upon my mind.

' Then at the end of the village is the church—which
Mamma at once called " the little grey church on the windy
hill "—and I 'm sure Math. Arnold had it in his memory
when he wrote the " Merman "—It is opposite our house
and the downs slope upwards behind it—and look lovely
against the grey sky as I write.   Mr. Charles Hallé (jun.) is
staying here in the village—and is giving me lessons in
oil painting—(portraits).   I am at present occupied in
trying to copy the ridiculous face of my little cousin Ambrose
Poynter—whose ideas of the art of sitting are most primitive
—Say I am copying his profile, and look up suddenly, he
meets my gaze with a bland smile—full face—and says
" do you want my side face ? "—And it 's impossible to

be angry with him because he sits out of mere good nature and I 'm only too glad to have anyone to copy, however plain. But there is only one Sitter that I know as yet, who combines every qualification for that duty—and I think you can guess who that is.

' We have been several expeditions from here—to Newhaven and other places. Yesterday we made a false start and got the pony carriage we had from the Sun, down a hill and covered with mud—and nearly broke the wheels on a pathless hillside—but we came out safe at last and drove to Brighton instead of going over downs. There is a most terrible omnibus which plies between Rottingdean and Brighton and is the butt of my most withering sarcasm—until I am on it, when I become abject—It is always so filled with humanity that I wonder anyone arrives whole at its destination. And the roof is so piled with luggage that on windy days, when the sea is rough with storm winds and the breezes blow from the ocean, the " 'bus " runs a good chance of being blown over bodily. And a provincial omnibus is, if it could be, a more detestable invention than a London " 'bus." Because it does not behave in the businesslike way, that its London namesakes do—but goes up turnings and waits for you if you 're not ready at your own house, and in other ways behaves as an amateur and fails to inspire confidence.

' But why should I send you in the centre of civilization these uninteresting details of village life ? Here in Bœotia we live bucolic lives—the great excitement of the day being the arrival of the omnibus with the mails or the appearance of a donkey on our village green. Corydon and Amaryllis are the only inhabitants and we know no one else. My young cousin goes out with a bottle of poison and a net to capture living things—butterflies and wingéd beetles—and when I remonstrate and suggest that they love sunshine as well as he, his reply is that if God did not intend him to kill butterflies He would in some way prevent it and that he (Ambrose) is an instrument in God's hand whereby the erring insect is righteously chastized—To which I can answer nothing—and he goes out again triumphantly with a bottle of poison and a net.'

In 1884, probably, Colvin asked Burne-Jones if he could name an illustrator for Stevenson's *Child's Garden of Verses*, and this was the reply :

'I know no one who can invent but Crane.—It seems the last thing one can ever find—so much else that is skilful and delightful but not that. And I think Crane would enter into it with love.'

Crane was Walter Crane, whom Colvin would of course remember as the designer of the frontispieces to the *Inland Voyage*, 1878, and *Travels with a Donkey*, 1879.

'Yes, the police, as usual, were violent and lied deeply—but I dread the rows and messes of the future of which this is only a little foretaste, and the dear fellow is so bent on carrying through with it, and there will be no more poems ever again. But I must say the police infuriate me so that I shall go and help on Sunday—my blood boils when I think of them.

'And yet, poor ignorant wretches, how should they know? Tomorrow then you are in the country, and Friday I can't, and Saturday people are here—and on Sunday who knows if I am not in prison—but next week surely will be luckier.'

A reference, I think, to the Battle of Trafalgar Square on November 13, 1887.

To Mrs. Sitwell about the accidental destruction of the picture 'Love among the Ruins' in 1893 : 'Yes that miserable news was true—the poor thing is entirely destroyed—I will tell you some day how it happened but at present it still makes me sick to talk of it—and I try to forget it—not much chance of that. I may try to do it again one day—but I cannot make myself young again—nor put into what I do now much of the ancient Spirit. It was a fool who did it, inspired by a company limited. Next week I shall be back in London for a little time and I will run across and see you at the end of a day, and, prythee, we won't even mention this mishap—for the devil is conceited and likes to have his works talked of like the rest of us.   There is only one way of hurting his feelings, *i.e.* not to mention him.

' Sidney has just written me a dear letter—

' So have you.'

In *Memorials of Edward Burne-Jones*, by his widow, I find this passage : ' It was in August, 1893, just after he had recovered from the fit of exhaustion described in his letter to Lady Leighton, that a grievous misfortune befell us in the destruction of his picture of Love in the Ruins. It had been sent to be reproduced by photogravure in Paris, where, in spite of a printed warning on the back that it was painted in water-colour and would be injured by the slightest moisture, it had been washed over with white of egg or some such substance, and every part of the surface so touched was destroyed.'

Of Rossetti, in *Memories and Notes*, Colvin wrote thus : ' Looking back lately through volumes of the *Westminster Review* some half a century old, I found under the date January 1871 an essay near thirty pages long enthusiastically quoting and praising the poetical writings, both translated and original, of Dante Gabriel Rossetti.   Recognizing the essay for my own, I was freshly reminded of the fascinated admiration which possessed me in those days, youngster as I was, for the poet-painter and his work.   By the time I left Cambridge I already took intense pleasure in some of his early paintings which I knew in the houses of friends ; and I held (as I still hold) his renderings from the early Italian poets, first published in the volume of 1861, to be unmatched among feats of verse translation for graceful, unforced fidelity to the spirit and even in most cases to the letter of the originals.   Drawn moreover by the glamour which invested Rossetti's personality as the main inspiring focus and source of impulse whence had sprung all I most cared for—that, is, whatever is most imaginative and impassioned—in the English art of the time, I asked Burne-Jones to take me to him ; was kindly received ; and saw much of him throughout the years 1868-1872, which were somewhat critical and fateful years of his life.

'I had come into his circle of course too late, and with the Cambridge stamp and direction too definitely impressed upon me, to undergo the full dominating force of his influence such as it had been exercised some dozen years earlier, when he suddenly determined the careers of men like Burne-Jones and William Morris, or earlier yet when along with Holman Hunt and Millais he was a leading spirit in the original Præ-Raphaelite movement. The best days of his life were indeed already over. Since the tragic death of his wife his passionately craving and brooding nature had been gradually losing command over itself.

'About the surroundings and the way of life so much has been written that I shall pass them over quickly. The handsome old red-brick house in a row looking on the Chelsea reach of the Thames ; the combined gloom and richness of its decorations, the sombre hangings, the doors and panellings painted in sombre dark-green sparsely picked out with red and lighted here and there by a round convex mirror ; the shelves and cupboards laden with brassware and old blue Nankin china (in the passion for collecting which Rossetti was, if I remember rightly, an absolute pioneer) ; the long green and shady garden at the back, with its uncanny menagerie of wombat, raccoon, armadillo, kangaroo, or whatever might be the special pet or pets of the moment ; the wilful, unconventional, unhealthy habits and hours ; the rare and reluctant admission of strangers ; all these things have already been made familiar by repeated descriptions to such readers as are curious about them. So have the aspect and bearing of the man himself ; his sturdy, almost burly figure clad in a dark cloth suit with the square jacket cut extra long and deep-pocketed ; his rich brown hair and lighter brown, shortish, square-trimmed beard, the olive complexion betraying Italian blood ; the handsome features between spare and fleshy, with full, sensual underlip and thoughtful, commanding forehead in which some of his friends found a likeness to Shakespeare ; the deep bar above the nose and fine blue-grey colour of the eyes behind their spectacles ; and finally, the round, John-Bullish, bluntly cordial manner of speech, with a preference for brief and bluff slang words and phrases which seemed scarce in keeping with the fame and character of the man as the most quintessentially, romantically poetic of painters and writers.

' During the years of our intercourse it was Rossetti's poetry more than his painting that interested and impressed me. His earlier water-colours, those of the Dante cycle especially, comparatively unambitious in scale and technic as they were, seemed to me (and still seem) to give by their fine new inventive colour-harmonies, their passionate intensities of expression and their rare originality and often, though not always, their beauty of group-composition and pattern, a more satisfying idea of his genius for painting than his ambitious oil pictures on the scale of life.

' But Rossetti's poetry, both by its own power and by the manner in which I learned to know it, for the time being enthralled me completely. The story is well known how, in a passion of grief and remorsefulness at the time of his wife's death, he had buried the original bundle of his manuscript poems with her, laying it in her coffin among the rich strands of her red-gold hair. Of a few of these buried poems he had drafts or copies by him, and would sometimes, when I first knew him, read out from them to a small circle of his intimates. . . . The manuscript poems having been rescued, and the question of their publication having next to be considered, Rossetti used on many evenings to read out from them to a few invited guests after dinner. He was good enough to care, or seem to care, somewhat specially for my opinion, and consulted me, both verbally and in many letters which I have lately re-read, about the revision of the poems and the order in which they should stand in the proposed volume, in the end adopting most of my suggestions.

JOHN RUSKIN AND DANTE GABRIEL ROSSETTI

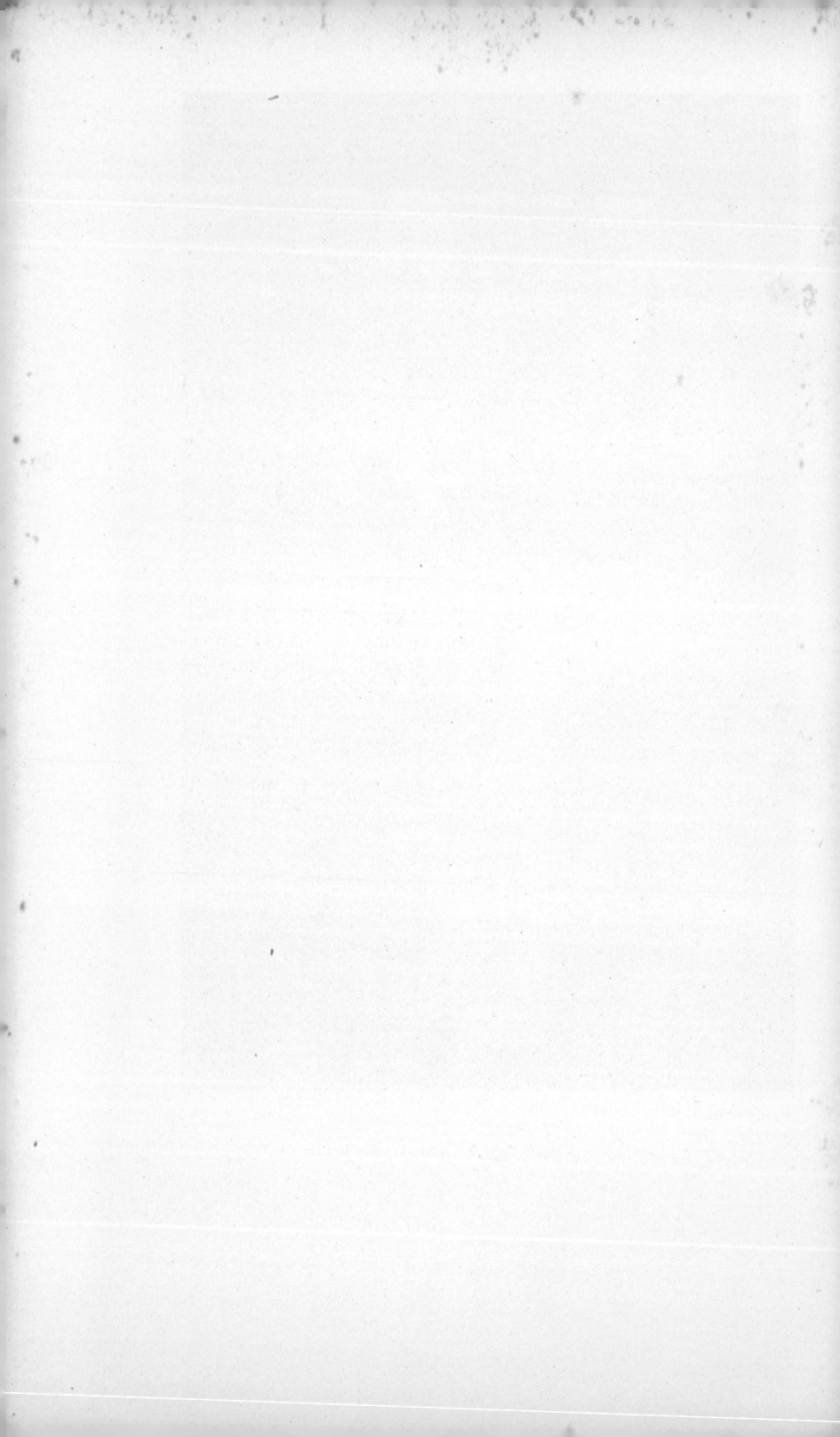

' But the readings themselves were among the marking events, and remain among the golden memories, of my life. Most of the poets I have known have had their own special way of reading, and it was generally interesting or impressive to hear. Rossetti's way was not dramatic in any ordinary sense of the word. It was rather a chant, a monotone ; but somehow he was able with little variation of pitch or inflection to express a surprising range and richness of emotion. His voice was magical in its mellow beauty of *timbre* and quality and in its power to convey the sense of a whole world of brooding passion and mystery, both human and elemental, behind the words. A kind of sustained musical drone or hum with which he used to dwell on and stress and prolong the rhyme-words and sound-echoes had a profound effect in stirring the senses and souls of his hearers. . . .

' Rossetti had little or none of Burne-Jones's fine self-sufficient indifference to criticism. It is not true, as has been said, that he took undignified pains to ensure that reviews should be favourable. Swinburne of course for one, and I for another, were absolutely unsolicited volunteers in the cause. But when there appeared the late Robert Buchanan's preposterous attack upon him, at first pseudonymous and then unveiled, in the pamphlet called *The Fleshly School of Poetry*, he was both agitated and angered beyond measure. In this matter again I did my best, together with a group of other ardent friends and admirers, and this time by the master's desire and request, to stand by him and make things as hot for his assailant as we could. At the same time I succeeded in dissuading him—I had forgotten the fact, but am reminded of it by his brother's biography—from printing a satiric effort of his own against the enemy which struck us as neither dignified nor effective.'

After referring to Rossetti's famous Limericks on his friends, Colvin quotes the beginning of one on himself :

' There 's an eminent critic called Colvin,
Whose writings the mind may revolve in.'

' Wild horses,' he adds, ' would not drag from me the sequel ' ; nor could I, with whatever power of persuasion I may possess, ever achieve this end.

Colvin mentions that he received from Rossetti a large number of letters, but I find no trace of them.

CHAPTER IV

JOHN MORLEY AND GEORGE ELIOT

1870–1873

ART study and criticism were only a part of Colvin's industry. He was also a busy reviewer and a keen conversationalist. In 1869 he joined the club now known as the Savile but then known as the New, and thus came into touch with some of the most congenial intellects among his contemporaries. The New Club had been founded in 1868 and had its quarters at 9 Spring Gardens. Among the original members were James Bryce, afterwards Lord Bryce, Andrew Clark, afterwards Stevenson's physician, G. L. Craik, Lord Dufferin, Michael Foster the chemist, Auberon Herbert, Lord Houghton, R. H. Hutton of the *Spectator*, Professor Jebb, Stevenson's friend Fleeming Jenkin, Norman Lockyer the astronomer, F. W. H. Myers, Simeon Solomon, and Henry Sidgwick of Cambridge. There were also three cherishable editors: John Morley, of the *Fortnightly Review*, Frederick Greenwood, of the *Pall Mall Gazette*, and Leslie Stephen, of the *Cornhill Magazine*.

In Colvin's year, 1869, were elected Oscar Browning, Basil Champneys, W. K. Clifford, Sir William Vernon Harcourt, E. Ray Lankester, Walter Pater and Frederick Pollock. Stevenson was elected in 1874, when the club's name had been changed to the Savile and its premises were at No. 15 Savile Row. They were afterwards in Piccadilly and are now in Brook Street.

In 1871 Colvin was made Honorary Secretary. In the dining-room hangs his portrait, painted by Theodore

47

Roussel in 1908, as a record of his paternal influence there.

We get some light upon Colvin as a reviewer and critical writer from John Morley's letters, which begin with 1870. Morley, then in his thirty-second year, seems to have found in Colvin a trustworthy and versatile supporter. Colvin's earliest article that I can find, is that on ' English Art in 1867 ' to which I have referred. Morley's first letter, however, bears upon the state of affairs in Europe and not upon literary contributions. The Franco-German War was then in full swing : ' You might gather from my little piece in the September *Fortnightly*, how much I am with you in protesting against the Piriturist and also the Odgeiran disparagement of Germany. Such disparagement seems to me equally unworthy of historical philosophers and practical politicians.

' The situation is very desperate. If Paris is taken, Bismarck may ask immoderate things and take them. If the Prussians are repulsed, wh. seems not impossible, then France becomes impracticable, and the whole game is once more open. The only comfort is that there must be a decisive stroke of some kind or other—decisive for a while— before the winter sets in, so that the mind of Europe may receive a little freedom, perhaps enough to discover some sort of new solution.

' Of the two subjects wh. you are kind enough to mention for the *Fortnightly* the Albert Memorial is one with wh. I gladly close, without further adv. As for Byron, I only wish to say that I have myself in hand an essay on him —of a very general kind—wh. I have some faint notion of printing in the *Fortnightly*, before it appears in a volume.'

It was not, however, the *Fortnightly* but the *Pall Mall Gazette* that printed Colvin's views on the Albert Memorial. Here is one sentence : ' The work of the Albert Memorial remains one probably of extraordinary credit to the engineer and mechanician ; it remains one certainly of extraordinary and ostentatious costliness in material and ornament ; but

JOHN MORLEY

it does not and cannot remain (we speak of it as a whole) a respectable work of art.'

Colvin meanwhile was thinking about the state of Europe and the two belligerent nations in his own way, and in 1870 issued, at a penny, his first published work: *A Word for Germany, from an English Republican*, 1870, an open letter to Professor Beesly. In this document Colvin urged England to intervene against France. Morley thus refers to it, in January 1871 : ' What is all this you say about William [the Emperor] and Providence ? The devil take Wm. by all means, if you choose ; but apart from that, I hope you have not swung round to France. I stick fast by a certain " word for Germany," and don't see that anything has happened that ought to make one wish ill to the side to wh. you then gave us such good reasons for wishing well. French republicanism is hollow, wordy, intolerant, and I at least have no faith in its stability, nor in its virtue, if it be stable. As I said to Harrison, France is the Marie Stuart of nations; lovely, atrocious, delightful, an adulteress, a murderess, exquisite, and irresistible to ardent young men. I love French people, and I detest all the German ditto with whom I have been brought in contact—*But* . . .'

To Morley's comments on the French might be appended a passage from a letter from Ruskin to Colvin in 1872. Colvin—as long ago as that—had been championing some good cause, and Ruskin, with his accustomed liberality, had acceded to a request for money. He writes: ' I send you the £100 ; of course good security means the assurance of any wealthy person that he will pay if the Frenchmen don't.—In the present case, I will waive such condition on your testimony to their good French character. Alas, I had rather now in general trust a French tradesman than an English.'

To return to 1871, I find Morley writing to Colvin in February : ' Your article on Rossetti in the *Westminster* is truly admirable. I read it with the warmest interest and pleasure. It is better than Swinburne's in my own *Review*,

D

because it is historical and philosophical in its base ;—because in a word it is true criticism.' [1]

In January 1873, as I have said, Colvin was elected Slade Professor at Cambridge. In the same month (to bring the first part of this chronicle to a close and clear the decks for what was one of the most important days in his life, later in the year 1873) I find this letter from George Eliot :

'MY DEAR Mr. COLVIN,—I was very glad to see Mr. Jebb, for I had a pre-established respect for him, and should willingly have invited him.

' In general, as you divine, we are averse to the enlargement of our circle by the hasty introduction of " friends," seeing that very charming people are capable of having decidedly uncharming friends.

' Thanks for your pretty intention of sending me the photographs. I hunted up Mr. Newton's article, but was little the wiser for its wise dubieties.

' The *Fortnightly* is not yet come to us. When it does come, my husband will hinder me, according to his usual prescription for my mental hygiene, from reading what is said about myself. All he will allow me is an occasional quotation of what he thinks will gratify me by its tone or bearing. But be assured that we should neither of us readily impute to you a conscious lack of courtesy.

' I have been keeping the New Year dolorously with face-ache and sore throat, and am still a prisoner in an upper room.—Yours always truly,   ' M. E. LEWES ' [2]

' The Sunday afternoon receptions at The Priory,' says Colvin, in *Memories and Notes*, ' were not always quite free from stiffness, the presiding genius allowing herself—so at least some of us thought—to be treated a little too markedly and formally as such. Perhaps, however, the secret was that she by nature lacked the lightness of human touch by

---

[1] From a letter in the Fitzwilliam Museum.
[2] In the Fitzwilliam Museum.

which a hostess can diffuse among a mixed company of guests an atmosphere of social ease.   Humour in abundance she had, but not of the light, glancing kind : it was a rich, deliberate humour springing from deep sources and corresponding with the general depth and power of her being. The signs of such depth and power were strongly impressed upon her countenance.   I have known scarce any one in life whose looks in their own way more strongly drew and held one.   She had of course no regular beauty (who was it that asked the question, " Have you seen a horse, sir ? Then you have seen George Eliot " ?) : but the expression of her long, strong, deeply ploughed features was one not only of habitual brooding thought and intellectual travail but of intense and yearning human sympathy and tenderness. . . .

' If it had been her nature to seek equality of regard and companionship from those visitors who came about her, Lewes, I think, would have hardly made it possible.   His own attitude was always that of the tenderest, most solicitous adoration ; and adoration, homage, was what he seemed to expect for her from all who came about them.   He never encouraged the conversation among the Sunday guests in the room to become equal or general, or allowed one of them to absorb her attention for very long, but would bring up one after another to have his or her share of it in turn, so that if any of us began to feel that talk with her was taking an easier and closer turn than usual, the next thing was that it was sure to be interrupted.   I recall the beginnings of several conversations which were thus broken before I had succeeded in getting more from her than sympathetic enquiries about my own work and studies, or perhaps about the places I had last been visiting in France or Italy.   Naturally I valued such enquiries, but was not at all seeking them : what I wanted was not to be drawn out myself but to draw out my hostess and feel her powers playing—the spell of her mind and character acting—upon me and upon the company generally.

'Besides entertaining the day's guests, or helping them to entertain each other, in groups, Lewes liked sometimes to get a few minutes' chat apart with a single one coming or going; but the subject was almost always connected in some way with George Eliot's work and fame. During the serial publication of *Middlemarch* I particularly remember his taking me apart one day as I came in, and holding me by the button as he announced to me in confidence concerning one of its chief characters, " Celia is going to have a baby ! "   This with an air at once gratified and mysterious, like that of some female gossip of a young bride in real life.'

CHAPTER V

MRS. SITWELL (AFTERWARDS LADY COLVIN) AND THE FETHERSTONHAUGH FAMILY

WE now come to August 1873, which was a very auspicious month for three people : Frances Sitwell, Sidney Colvin and Robert Louis Stevenson. This book is not primarily about Robert Louis Stevenson, yet but for him it would never have been written ; for it was he who gave Colvin, a born devotee, the principal literary devotion of his life ; and it was he who put the capacity for sympathy and stimulation that marked Lady Colvin, then Mrs. Sitwell, to its most notable test. The two persons who brought Colvin, Mrs. Sitwell and Stevenson together were Professor Churchill Babington, a Cambridge colleague of Colvin's, and his wife, who had been a Miss Wilson and was both a first cousin of Robert Louis Stevenson and by marriage a kinswoman of Mrs. Sitwell. The meeting-place was the rectory at Cockfield, near Bury St. Edmunds, in Colvin's own county. Mrs. Sitwell and Colvin had already met ; Robert Louis Stevenson, then twenty-two, was new to both of them.

Before proceeding with the story, something should be said of Mrs. Sitwell and the Fetherstonhaughs. According to a memorandum in Lady Colvin's handwriting, 'the Fetherstonhaughs descended from a Saxon warrior named Frithestan, who founded the family in Britain about the beginning of the eighth century : he built his house upon a hill and held the surrounding valleys by his sword, but time and Border Scots having destroyed this stronghold the chieftain of that line selected a more sheltered site in the " nalgh," which in the old Saxon dialect means a valley,

and built Fetherstonhaugh Castle in one of the valleys of
the Tyne. The lord of the Castle was known [as] Frithestan
de Nalgh at the time of the Conquest—he took for his arms
gules on a chevron between three ostrich feathers argent,
a pellet with the motto *Volens et Valens*. An unbroken
male line held the Castle down to 1659. There are tablets
in St. Dunstan-in-the-West, London, and Stanford-le-Hope
in Essex. The Irish family descends from Cuthbert F.
of the Heather Cleugh branch, who after the battle of
Worcester, 1651, fled to Ireland, where he settled and had
five sons.'

From another memorandum in, I think, Cuthbert
Fetherstonhaugh's handwriting, I take this note: ' Our
grandmother, our mother's mother, was Susan Rolleston—
the Rollestons I may mention trace their descent from Rollo,
Duke of the Normans, and before him until it is lost in the
mists of antiquity. Our great-grandmother was Marjorie
Synge, daughter of the Bishop of Killaloe, granddaughter
of the Archbishop of Tuam—they had a protestant Archbishop in those days ; there 's an R.C. one now. Marjorie
Synge married William Curtis a parson, our great-grandfather.
—Our father's mother was Mary Hardiman, and I *think* our
grandfather's mother's maiden name was Wollf—that is all
the information I have been able to collect—if I meet any
relative who can give me more details about the family
I 'll make a note of it.'

From the racy pages of Lady Colvin's brother Cuthbert's
reminiscences, *After Many Days*, published in Australia in
1918, I take some passages illustrating the family life of
the Fetherstonhaughs. Lady Colvin had been born on
January 25, 1839. ' I have the honour,' writes her
brother, ' of having been born on the day Queen Victoria
came to the throne, the 22nd of June, 1837. My birthplace
was Dardistown, my father's home in County Westmeath,
Ireland, not far from Mullingar, famous for its fat cattle,
from which originated the saying applied to girls with thick
ankles, " beef to the heel like a Mullingar heifer."

MRS. SITWELL
AFTERWARDS LADY COLVIN

' I remember but little of the first six years of my life, beyond, from a window, seeing my father driving with long reins a colt from whose mouth flew foam, flecked with blood. Also I just remember one night seeing a four-in-hand drag, lamps lighted, leaving Dardistown, having on board a lot of my uncles, all smoking cigars, bound for my grandfather's place " Mosstown." The late Beresford Cairnes, of Parramatta, seemed to know a lot about my people, for he told me that not only were there usually forty blood horses in the Mosstown stables, but that often forty people sat down to dinner there. This is not to be wondered at when I mention that my grandmother bore no less than twenty-eight children to my grandfather. She outlived her husband, to whom she was married at sixteen. In her old age she used to go to sleep in her armchair after dinner, and one evening in her seventy-fifth year she did not awaken again in this world. Seventeen of the children grew up. The men were tall and handsome, all of them good horsemen and good shots, and I think there were some pretty gay boys among them. Some of my aunts I can remember as beautiful women.

' With such a family, accompanied too with proverbial Irish prodigality, is it any wonder that my father sold Dardistown in 1843, under the Encumbered Estates Act, and took his family to Germany for economy's sake ? Living and education were very cheap then in Germany. My father's family consisted of my mother, three sons and five daughters—so that moving to Germany with our belongings was no joke. We went to " Neuwied-am-Rhein " for a year, and I remember a big flood on the Rhine, and going up to the counter of a shop in a boat. From Neuwied we went to Frankfurt-am-Main, where we lived for four years until the revolution in 1848 scared us back to old Ireland. I must confess that we carried away very happy memories of Germany and of the Germans. . . .

' Frankfurt is still very real to me—the Zeil, the Ross Market, the Hotel d'Angleterre, Bethman's beautiful place with the far-famed Ariadne sculpture, the Promenade round the town, made after the fortifications were taken down, and finally the Judenstrasse where the Jews had to live. Our house, the " Burgenmeisterhaus," a large three-storied building, fronted the Promenade, and a very happy and cheerful life we young people lived in it. There were a good many British families living in Frankfurt, but we were on very friendly terms with a number of nice German families also. My eldest sister and my brothers used to go to the German balls and parties. We Irish seemed somehow to get on better with the Germans than did the English. We were, I take it, more free and easy, not so stand-off, " don't you know."

' My father was then forty, quite a young man, though to me he seemed quite old. He was a splendid shot. (Years afterwards, on the morning of his eightieth birthday, he came to my bedroom and held out a bag of snipe he had shot before breakfast.) He and a great friend of his, Robert M'Carthy, used to go on shooting excursions in Germany. They imported a fine upstanding Irish mare, and a real Irish jaunting car, which rather amazed the Germans and caused some amusement.

' In Frankfurt I went to a German school, and for four years I was taught as if I were a German boy (how I praise God that I was not !), with the result that when we left Germany I spoke German better than I did English. . . .

' Among the English living in Frankfurt when we were there was a Dr. Leighton and his family. His eldest son Fred, who afterwards became famous as Sir Frederic Leighton, was much at our house, and became a prime favourite with my father, who always called him " Fritz." He was a handsome boy then, about eighteen, and very attractive. He was studying to be an artist and was a clever caricaturist. My brother had quite a collection of his caricatures and little sketches of friends. I had a little oil-painting of his done on the cover of an old book, and I have still a pencil sketch of what he intended to be a painting of the Babes in the Woods. " Fritz " thought himself at that time to be very much in love with my eldest sister. . . .

' Then came the troublous upheaval year of 1848, and not thinking it safe to remain in a country seething with revolution, we decided to leave. Even before we left there was street fighting in Frankfurt. . . .

' We returned to Ireland at about the end of the frightful famine of 1847 and 1848. The worst was over before our return, but of the many terrible times of trouble and distress through which poor old Ireland has passed, none pressed more hardly on her than the disastrous famine caused by the failure of the potato crop, the staple food of my countrymen. The poor people died in hundreds of thousands, of absolute starvation. . . .

' As our old home " Dardistown " had been sold when we returned to Ireland, we rented a place in County Westmeath called Rath-Caslin, where we were near many relatives. I then went to a large school in Wales. All I learned there was to fight and be a blackguard. . . .

' After a year in Wales I went to school at Belfast at the old Academy, over which reigned a Dr. Bryce—a Presbyterian clergyman and a gentle good man. It also was a large school—about one hundred boarders and a large number of day boys. While in Wales I had to fight every boy in the school anywhere near my own age. At Belfast I really do not remember having had a fight at all. . . .

' After a while we left Rath-Caslin and went to live at Kingstown, on the sea near Dublin. Our greatest friends there were the Brookes. The Reverend Mr. Brooke was a delightful man, and he had an equally delightful family. There was a charming Roman Catholic clergyman in Kingstown at the time, a tall thin man, and these two men, Mr. Brooke and Father Germaine, might often be seen coming along the street arm in arm, the best of friends, and yet probably the very same evening Mr. Brooke would be preaching a controversial sermon and dealing sledge-hammer blows at the other's church.

' The eldest son, Stopford, who took holy orders, died
lately.   His name has become a household word in religious
and literary circles.   His life of that magnificent and most
lovable man, the Reverend F. W. Robertson, is an enthralling book. . . .

' In our avenue lived the Wolseleys.   Garnet, afterwards
Field-Marshal Sir Garnet Wolseley, was then a lad, bright
and winning.   Another brother, who was a constant visitor
at our house, became an army surgeon, and there I first
met my great friend Fred Wolseley, so well known in
Australia as the inventor of the shearing machine, of whom
more anon.

' In 1852 my father, two brothers and a cousin, Travers
Adamson (afterwards for years Crown Prosecutor in Melbourne) started off for Melbourne to try their luck at the
diggings.   I pulled out into Dublin Bay in my boat, met
them in the Bay and waved my last farewell to them. . . .

' Most of the twelve months after my father left for
Australia I spent at home and at my uncle's, as I was
delicate and had to leave school several times.   My mother
(a Curtis) came of a clever, talented family—she was very
musical and well read, and to a certain extent a classical
scholar.   She could read her New Testament in the Greek
text, and had a little knowledge of Hebrew.

' Just at this time Dickens' works were coming out in
serial form, and I remember how eagerly we all looked
forward to a new number of *David Copperfield*.   Truly, our
home was a happy one.   My mother used to read Dickens
and Thackeray to her five daughters, and to me when at
home.   She was deeply religious—hers was not the church-
going and psalm-singing and pulling a long face sort of
religion, but real religion—the religion of Christ.   Withal
she was strictly orthodox. . . .

' Four of my sisters are still alive [1917]—one married a
French engineer, M. Ponsarde.   She and he went through
the two sieges of Paris.   *Mon Dieu!* how she did hate the
Prussians—" cochons " she always called them—and I can

now readily believe all the atrocities she attributed to them. The Ponsardes' sympathies were with the Communists until they murdered the Archbishop of Paris and started burning the beautiful city. For many years I had in my possession a letter from my sister with *Par ballon monté* (by balloon post) on the envelope. I wish I had managed to keep some of her letters from Paris under siege. She nursed in the hospitals most of the time. Her husband was afterwards at the Panama Canal doing engineering work.

'Another sister, Fanny Sitwell, when a widow, married late in life Sidney Colvin.'

Madame Ponsarde, I might mention here, died shortly before Lady Colvin. Their father, meanwhile, having failed as a digger, was appointed Police Magistrate at the Buckland River, and in 1853 the young Cuthbert went out to join him. Two years later the rest of the family followed.

It was not till 1892 that Mrs. Sitwell's father died. I will insert here a character sketch of him from the Hamilton *Spectator*, printed in his son's book : ' A well-known, venerable, but, nevertheless, sprightly figure, that of an old colonist, respected by all ; the man who had a kindly word and smile for everybody, and upon whom everybody smiled in return, will be seen amongst us no more. " The dear old Governor " is dead. Not an Excellency, but " The Governor," for by this name Mr. Cuthbert Fetherstonhaugh, who reigned in the hearts of many people of this district, will be better and more fondly remembered than by his ancient and historical family patronymic. Now and again he might be addressed as " Mr. Fetherston," for short, but the nonagenarian who expired at his residence, " Correagh," at five o'clock on Wednesday, better liked to be addressed by the title given him by his many friends years ago. How it came to be conferred upon him we know not ; but we do know that he was from time to time introduced to various Excellencies, including Lord Hopetoun, as " The Governor," and acknowledged by them as such. Many hearing of his death will be apt to exclaim, " Shall we ever look upon his like again ? " He was a man amongst men, a genuine unaffected Irish gentleman—which, all the world over, is admitted to be the best type of a man.

' Cuthbert Fetherstonhaugh, born at Grouse Lodge, County Westmeath, Ireland, on the 27th November 1803, was a son of Theobald Fetherstonhaugh, of Mosstown, and had no fewer than twenty-seven brothers and sisters, seventeen of whom grew up tall, handsome men and women. In 1827 he married Miss Susan Curtis, who bore him six daughters and three sons, of whom five daughters and two sons are still alive. Of her it is said by those who had the pleasure of her acquaintance, " She was a devout Christian and faithful friend and helper of the poor and sorrowful." This lady went to her rest in 1871.

' In 1852 " The Governor " came out to Australia, where about that time gold was said to be so abundant that one could hardly avoid making a fortune. " The Governor," however, managed to avoid it. Two of his sons came out with him, and in 1853 he was joined by his younger son, Cuthbert. In 1856 he was followed by his wife and five daughters, and thus happily united with his loved ones, he strove to make his way in the world. Like many other scions of old families, he tried his luck on the goldfields. He endeavoured in various ways to make a fortune, but felt his lack of commercial knowledge, and, whilst making a large pecuniary loss, merely gained experience. But he was an educated man, and his attainments in 1854 enabled him to secure the position of Police Magistrate at the Buckland River. He soon became a well-known figure to the diggers, and his cheery manner, straight-forwardness, and never-failing courtesy quickly gained for him the popularity he never subsequently forfeited.

' About 1855 Mr. Fetherstonhaugh came to Hamilton, then known as " The Grange," when Acheson ffrench was squire of Monivae, F. Hale Puckle Commissioner of Crown Lands, and wire fences an unknown quantity. " The Governor's " jurisdiction extended from Hamilton to

Casterton, Coleraine, Digby, Branxholme, and in fact all over the country of which those were and still are the centres. There were no shire councils in those days, no roads level as bowling greens, no bridges across rivers or creeks, but blow high blow low, with rivers running bankers, he had periodically to put in an appearance at all those places and administer the law. He was always well mounted, was as regular as clockwork in official appointments to the day, nay to the very minute. There was no waiting for the Police Magistrate to appear, no cause to wonder where he could be ; this, although many a time and oft he, in order to reach his destination, had to swim the Wannon, and the creek on the banks of which the town of Coleraine is situate, when in flood. Many were the narrow escapes he had from being carried away. Needless to add that such a man received a hearty welcome wherever he went. And so he continued honestly and zealously to perform his allotted tasks until the year 1869, when, owing to some political jugglery, whilst in possession of all his vigorous faculties, his mind and judgment unimpaired, his services were dispensed with, and he was superannuated. Twenty years after his superannuation, when on a visit to New South Wales, he rode over fifty miles to and at a kangaroo hunt, and, as our informant tells us, " came in as fresh as a lark," which, we submit, no man with impaired physical or mental faculties could have done. As a magistrate, who knew him well, says, " His decisions were not only considered equitable, but always good law."

' No keener sportsman ever hunted fox or put gun to shoulder. Even in his youthful days in Westmeath he was known as the daring fox-hunter, and his prowess on Lancer is not yet forgotten in that county. As a snipe-shot he could, even during recent years, " wipe the eye " of many a younger man. In fact, we have never known of anyone possessed of a finer constitution, and one could easily believe him a year or two ago when, his heart's action commencing to fail, he was wont to say, " I have never had a headache

or taken a dose of physic in my life, and don't know what
a liver is."

'In a somewhat hastily, and must we say, sorrowfully,
written account of a long and good life like "The Governor's,"
many circumstances in connection therewith are apt to be
overlooked, but we can mention a few episodes in connection with him as a sportsman. On one occasion he was
riding to hounds near Hamilton and smoking a short pipe.
His horse slipped in taking off at a rasper, and he came a
regular cropper, landing on his head and smashing a new
hat. Coolly he rose to his feet, and laughingly remarked
to the late Thomas Seymour, who was close behind him,
"Ah! Tom, I've smashed my hat, but I've saved my
dhudeen; see, it is still going," and he mounted again,
puffing away as though nothing had happened. On another
occasion, whilst hunting in Westmeath, he at almost the
very commencement of a long run fractured a shoulder-
blade, but went throughout the hunt without a murmur,
or letting anyone know what had happened. Again, in
1867, an irate Teuton, who, strange to say, did not know
"The Governor" even by sight, followed him through his
paddock, vowing vengeance, and called out to him, "I'll
have you up before old Fetherston!" Imagine the man's
surprise when "The Governor" turned round, snapped his
fingers, and exclaimed, "I don't care that for old Fetherston." Such a contempt for the majesty of the law, as
represented by a known terror to evildoers, quite staggered
his accuser, who refrained from further trouble. It is also
said (but indignantly denied by the lady) that "The
Governor" having come to grief over a rail fence, one of
his daughters being rather close behind him, called out,
"Don't move, Governor," and forthwith cleared fence,
father and horse.

'We are indebted to one of "The Governor's" nearest
and dearest friends for the following tribute to his character:
"He ever looked upon the best side of human nature,
but when a cowardly or dishonest action came under his

notice, his denunciation of the offender was scathing and
severe. In religion, he kept to the old well-beaten path,
that of an English churchman of the Evangelical school,
but by no means a bigoted one, being liberal and tolerant
to others who were striving to reach the same goal by other
avenues." With Tennyson he believed in "the larger
hope." . . .

'During his last illness, which extended over five or
six weeks, his kindly consideration for others continued to
be as conspicuous as it had ever been. Though, at times,
suffering intense pain, his thoughts were for those around
him. Patient and resigned, he would sometimes exclaim,
"The Lord has been very good to me. I wish He would
take me now and give me rest," and his supplication was
mercifully granted. A more peaceful death-bed was never
witnessed. Cheerful to the end, confident that he was
amongst those whom Christ died to save, "The Governor"
sighed his last and glided away into

"The quiet haven of us all."'

Frances Sitwell went out to Australia with the family in
1855, but she did not stay long, returning to marry, at
the early age of sixteen or little more, the Rev. Albert
Sitwell, whom she had known, and was betrothed to, in
Ireland. The next event in her life was an attack of cholera
in Calcutta, where her husband had a chaplaincy, and this
made necessary a return to England, to a living in the East
End of London. Two boys were born.

In what year Colvin and Mrs. Sitwell first met I have
not ascertained: but it was the late eighteen-sixties. In
1870, says Mr. Champneys, Colvin, with whom he was then
sharing a house at Hampstead, with Appleton, editor of
the *Academy*, 'invited me to go with him to dine in Bethnal
Green with Mr. and Mrs. Sitwell, with the latter of whom he
was forming a close friendship, and who, many years later,
became his wife. I fully shared his appreciation of the
lady, and she became equally my own friend, giving a new

charm and increased intimacy to my already mature friendship with Sidney Colvin.   Not much later the Sitwells removed to Minster in Thanet, on his appointment as vicar. I visited them there on more than one occasion.   In our constant intercourse and ever-ripening friendship I realised how admirably Mrs. Sitwell supplemented Colvin's natural qualities.   Her bright intelligence and instinctive appreciation of excellence of various kinds seemed as it were an efflorescence of the more solid and scholarly judgment of Sidney, while her social tact and ready sympathy supplied whatever might have seemed lacking in him of the lighter graces which conduce to enjoyable social intercourse.'

Among the Sitwells' friends were their neighbours at Stepney, the Rev. J. R. Green the historian, Stopford Brooke and H. R. Haweis.   All might have gone well had not Mr. Sitwell been a man of unfortunate temperament and uncongenial habits.   It soon became clear that a rift was probable, and when Mr. Sitwell was given a country living in the heart of distant Thanet, a crisis could not be averted. Mrs. Sitwell, with the amelioration of visits to London friends, managed to endure ; but when a new trial came in April 1873, in the death of her younger boy, she broke away. I find Lady Carlisle thus writing to her :—

' MY DEAREST FANNIE,—Thank you so much for your Photo of yr. two dear boys.   It was good of you to let us have it, and I well sympathize with the thought you have that they should not be separated in our minds. . . . I cannot tell you how glad I am that I really know you and love you now.   I shall never change now towards you—I shall always feel the most tender loving fondness for you— and rejoice that we have got to understand one another. You have been so very dear and affectionate to me—and I am very grateful to you for it.   I do not know whether any friend can be much to you who have such a hard life and who have lost so cruelly much—but if ever I can show you my affection in deeds, I will do so—for it is very real—

and it may be that some day you may want me. If ever you do, be *quite* certain that I will faithfully do my very utmost for you. . . .'

By the time that the Cockfield visit occurred, in August 1873, Mrs. Sitwell was apparently sufficiently independent to be acting as secretary of the Working Men's College in Queen's Square, but there had been no official separation.

That this was imminent a year later we learn from a letter from Lady Carlisle to Colvin in May 1874 : ' I know that this will involve a most trying storm, and I think as I told her (and I am afraid she was vexed at my saying so) that she will have to defy a good many people just at present ; but all that will soon blow over and everyone will recognize that she has done the right, the wise thing. . . . I have often and often been thinking of her since I left England, and wishing with all my heart that her life could be set going on a quiet, if not on a happy basis. But her health requires her to be freed from any more shocks—No more demands must be made on her extraordinary courage. Why should she be allowed to be quite worn out before her youth is over ? '

CHAPTER VI

MRS. SITWELL AND R. L. STEVENSON : I

1873

HERE, from *Memories and Notes*, is Colvin's account of the Cockfield visit : ' I had landed from a Great Eastern train at a little country station in Suffolk, and was met on the platform by a stripling in a velvet jacket and straw hat, who walked up with me to the country rectory where he was staying and where I had come to stay. . . . I could not wonder at what I presently learnt—how within an hour of his first appearance at the rectory, knapsack on back, a few days earlier, he had captivated the whole household.

' If you want to realize the kind of effect he made, at least in the early years when I knew him best, imagine this attenuated but extraordinarily vivid and vital presence, with something about it that at first sight struck you as freakish, rare, fantastic, a touch of the elfin and unearthly, a sprite, an Ariel. And imagine that, as you got to know him, this sprite, this visitant from another sphere, turned out to differ from mankind in general not by being less human but by being a great deal more human than they ; richer-blooded, greater-hearted ; more human in all senses of the word, for he comprised within himself, and would flash on you in the course of a single afternoon, all the different ages and half the different characters of man, the unfaded freshness of a child, the ardent outlook and adventurous day-dreams of a boy, the steadfast courage of manhood, the quick sympathetic tenderness of a woman, and already, as early as the mid-twenties of his life, an almost uncanny share of the ripe life-wisdom of old age.

66

He was a fellow of infinite and unrestrained jest and yet of infinite earnest, the one very often a mask for the other ; a poet, an artist, an adventurer ; a man beset with fleshly frailties, and despite his infirm health of strong appetites and unchecked curiosities ; and yet a profoundly sincere moralist and preacher and son of the Covenanters after his fashion, deeply conscious of the war within his members, and deeply bent on acting up to the best he knew. . . .'

I quote again from Mr. Champneys : ' It was late in the year 1873 that Robert Louis Stevenson first appeared on the scene. I was among the very first who was introduced to him, and I remember that he spent a week as my guest in the cottage on the top of Hampstead Hill which I then occupied as a bachelor. Indeed, I am almost certain that during this visit he wrote his first paper for an English publication—the *Portfolio*, to which both Colvin and I were contributors. Colvin was the very friend Stevenson needed at this juncture, for he had already won his spurs in art and literary criticism, had an extensive acquaintance with editors, and was both in attainment and judgment specially fitted to preside over the start of a literary career—the more, not the less, because by genius and temperament these two were so widely different. I have both read and heard insinuations that Sidney's Colvin's fame rested mainly on his special association with Robert Louis Stevenson. Any dispute as to the proportion in which each profited by the other is as distasteful to me as it would have been to either of them, and it need only be said that the association was mutually beneficial, that Mrs. Sitwell was fully a partner in it, and that it endured till death.'

' Among the guests at Cockfield,' Colvin continues, ' I found one, a boy of ten, watching for every moment when he could monopolize Stevenson's attention, either to show off to him the scenes of his toy theatre or to conduct him confidentially by the hand about the garden or beside the moat ; while between him and the boy's mother, Mrs. Sitwell, there had sprung up an instantaneous understanding.

Not only the lights and brilliancies of his nature, but the strengths and glooms that underlay them, were from the first apparent to her, so that in the trying season of his life which followed he was moved to throw himself upon her sympathies with the unlimited confidence and devotion to which his letters of the time bear witness.'

Certain of these letters are printed in the four-volume edition of Stevenson's correspondence, where they fill many pages. Day after day Stevenson poured out his news—news from within and news from without ; but it was necessary when that edition was published that certain parts should be withheld, on account of their intimate character. The whole correspondence is now in the Advocates' Library at Edinburgh, to which Colvin bequeathed it. In 1923, however, he made a selection from it which ran through three numbers of the *Empire Review*, and from this I now make a further selection, choosing such passages as show most vividly how dependent the young man had become upon his new and understanding friend. Taken together with those published in the four-volume edition of Stevenson's Letters, which are well known, they prove the strength of the hold which she was exercising.

Colvin, in introducing the extracts in the *Empire Review*, wrote thus : ' It must be borne in mind that the years to which most of these letters belong were years when Stevenson's character was as yet unformed and his life beset by many difficulties—his years, in a word, of *Sturm und Drang*. In his case the *Sturm und Drang* were specially severe ; partly from the native fire of genius in his blood, partly through his extreme diffidence and uncertainty as to his own powers and purposes, still more by reason of the painful misunderstanding, chiefly on religious grounds, which existed for the time being between himself and his father ; and not a little, lastly, through the reaction of his nature against the uncongenial austerity of the climate, moral and mental, of his native Edinburgh.

' All these elements of disturbance were working danger-

COCKFIELD RECTORY, SUFFOLK
WHERE R. S. L. AND COLVIN FIRST MET

ously in him, together with the strain arising from physical ill-health, when he first met Mrs. Sitwell in his twenty-third year.   In her he found from the first the full measure of womanly understanding and sympathy of which his nature was in need.   Her helpfulness was presently backed by the technical advice and encouragement of Sidney Colvin ; and under these joint influences he quickly began to find his feet in literature, and to win acceptance for his work in the best periodicals of the day.   Several of the schemes begun at this time and mentioned with eagerness in his letters came in the end to nothing ; others of his efforts were readily accepted by such editors as Philip Gilbert Hamerton (the *Portfolio*), George Grove (*Macmillan's Magazine*), and Leslie Stephen (*Cornhill Magazine*).'

Here is a passage from the letter dated September 9, 1873 : ' I am afraid this letter is incoherent a little ; but this and yesterday have been rather bad days with me. How poor all my troubles are compared with yours ; I am such a scaly alligator and go through things on the whole so toughly and cheerily.   I hope you will not misunderstand this letter and think I am *Werther*ing all over the place.   I am quite happy and never think about these bothers, and I am sure if you were to ask my father and mother they would tell you that I was as unconcerned as any Heathen deity ; but "heartless levity" was always one of my complaints.   And a good thing, too.   "Werena my heart licht, I wad die."

' I take it kind in Nature, having a day of broad sunshine and a great west wind among the garden trees, at this time of all others ; the sound of wind and leaves comes in to me through the window, and if I shut my eyes I might fancy myself some hundred miles away under a certain tree. And that is a consolation, too ; these things *have been*.

> ' " To-morrow, let it shine or rain,
> Yet cannot this the past make vain ;
> Nor uncreate and render void
> That which was yesterday enjoyed."

I have the proof of it at my heart, it never felt so light and happily stirred in the old days.   Just now, when the whole world looks to me as if it were lit with gas, and life a sort of metropolitan railway, it is a great thing to have clear memory of sunny places.   How my mind rings the changes upon sun and sunny !   Farewell, my dearest friend.'

Mrs. Sitwell seems to have written to her young friend's mother soon after this London visit, for I find Mrs. Stevenson replying thus on October 30 :—

' DEAR MRS. SITWELL,—Very many thanks to you for your kind note & for all your goodness to my boy.   I can assure you it has been a great comfort to me to know that he was among kind friends & well cared for, particularly just now when I know he is not strong.   I was just thinking of writing to tell you how grateful both his Father & I felt to you when I received your note.   I daresay you do not wonder that I cannot think of letting him go farther away without getting another sight of him, so I have determined to go to London with Mr. Stevenson on Saturday, so I shall hope soon to have an opportunity of telling you in person how grateful I am to you.   Louis has talked so much of you that I quite feel as if I knew you, but still a meeting face to face will make correspondence easier.   I do trust we shall find our dear boy improving & that a complete change & rest may with God's blessing soon restore him to health & strength.   He makes a great blank here, as I daresay you can understand.   As I hope very soon to have the pleasure of seeing you I shall not write more at present, but with renewed thanks & very kind regards I am ever,—Yours most truly,   M. I. STEVENSON '

In November Stevenson was in London again, to consult Sir Andrew Clark, who at once despatched him to the Riviera.   *En route* he wrote a long letter. to Mrs. Sitwell, beginning at Dover, November 5 : ' My father was much delighted with you, as I knew of course he would be ; but you and Colvin have so lamentably overdone your

solemnity that you have given rise to an entirely new
theory of my illness. I have been in " the very worst
possible hands," my illness is almost entirely owing to your
society ; and so forth. Are they not perplexing people to
deal with ?

' I have an article in my head which I think might do for
the *Portfolio* ; you see you always inspire me.'

From Paris, November 6 : ' There were two English
ladies in the carriage with me going to Italy under the
guidance of a man ; all three stolid, obtuse, and unemo-
tional. It did make me angry to think that a third of the
money that will be spent in hawking these dull creatures
through all that is sunny and beautiful would suffice to
take you, with all your eager sensibilities and quick nerves.'

CHAPTER VII

GLADSTONE, GAMBETTA, HUGO, SIR CHARLES
NEWTON AND TRELAWNY

1873-1876

WE can now return to the year 1873 and resume the story of Colvin himself. Stevenson, he tells us, spent a few days at his cottage at Norwood with him in August, after leaving Cockfield, and then returned to Edinburgh ; Colvin seems to have gone to the Howards at Naworth for a short visit, among his fellow-guests being Mr. Gladstone, who was then ' in his fourth year of office as Prime Minister and the sixty-fourth of his age. He had been on an official visit to the Queen at Balmoral, and the route by which he had chosen to leave was a long day's walk, over some of the roughest tracks and through some of the wildest scenery in the Grampians, to Kingussie Station on the Highland Railway. Having slept one night at Kingussie, he took train the next day to Carlisle, and arrived at Naworth in the evening, to all appearance perfectly fresh and un-fatigued by his long tramp of the day before.'

But first a word of description, from *Memories and Notes*, of Colvin's host and his home. ' Naworth, near Brampton in Cumberland,' he says, ' was one of the two family seats of the Earls of Carlisle, romantically placed on the steep side of a glen overhanging a beck which runs down to meet the Irthing near Lanercost Abbey. It was the country home at that date of George Howard, after-wards ninth earl, and of his wife Rosalind, by birth a Stanley of Alderley. No more exceptional or attractive young couple gathered about them in those days a more varied company of talents and distinctions whether in art, literature, or politics. George Howard had married fresh from Cambridge, where he was a couple of years my senior. His ambition was to be a painter, and he worked sedulously at the art under the teaching of that fine austere craftsman and vigorous, caustically tongued personality, Alphonse Legros.

' Besides his painting George Howard cared for nearly all forms of culture. He had a range of manner varying from the most captivatingly cordial and urbane to the cynically sceptical and ironic. He was a born lover of Italy and things Italian. Nature had even modified towards the Italian his strongly marked hereditary Howard type of countenance, and in Tuscany, where the features of the people generally are apt to bear a special stamp of race and finish, I have often enough observed to myself in driving through some provincial market-town, " Why, here is a whole population of George Howards." '

We return now to Mr. Gladstone, in Colvin's words: ' In those first days at Naworth, I remember, I came in for a sample of what struck me as not being by any means his best. An opportunity presenting itself, I strove hard to make him, with the photograph before us, share my enthusiasm for a certain splendid and almost uninjured Greek fourth-century head of a goddess, in all probability Aphroditè, discovered not long before in Armenia and then under offer to the British Museum by the dealer Castellani. Any and every Greek subject that might be broached led Mr. Gladstone's mind at once and inevitably to Homer. Naturally I did not disclose the fact that I was one of the reviewers who some time earlier, in dealing with his volume *Juventus Mundi*, had expressed without compromise the opinion (shared by practically all trained scholars and archæologists) that no Homeric critic had ever shown, along with so minute and systematically tabulated a knowledge of the text, such ingenious perversity as he in comment and interpretation. For one thing, Mr. Gladstone held, and worked out with insistent affirmation and detail, the theory that the *Iliad* and *Odyssey* were indisputably the work of a single individual poet ; that so far as concerns the war of Troy in its human aspects the *Iliad* is strictly historical, and that as to the gods and goddesses who play so large a part in the story, they and their several characters and the Olympian system to which they belong are the actual creation of Homer himself. I found that these rooted convictions concerning Homer stood in the way of his being much interested in my Aphroditè head, or even admitting that it could be Aphroditè at all.'

Here is an extract from Colvin's review, in the *Pall Mall Gazette*, August 5, 1869 : ' Mr. Gladstone affords a highly remarkable instance of versatility in industry, of that habit of mind which for relief seeks no relaxation, but only what may be described as a change of tension. It would, however, be a poor compliment to Mr. Gladstone to discuss either division of his labours with the other division before our eyes—to remind ourselves that his politics and his scholarship, taken separately, are only parts of a feat of double activity, and to assume that, as such, they demand lenience of separate criticism. Neither politics nor scholarship are things that can be done by halves. When, therefore, we find a Prime Minister who is also a Homeric commentator, we expect, in justification of such duality, that his administration on the one hand and his commentaries on the other shall be as well done as if he were pure statesman or pure scholar. Everyone admits this so far as the politics are concerned. No one would think of congratulating Mr. Gladstone on the comparative merit of his Irish Church Bill, considering the pressure of his classical pursuits. But the same principle does not find equal recognition in the case of Learning. Although the days are past when Learning was supposed to have received a compliment if men in high places condescended to meddle with her, there is yet a strong disposition to receive with indulgence a work of hard scholarship from the hand of the foremost statesman of his time. That Mr. Gladstone stands in need of such especial indulgence we by no means say. On the contrary, whatever faults we have to find with his work, lack of thoroughness or pains will not be among them. But it is necessary to premise that in treating of the present book we decline to take into account, what in a general estimate of its author's powers we should be bound to insist on, the difficult circumstances of its production ; and that we propose to deal with it simply in its relation to the subjects which it handles, simply as a contribution, no matter by whom made, to European scholarship.'

' I was half inclined at the time to suppose,' the account continues in *Memories and Notes*, ' that his coldness in response to my enthusiasm must arise from caution lest I should have designs upon the public purse in connection with the purchase of this head. If so, his caution was belated, for the purchase, though I did not know it at the time, had actually been concluded ten days before. But his mind, as I had occasion more than once to observe, seemed always in an alert attitude of self-defence against any suggestion that seemed to point to an increased expenditure from the public purse. Conversation having one day [this was at a later period, after Colvin had gone to the Print Room] turned on public salaries and the relative scales of pay for this or that kind of service, Mr. Gladstone said to me, " I for one would never be a party to increasing the salaries of you gentlemen of the British Museum, for a more delightful occupation I cannot conceive." '

In the winter of 1873-74, as we know both from Colvin's *Memories and Notes* and Stevenson's correspondence, Colvin was twice in the south of France with his new friend. According to *Memories and Notes* he dallied in Paris on his way thither or back, for it was then that he met Gambetta, Madame Adam and Victor Hugo, of whom he writes in that book. His first meeting with Gambetta, he says, was by appointment at his modest quarters in the Rue Montaigne. ' I had till then never seen him either in

the tribune or elsewhere.   From his reputation as the most
impassioned of combatant political orators and leaders—
or, as his enemies had it, the wildest of demagogues—I
had expected to find in him a typical, high-strung, rest-
lessly excitable and volatile son of the South.   It was
therefore with some surprise that I found, instead, a sub-
stantial rubicund person, occupying solidly the middle
of a broad settee, who welcomed me with quiet geniality
and proceeded at once to discuss gravely a question which
was then deeply agitating France, that of the freedom of
the Press.

' For the next four years or more I seldom passed any
time in Paris without seeking opportunity to know him
better.   Once or twice I heard him speak in public debate
at Versailles, once or twice at semi-private political gatherings of his supporters.   More often, that is perhaps four
or five times, I saw him in the character of host at his own
breakfast-table, and about as many times as chief guest
at the evening parties of that most zealous and cordial of
political entertainers, Madame Edmond Adam.

' Among the habitual guests at these breakfasts, and one
of the host's most intimate and trusted friends, was the
famous actor Coquelin, whom I knew independently.   I
have a lively recollection of a day when, after the meal
was over and cigarettes lighted, Coquelin, seated straddle-
wise and talking over the back of his chair, held forth on the
manner in which, if he had the chance, he would wish to
play the part of Alceste in Molière's *Misanthrope.*   " *On
peut être distingué quand on veut,*" he interjected of himself,
with a gesture meant to indicate as much : but the idea
that such a part could fit him only showed that an artist
incomparable within his range, and brilliantly intelligent
to boot, could be very imperfectly conscious of his own
physical limitations.'

In a letter to Henley after Gambetta's sudden and tragic
death, Colvin writes : ' I am sad about Gambetta : there
was a cruel incompleteness in his destiny : and there are

LÉON GAMBETTA

FROM THE MEMORIAL IN THE PLACE DU CARROUSAL, TUILERIES

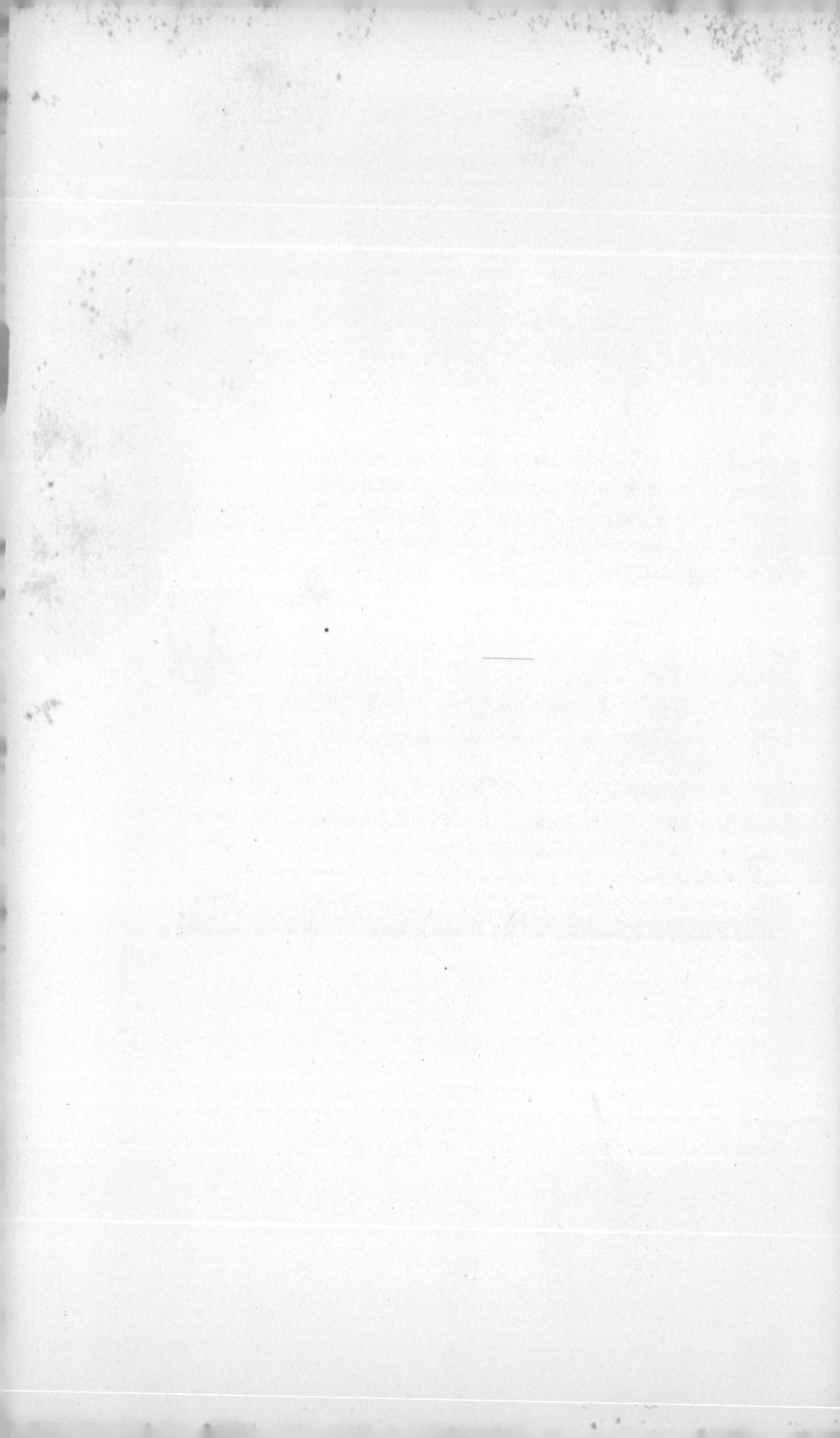

so few spirits of power in the world, and his was one : and when I used to see him, which was I suppose about his best time, he certainly always seemed the bravest and most genial of strong men and fighters.'

At the same time Colvin had been taken to see Victor Hugo, and on his subsequent visits to Paris—in 1874 to 1876—he used always to present himself at the great man's door, and sometimes attended his receptions. ' At these evening gatherings,' he says, ' the ex-actress and ex-beauty Madame Drouet, the housemate and companion of all Hugo's later life even from before his wife's death, used to do the honours. He had just turned his seventieth year, and his strength of body and mind showed no sign of abatement. . . .

' He had a gracious and not too self-conscious patriarchal courtesy and cordiality in welcoming his guests. His voice was mellow, subdued rather than loud, and even when the matter of his utterance was declamatory its delivery was serene. His sturdy figure and abundant—though not wild or untrimmed—white hair and beard, with his firm, easy movements and gestures, were full proofs of vigour. His bearing, which was that of one conscious of authority and tempering it not with condescension but with a benignant old-fashioned grace, I thought became him well. But I thought also that the demeanour of his *entourage* was too submissive in homage, and that the silence for which those nearest him gave sign when he was about to speak was inconsistent with social ease. *" Chut, le maître va parler "*—surely it is no false trick of memory which makes me hear one of the group of satellite friends, Paul Meurice or Vacquerie or Claretie or Lockroy, thus whispering peremptorily to those about him, with a corresponding gesture of the hand, on one evening when the conversation threatened to become general. At any rate to become such it was never, in my experience, allowed.'

It is amusing to recall here how, in London at the same time, George Henry Lewes was stage-managing George Eliot in just the same way.

In March 1875, Colvin, impelled by his interest in classic art, went out to Greece to watch the excavations of the temple of Zeus at Olympia, which were then in full force under German supervision.   His companion was Sir Charles Newton (later to be a colleague), who was then Keeper of the Greek and Roman Antiquities at the British Museum. Colvin describes, in *Memories and Notes*, this learned administrator.   He was not, he says, ' in the full sense of the word a man of genius.   That is to say, he had not the intensity of being, the radiating fire of the spirit, which gives to the personality of genius its power to dominate or enthral.   But he had a character, and a very marked character, of his own : his actual achievement was a considerable one in the history of English, nay, of general Western culture, and in the absence of any full or formal biography it is right that some picture of him, as living as may be, however brief, should be attempted by one who like myself enjoyed the honour of his regard and the advantage of his teaching.   He was my senior by all but thirty years, and I first knew him when I came to London fresh from my Cambridge degree in 1867-68 and threw myself— among other studies which I did my best at the same time to master and to expound in popular reviews and journals —into the special study of classical archæology. . . .

' As he moved about with a somewhat shuffling or flinching gait (for his feet did not in later years carry him very well) among the noble damaged marbles at the British Museum, the kinship between him and them seemed to strike obviously upon the eye.   True, his tall figure was too spare for that of a rightly proportioned Greek god or demigod or sage, but his head was truly Olympian.   The hair grew outward from the parting in rich and waving grizzled masses, to which corresponded a square grizzled beard somewhat roughly kempt : the brow was intent and deeply corrugated, the features severely handsome save for a broken nose, the result of a fall ; but this seemed only to complete his facial likeness to a Greek Zeus injured and

SIR CHARLES NEWTON

imperfectly restored. A great scholar and a great gentleman, he was in all companies a distinguished presence and in all the best was made welcome. . . .

'After their triumph and the establishment of their empire in 1870 the Germans, keen, to their credit be it said, in the pursuit and organization of every other science no less than of the sciences of conquest and spoliation—were determined to take a practical lead in archæological research on classic ground. Their first great undertaking was the excavation, by arrangement with the Greek Government, of the site of the ancient temple and sacred enclosure of Zeus at Olympia, a scheme which had been for a while ardently entertained, but never put in hand, by Lord Elgin, and at which a few tentative scratchings had later been actually made by the French under General Maison. By the winter of 1874-75 this undertaking was in full swing. I was eager to visit and watch it, and with some difficulty persuaded Newton to meet me towards the end of March at Athens in order that we might arrange to travel thence to Olympia together. Some years had gone by since he had last been in the Levant. It was my own first visit to Greek soil. . . .

'The immediate daily fruits of the excavation were such as to leave little time for dreaming, and to raise in trained minds a hundred absorbing problems. Fragments of sculpture and architecture were coming up as thick as potatoes under the spade : the flying Victory of Paionios, duly identified by its inscribed pedestal ; many drums of the columns of the great temple lying regularly in rows as they had fallen outward ; the sculptured figures, one after another and all more or less shattered, of the east pediment of the same temple.

'When I was in Greece,' Colvin adds, ' the German minister there was Herr von Radowitz, a brilliant, still young diplomatist who had been until lately Bismarck's secretary and stood very high in the great Chancellor's favour. He and I saw much of each other at Athens, and were com-

panions on several excursions and for the time being great
friends. He having to depart for Berlin and I for London
about the same time, we had agreed to come away together
by one of the Austrian Lloyd mail-boats proceeding round
Cape Malea to Trieste. An invitation to dinner for both
of us at the English Legation coming for the night on which
we should have started, we decided to change our plans,
stay for the dinner, which we knew was bound to be pleasant,
and travel from Athens by way of Corinth and Patras, a
short cut which would enable us to reach Corfu before the
arrival of the Austrian mail-boat and be picked up there by
her. Carrying out this plan, we came to Corfu accordingly,
and after a few hours' rest went down to the harbour for the
mail-steamer at the hour when she was due. The hour
passed and she did not appear ; and then another hour and
another, and another, until late in the afternoon there came
the news that she had been in collision with an English cargo
ship at three o'clock in the morning and gone down like a
stone with absolutely every soul on board. Thus we two
had had as narrow an escape for our lives as it was possible
to have without the least touch or thrill of adventure in it.
Inasmuch as the change of plan which had brought it about
was of my proposal, Herr von Radowitz, and afterwards
his family, chose to look upon me as having saved his life,
and made much of me accordingly when I went to carry
out some studies at Berlin the next year.'

Colvin and Newton remained on intimate terms until
Newton's death, in 1894. It was with him, I may interpolate here, that Colvin paid his very interesting visit to
that aged Berserk, E. J. Trelawny, the friend of Byron
and Shelley and the author of *The Adventures of a Younger
Son*, 1831. This was in 1881, when the old fellow was
rising eighty-nine. In Colvin's story of the visit he is at his
best : ' Newton and I,' he says, in *Memories and Notes*,
' were the guests for a winter week-end of our friends
Captain and Lady Alice Gaisford in their Sussex home,
distant about a mile from the cottage in the village of

EDWARD JOHN TRELAWNY

Sompting, where Trelawny had then long been living. Our
host, a brother Dilettante of Newton's and mine, was a son
of the once famous Greek scholar and dean of Christ Church,
Thomas Gaisford, and was himself a fine type of handsome,
chivalrous, cultivated English gentleman. He was on
terms of friendly regard and intercourse—under some
degree of protest, if I remember aright, from Lady Alice—
with the old rebel his neighbour, and by previous arrangement walked over with us and introduced us. The house
where Trelawny lived was a large cottage painted red and
set back a little way on the left-hand side of the road, not
far from the entrance to the village. The veteran received
us in a small, old-fashioned room on the ground floor,
where he sat in an arm-chair with a couple of black-and-tan
terriers playing about his feet. I had been accustomed to
hear much of his extraordinary vigour. He had always
been of abstemious habits, and although past eighty-eight,
and a water-drinker, and although he had still inside him
one of the two bullets which had been lodged there by the
assassin Fenton during the Greek war of liberation, he was
nevertheless, it was said, so strong that he had only lately
given up the habit of bathing in the sea in all seasons,
and of warming himself on the coldest mornings, not at
the fire, which he refused to have lighted before noon, but
by the exercise of chopping wood. I was therefore somewhat surprised to perceive in him at first sight all the appearances of decrepitude. He scarcely moved himself in his
chair on our entrance, but sat in a shrunken attitude,
with his hands on his knees, speaking little, and as if he
could only fix his attention by an effort. He wore an embroidered red cap, of the unbecoming shape in use in Byron's
day, with a stiff projecting peak. His head thus appeared
to no advantage ; nevertheless in the ashen colour of the
face, the rough grey hair and beard and firmly modelled
mouth set slightly awry, in the hard, clear, handsome
aquiline profile (for the nose, though not long, was of
marked aquiline shape), and in the masterful, scowling

F

grey eye, there were traces of something both more distinguished and more formidable than is seen in Sir John Millais's well-known likeness of him as an old seaman in his picture "The North-West Passage," a likeness with which the sitter himself was much dissatisfied.

'Passing to the circumstances of Shelley's death in 1822, Trelawny, after showing us the scar where he had burned his hand in plucking the poet's heart out of the ashes, detailed at length his reasons for believing that the sinking of Shelley's boat the "Don Juan" (rechristened the "Ariel"), in the squall after she had left Leghorn Harbour, was due to foul play. He repeated without variation the account of the matter given in his published volume of *Records*, dwelling particularly on the circumstance that he had been himself prevented from putting out in company with his friends in Byron's schooner "The Bolivar" by warnings of the quarantine to which he would thereby make himself liable, addressed to him from the pier by men affecting to be custom-house officers but who turned out not to be custom-house officers after all. And he insisted on the fact that when the wreck of the "Ariel" was brought to the surface her bows were found to be stoven in. This belief that the "Ariel" had not gone down by accident in the squall but been deliberately run down, was one which had by degrees gained complete possession of Trelawny's mind, but is not shared by those who have inquired most carefully into the evidences. When we rose to go he accompanied us into the hall. Newton, in shaking hands, congratulated him on looking so very well considering his age, and then turned to put on his coat: whereupon I could hear the old man, standing behind him, and conscious no doubt of his own fast declining health, growl to himself, "'S very well, 's very well: that's the kind o' lies I was talking of: lies, lies, lies." . . .

'To have shaken the hand which plucked Shelley's heart out of the ashes was,' Colvin ends, 'an experience one was not likely to forget.'

CHAPTER VIII

MRS. SITWELL AND R. L. STEVENSON : II

1874–75

THE letters from Stevenson to Mrs. Sitwell continued to pour forth, and I resume the pleasant task of extracting passages from them.

From Mentone, in February 1874 : Mrs. Sitwell had been in Paris and was now returning to England : ' To-morrow you go, and to-morrow night the Straits will be again between us. Absence from you brings home distances to me wonderfully, and I have a sort of bird's-eye picture of the space that separates us always under my eye. . . .

' No, my paper is not good ; it has the right stuff in it, but I have not got it said.

' I am afraid S. C., when he comes, will be disappointed. I did not tell you he had written me such a jolly note, saying he hoped a great deal from me. It is very nice of him, but I am not so good a card as he thinks ; it is very doubtful to me if I shall ever have wit enough to do more than good paragraphs. However, a good paragraph is a good paragraph, and may give tired people rest and pleasure, quite as well as a good book, although for not so long ; a flower in a pot is not a garden, but it is a flower for all that, and its perfume does the heart good. So let us take heart of grace and be happy.'

The essay on which he was then engaged was that on Walt Whitman.

S. C. went out for a while twice during that winter—1873-74—and was with Stevenson at Mentone and Monte Carlo. Colvin has often been accused of a want of humour ;

but this I think is unfair. He relished humour but did not
seek it or much roll it on the tongue. The reason probably
is that his prevailing desire was to find things to praise,
to become lyrically enthusiastic upon, or even to censure
and dismiss ; and that kind of highway mind has not time
or inclination to loiter in the lanes. Lady Colvin, on the
other hand, loved a joke and laughter. To return to
Colvin and the more frivolous side of life, one performance
in literary facetiousness can be traced to him, or rather to
him as a collaborator, and that is the burlesque hotel
advertisement which he and Stevenson composed together
when they were in the south of France. The only copy
of this card that is known to exist is in the possession of
Mr. Basil Champneys. It is in two languages and runs
(or stumbles) thus :—

' GRAND HOTEL GODAM

' (Englisch—House)

' PLACE DU PARADIS.—ALCIBIADE KROMESKY, PROPRIÉTAIRE

' Tous les agréments du *Hihg-Life* se trouvent réunis dans
ce magnifique établissement, nouvellement organisé et
entretenu sur le pied du confortable le plus recherché.—
Salons de Société, de Lecture et de Billard.
' Pension à prix modérés. Cuisine et service hors ligne.
Spécialités de rosbif, rhum, thé Pekoé, porterbeer, wischky,
old Thom et autres consommations dans le goût britannique
—On parle toutes les langues.

' THE GREAT GOD-DAMN HOTEL

' PLACE DU PARADIS—ALCIBIADES KROMESKY, PROPRIETAR

' All the agreements of hihg-life are reunited in this
magnificent establishment, newly organised, and entertained upon the footing of the most researchd confortable.
—Salons of Society, Lecture, and Billiard.

' Pension to moderate prices. Kitchen and service out of common. Specialitys of roasbeef, rhum-punsch, Pekoë tea, porterbeer, wischkey, old Thom, and other consummations in the britisch taste.—One speaks all the languages.'

' Of the literary projects broached between us at that time,' writes Colvin in *Memories and Notes*, ' the only one I remember was a spectacle-play on that transcendent type of human vanity, Herostratus, who to keep his name from being forgotten kindled the fire that burned down the temple of Ephesus. Psychology and scenic effects as Stevenson descanted on them come up together in my memory even yet, not in any exactness of detail, but only in a kind of vague dazzle and flamboyance.'

We may suppose that Mrs. Sitwell was not unaffected by the ardency of her young adorer, for in March 1874 Lady Carlisle writes to Colvin : ' I daresay I have been lazy about writing owing to the fact that I hear about you from F. S. How very delightful it is to see her so well. It is years since I have seen her anything like what she is now, bright and well and comparatively free from trouble—She laughs so merrily once more and looks as if she could enjoy things—I think she will get through the year tolerably well if only she can manage to keep away from Minster except for Bertie's summer holydays.'

Stevenson returned to Edinburgh in the spring, and I continue the extracts from the *Empire Review* correspondence :—

' *Swanston* [*May* 1874], *Friday*.

' Again very cold. I have been out walking in a sheltered bit of the garden, in a sun-blink. When there is wind, here, it makes a wonderful noise in the trees, that fills the ear agreeably ; and to-day this was broken up and accentuated with the most delightful love songs from all sorts of birds, the blackbird supreme, of course. It was delightful ; one seemed to hear the whole air full of the rustle of the wings of Spring. Only it was strange it should be so cold.

' I find I must write to you pretty often for dear life. I am not so strong as I thought I was and—'

' *Saturday.*

' So far had I written yesterday and the best thing I can do this morning is just to continue—

and I require to keep always present to my mind that there are other people, not here in Edinburgh, and that I have another life to lead all over. And you can't tell how it strengthens me to write to you and to hear from you ; your letters are always tonic to me ; I just say, " Very well— there she is—now look here, old man, you must be as nice as you can." It doesn't matter what, or how, you write, the effect has been always the same in that particular.'

' *Yacht " Heron,"*
' *Oban [Early Summer,* 1874].

' The news, such as it is, has gone to Colvin ; what am I to say ? I am so stupid, I just wish to put in a word to you. I am quite happy, and very well for me. I read away a good deal at odd times, so it isn't all waste time, and during the rest I go in hot for health, and my health is better. I work like a common sailor when it is needful, in rain and wind, without hurt, and my heart is quite stout now. I believe in the future faithfully. I am fully content and fear nothing, not death, nor weakness, nor any falling away from my own standard and yours. I shall be a man yet, and a good man, although day by day, I see more clearly by how much I still fall short of the mark of our high calling ; in how much I am still selfish and peevish and a spoiled child. You will see that I am writing out of a great blackness. It is true, but it does not apall me (I don't know how to spell that word). And there is a good deal of it due to the tempest that is roaring over my head and filling the little cabin with draughts and shudderings of the air. We lie here in a good roadstead ; and so do I in my own constancy. Let the wind blow.'

'Edinburgh [Autumn, 1874]. Saturday.

' I have found what should interest you. A paper in which I had sketched out my life, before I knew you. Here is the exact copy even to the spelling ; the incertitude of the date is characteristic :—

' " I think now, this 5th or 6th of April, 1873, that I can see my future life. I think it will run stiller and stiller year by year ; a very quiet desultorilly studious existence. If God only gives me tolerable health, I think now I shall be very happy ; work and science calm the mind and stop gnawing in the brain, and as I am glad to say that I do now recognise that I shall never be a great man, I may set myself peacefully on a smaller journey ; not without hope of coming to the inn before nightfall.

O dass mein Leben
Nach diesem Ziel ein ewig Wandeln sey !

DESIDERATA

1. Good health.
1. 2 to 3 hundred a year.
3. O du lieber Gott, *friends !*
    Amen.

Robert Louis Stevenson."

' I can't quite say that I know what the " inn " was, therein referred to, but I think I do. It was rather an interesting find, wasn't it ? '

' [Edinburgh, Autumn, 1874.]

' You remember, perhaps, at least I remember, I once wrote to you to tell you how you should do with me ; how it was only by getting on my weak side, looking for the best, and always taking it for granted that I should do the best before it is done, that you ever will get the best out of me. This is profoundly true. . . . I shall be in London this week, or early next : Isn't this good news ? and I think we shall pass a few happy days ; I want you to be the better of

my visit, if only it is possible—do you think it is ? I think
so, and mean to make it so. . . . In a few days, I hope—
hurrah, hurrah, que je suis bien aise ; You shall get better
and be fit for your work and do it well—you *shall* get better.

' Due in London, Euston, 2.30 on Thursday. Shall go to
Savile Club for orders ; do have orders for me there, and
let them be to come early.'

' Swanston, Saturday [Autumn, 1874].

' O !—I 'll tell you something funny. You know how
rarely I can see your face : well, last night I kept dreaming
I saw you arrive at the Finchley Road Station, as you did
the afternoon before I left : and I never could catch more
than a glimpse of your face before it turned into somebody
else's—a horrible, *Scotch* face, commonplace and bitter.

' You don't know how I yearned to-day to see you all.
I feel myself in the uttermost parts of the earth, alone with
ugly puppets, and my heart just melts within me when I
think of you, and S. C., and Mme. G., and Bob [his cousin,
R. A. M. Stevenson]. Any of the four of you I want to see
badly ; and somehow S. C. most, I feel as if I could be
good for him and am so vexed that he is not well.'

' [Edinburgh, late Autumn, 1874.] Saturday.

' I was so glad to get your letter, in spite of bad news. It
is strange to think of you so feeble and with all these troubles
about you ; and then to think of your just holding me by
one hand out of the gulph, which, alas ! is true. I know
that very well ; as the effect of my last stay with you died
away, and the cold weather came, I have had a bad struggle
with myself day by day, and night by night. . . . O don't
let go my hand.'

' I shall (if I can manage my parents, to whom I have not
yet spoken in the matter) arrive at King's Cross on Wednesday evening. Is there a hotel at King's Cross ? I shall
come to the College for you, shall I not ? '

' [*Edinburgh, December*, 1874.] *Wednesday.*

' Thank you, my dear lady, for your letter : O, yes, God knows every word of it knocked at my heart, and I will try to be what you would have me ; and I do feel the ground stable under my feet as I have never felt it heretofore.'

' *Friday.*

' Madonna, I am so glad you are in the world, and I do want to be reminded of it often. . . . Good night, Madonna —I pray all my Gods for you fervently, and if they are impotent, they are yet beautiful—look at them, and you will be good and brave.'

' *Thursday.*

' By the by, if I am to do a paper that S. C. suggests—and I think I will—I should like any letter of mine in which I say anything about winter, snow, ice, Duddingstone, or even sunsets, to give a look over ; I shall see if I want them, or not ; I hope I may do without them ; but you see my letters to you are the only notes I make, and especially when I am skating my mind runs miles away from literary intentions, so that my impressions are rather fragmentary to work upon.'

' [*Edinburgh, December*, 1874.]

' Colvin's article on Champneys' book is very wise, but I think he went too far in admitting that the sensations given us by the Alps were, in themselves, greater than those given by the Romney Marsh. I don't think so. A great dead flat is at least a more ideal, more perfect, more satisfactory thing than ever so high a hill ; because the hill might be ever so much higher, whereas the marsh can be no flatter if it bust itself. Besides, big hills may be more of a sensation to a person brought up in Suffolk ; but, if novelty is to come in at all, quite a flat is a violent sensation to me ; for I come from the hills—I had not seen anything quite flat, except the sea and here and there a billiard table, until I went abroad and spent some days in Holland. Please communicate this to Colvin, unless he has quarrelled with me by

chance—he studiously will not answer my letters. I have
been a bad correspondent, but he has been so much a *badder* !
Indeed, if you won't think me getting insane, I think the
world in a conspiracy against me ; for devil a one will write
to me except yourself. Even Bob sends me scraps only
fit to light a pipe with.

' At last I can write ; I could not make a mark on this
paper with a steel pen, and you do not know with how much
sweat of the brow my former letters were written. Now I
have taken to a quill, all goes well. . . .

' I want to know how you are badly. I say, you have
much need to take care of yourself, if it were only for the
sake of a young gentleman in Edinburgh alone—you don't
know how the thought of anything going wrong with you
haunts and disquiets me.'

' *Wednesday.*

' Dear, I am wonderfully happy. Pleased with my work,
not disquiet about you ; I must never disquiet myself
about you any more ; you will have strength for all that
comes, after you have found strength for what has come.'

Mr. Champneys' book, *A Quiet Corner of England*,
describes the Romney Marsh and Rye district. Stevenson,
Mr. Champneys tells me, reviewed the book in the *Academy*.
Further extracts :—

' [*Edinburgh, early Spring*, 1875.]

' The best trumpet that I can suggest is to read Thomas
Carlyle's Essay on Burns. Sick as I am of reading anything
in which so much as the name of Burns appears, I was really
electrified (beg pardon for such a *Daily Telegraphism*) by
this. It is full of very fine criticism, expressed here and
there in rather an old-fashioned, academical style, full of
beautiful humanity—see the whole passage about Burns
having refused money for his songs—and full of wonderful
wisdom. The whole conclusion is indeed admirable ; as
where he says that all fame, riches, fortune of all sorts is to
true peace no more than " mounting to the house top to

reach the stars " ; and again about Byron : " the fire that
was in him was the mad fire of a volcano ; and now we look
sadly into the ashes of a crater which ere long will fill itself
with snow."

' I subscribe to that essay.   My own is quite unnecessary.
Do read it, it will do you good ; it would do the dead good.
It has reminded me once again of the great mistake of my
life—and of everybody else's ; that we are all trying to gain
the whole world if you will, except what alone is worth
keeping ;   our own soul.   God bless T. Carlyle, say I.'

'[*Edinburgh*, 1875.]   *Monday*.

' DEAREST MOTHER,—This is E. A. Poe :—

'" Because I feel that, in the heavens above,
    The angels, whispering to one another,
Can find, among their terms of burning love,
    None so devotional as that of " Mother";
Therefore by that dear name I long have called you,
    You who are *more than mother unto me*,
And fill my heart of hearts."

' I do not know to whom it was that I wrote last spring,
when I was at the bottom of sorrow at Mentone—but I
think it was to Bob ; if it was not to him it was to you—
calling for a mother ; I felt so lonely just then ; I cannot
tell you what sense of desertion and loss I had in my heart ;
and I wrote, I remember, to someone, crying out for the
want of a mother—nay, when I fainted one afternoon at
the Villa Marina, and the first sound I heard was Madame
Garschine saying " Berecchino " so softly, I was glad—O, so
glad !—to take her by the hand as a mother, and make a
mother of her at the time, so far as it would go.   You do
not know, perhaps—I do not think I knew myself, perhaps,
until I thought it out to-day—how dear a hope, how sorry
a want, this has been for me.   For my mother is my father's
wife ; to have a French mother, there must be a French
marriage ; the children of lovers are orphans.   I am very
young at heart—or (God knows) very old—and what I want
is a mother, and I have one now, have I not ? '

' [17 *Heriot Row, Edinburgh, March* 1875.] *Wednesday.*

' DEAREST MOTHER,—I am all right again, I think, and write to tell you so at once. Forgive me if I write no more. I am reading " The Village on the Cliff," and cannot tell you how beautiful I think it. I am inclined to give up literature. I can't write like that. Never mind, je serai fidèle.

' Goodbye, dear.'

' [17 *Heriot Row, Edinburgh, March* 1875.] *Tuesday.*

' Your son is very sad to-night, dear, very cold in body and black at heart. The snow lies melting outside under a thin north-easterly rain. It is bitter cold ; and the thickest shoes are wet through in the length of a street. I have done no work to-day—it would not come ; and I have been so sad ; so sad, and longed for a sight of you, and a few moments of speech with you, more than I can say. Did I tell you—yes, I did, I remember—how I thought I saw you in the street ? Do you know I wish so much to meet you by chance somewhere ; and I keep telling myself I shall see you at the next corner, and making long stories as a child does ; only you never come. . . .

' My vitality is very low in every way ; although I am not at all ill—all I want is a little warmth, a little sun, a little of the life I have when I am by you.'

' [*Edinburgh, Spring,* 1875.]

' I do not know if you are aware how much you help me in my work ; it is not only that I have a strong motive ; it is that I have always a woman to think of ; and that is for so much.'

' *Swanston* [*Spring,* 1875]. *Friday night.*

' I am so glad to hear no ill of your health. You must not die. I cannot think of what life would be to me if you were gone ; a great black hole, without form and void. Please keep this in view. Although I speak jocularly I am grave at heart. I should be left to speak in the words of

surely the most affecting historical document in the world—
Emery Tylney's character of George Wishart, " O that the
Lord had left her to me, her poor boy, that she might have
finished what she had begun." I can't tell you how beautiful that whole paper is from which these words are imitated.
I was reading it again the other day, and my heart came into
my mouth when I got to that passage : one is so little
prepared for such a cry of the soul amid the succinct details
of life and manners that surround it. And the saying, in
my mind, attaches itself to you : I have had to explain all
round that you might understand the full meaning of the
words and how they are not simply my words, but have
been sanctified by the fire of martyrdom and the name of
one of the good, pure, quiet delicate spirits of the Earth ;
and you needed to know that to know why I like to apply
them to you.'

' [*Edinburgh, late February,* 1875.] *Friday.*

' First, the Wagner Concert. Yes, it was a great success,
and what do you think ? Baxter said the very thing of
him that you had said, to wit, that he was like Walt
Whitman. Baxter and I go together to all the concerts that
are going ; however, we generally come and go with
Beethoven—we have now added Wagner to the list ; he
is jolly and fresh, like a wind.'

Baxter was Charles Baxter, Stevenson's lawyer friend
and, later, executor : one of the ' Three Musketeers ' in
Henley's poem.

' [*Paris, Spring,* 1875.] *Friday.*

' My dear, the Gods are against me. I have missed
the trains so freely that I am stuck here for yet another
night. I shall be in London, however, to-morrow at six.
I shall go straight to the club, in hopes of finding Colvin,
or a note from you. It is the most splendid weather, the
trees are out along the bright streets in their first greens,
and the whole town sounds and shines about one, so that
it goes to the head like wine.'

' [*Edinburgh, Spring*, 1875.]   *Friday.*

' This spirit of mine must ever be somewhat holy ground ;
your son must be better than the sons of other people,
madonna.'

' [*Swanston, Spring*, 1875.]   *Saturday.*

' Life is a curious problem (original remark : copyright) ;
and I do not see my way through it very distinctly at
. present.   I do so hunger and thirst after money (i.e. happiness) ; *and yet to get that, I must give up my hope of making
myself strong and well (i.e. happiness).*   Two birds are
building a nest in the holly before my window ; you should
see them fly up with great straws in their mouths ; God
prosper them.   They are better off than we ; they are not
obliged to play other people's games, wear other people's
clothes, walk with other people's gait, and say other people's
silly words after them by leaden rote, under pain of breaking
hearts and drawing hot tears and driving home the gross
dagger of disappointment into breasts full of hope.   There,
you see, I am as moral as ever, again, God help me.

' Wild work, madonna, wild work—this decency to others.
I may say with Sir Andrew, " Nay, I care not for good life ! "
It seems to me the wildest of follies, the most indecent
prodigality of our little hopes and chances ; and yet—Hey,
diddle diddle, the cat and the fiddle, the cow jumped over
the moon.   From circumference to middle, the whole is a
riddle, and I hope to be out of it soon.—Impromptu verses :
copyright.   Adieu.   Well, one thing I have to be thankful
for to " whatever Gods may be."   I am no longer the
miserable perverse tremulous childish DEVIL, who came
down to London in March.   I could throw my hat over the
house when I think of it—over the house ?—over Uranus.'

' Whatever Gods may be,' introduces W. E. Henley,
' my poet,' as Stevenson calls him in an earlier letter.   The
words are from the famous lyric which begins ' Out of the
night that covers me.'   The two men had just met,
Stevenson visiting Henley when he was ill in the Old
Infirmary in Edinburgh.   It was Leslie Stephen who

introduced them to each other and who published Henley's first Hospital poems in the *Cornhill*.

None of the later letters are so intimate. Stevenson was now seeing more of his cousin R. A. M. Stevenson and going more often to France, where in 1876 he met Mrs. Osbourne and fell under her spell.

Before leaving this period of his life, when he was within the aura of Mrs. Sitwell, let me quote a poem which he wrote to her. Undated, it belongs to 1873 or 1874 :

> ' I read, dear friend, in your dear face
> Your life's tale told with perfect grace ;
> The river of your life I trace
> Up the sun-chequered, devious bed
> To the far-distant fountain-head.
>
> ' Not one quick beat of your warm heart,
> Nor thought that came to you apart,
> Pleasure nor pity, love nor pain
> Nor sorrow, has gone by in vain ;
>
> ' But as some lone, wood-wandering child
> Brings home with him at evening mild
> The thorns and flowers of all the wild,
> From your whole life, O fair and true,
> Your flowers and thorns you bring with you ! '

CHAPTER IX

THE FITZWILLIAM MUSEUM AND ROBERT BROWNING

1876–1880

IN 1876 Colvin was appointed director of the Fitzwilliam Museum at Cambridge, a post he held until 1884. The following words from *Memories and Notes* tell us something of his activities there : ' In the years when I had charge of the Fitzwilliam Museum at Cambridge, my main endeavour had been not so much to enrich its collection of miscellaneous original objects of art as to save out of its revenue a fund for providing the first and indispensable apparatus for archæological study in the shape of a gallery of casts from antique sculpture. The new gallery was built and stocked, and in April 1884 a representative company came to the ceremony of its formal opening. The Prince of Wales was present, and among the speakers were such practised celebrities as James Russell Lowell, then American minister in London ; Lord Houghton ; Professor Jebb, who had lately been public orator of the university ; and the President of the Royal Academy, Sir Frederic Leighton. I can see and hear them now. Lowell, with his square and vigorous presence and his great square-cut tawny beard already beginning to grizzle, spoke without technical knowledge but with practised readiness and genial good sense as he regretted the absence of a brother diplomat who chanced to be a past master of these subjects (that was the then French ambassador in London, M. Waddington). Lord Houghton, on public occasions always eloquent and elegant in spite of a slipshod habit of dress and person, spoke, with sweeping gestures of the arm and his scarlet gown half slipping off his back, more aptly and graciously even than usual. Jebb, classically pointed and polished both in phrase and delivery, and Leighton, floridly handsome and winning in person and in the use of tongue and brush alike ever gracefully accomplished, were both at their best.

'But far the most effective speech of the day, despite its somewhat antiquated style and stiff delivery, was Newton's. For many years of his life he had laboured in vain to get his beloved studies officially recognized and admitted into the curriculum of his own university of Oxford. To see the object achieved at Cambridge, with the certainty that Oxford must soon follow, was to him like a view from Pisgah. His fine, worn and furrowed, now ageing face took a touching look of relief and happiness as he defined and defended with a master's insight the studies to which he had given his life, declaring as he wound up, " I rejoice to have seen this day ; it is a day I have waited for, and prayed for, and toiled for—in many lands—and when I looked this morning at the cast of the little figure of Proserpine I myself discovered at Cnidos, I was reminded of her ἄνοδος when she came back from the darkness of Hades into the light of the upper world, and the thought came to me that this was the ἄνοδος of archæology, so long buried in England." '

A few sentences from John Morley's letters at this time, 1876. On September 15 he wrote : ' Of course, say what you like about G. Sand. You will naturally spare G. Eliot's feelings as much as critical honesty will permit.' Colvin was reviewing *Daniel Deronda* for the November number, and I find a characteristically candid letter from Lady Carlisle on this theme :

'1 *Palace Green, Kensington, W.*
'*Nov.* 2, 76.

'MY DEAR MR. COLVIN,—I have just read your article on *Daniel Deronda* and I cannot refrain from writing you a little note to express my great pleasure therein. The

G

criticism from beginning to end is truly admirable : I had no idea how good it was likely to be—but indeed in my humble opinion it is first rate. It is very long since I have read anything of your's except an article on University Reform and that Homeric hymn which you kindly sent me, so that I scarcely knew how exceedingly good you were likely to make a piece of difficult criticism. For surely *Daniel Deronda* is most hard to judge rightly. What a wretched performance the *Edinbro' Review* article was !— you have done Mrs. Lewes full justice, and chosen all your points with most acute discrimination—I daresay it will seem to you somewhat presumptuous on my part that I should think my opinion worth giving, but after all, you write magazine articles for the public and I am one of it. Moreover my pleasure was considerable and I like for my own satisfaction to express it. What a pity that your political opinions on foreign matters are so sadly inferior to your literary criticisms !—By the way I must take objection in yr. article to your passing depreciation of G. Sand's theism—How incorrigibly intolerant you are on that subject.—Yrs. sincerely,

'ROSALIND HOWARD '

Before leaving Lady Carlisle, who ceased about this time to be an active correspondent, let me quote from another characteristic letter : ' All George's Flaxman drawings are entirely at yr. service—as is anything and everything else in our house. Borrow or take anything you like at any time from 1 Palace Green. We are enduring anti-quarianism now—a thing George likes and I detest. Col. Fox my brother-in-law is here and digs up Roman camps and cares for nothing from wᶜʰ he cannot gain some know-ledge ; cannot even enjoy a view unless he can glean fr. it some information about the geological course of a river. It is so tedious. Then Dr. Bruce arrives to-day. He is the man who has written that great big book on the Roman Wall. I hope Col. Fox will amuse him for I am sure I am

incapable of doing so—I wish you were here for it might
interest you to go to the Roman camp ; they are going to
to-morrow. It is 18 miles off and we have never seen it.
George is doing much drawing and, as you will have observed,
answers no letters. Bad boy !—He does not deserve to
get letters.'

From Morley, in November 1876 : ' I am just back from
Berne and Florence. Many a time did I wish you were
there to instruct and guide my crude judgments.'

A more serious matter than reviews of books was occupying Morley's mind a little later in the same month : the conference regarding the aftermath of the Crimean War that
threatened us at that time. ' I go wholly with you,' he
wrote, ' as to the Conference—and declined to have anything to do with it. A public meeting to express in a
broad general way the resolution that we won't go to war
is one thing ; but for a miscellaneous crowd, even of accomplished men, to pretend to settle details of administration
in the Provinces—and that is what the Conference pretends
—is surely a piece of nonsense. I feel so uncertain (as every
sensible man who has not thought about the matter with all
his mind and for years and with good counsel from soldiers
and sailors must feel uncertain) about the peril to us of
Russia, that at present I am content to say this : ' Let
Russia smash the Turk, if she likes : but if she advances
on Constantinople, or comes within a certain distance,
then we will occupy Const., not as enemy of Russia or friend
of Turk, but as European constable.'

Colvin's duties as Slade Professor led Morley to remark
at the end of this letter : ' Tell me if you hear of a good
literary contributor, who won't go and be made Slade
Professor and desert me.'

On November 29, 1876 : ' What do you say to writing
a charming little article for me on *Florence*—with Mrs.
Oliphant's new book for a text on which to hang a delightful discourse ? Do, I beseech you. The man, the
subject, the place, the public—all in accord.'

A month later : ' I wrote to you some time ago about Florence, and an article thereon. You deigned no response to my poor letter. So that is at an end. Now will you write an essay, narrative, historical, descriptive, pictorial, on *Titian*, à propos of the new life of said Titian ? Please answer—and answer Yes.' I do not find this article.

In the spring of 1876 I find George Howard writing to Colvin from Rome : ' I was so glad to get your letter and to hear that you were going to have the delight of a travel in Greece. I was also delighted to hear of your renewed professorship—though I suppose that there was no danger about that. I certainly envy you your Greece—I daresay Newton will come out more lively when he gets his foot on his native marble. By the way, I am not at all prepared to believe in all your superlatives about these Olympian things—even though I read Newton's paper about them. The last thing dug up is always cracked up in that way. Now you and Newton will be able to arrange together what you shall say —but we won't believe you—just wait and see. I have been revolving in my mind some excellent subjects for great decorative work—When you get your job done at Cambridge do you think you could give me a commission for frescoes ? Here are the subjects :

' 1. S. C. re-elected to his Professorial chair by acclamation.
' 2. S. C. embarks for his travels in Greece.
' 3. S. C. travels with Newton.
' 4. S. C. inspects the marbles at Olympia.
' 5. a difference of opinion with German professors.
' 6. S. C. captured by bandits.
' 7. S. C. proclaimed president of the Greek Republic.
' 8. S. C. returns to Cambridge and opens a museum of casts & gallery of chromolithographs.

' There—don't you think those would look well on the walls of the Fitzwilliam ? It would be doing something for the way of fostering a real spirit of art in the University, and

ROBERT BROWNING

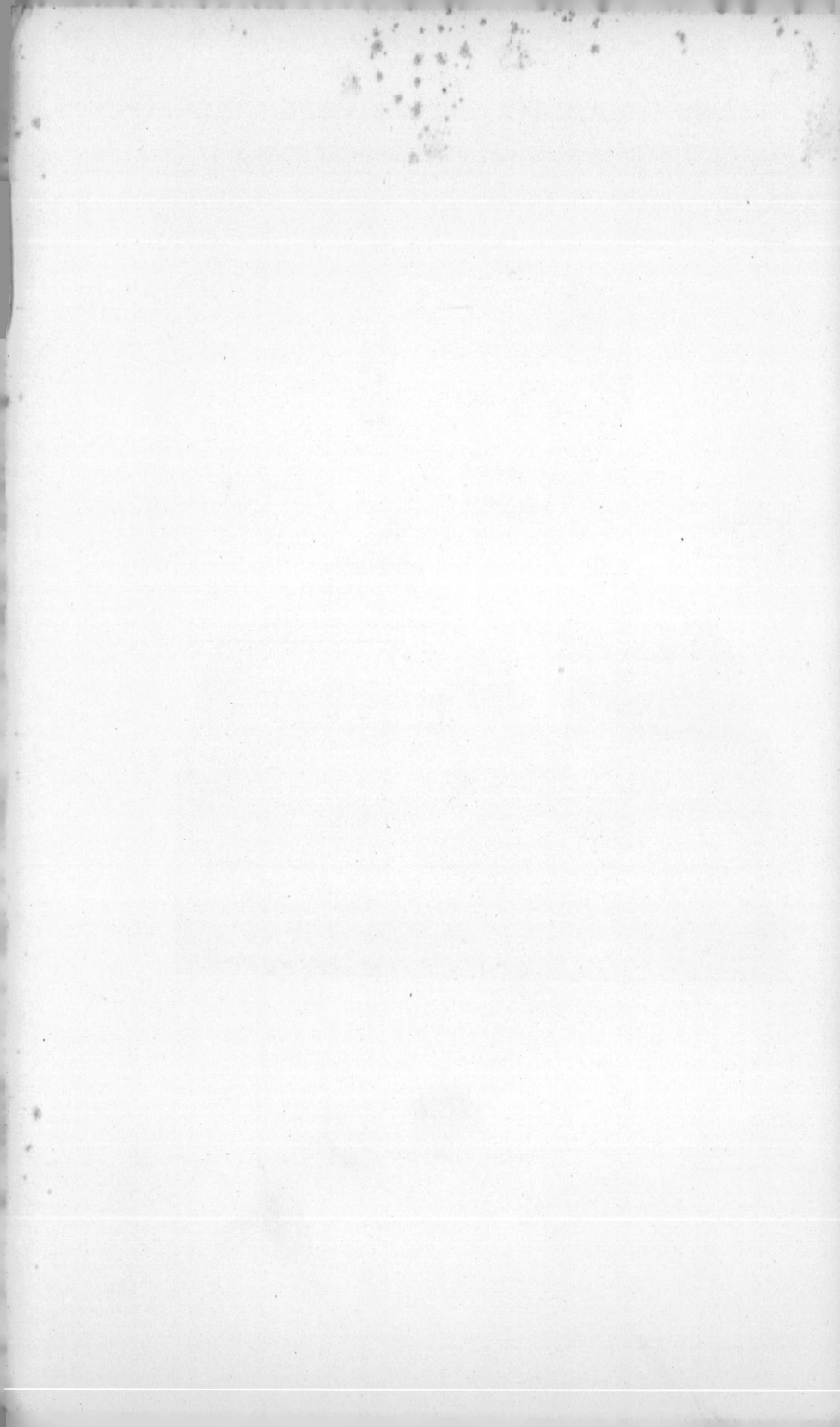

I would promise to employ none but women as my assistants. This would probably cause a great rush of students to Girton & Merton.

'Of our proceedings here there is nothing to say. Every day I work—very slowly though—Once a week I ride on the Campagna—which is more heavenly than anything that you can imagine. Yesterday I rode where the whole country looked like a Cumberland moor covered with asphodel instead of heather.

'My wife and children are deep in antiquarianism and I think of running them all for the next professorship that turns up. So look out. Of painters here, there is Costa—whose work you do not know well, I think; it is splendid. You ought to come here in order to acquaint yourself with the certainties of modern art, after having muddled your mind with the uncertainties of antique ditto. . . .'

It was, Colvin tells us, at Naworth that he first met Robert Browning, from whom, in this period of the 'seventies, I find two or three letters, not, however, of importance. Colvin's description of the poet has much life : ' Loudness of voice and a vigorous geniality of bearing were what, on the surface, chiefly distinguished Browning from other Englishmen in social life throughout these years. Needless to say, the veriest oaf could not have mistaken them for vulgarity. The poet's biographer and most confidential friend, the late Mrs. Sutherland Orr, used to say that they were originally the mask of a real shyness and diffidence on first confronting, in advanced middle life, the ordeal of mixed general society. I should rather have supposed that they were the natural symptoms of an inborn vital energy surpassing by threefold those of other men. Certainly the poet's shortish robust figure, held always firmly upright with the powerful grey-haired and bearded head a little thrown back, his cordial greetings and vigorous confidential and affectionate gestures, would have conveyed the impression of such vitality, even had the same impression not been forced upon those of us who were readers by the

surprising prodigality in these years (I speak of the early
'seventies) of his work in literature. . . .

'It is a curious fact that in spite of the intensity of intellectual and emotional effort to which for the most part
they bear witness, Browning's poetical labours,—excepting,
no doubt, those he was accustomed to read aloud among
his friends,—were wont to leave little trace or echo in his
own memory.   Was this perhaps because of their very
rapidity and abundance ?   Such was at any rate the case ;
and I remember with what amused gusto he related one
day how a lady friend had been reading him out certain
verses, and how he had slapped his thigh (a very characteristic action, by the way) and said, " By Jove, that 's
fine " ; how then she had asked him who wrote them and
he could not say ; and how surprised he was when she
had told him they were his own.

'Browning's talk had not much intellectual resemblance
to his poetry.   That is to say, it was not apt to be specially
profound or subtle ; still less was it ever entangled or obscure
. . . (The mere act of writing seemed to have a peculiar
effect on him, for I have known him manage to be obscure
even in a telegram.)   Rather his style in talk was straightforward, plain, emphatic, heartily and agreeably voluble,
ranging easily from deep earnest to jolly jest, rich and varied
in matter but avoiding rather than courting the abstruse
whether in speculation or controversy, and often conde-
scending freely to ordinary human gossip on a level with the
rest of us.   Its general tone was genially kind, encouraging
and fortifying ; but no one was more promptly moved to
indignation, indignation to which he never hesitated to give
effect, by any tale or instance of cruelty or calumny or injustice: nor could anyone be more tenderly or chivalrously
sympathetic with the victim of such offences.   Not to quote
instances known to me of a more private and personal kind,
I remember his strong and reiterated expressions of anger
against Froude for having, as he thought, misrepresented
the character of Carlyle.   Instead of being the hard man

figured in Froude's pages—inconsiderate in relations with his wife, unkind, in one instance at least, in his treatment of a horse—Carlyle, maintained Browning, was the most intensely, sensitively tender-hearted of men : and he went on to tell how, as he walked one day in Chelsea with Carlyle's arm in his, a butcher-boy drove by savagely flogging his horse and he felt the sage shake from head to foot in a spasm of righteous indignation. . . .

' One of my vividest recollections is of an evening when he made one of a party of three to see the great Italian tragedian Salvini play King Lear.   Everyone had seen Salvini play Othello, his most usual Shakespearean part; but this performance of Lear was new to us all.   It turned out to be overwhelming, an absolute, ideal incarnation of ruined age and outcast greatness and shattered reason and unchilded fatherhood and fallen majesty in despair.   Browning sat there between us, his face set firm and white like marble, but before the end tears were coursing down it quite unchecked.   He seemed unconscious of them, and as we came out could only murmur with a kind of awe, " It makes one wonder which is the greater, the poet or the actor." '

Here is a note from Browning to Colvin on his theory of translations.   It belongs to 1877 : ' I am probably more of your mind than you suppose, about the sort of translation I should like for myself and for you : but I only undertook to " transcribe "—esteeming it sufficient success if I put anybody ignorant of Greek in something like the position of one acquainted with it.   This latter person recognizes *under* a given word the corresponding modern sense—but he sees the—perhaps grotesque—word *first*, and supplies the elucidation for himself : so I expect an intelligent reader to do, because it seems part of my business to instruct him that, for instance, the Greeks called πραπίδες what we call " understanding."   But it is ungracious work and I have done with it.' [1]

<hr>

[1] In the Fitzwilliam Museum.

On the publication of Mrs. Sutherland Orr's *Life and Letters of Robert Browning*, Mrs. Sitwell, who supplemented her slender resources by journalism and translation, said in the *National Review* : ' Those who knew Browning need no written reminder of him. The stimulating geniality of his presence, the warm grasp of the hand that sent us on our way rejoicing if we met him but for a moment in a London crush, made a difference in the day. And those who have heard his somewhat strident voice grow tender even to tears in reading out his own *Andrea del Sarto* have a memory of him that will remain with them for life.'

That, and a passage about the women in Meredith's novels (to be quoted later), are the only specimens of Mrs. Sitwell's literary work that I have found, except a few musical criticisms for the *World;* but I know that she worked very hard with her pen. Latterly she wrote nothing but letters : warm, impulsive, gossipy, but not remarkable for style.

The years 1878 to 1881 are not very fruitful. Colvin was in residence in Cambridge, busy with his two Cambridge appointments and in constant correspondence with Stevenson and, as we are about to see, with Henley. At Easter of that year he was in Paris with Burne-Jones.

John Morley again, after being appointed editor of the *Pall Mall Gazette*. On May 14, 1880 : ' Your collaboration on my small paper will be most welcome. We are in urgent need. Can you not send me an occasional note—from 8 to 15 lines—now and then, while we wait to arrange for more serious matters. Pray help me, if you can. The shortest note will be useful. Avoid the beaten track as you would naturally do. Anythg. literary, social, educational, academic.'

The *Pall Mall Gazette*, it will be remembered by students of the history of London journalism, after a long career as a Tory organ, under Frederick Greenwood, was suddenly, in April 1880, bought by George Murray Smith, the publisher and founder of the *Dictionary of National Biography*, as a gift to his Liberal son-in-law, the late Henry Yates Thompson, who appointed Morley as its editor. Greenwood, finding himself out in the cold, lost no time in collecting capital to establish the *St. James's Gazette* in which to carry on his True Blue policy. Colvin would naturally gravitate to a Conservative rather than a Radical paper, but he seems to have worked for Morley now and then. On December 12, 1880, for instance, I find him telling Henley to look at tomorrow's *Pall Mall Gazette* for his article on Hall Caine's account of the last days of Dante Gabriel Rossetti.

On March 29, 1881, Morley wrote : ' I wish Comyns Carr would work a bit harder for me. Why does a taste for the fine arts make men so tardy with their copy ? '

In 1879 Colvin became a member of the Athenæum Club, and to the end of his life was closely associated with all its activities.

In 1880 appeared the first volume (not yet followed by its second) of *A History of Painting*, from the German of Dr. Alfred Woltmann and Dr. Karl Woermans, edited by Sidney Colvin, M.A. The name of the translator was not given.

CHAPTER X

W. E. HENLEY

1879–1881

IT is not, I fancy, generally thought that Colvin and Henley were ever intimate; but as a matter of fact there was a time when Henley constantly sought Colvin's advice and help and corresponded with him in the freest possible way. This is abundantly proved by the letters from Henley to Colvin which Colvin preserved, and the letters from Colvin to Henley which Mr. Charles Whibley has kindly placed at my disposal. From 1879 to 1881 the correspondence was continuous and of the most cordial. It is regrettable that after this the two men drifted apart. The reason is supplied by a curious note on the broken relations between Stevenson and Henley, culminating in the famous article by Henley after the appearance of Sir Graham Balfour's *Life of Robert Louis Stevenson* in 1901. This note was written by Colvin not long before his death, and it runs thus :—

' TO FUTURE BIOGRAPHERS OR COMMENTATORS ON THE BIOGRAPHY OF ROBERT LOUIS STEVENSON

' With reference to the causes of estrangement, and in the end actual quarrel, between Stevenson's widow and his sometime close friend William Ernest Henley, it ought to be publicly known that the wife had ample & just cause for regarding the friendship as one that entailed risks to Louis's health and should be discouraged accordingly. For all his crippled bodily condition, Henley was in talk the most boisterously untiring, the lustiest & most stimulating of companions, and could never bring himself to observe the consideration due to Louis's frail health & impaired lungs. Anxiety on this acct was the main cause of the wife's disliking his society for her husband. I can testify from my own experience that she was not moved by the kind of jealousy which a wife commonly feels towards the friends of her husband's bachelor days : I had been an even closer intimate of Stevenson than Henley had, and without attempting to come between us she took me into her own engaging affectionate intimacy during their married life ; simply, I believe, because I showed a reasonable consideration in forbearing to tax his energies as a companion too much.

' No doubt, also, experience of the practical failure of the experiment in play-writing on which Stevenson spent so much effort with little or no result in conjunction with this same friend made the wife regard the friendship as one that brought a dangerous amount of exertion with no corresponding advantages.'

Into the particulars of the case I cannot go, having no knowledge, nor does it seem to me now worth while. But I may say that the perusal of Mrs. Stevenson's letters during the Bournemouth period supports Colvin's view. Colvin, whatever his own feelings as to Henley may have been, was so pledged to the Stevensons, so involved in their affairs, that he went with them in the matter. I never heard him say anything about it. Later, we shall see, in 1895, Colvin asked Henley's advice about *Weir of Hermiston* ; but the last preserved letter in this period of cordial correspondence belongs to 1881.

Henley's letters in this period are frank and vigorous, as he always was, but the letters from Colvin are by no means lacking in spirit and they reveal also his untiring kindness. Most of them are concerned with Henley's efforts to establish himself in London journalism and Colvin's aids to that end ; there are also many sidelights on the Stevensons, and a number describe Colvin's campaign among the theatrical managers to get *Deacon Brodie* accepted.

In 1879 Henley was thirty and, on the cessation of his paper, *London*, in need of work. In *London* had appeared Stevenson's *New Arabian Nights* and many of Henley's poems and criticisms.

The first letter, which I quote in full, is dated from Stevenson's paternal home, January 20, 1879, and refers to *Deacon Brodie*, which Henley was then writing in collaboration with Stevenson. It is a joint letter :

' MY DEAR COLVIN,—This should be " Our dear Colvin," or " Our Colvin which art in heaven," Act IV is complete. We are of opinion that it ain't so damned bad, tho' in some ways Act III, as it ought to be, is the flower of the flock for passion.

' About the transposition of tableaux demanded. I (*this is R. L. S.*) think there's a sight of good in your reasons (*W. E. H.* adheres). But, first—the act must progress in emotion, not in time. Chapel's Court is a piece of pure stage business, & stage talk, with nothing but one very moving incident and that at the end. After the deep human emotion of the "Two Women" you would simply lose in Chapel's Court all you had already gained before Burke's Door, and have to begin your last act again on a cold iron with the beginning of the last tableau. Remember, a play is emotion as a statue is marble. Incident, story, these are but the pedestal. Sophocles tells you a story which is a mass of tangle & contradiction ; yes, but the emotion steadily progresses to the end. We can't do that ; but we must not stumble back in the full course of the last act. This is the reason on which I (*complete adhesion of W. E. H.*) we stand or fall.

' Secondly. You will see when you read Tableau X that Tableau IX requires immediately to precede it. The Doctor enters ; well, here is what the Doctor does.

' Thirdly. Tableau VII is not a burglary; rightly looked at, it is a scene of passion. The two scenes, although formally alike, are essentially opposed in character, feeling & appearance.

'Fourthly. Chapel's Court is not an exhausting scene to the actor ; and when you see what he is called upon to do in Tableau X you will recognise the necessity of a rest *immediately preceding it*. It is a case for pegs—of soup or other stimulant—say liquorice water.

'Fifthly, and of course it's just as well that it should be a set scene and not a flat.

'The last four are just thrown in. Number One's the clincher. Number One's the art of writing plays : mind you, neither more nor less.

'The second act of " Rogue Denzil's Death " or a " Word from Cornwell," or whatever it is, was made yesterday afternoon. It is the finest act in dramatic literature. " Whaur 's Wullie Shakespere noo " ? As they say in Kirkcudbright. (*Entire & passionate concurrance of R. L. S.*)

'Next letter to Heriot Row. Let us know by what time you want the whole MS. We send you fourth act ; send it on registered as before to same address as before. The copyist will be readin the sooner.

'Our one doubt about the success of the play is the loathsomeness of Brodie in Tab. X.

'We are, Dear Sir, yours very truly,

'W. E. H. & GEORGE THE PIEMAN.'

'Loathesomeness of Brodie throughout, without predjudice to Moore and Ainslie. A play never fell by a last scene if it had any strength ; you get the emotion up ; well, the curtain has to come down, if it comes down in " blood and bones and the name of God," 'twill do.

'Louis has proposed an " Imaginary conversation " between Boswell and the Dook in his condemned cell. Think you it were worth gold ? publishers' gold ? '

—George the Pieman was a character in the play and a pseudonym sometimes used by R. L. S.

The next letter is from Henley's lodging in London, on January 26, 1879 :

'DEAR COLVIN,—You are a good man to write as you

have written. Whether Irving takes the play or not, it is
of not much consequence now. It has excited your interest
& gained me (I hope I may say it) your regard ; & the best
of its work is done. I think I shall be grateful to you while
I live.

'I got the telegram all right ; I posted it to Louis. I
have also posted him your letter. I suppose that on occasion he could come up to London. In any case, I am always
here, & Irving, if he wants me, (God send he may !) can find
me when & how he will.

'I found out about the Johnson while in Scotland. My
wife's people knew some of his people, & told me a pleasant
story of his relations with Irving. Whether he's up to the
Procurator I know not. A good Ainslie is a necessity too,
you know, & where are we to look for that ?

'I have intended the Dook for Kyrle Bellew ever since I
saw that lovely Osric of his ; but Jenkin, who saw that
delightful young man play Claudio in *Measure for Measure*,
says he has passion as well as grace & gaiety ; & if this be
so there's our Leslie found. My heart would break to see
the Dook made vulgar & horrible & like a bad low comedian.
But what could I do ? Forrester is a stick as Claudius ;
but he might play Leslie, & who but Bellew could play
George the Pieman ?

'All this is in the air,—miles & miles in the air ! But I
can't help it. It's pardonable, is it not ? To come back
to my senses, you saw the alterations we had made, I hope.
I think we are very greatly indebted to you for your suggestions. They have strengthened the piece amazingly. The
soliloquy after the interview with the Procurator (Act II)
in particular has been immensely improved. And so has
the end of the scene (Act I Tableau I) between Smith &
the Deakin. I think we shall have to put you in the bill
as a collaborator.

'The news I have is principally connected with future
work, & will come better orally than thro' the eye. So I'll
reserve that much of it. But I've seen Louis' book [*Travels*

with a Donkey]. It is better than the [*Inland Voyage*].
And Douglas, the Edinburgh publisher, offered thro me,
to open negotiations with Louis for its purchase. The
young man is greatly pleased with this little incident ; so
am I ; so, I doubt not, will you be. Douglas told me he
thought he could make it pay ; & told me that he should
have thought that at least a thousand of the *Voyage* had
been sold. You know how far he is, or is not, mistaken.——
' I 've Darwin's copy of the " Fairhaven " to give you
when I see you. I 'm to ask you to take charge of it &
restore it to its owner for Louis.
' Mrs. Jenkin has a part in hand. I will tell you what
presently. She told me not to speak of it for awhile, as to
no other living soul but myself had she communicated &
even yet in doubt as to whether it would come off. Next
day I saw her again, & she announced that she had determined on it. So in May, my dear Colvin, you will have to
come North with us. I & my wife have determined to go ;
& neither you nor we will regret the journey. Shakespeare's greatest woman will at last be greatly played. I
suppose I must ask you to keep silence about the whole
business. Please do so.
' When I may see you let me do so.—Faithfully yours,
                                   ' W. E. HENLEY '

Of Mrs. Fleeming Jenkin, who was one of the Suffolk
Austins, Colvin writes thus in *Memories and Notes* : ' Her
own special gift was for acting and recitation. It was only
privately exercised, but those of us who had the privilege
of seeing and hearing her will never forget the experience.
Her features were not beautiful, but had a signal range and
thrilling power of expression. In tragic and poetic parts,
especially in those translated or adapted from the Greek,
she showed what, as I have already hinted, must needs, had
it been publicly displayed, have been recognized as genius.
To hear her declaim dramatic verse was to enjoy that art
in its very perfection. And her gift of dramatic gesture was

not less striking. Recalling her, for instance, in the part
of Clytemnestra, I can vouch for having seen on no stage
anything of greater—on the English stage nothing of equal
—power and distinction. Besides these and other figures
of Greek tragedy, Mrs. Jenkin showed the versatility of
her gift by playing with power and success such contrasted
Shakespeare parts as Cleopatra, Katherine the shrew, Viola,
Mrs. Ford, as well as, in other fields of drama, Griselda,
Peg Woffington, and Mrs. Malaprop. Needless to say that
Jenkin, who delighted both passionately and critically in
everything his wife did and was, took especial pride and
joy in these performances, and in getting them up was the
most energetic and capable of stage managers, whether in
the private theatre which he and his friends established for
a while in Edinburgh (and in which the young Louis Stevenson occasionally bore a part), or on the rarer occasions when
she was able to appear in London.

' Of the wise and warm and perfectly unassuming private
virtues of this admirable woman, her tactful human kind-
nesses and assiduities, constant and unfailing until the end,
among her friends and descendants, the present is no place
to speak. The affection with which Stevenson never ceased
to regard her, the value he set upon her practical wisdom
and advice as well as the zeal with which he bent himself to
carry out the heavy task his friendship had undertaken in
writing her husband's life—all these things are made
manifest both in that *Life* itself and in his published letters
written to her during his invalid years at Bournemouth.'

A letter from Colvin to Henley on February 6, 1879,
tells us what was happening to R. L. S. Mrs. Osbourne
had gone to America to put her house in order and prepare
for their marriage.

' DEAR HENLEY,—Forgive the tardiness of a badgered
Professor-Director vainly trying to do his own work and
keep his friends in mind in the midst of a hundred
occupations.

'Louis had been to pieces, and was together, or nearly together, again, when he went away yesterday week. He had got a quite sane letter from an intelligible address in Spanish California, where, after wild storms, intercepted flights, and the Lord knows what more, she was for the present quiet among old friends of her own, away from the enemy, but with access to the children. What next, who shall tell ? Louis had eased his mind with a telegram, without, however, committing himself to anything. He won't go suddenly or without telling people.—Which is as much as we can hope at present.

'I am so sorry about your overwork, and so vexed and angry that nothing can be got out of that Irving.—After our efforts to get at him when Louis was here, you see it is not possible for me to do anything more unless in a manner that would show I was offended, both on the authors' a/c and on my own : and it is not desirable to show that feeling so long as there is a chance his behaviour may be only the consequence of dilatoriness and slipshoddery, and not the consequence of his having read and rejected the play. Damn him. I do, at frequent intervals ; but that is no consolation to the persons principally concerned : and I did hope that by this time you might be taking a holiday with a mind relieved. Let me know if you do get a holiday all the same, and believe me—Yours very sincerely,

'SIDNEY COLVIN'

Although Irving was not interested in *Deacon Brodie*, he seems later to have commissioned or half-commissioned a play on the life of Robert Macaire, by the same authors, which was, however, still-born. Colvin seems never to have much admired the great Lyceum hero, yet when *Much Ado About Nothing* was produced in 1882 I find him writing : 'It's a pretty thing on the whole, about two-thirds of the Beatrice really brilliant and delightful, and even old automatic-legged Irving does some good comedy, especially in the last act.'

H

In August 1879 Stevenson followed Mrs. Osbourne to America, reaching San Francisco on the 30th. *The Amateur Emigrant* tells the public portion of the story. Here is Colvin's comment on his departure : ' So you see he has gone on to the far West, ill, and with every condition to make him worse. If it wasn't for the frailness, I wouldn't mind, but if that spirit will go playing fast and loose with its body, the body will some day decline the association—and we shall be left without our friend.—Of course if he does live, he will come out somehow or another having turned it all to good—and it 's no use doing anything but hope. But I can't help fearing at heart as much as hoping.'

From Henley [undated] : ' I 've not read " Fine Arts," but I will soon. The *Pall Mall* Meredith well nigh killed me ; & last night I 'd to see *Nicholas Nickleby* & do a notice ere I went to bed. I wrote a very decent little article, but I won't ask you to read it. I don't know how much will be left of it. A brutal & licentious editor, & so on ! I missed *Light & Shade* ; but I 've got Irving for to-morrow night, & I shall probably do *Henry V*. also.

' Send *Maîtres et Petits-Maîtres* when it comes, also *Histoire du Romantisme*, if possible. In return, my verses —second hospital series—herewith. Please read 'em & if you 've any remarks to offer, chalk 'em on the margin.

' As you are going to do a Gautier, it might be as well for you to read Louis Veuillot on him as a stylist. The criticism, which is very severe, is also very instructive. You 'll find it in the *Odeurs de Paris*. Don't be at the pains of buying the work ; I have it. Let me know if I shall send it to you.—A Vous toujours.

' Have just had a rasping lecture on Style from the Greenwood. Will show it to you next time I see you. It appears I don't write English, & am a copyist of other gents.

' I shall knuckle under ; I must keep the *Gazette* (if I can) till our new Journal is a fact, or till I 'm Editor of *The Times* or something of that sort.'

Nicholas Nickleby was a revival, in October 1879, of Andrew Halliday's dramatic version of the novel.

The complete MS. of the second series of Henley's Hospital poems was among Colvin's papers, with a large number of suggested variations.

Henley writes on December 9, 1879 : ' There is no news of the Wanderer [R. L. S.]—at least not much. Bob (still hippodromically given) declares he has had a letter from the Wanderer, & that the Wanderer " expects to be married soon."

' To-morrow I am going to see Irving's Digby Grant [in *The Two Roses*]. The merry greenwood has sprung a guinea for the stall, & expects an article of " good quiet *criticism* "—the merry one's own words ! I am afraid, my dear Mr. Sidney Colvin, that I am found out at last. Privately, I 've always known I wasn't a critic ; but I fancied I had concealed the fact with some success. Then Meredith spotted me ; what *he* wanted was " criticism " ; & now here 's the good greenwood reechoing with the same pathetic overword. I think I shall begin to take in the *Daily Telegraph* at once. I must try & be critical about the Irving. Please tell me in your next what criticism is ; where it is to be procured ; how they sell it ; & whether, adds the Dook's own, whether there 's any reduction on taking a quantity.

' As to that little family event you speak of, we haven't yet made up our minds when it is to come off. We are not, my dear Mr. Sidney Colvin, so gay & free as we ought, having had little practice & no experience in these matters.

' You do not seem to be going to Italy this trip ? I 'm not sorry, as there will be some chance of seeing you, & also some chance of reading you on some other subject than one antient & fishlike & Florentine. Did you read of your Fine Arts this morning ? What a good review it was ! how carefully the reviewer had read it ! What a fortunate writer you are ! There 's criticism, if you like, now. It seems to be your fate (as witness Fine Arts & Flaxman) to be better & more ardently read than Charles Dickens himself.

' I got on to that Balzac bibliography today for the first time. What a man ! What a life ! '

The merry greenwood was Frederick Greenwood, editor of the *Pall Mall Gazette*.

Colvin's ' Fine Arts ' and ' Flaxman ' were his articles under those headings in the *Encyclopædia Britannica*, to which he was a valued contributor, among his other articles being those on Botticelli, Leonardo da Vinci, Giotto and Michelangelo. The reference may also be to Colvin's early privately-printed book from which I have quoted : *A Selection from Occasional Writings on Fine Art*, 1873.

Colvin to Henley, from Paris [no date] : ' All sorts of exhibitions going on here ; including one of Delacroix, which I am glad to find has had the effect of opening people's eyes to the mistake they had made in fancying him a good artist : believe me, it is a *far* hollower bubble of a reputation than that of the literary romantic, Victor Hugo, which you are so fond of puncturing : a man of an ardent—at least of a feverish—temperament, agitated with a tumult of second-hand ideals and aspirations—essentially *common* as well as essentially febrile—false and violent in sentiment as in colour—alike incapable of sane workmanship and of living imagination : voilà.'

From Henley on January 2, 1880 : ' Write by all means. If you 've not sent what you had written, send it. Don't defer expostulation because he [R. L. S.] is ill. On the contrary. It is absolutely necessary that he should be brought to see that England & a quiet life are what he wants & must have if he means to make—I won't say reputation—but money by literature. We shall pass off all he 's done, but I won't answer for much more. Come back he must, & that soon.

' I don't believe that our letters (I 've not yet written,

W. E. HENLEY

FROM THE PAINTING BY WILLIAM NICHOLSON IN THE TATE GALLERY

being too blasphemously given towards California & California things to trust myself) will have any effect at all in diverting him from his project. . . . All we can hope to do is to make him get through his book quickly & come back quickly.

'I shall try & write to-morrow, though I don't quite know what to say. I am hopeful as far as Louis himself is concerned—very hopeful. . . . You may expect that Louis will resent your criticism of the last three works ; I know he will. But I think it right he should get them ; et avec, a confident expression of hope for the future, & as confident a prediction that Monterey and he will never produce anything worth a damn.

'You are too rough on *The Egoist*. I read over my *Athenæum* article yesterday (first time since Cambridge) & stand by it. The book is as good & not as bad as you say. It is an attempt at art by an elderly apprentice of genius. It is the material for a perfect comedy—not of intrigue ; d——n intrigue ; intrigue is not comic—but of character—the missing link between Art & Nonsense. An inorganic "Misanthrope." Do you know the French for jelly-fish ? Then Meredith, c'est Molière—méduse. The devil will surely damn him hot and deep. I hate & admire him. Won't you try an article on *The Egoist* somewhere ? Surely you could get *The Times* & three columns to do it in ? How I wish—how I do wish you would !

'Try & see the Bob. When you return you will look upon the face of one who has read " Fine Arts," by Professor Colvin. I swear it.

'I dine with Lang to-night. Let me see you soon. I won't detain you long, & I 'll do my best (in return) to see you often. Don't imagine you are going to effuse wisdom at the cost of me. I look upon you for the vacation as partly bound & beholden to me, & I shall worry you as much and as fully as ever I can.

'The Deacon 's got as far as " O hevving of hevvings that I were a good man ! " It looks nice in print. Read

H. James's *Confidence*. It will console you for much in G. Meredith's *Egoist*. There's a hartist if you like.'

Stevenson's ' last three works,' if by works Henley means books, were *An Inland Voyage*, *Picturesque Notes on Edinburgh*, 1878, and *Travels with a Donkey in the Cevennes* (dedicated to Colvin), 1879. I think Henley must have referred to magazine articles. At the time Stevenson was engaged on *The Amateur Emigrant*, and in March Colvin writes : ' And joy—(but this is a digression)—I've got the second half, nearly all, of Louis's *Emigrant* ; and it's as good as the first half was bad ; so that reading it in the train I found myself chortling at frequent intervals, to the discomposure of my fellow-travellers, who thought of requesting the guard to remove the lunatic.'

From Henley [Spring 1880], undated : ' F. W. G. [Greenwood] & I are really very thick. He had a couple of books waiting for me (He told me, by the way, that Meredith, whom I stumbled against at the door in the most extraordinary fashion, had not exactly battened on the *P.M.* notice any more than on the *Athenæum*), & we arranged that though I may not do the Méryon exhibition, as he has a gent attached, I'm to work off Burty & Wedmore in an article. I says, then, says I : " Have you given out Yriarte's *Venice* ? " And says he, " Yes, I have. Why ? " Then I says, " Because," I says, " I should have liked to say something about it." And he says then, " Any particular reason ? " he says. And I says, " Yes," I says, " it's a much better bit of translation than we usually gets," I says. " Aha ! " says he, " I'll remember that when I see the article." And I says, " Do ! because," says I, " it will be worth your while."—And then I laughed in my sleeve, & dissembled so beautifully that Louis, could he have seen me, would have been jealous, & handed me over the wall-coloured cloak incontinent. So there the matter rests.

' I saw Maccoll yesterday too. The Dickens article (7½ cols.) appears to have pleased him well. It is curious

that Meredith should have winced under my articles as he
seems to have done. Maccoll told me the *Spectator* had
pronounced *The Egoist* a failure, because its characters
were not human beings. And I go & worry my guts out
& try to teach the blasted public something of the author's
meaning & games, & the author repudiates me on all hands,
& says that he " should have preferred to have been
criticized " ! F. W. G., by the way, was quite under the
Meredithian spell. Decidedly Meredith has the comic
muse attached to his tail, & drags her about with him
wherever he goes.

'About Louis. I 've sent him the cutting & some
journals. Also a brief note, begging him to work off his
games & return most speedily to his sorrowing friends,
when all will be forgotten & forgiven. Also urging him to
try & think out the story of the Pied Piper, with a view to
the improvement of the British Drammy. If he can only
get an intrigue, we will do a real fantasticality on it ; in
good sound verse & careful, well-minted prose. Gautier's
ballet set me a-thinking. It 's not much good in itself,
I fancy ; I liked it worse when I reperused it at home here.
The one notion in it is the enslavement *des jeunes filles*,
instead of the blessed babes. I really believe, Colvin, that
if Louis will only imagine something, we could found a new
genre in fairy plays, & make our fortunes & the Gaiety's at
the same time.

' I think I 'm gradually getting through my information
somehow. It 's a good deal mixed with pink & the gay
young feller called the Dook ; but it 's coming. To-day
I 've finished an article for Stephen, & I feel pretty confident that Stephen will not take it. The subject is Molière,
or rather Molière's first lieutenant, La Grange. But there
are many original views in it about Molière, Shakespeare,
the musical glasses & the Misanthrope, & the Stephen
(Old Mumblepeg, as George persists in calling him) will not
bite, I believe, & the original views will take their virginity
to the butterman. Such, my dear Colvin, is Life !

' I shouldn't wonder now if I could manage at last to get back on the *Deacon*.   And I think there is every possibility of a certain immortal work on the Fine Arts being read ere I next foregather with the author.'

Norman Maccoll was the editor of the *Athenæum*.

The point of the conversation about Yriarte's *Venice* is that Mrs. Sitwell was the translator.

From Henley [April 1880] : ' This morning I saw Thompson.   I found him very agreeable & quite willing to take of my copy.   The dramatic criticism he told me, I must work into my own hands ; there were one or two at it already, & if I wished to get it, I was to beat them out of the field.   Good, of course, but not easy to do !   However, I put a capital face on the matter, & offered to do *King René's Daughter* ; accepted ; so on 20th May, I am hon the spot.   I shall leave Edinburgh in mornıng & assist at Lyceum in evening.   I am also, I believe, to have the French plays ; & just now, am going into town to get programmes, & so have occasion to come down on him about tickets.   To conclude, I made a raid on his bookshelf and gobbled down a lot ; how many of 'em will actually reach me, I know not.

' Payn says that most of the Greenwoodians are yet in possession ;   also, that nothing could be fairer than that idea of Thompson's, of putting us all to work & taking the best one.   I think it bosh, & believe that *jamais, au grand jamais*, I shall have it—the matter—in my hands.'

Owing largely to Colvin's introductions Henley now had two evening papers open to him, instead of one, on account of the *Pall Mall* becoming Liberal under John Morley, as I have described in an earlier chapter, and Greenwood founding the *St. James's* ; but he does not seem to have been able to adapt his very idiosyncratic style to the complete satisfaction of either.   Here is a very sensible letter from Colvin on this point : one typical of several :—

' MY DEAR HENLEY,—I 've read your Sarah article

(in *Guardian*) and think the substance of it quite admirable. But I want to speak again about style ; to make yourself acceptable to editors—and readers, if you will forgive my saying what I think—you *must* get rid of a tendency to a quaintness which is rather slangy than quaint, and to a use of eccentric forms and dubious constructions not at all really serving to improve the colour or life of your writing. " Fillip up " is slang and bad form. " With lacking " is quaint and obscure when what you mean is " for want of." The paragraphs describing S. B.'s gifts and failings, excellent as criticism, are too large and involved ; you have, as a correction, introduced more semi-colons and fewer full-stops, when what they wanted was fewer semi-colons and more full-stops, inasmuch as sentences of that length can only be ventured by a master of structure, movement, and articulation like Newman or Ruskin. " Reticient " of course is a misprint for reticent. " Elocutionist " is a beastly Yanke[e]ism. " A something of " is not English at all. " All too many " belongs to archaic poetry and not to modern prose.

'Etcettery, etcettery. Says you, it's only a hurried article in a provincial paper. But in great things or little, these tricks are a disfigurement and should be unlearnt. I notice them in the Butler piece, in Ward's book, as well. " Rhythmist " for instance is a still beastlier Yankeeism than elocutionist. " A someone " is as bad [as] " a something." "Intelligence of," for " comprehension of " or " insight into," is bizarre, and more Italian than English. To be bizarre, that is in one word your temptation ; whether it is the knack or the habit which you have to unlearn. To afford to be bizarre, as I have often told you, you must be Charles Lamb, with his genius and his leisure for polishing. Damn bizarrerie, says the ordinary editor, and not unwisely. Forgive me ; yet, besides your faculty of criticism, the faculty of clear straightforwardness in writing, and, besides doing better, you will earn guineas where you earn shillings.

' And above all do not be offended with the above from,—
Yours ever,   SIDNEY COLVIN

' You know, don't you, that I may be right or wrong in
all this, but my telling you out is the best proof that I take
both your work and your friendship seriously ?   S. C.'

From Henley [April 1880] : ' I 've just written volunteering
a notice of Swinburne's *Songs of the Springtides*. Drop
me a line to say how—in what tone—I ought to treat it.   If
they say yes, it will be awful.   The book 's an ecstasy of
exaggeration, a rapture of superlatives.   Such a son of
Thunder & small beer I never did see.
    ' I would have written yesterday, but had my review to do
—a long one it is ; & had a bad & dreadful cold, besides ; &
had withal an appointment with R. A. M. S. to see the Millet.
I saw it.   O Colvin, Colvin !   Why will you not make an
art-critic of me ?   I am not a bloody fool, for I can feel &
see & be religious over great art.   We went & looked through
the Grosvenor afterwards, & Lord ! how poor it all seemed !
Beside that solemn fateful figure, those mysterious birds,
that fatidic landscape, that prophet's tree—but why do I
rave ?   Let me rather direct your attention to the words
of T. Taylor, Esquire in *The Times*, in a comparison of
Millet & B. Lepage.   As reported by Bob, it 's hard to say
whether he misunderstands the man of genius or the man of
talent, art or nature, intention or accomplishment, worse.
Make me the art-critic of the *P.M.G.* !   I would T. T.,
Esq. had a new play coming out to-morrow, that I might
show him what criticism is—what it is to be right.   For
God's sake make me an art-critic.   What with you, Bob,
& Legros, I could thrive.'
    No one who has read Henley's *Views and Reviews* will agree
that he needed tuition in art criticism.
    From Colvin, about *Deacon Brodie* [Spring 1880] :
' *Deacon* went to Clayton on Saturday—so as to *reach* him
on that day.   I hoped you would have heard by this.   You
are certain, I think, to hear soon.   I shall be in town

Friday, Saturday, Sunday, and will ask for a long jaw one
of those days. . . . If there were time for the Clayton experiment to come (as I hope it won't come) to nothing first,
it might still be worth while to get up this performance.—
But of course the Mary scene must be written in. A little
more phosphorus, and you 'll work it off all right. The
draft you have is better than you think ; at least, those
lines and none other, with the speeches amplified and sustained, are the right, just human and natural lines for it
to go on : of that I am certain, with the unalterable
certainty of what, as I put it to myself, is actual experience.
—Have you read Coquelin's *L'Art et le Comédien* ? The
red-ribbon silliness apart, it is one of the cleverest and
justest pieces of work I have read for many a day.—Also
I 've read *Cannosine*.—Consequently have heaps to jaw
about.—And here is a letter from Louis. Will he live ?
will he die ? He has taken quite the right measure of his
Thoreau ; only it is a shade more sententious than he
thinks.'

Clayton was John Clayton, the actor.

The essay on Thoreau appeared first in the *Cornhill*, and
afterwards in *Familiar Studies of Men and Books*.

From Colvin to Henley [April 18, 1880] : ' A letter from
Mrs. O. . . . Louis has been, and is, dangerously ill. The
letter isn't to me, but I expect it will be sent on to you. It is
confused, but refers to a worse time, not specified, when she
had got " her own doctor " to make a " most thorough
examination " of him (that can only be the same examination about which he wrote to you in that cheery fashion).
Doctor had at first thought there could be no hope, but
afterwards " said he could save him, though it would be
with the greatest difficulty." " In five weeks, he said,
there would be a wonderful improvement "—" after which,
Louis is to go to the mountains " (that means lungs). " A
sea-voyage would simply kill him at once in the present
state of his health." " No work to be done meantime,"
and money would be wanted. Money, therefore, had been

asked for from home. "Decidedly better" at time of writing. "I am trying to take care of my dearest boy, and do believe that he is not only going to be better soon, but in time quite well."'

From Colvin [May 5, 1880] : 'I 've two letters from Louis at once ; you, I expect, have a letter and a scenario. Does he tell you about the £250 a year which his people promise ?— that 's a big weight off our hearts—and about his plans for a home in the hills ?—which are all very well, but look like anything rather than like coming back to the old country. . . . I broached to the Carrs the idea of a Warner reading of the Deacon in their house : at first they jumped at it ; but I wouldn't let them settle until they had read it, and therefore sent them the piece.'

Colvin had failed to interest John Clayton in *Deacon Brodie*. Warner was Charles Warner, famous as Coupeau in *Drink*, the English version of Zola's *L'Assommoir*.

It was very shortly after this, on May 19, 1880, that Stevenson and Mrs. Osbourne were married.

From Henley [May 21, 1880] : 'Last night, late, the enclosed from Morley. I was in three minds to send the ticket back, with a polite hint that he had my permission to retire hup. Of course I conquered the impulse, & to-night I shall leave my Berlioz, & go in unto Iolanthe. My own opinion of my fortune is poor. I wouldn't give sixpence for my chance with J. M. ; I shall find that person's finger thicker than the Gay one's loins. As he cut my "Whole Duty," so, I am positive, he has suppressed my Swinburne altogether & my Blackmore as well. I am very sorry indeed, for, if it is so, it means ruin. However, *je m'en fiche!*

'Here 's a sigh for those who love me
And a smile for those who hate,
And whatever sky 's above me,
Here 's a heart for every fate—·

whether it calls itself John Morley or Walter Good, or—no matter what. Meanwhile, of course I ain't so gay & free as I pretend to be. I shall go & see Morley to-morrow, & ask about the French plays. If they, too, are to be done on approval—*bon soir!*

' Let me see you soon. Life is a bore unless one has a heritage of some sort. A good wooden spoon, now ? What say you to a good wooden spoon ? I wish I had had one. In the meantime, j'ai des amis et j'ai une femme—& life is —well, it 's devilish enviable.'

I interpolate some mixed Colvin letters here. This, in August 1880, refers to the book on Landor which he had been commissioned by John Morley to write for the ' English Men of Letters Series ' :—

' MY DEAR HENLEY,—Life is not the least worth having at its present rate, at least for me, of busytude. I got back from Paris on Wednesday night, spent Thursday in town— the whole mortal day taking Landor notes at the B.M. and elsewhere, which I have since lost ; no time for Coupeau, no time for talk, nothing—came back here on Friday, and have been up to the eyes in work and correspondence ever since. Work which don't pay either ; that is to say learned contribution — real old out-and-out Bummkopf — to the Journal of the new Society for Hellenic Studies, in which I 'm going to publish three (ugly) unpublished vases, and a text that 'll just knock down the entire human species by its learnedness. That 's what 's the matter with me,— that, and entertaining a pack of beastly medicoes belonging to the Association, which meets here this week,—until the 20th ; from which date I dedicate myself for six weeks without a break to the complete writing of ye immortal Landor ; first three weeks, most likely, at his own old home of Llanthony in South Wales ; next three weeks, here. After which my lecture work will be beginning again. So no holiday for the likes of me.

' I am most anxious to hear your view of Coupeau as you were going (I was told) to see it at the Surrey. Also to know if the melodrammy is under weigh. Still more to know whether your liver is better—was so sorry to hear of

its being bad.—Found the article on the littler cardinals ;
good ; but see, Yates [in the *World*] never has any formal
reviews, only Book-Table, or Paper-Cutter, or some such
rubbish.   It ought to make a right good *Sat. Rev.* article ;
do you think I may try there ?

' Saw no play at Paris—would have gone to Garin, but
was engaged to dine, and the next night, being very tired
with Bummkopf—researching and hunting up of draughts-
men and lithographers, chose, instead of the *Gendre de M.
Poirier*, an open-air dinner in the Champs Élysées and an
early bed.   Saw no actors in the flesh either, but had a
great pleasure in seeing again my old and fast friend Radowitz (future Chancellor of German Empire—you bet).   My
first and probably last intermixtion in politics consisted,
two years ago, in establishing a curious kind of friendship-
before-acquaintance between him and Gambetta, the coming
and the come statesmen of Europe.   Curious, but true.

' Had a fearful ironical sell on the way out.   Ellen Terry
travelled with her chicks to Boulogne by the same boat
with me, and without her husband, who is the green-eyed
monster incarnate.   There was my chance, to have a good
time and make myself of service to the gifted and engaging ;
which I proceeded to do ; but lo, the sea uprose, and while the
gifted and engaging continued to beam, the most devoted
of her servants and adorers had to interrupt his assiduities,
and go off to lie down dejectedly beside the gunwale, with
a cheek from which its genial glow had departed.—And
as the G. and E. is not deficient in the sense of humour,
she must have fully appreciated the situation.

' This is a long jaw, for a man who considers himself busy,
but it may be my last for some days.—Oh, did you hear
that Louis had written his people he hoped his health would
enable him, travelling by easy stages, to reach England by
the middle of September ?   That sounds pretty dicky, I 'm
afraid.   Write to me.—Yours ever,   S. C.'

G. and E. meant probably Gifted and Engaging.

The next letter is very interesting. Mr. and Mrs. R. L. Stevenson, sailing from New York on August 7, 1880, had just arrived at Liverpool :

' MY DEAR HENLEY,—I have behaved like a brute beast to you ; but such, as you pretty well know by this time, are the ways of the animal. Only it has been worse than usual because I had things to say which you would have wished to hear. Did you know that I went off to meet Louis and his family at their landing ?—suddenly made up my mind at dinner here last Monday, took the night mail, and was just in time to welcome them at early morning on the quays of the grey Mersey. They were pleased, and I was glad to have gone, though I 'm not sure that I should have done so had I known that the old folks were going too. However the said old folks were not enterprising enough to go down to the river, so that in point of fact mine was their first greeting. And I stopped four or five hours and lunched with the united family—old Mrs. Stevenson (who looks the fresher of the two), young Mrs. Stevenson, old Mr. Stevenson, Mr. Louis Stevenson, and Sam—who distinguished himself (it should be said in passing that he is not a bad boy) by devouring the most enormous luncheon that ever descended a mortal gullet.

I daresay it made things pleasanter my being there ; and I 'm bound to say the old folks put a most brave and most kind face on it indeed. They were all going off by way of Edinburgh to the West Highlands—I wonder whether you 've heard from Louis since ; but I suppose of course you have. It was too soon to tell yet how he really was ; in the face looking better than I expected, and improved by his new teeth ; but weak and easily fluttered, and so small you never saw, you could put your thumb and finger round his thigh. On the whole he didn't seem to me a bit like a dying man in spite of everything. It would have done, and will do, your heart good to shake hands with him again.

' The plan is, or was on Tuesday, that they are all to be

in the West Highlands till towards mid-September ; then Louis and family coming to town or neighbourhood, for a month ; then somewhere (uncertain where) in a warm climate for the winter. When I had him alone talking in the smoking room it was quite exactly like old times ; and it is clear enough that he likes his new estate so far all right, and is at peace in it ; but whether you and I will ever get reconciled to the little determined brown face and white teeth and grizzling (for that 's what it 's up to) grizzling hair, which we are to see beside him in future— that is another matter.

' We didn't talk much about work—he has been able to do almost nothing for some time—but I saw the blank-verse poems he wrote when he was very bad to his friends : they 're fetching (to you and me) but not very good ; two of them are going to appear in the *Atlantic Monthly*.

' Am off at cockcrow tomorrow morning for fresh air and the genius loci at Llanthony and the neighbourhood ; am taking tons of books, and mean to come back tomorrow three weeks weighing 14 stone and with half my Landor finished. Let me have news of you. Address P.O. Abergavenny, S. Wales. Yours ever, S. C.'

In September, from Llanthony Abbey, Landor's old home : ' Landor has been on the go too ; not so fast as I could have wished ; but every page goes faster than the last, and I have a real hold of it and could almost spout you the book from title to colophon ; colophons are unluckily no longer in use, but they sound nice.—From Bummkopf and Landor together I 've only had three whole holidays at all ; one on the way to, and one on the way back from, Llanthony, and one to do a big day's walk while we were there. Llanthony is one of the most beautiful places in the world ; one of the most winning in fine weather and repelling in bad ; we had it all fine, and were happy, but not idle enough.

' Llanthony shall have three pages in the immortal work.

Llanthony, and a young woman with eyes, who wanted
something for her album, produced the following, see
separate enclosure. Poesy with me is a pure sign of im-
becility. I only wish it wasn't with somebody else [R. L. S.]
a sure sign of ill health. That line of L.'s to you is to my
mind quite discouraging, and I have a great fear that he
has got his death blow.'

Here are the Album verses, the only example of Colvin's
muse that I have been able to find :—

'Extempore effusion, composed while waiting for the
midday meal at Llanthony Abbey, August 30, 1880, in
answer to the request of a young lady who desired a
contribution to her album.

'*N.B.*—The critical mind will perceive that the
young lady is herself supposed to be the speaker.

> ' Beneath the shade of Cambrian hills,
> While August air the valley fills
> With music of the woods and rills,
> I take my holiday.
> Amid the ruin'd aisles and piers,
> Where holy men in other years
> Abode with orisons and tears,
> I play my summer play.
>
> 'What do I play at? Who can tell?
> Lawn tennis I could play at well,
> But tennis nets in Honddu dell
> Are none: instead of this
> I ride or sketch or sing or chat,
> Or stroll, or shoulder little Matt,
> Whose cheek is clean enough to pat,
> Not clean enough to kiss;
>
> 'Or tease papa, who sallies out
> To bring us home a dish of trout,
> But brings instead, poor dear, the gout,
> And limps with padded toe;
> Or take this book, where here a friend,
> And there another, rhymes has penned,
> And read them o'er, and where they end,
> Ask prettily for mo'.'

I

'Ahem! I should like to know if that is not a contribution to the elegant literature of my country.'

Henley's next letter is chiefly concerned with Colvin's monograph on Landor in its published form in 1881. I keep the Landor portions for later quotation and retain here only the other part : ' Louis' story, " The Merry Men," is first-chop indeed. It contains some stunning dialogue, heaps of good descriptive writing, no end of real imagination, & a character who is a veritable creation. You will enjoy it greatly, & be prouder of our young man than ever. He is not, I am sorry to add, so well as he ought to be ; but of that we are not to speak. I go on hoping for the best ; & as all that 's the matter with him is a slight cold, I don't see that I 'm wrong.

' Oscar's book has come out at last. The *Athenæum* wigged it horrid. A writer in the *D.N.* whom I suspect to be Lang, was more kindly, but scoffed at it too. It seems, by the extracts I 've seen, to be tolerably putrid. Oscar's self-sufficiency is the best thing about him, so far as I know. You think differently, I am aware : but I can't help fancying that your indomitable charitableness leads you astray. At all events, I can't believe that anyone worth a rush would have allowed himself to print such stuff as I have seen quoted. It 's a pity ; for the young fellow seems to have had good parts to begin with. What he has done with 'em I don't like to think. His is a strange figure, truly, & one that painted at full length—like Rastignac's, for instance ; or like Barry Lyndon's—would be uncommonly interesting. Had I seen what you have seen, & lived abroad as you have lived, I might be tempted to try it. I should at worst produce the history of a very odd & fantastic movement & sketch the outline of a very odd & fantastic career. Don't you think it ought to be done, & well—that is to say dispassionately & temperately & cruelly—done ?

' Talking of Barry Lyndon reminds me that I 've seen & met & talked with Sheil Barry the actor. I wrote a

flaming account of his Gaspard in *Les Cloches de Corneville*
some years ago ; & Teddy [Henley's brother Edward, an
actor] found that he thought it the best thing ever writ
about himself—an opinion with which, on reperusal, I am
disposed to agree. So I went to the Crystal Palace & saw
him play Danny Mann in the *Colleen Bawn* and Harvey
Duff in the *Shaughraun* : two magnificent performances,
the work of a man who 's an actor in every fibre. We had
a good long talk, & I found him a very quiet, modest, &
intelligent man—as different from Warner, and from what
I hear of Irving, as light is from dark. I feel sure that we
shall be friends, for I like him much. And I feel sure that
if I do not die, & can only get fairly on to the drama, I shall
make him a part in which he 'll be the talk of London.
Meanwhile he is an Irish comedian. Teddy admires him
passionately, & I was glad to find that he thinks well of
Teddy. This is one reason why I was so anxious that
the lad should go touring with Boucicault, to whom the
little man is for the moment indispensable. He promised
to come & see me ere he left, but he hasn't been, & I 'm
more disappointed than I can say. However, the tour is
to be but six weeks long, & I shall see him on his return
no doubt. I can't help thinking that I 've found my man
in him ; for he 's not addicted to sympathetic parts, is
longing to get on, & has pluck (O Landor, forgive us !) &
strength & art enough for anything. In fact, if I weren't
so stupid over the Russian play, I think I 'd start on my
" Admiral Guinea " at once. You don't know the admiral,
do you ? I don't yet. But I think he may one day be a
good deal on the spot.

  ' I dined on Wednesday with Austin Dobson—for whom
I have a great liking & esteem & who seems, I am proud to
say, to think well enough of me—& an American journalist,
a J. Brander Mathews. He, the A. J., is a rum creature. He
reminded me of a Bas-Bleu in bags. I know the Americans
now, thank you. They have plenty to say & no remarks
to offer, but they are, before all things, Up to the Mark.

That's their great quality. Henry James is the supreme
expression of it. Mathews is Up to the Mark, too; but in
another style & to a less degree. . . . He was full of amiability,
& volunteered any amount of assistance in the States. When
this was made plain to me, I began asking for information
for Louis' sake. I found his " Whitman " & his " Thoreau "
very well known & very highly esteemed in the States; I
heard that for the " B. Franklin " he has in view there
would be instant & splendid sale : & it was intimated to me
that if he would print his Americanisms in a volume for
sale in the States he would make a good thing of it. The
idea indeed is admirable. I have communicated it to
Louis. There's much more to say about it, of course ;
but say it by letter I can't. You shall hear all when you
return.

'Bob is well. He is bent on the figure & on portraiture.
Legros has been careering round with Ionides in a yacht.
Anthony has painted another picture, & is burning to get
at Geo. Howard with it, & with the preceding one, which
is yet unsold. Baxter has gone daft over Piranesi, with
whose etchings he will decorate his dining-room, while with
three Canalettos he proposes to adorn his drawing-room.
I am excessively poor, excessively idle, excessively hopeless,
& excessively careless. I have been going to write an
article—a *Cornhiller*, I hope—next week any time since you
left ; & I haven't begun it yet. The Châtelaine is well
in body & mind. Our love to you & everyone. A note
will please us much, however brief it may be.'

Oscar Wilde's book was his *Poems*. Stevenson never
carried out his project to write a study of Benjamin Franklin.
The essays on Thoreau and Whitman, reprinted for
periodicals, will be found in *Familiar Studies of Men and
Books*. Bob, Stevenson's cousin, in 1882 was to join
Henley's staff on the *Magazine of Art*, and become known
as one of the most sensitive art critics of his time. Anthony
was Henley's artist brother ; Teddy, his actor brother.

That is the last letter from Henley which Colvin pre-

served, until those of the year 1895 ; but Henley kept
letters from Colvin written constantly until 1885. Extracts
from these will be found later in this book.

I close this chapter with Colvin's appreciation of the
Magazine of Art, to which he was a steady contributor :
' Hooray for the mag. It 's a first-rate [one], and the firm
is an ungrateful firm if it don't vote a testimonial of several
thousand pounds and an épergne to the editor.'

CHAPTER XI

LANDOR IN THE 'ENGLISH MEN OF LETTERS SERIES'

1880–1882

THIS is the letter in which, early in 1879, John Morley invited Colvin to contribute a volume to his 'English Men of Letters Series,' leaving the choice to him : 'Long ago,' he says, ' should I have written, but in the first place we did not know how far the success of the early volumes would encourage us to go on. Well, that is now settled. Nothing could be more satisfactory.'

Colvin having chosen Walter Savage Landor, Morley replied thus : ' I close with your proposal of Landor, most cheerfully. He will make an excellent subject. Only let me petition you to give us plenty of the man himself, letters, talks, and personality generally. Symonds' *Shelley* seems to me a model of what one of our books ought to be.

' Of course I quite understand that you are to take your own time, and there is no sort of hurry. But it would be perhaps as well if you could name some sort of date—say a year hence, or eighteen months, or what you please—just to give my hopes a happy tinge of definiteness.

' Length, then, not less than 180 pp.—nor more than 200 pp. Give us as many extracts as you please.

' I am delighted to add you to my band, for many reasons.

' The Dean's [Dean Church] *Spenser* goes to the printer next week—else you should have taken him, with pleasure. [F. W. H.] Myers' *Virgil* is talked about in a way that ought to please his friends.

' Jebb is going to do *Bentley* for my series.'

The *Landor* duly appeared in 1881, and among the letters are several that bear upon this accomplished study, none more interesting than the very long one, in two parts, from Henley, to which I have referred and which I now quote :
' The *Landor* turned up yesterday. I read it very carefully, & with immense pleasure. It is an admirable bit of work, & does you honour, & no mistake. The style is wonderfully easy & smooth, & wonderfully lucid & expressive ; & you know your man. Oh yes, you know him very well indeed ; and you make us know him too. I congratulate you with all my heart, & wish with all my heart you were set at some more work of the same sound, authoritative, entirely human type.
' The final chapter would have been a loss indeed. All thanks to Morley who allowed you to retain it. I forgive him his Old Friend ; I forgive him his Mediaevalism even. All thanks to you, too, for your definition of Style. I see you were thinking of me when you formulated it. Were you not ? Anyway I think you were. I shall make much use of it.
' Honestly, I think your *Landor* the most vivid & human book of all the series. I have a great admiration for Stephen's *Johnson*, it's true ; but I haven't read it since it came out, & I may be mistaken about it. If I am you must forgive me. But I think more of it than of any one of its companions excepting your *Landor*.
' I must add that I don't at all agree with your estimate of Landor as a creative & dramatic artist. As an artist in style you have done nobly & brilliantly by him. You are no end good about his verse, though I think your " titanic " & so forth, as applied to such marmoreal Ossianisms as *Gebir* & *Count Julian* a little my eye. But I am a bit disappointed by your treatment of Landor the (so-called) dramatist. I can't but disagree with your estimate of him, & qualify this particular element in his genius very much. It appears to me that Landor was a man of vast capacity, but that he never cared to rightly understand the meaning

of the word " dramatic," & that, for all his gifts of fancy &
intelligence & imagination, he is no more a dramatist than
most of us. That quality of disconnectedness which you
note as a principal attribute of his is as fatal to his dramatic
power as to his power of argument & his power of narrative.
His scenes—even at their most dramatic, at their most " intense," at their most " passionate "—are never scenes. If
they advance, it is in their author's despite, & by circuitous
routes & after retreats & digressions innumerable. They
are not scenes ; they are mere talks—they are what Landor
called them in fact, " Imaginary Conversations." And to
set them up for drama, & their author for the nearest Shakespeare, seems to me to misunderstand drama & to be not
very good at Shakespeare.

'Landor was much too personal, too passionate, too
egoistic, & (I think) too selfish to be dramatic. If I were
not afraid of your sending me an ounce of dynamite in your
answer to this, I would add that perhaps, also, he was a
little too stupid. I mistrust those groans & tears of his ;
they remind me of the real emotion that kills the actor ;
they are honourable enough to the man, but they rather
bust the artist. I am afraid that what he did, when he set
himself to write such a conversation as the " Libraries of
Vipsania " (for instance), was the reverse of what he ought
to have done. He felt a good deal *for* his characters, but
he did not feel *with* them ; he was satisfied with the impression they were producing upon him, & took no care of the
impression they should have been producing on each other ;
he worked, in fact, stupidly & selfishly, like the solid,
generous-hearted, blundering old British Lion that he was.
And he fails to impose any sort of conviction upon me
either that he understood the nature & object of emotional
portraiture, or that he apprehended to any considerable
extent the character of the emotional processes of the men
& women he chose to think he was portraying. The
" Leofric & Godiva " is one long proof of this. Leofric is
Landor, & Godiva is Landor ; the talk engaged in between

them has no very obvious raison d'être, & starts from nowhere to end nowhere. It contains some beautiful things in the way of emotion, & still more beautiful things in the way of expression. But it is too full of impertinences & irrelevancies, of lapses & breaks, of blunders & ineptitudes even, to be called drama. And to me, except as a piece of writing —not of dramatic writing, mind you, for in dramatic writing I should ask for more of swiftness & less of weight, for more of variableness & appropriateness & less of majesty & fulness, for more matter & less of manner—it hardly seems creative art at all. It is stenography in marble, it is reporting on a bronze tablet, if you will. But it lacks thrill & tact & movement ; it lacks passion & height & apt & definite imagination ; that selectiveness (you know what I mean) which all we English want so much is apparent, not in the matter—for the old boy seems to have set down pretty much what came uppermost as it came—but only in the manner. And you call this drama ? My eye, sir, my eye !

' It is odd that, having put your finger on that quality of disconnectedness aforesaid & bowled over Landor as an arguist & a story-teller with it, you should not have seen that such a quality must needs be doubly fatal to him as a dramatist. If he could not contrive to imagine a sequence of facts, how do you suppose he was to imagine a logical sequence of emotions ? The truth is, my Colvin, that your admiration for Landor as a writist has somewhat got the better of your better judgement as a critic of the creative in art. You seem to me to have approached the old man in a glow of admiration, & to have taken one or two of his bladders for lanterns. I wish we had talked these " Conversations " over more fully, book in hand, ere you wrote. And I wish, too, that I 'd minded my *Count Julian* better. That scene you quote ought to have settled the dramatist with you for ever. It is really too stupid. No man could gravely write & as gravely publish that for passion & for a scene, & ever become a dramatic poet. It proves the root

of the matter to have been out of him. It proves him to
have been unintelligent as far as drama & the human heart
are concerned. It proves his imagination to have been
rather a creation—a resultant, so to speak, of Alfieri, & the
Roman temper, & the Greek tragics, & the English want of
taste—rather than a natural quality. And it proves that
he didn't always know what he was writing, nor why he
wrote it, & that he was capable both of missing his aim &
misjudging his means.

' A great artist in style ? By all means. You do not say
a word too much about him there, though, as it seems to
me, you are perhaps not critical enough of his fondness for
interjections & exclamatory sentences. But a great artist
in sentiment & emotion ? Not if I know it. His own
instinct was righter than yours, for he called his work
Imaginary Conversations. Let them stay at that ; & they
will do nobly. Claim much more for them, & you 'll oblige
me to become a serious personage, & formulate the drama,
& take to lecturing you. Which would be dreadful.

' It 's for this reason that I love my Epicurus & his two
girls, & my *Caesar & Lucullus.* There 's no pretence at
drammy there. It 's all Landor pure & simple ; everything is apt, cheerful, stately, discursive, broken, impetuous,
irrational, & splendid ; a talk of the golden-mouthed gods.
Decidedly, I am a better judge of literature than you.
Than you, even ! O Sidney Colvin, M.A., & Fellow of
Trinity ! Than you—than you—than you ! Think of that,
& be confounded.

' Now I 'll go drink a whiskey & soda, & go to bed. I
am tired, & it 's doosid late. Good night.'

' *Sunday Night.*

' To go back to our text. You seem to have seen that
there was something wrong about Landor's drama, for you
advise readers not to hanker after stage directions, but to
wade in & read between the lines. It is not the absence
of stage directions, you may rely upon it, that plugs us up ;

it is, as I have said, the non-dramatic quality, the disconnectedness, the solutions of emotional continuity. And
nothing else.

' Looking over what I 've said, & remembering what I 've
written elsewhere, I perceive myself a pedant, & could
almost resolve never to say a word about the drama more.
I seem to credit myself with a monopoly of the dramatic
fakement, don't I ? It 's really abominable, & I 'll leave
off talking about the subject. If I don't, you 'll have
my blood one of these days ; & if you don't somebody else
will. So please look upon this as my last appearance as a
dramatic critic.

' One of the great virtues of your work, my dear Colvin,
is it 's excellent humanity and the pleasant & wholesome view
of life it sets forth. You are full of felicities of all sorts ;
but none are more felicitous than those that treat of
morality. In one passage, where you speak of the " domestic
artist," I like to think you had the Châtelaine in view as
you wrote. Whether or no, I am particularly pleased with
it ; & there are many others. As I said last night, your
book is a real one, & you may well be proud on 't.

' A remark to make :—I am grateful to you for proving
indubitably that if Landor had been a contemporary, he 'd
have been as determined a Jingo as Louis, as I, or as A. C. S.
[Swinburne] himself. . . .'

Mrs. Henley was the Châtelaine.

This is the definition of style in the Landor book : ' But
harmony and rhythm are only the superficial beauties of
a prose style. Style itself, in the full meaning of the
word, depends upon something deeper and more inward.
Style means the instinctive rule, the innate principle of
selection and control, by which an artist shapes and regu-
lates every expression of his mind.'

Among the other letters is this from Sir George
Trevelyan : ' I have twice tried, first to read, and then to
read in, Forster. Your book is just what a book should be.
None the less am I of the vulgar with regard to Landor's

writings. The only things I can read at all with pleasure are the little bits you take from his poetry. Even those selections you make from his prose do not affect me. There always seems to me to be nothing to *get* out of him, in the sense in which you get something out of Fra Lippo Lippi, Bishop Blougram, or the conversations in *Quentin Durward*. But I cannot help thinking that even in this we do not disagree.'

From the author of *The Angel in the House* :—

'*Hastings, July* 20, 1881.

' MY DEAR COLVIN,—I have just received your book on Landor and thank you much for it.   I hope it may do something towards making known the best prose writer since Hooker.   But there is a charm about what is sincerely good that secures it being overlooked and neglected even by the best.   Even they pass such a spirit by saying, as it were, to themselves : " This is none of us.   We do not meddle with it.   It is only a god."—Yours very truly,

'COVENTRY PATMORE'

In the following letter we meet with a name of great distinction in Victorian days, Sir Henry Taylor, author of *Philip van Artevelde* and grandfather of the Colvins' very intimate friend Mrs. J. L. Garvin :—

'*The Roost, Bournemouth,*
'13 *Jany.* 1882.

' DEAR MR. SYDNEY COLVIN,—It has been a great pleasure to me to read yr Life of Landor & as I think you could not write it in the way it is written without taking an interest in everything relating to the subject, I will give you an account of the only two interviews I had with Landor after the death of Southey.   I was staying with a friend at Kiloten Knoll about three miles from Bath, & I called upon Landor to ask him whether he would allow Southey's Letters to him to be published with Southey's Correspondence.   I was shown into an empty drawing room, & standing by

the fireplace I saw over the chimney piece a painting of
Landor's house & grounds at Fiesole. Presently Landor
came down-stairs ; we shook hands, & I pointed to the
picture & said I had passed by the place on my road from
Florence to Fiesole & had admired it very much :—" Yes,"
he said, " a beautiful place, a charming place, I was very
sorry to leave it, but my wife used me so ill I was obliged
to come away." Then we went round the room to see a
considerable collection of pictures on the walls. I expressed
my admiration of a landscape by Wilson. He said:—"You
shall have it." I demurred & declined, as being in no way
entitled to such a gift. He said no more, but the next day
made his appearance at Kiloten Knoll with the picture,
which is now hanging on the wall of my dining room of my
house at East Sheen.

' These two interviews were the first & last of what I
saw of Landor. In previous years I had talked about him
with Southey, who described him as " a man of clear intellect
& insane temper." Your life of him is in accord with that
description. Those who take the interest that I do in his
works have much to thank you for.—Believe me, Yours
Sincerely,   ' HENRY TAYLOR '

The following letter from Fleeming Jenkin, Colvin's
friend and later the subject of Stevenson's biography, is
an example of the literary criticism of a man of intellect
who was not by calling or practice a literary man :—

                              ' *Glen Morven, Augt.* 2, 1881,
                                 ' *Morven, N.B.*

' MY DEAR COLVIN,—I have just read with great interest
& pleasure your life of Landor. I have for long time been
curious concerning him and his writings, and you have
told me what I wished to know and by your telling, you have
conciliated me (for I own to a natural antipathy to the man
you wrote of). I feel sure you have written very honestly
and with a perception of all your hero's failings, and with

a human perception of them which quite disarms me. There
are very few biographies I would rank higher than this &
those which I would so rank owe very much to the subject
chosen. Not but that Landor is a good subject—and one
which might have led many men astray but, I never read
any life in which kind taste, kindly reticence so naturally
and wholesomely combined with honest outspokenness.
All I ought to know, you tell me. Many things I see there
are which might have been told, which might have given
pain to many—none of these are told and I wish to hear
none of them.

'I agree to an amazing extent with your literary criticism and on the one point on which I differ, I feel it is almost
hopeless to speak, for the statement can only be dogmatic
assertion on the one side or the other and you have a much
better right to make dogmatic assertions in literature than
I have.

'But a man's a man for a' that and cannot but have his
opinion & you probably take enough interest in humanity
at large to be faintly interested even in my literary
impressions.

'I have only one fault to find with Landor but a great
one—

'to me Landor seems wholly deficient in truth of *imagination*. The irritation which I invariably feel when reading
his conversations arises from this—I make no cavil about
the sedateness of his style, nor about the gaps left without
stage directions. On the second reading (and all good
dramatic writings require at least a second reading) I can
supply and would willingly supply these ; but when I have
supplied them, when I have Godiva off her horse at the
proper moment I still feel that she and her husband are
often saying what no human being ever said or could say
under the circumstances—and if I feel this in a dialogue
which contains occasional passages which are not only
beautiful, but which a woman could say (as for the man,
No No No) you can suppose what my feelings are in reading

the utterances given to a Henry VIII. or any other man whom Landor hates. I had supposed that Landor's imagination was verbal, but your book teaches me that he really did imagine the people, & that with tears and laughter I am surprised—*you* see the falseness of his humour. Well! to *me* the pathos seems quite as false. The noble things his heroes say are usually as little like anything which I can imagine a man saying as the funny or giddy things his funny & giddy people are made to utter.

‘ Of course whether you or I be right depends simply on the relative truth of our imaginative ear—I cannot make you believe a note is out of tune if you do not hear the discord. You cannot make me hear a harmony if my ear is too sluggish. What, however, confirms me in my impression is this. I perceive every merit you claim for your writer except this one—the nakedness far from being repulsive has charm for me. The general line of thought is quite in harmony with my own. I have no quarrel with him because his Pericles is not *any* Pericles, his Henry VIII. not any Henry VIII. but simply because his pictures of these people are pictures of dummies not of human beings. I see Landor speaking behind an ugly mask with quite a schoolboy's pleasure in making the objects of his antipathy speak in a way which shall be loathsome. I hear Landor being charming & humane & playful (Ah !) behind a pretty mask which he calls by some nice woman's name. Consequently it is only in those dialogues where Landor's *opinions* have weight that I can enjoy him at all. All his critical dialogues give me pleasure—none of his political none of his dramatic. I can read all about “ prodame ” & Vail with interest but I dance about in agony over Joan of Arc & Agnes Sorel—and such admiration as I give to parts of this dialogue or Leofric & Godiva would be given equally if the speaker were avowedly Landor.

‘ The life and the writings of the man are to me all of a piece—the intention admirable—the shortcomings deplorable—and due to the same cause, lack of imagination—not knowing how things would be—not being able to project himself into the mind of his adversary.   You speak of his being blinded by imagination.   I say he was blinded by the want of it.   He would reform Llanthony ! but what that meant —what that little word reform implied, he had no more notion of than his bailiff ; perhaps not so much.

' I beg your pardon for this long scrawl.

'FLEEMING JENKIN '

In the following year Colvin prepared for the 'Golden Treasury Series ' a volume of *Selections from Landor*, from the preface to which I take this illuminating passage : ' Landor had two personalities, an inner one, so to speak, disguised by an outer ; the inner being that of a stately and benign philosopher, the outer that of a passionate and rebellious schoolboy.   Of the external and superficial Landor, the man of headlong impulses and disastrous misapprehensions and quarrels, enough and to spare has been said and repeated.   But together with this indignant, legendary Landor, we must not forget that there existed the other Landor, the noble and gentle heart, the rich and bountiful nature, the royally courteous temper, which won and held the loving admiration of spirits like Southey and the Hares, like Leigh Hunt and Forster and Dickens, like Robert and Elizabeth Browning, and even of one so grudging of admiration as Carlyle.   That Landor's inner and nobler self had little hold on or government over his other self must be admitted.   From his nature's central citadel, to use a mediaeval figure, of Pride, High Contemplation, and Honourable Purpose, he failed to keep ward over its outlying arsenals of Wrath, which Haste and Misjudgment were for ever wantonly igniting, to the ruin of his own fortunes, and the dismay of his neighbours and well-wishers.'

Although chronologically out of place, I am disposed to insert here two very interesting letters from Mr. George Moore.   I give them in full :—

'121 *Ebury Street, London, S.W.,*
March 8th, 1917.

'DEAR SIR SIDNEY COLVIN,—I daresay that you remember that it was your little book about Landor, little in size, but great in quality, that set me reading him. After exhausting your extracts, I bought another volume of extracts, and when these were exhausted I turned to the complete edition and every fortnight a volume comes to me from the Lending Library in Buckingham Palace Road. It seems to me now that I should like to have an edition of Landor of my own, and I am writing to ask you which is the best edition to buy. I should like to have the poems as well as the conversations.

'And now, Sir Sidney, I have to thank you for your edition of Stevenson's letters, which have given me the very greatest pleasure, revealing Stevenson to me even more perfectly than *Travels with a Donkey, An Inland Voyage, Men and Books,* etc. Story-telling seems to have been outside of his talent. The moment the story commences it seems to pare from him, to strip him of all the qualities that we admire. In a story we get Stevenson as if skinned. Perhaps I should say a skeleton Stevenson, a mummified Stevenson. I think from your admirable explanatory notes scattered through your edition of his letters that you yourself suspect that he was not a natural story-teller, and I am sending you a preface of a book of mine that is just coming out. You will read in it an appreciation of Stevenson that has not, I believe appeared before.—Very sincerely yours,   GEORGE MOORE '

'121 *Ebury Street, London, S.W.,*
'*March 15th,* 1917.

'DEAR SIR SIDNEY COLVIN,—I am very much obliged to you for your advice regarding the best edition of Landor. It will be very satisfactory for me to have all the volumes, and one pound fifteen shillings is not much to pay for conveyance to the summits of Parnassus where he dwells always,

K

never descending beyond the lower slopes. I admire half of Stevenson very much, but I only look even upon this half as a sort of trinket that Landor could wear on his watch chain and which might drop off without him being aware of the loss. You tell me that you cannot understand my attitude of mind towards the stories. Without proposing to attempt your conversion which would be an impertinence I may say a few more words on the subject. *Robinson Crusoe* and *Treasure Island* seem to me to be the childhood of prose narrative, the babyhood, for in my view the difficulties of prose narrative do not begin until we introduce man's inner entity into the story. Last night I came upon a passage in Landor which seems to state very well this point of view. " We do not want strange events," he says, " so much as those by which we are admitted into the recesses, or carried on amid operations, of the human mind. We are stimulated by its activity, but we are greatly more pleased at surveying it leisurely in its quiescent state, uncovered and unsuspicious. Few, however, are capable of describing or even remarking it ; while strange and unexpected contingencies are the commonest pedlary of the market, and the joint patrimony of the tapsters."

' There we have it. As soon as we attempt to introduce the reader into the recesses of the human mind the difficulty begins. But stories about digging in the sand are related to literature very much as Mozart's early sonatas are related to Wagner's *Mastersingers*. You will not agree with me in this, but perhaps you will now understand my point of view regarding Stevenson's stories. But although his stories seem to be purely mechanical, I greatly admire his critical discrimination. His articles in *Men and Books* are as good as Sainte-Beuve, though it may be doubted if the Frenchman would have plumed himself so ostentatiously that he was not like poor Villon.

' You will perhaps be interested to hear that in reading your edition of the letters the reader is as much interested in you as he is in the author of the letters, and I think the reason of this interest arises from your reticence ; most editors of the letters would have introduced a great deal of irrelevant matter but you refrained and the result is that the reader says : " I should like to hear more about Colvin." Altogether your attitude towards Stevenson is a pleasure to me to think about and an honour to you both.—Yours sincerely,   ' GEORGE MOORE '

CHAPTER XII

THERE is, I think, an impression that Mrs. Sitwell and Mrs. Stevenson were not too friendly. How true this may have been in the early days I cannot say ; it would not have been unnatural had Mrs. Osbourne, as she was in 1876, resented Stevenson's dependence upon her predecessor. But I have no reason to suppose that she did ; and we shall see that when the time came for them to meet, after the Stevensons returned from California in 1880, at Davos in 1881, and during the Bournemouth years, 1884-1887, some very affectionate letters were written by Mrs. Stevenson to Mrs. Sitwell, and I have no doubt, although none seem to exist, that the replies were punctual and equally warm.

I am now grouping together some of the letters of the years 1881-1887, none of which have been published before in book form, and only a few, marked by a footnote, in periodical form, when in 1924 Colvin selected them for two articles in the *Empire Review* in England, and in *Scribner's Magazine* in America.

As a preface let me quote Colvin's character sketch of Mrs. Stevenson. On their arrival in Edinburgh, he says, after their return from California in 1880 : ' She made an immediate conquest of them [her husband's parents], especially of that character so richly compounded between the stubborn and the tender, the humorous and the grim, his father. Thenceforth there was always at Louis's side a wife for his friends to hold only second in affection to himself. A separate biography of her by her sister has lately appeared,

148

giving, along with many interesting details of her early life, a picture of her on the whole softer and less striking than that which I personally retain. Strength and staunchness were, as I saw her, her ruling qualities; strength and staunchness not indeed masculine in their kind, but truly womanly. Against those of his friends who might forget or ignore the precautions which his health demanded she could be a dragon indeed ; but the more considerate among them she made warmly her own and was ever ready to welcome. Deep and rich capacities were in her, alike for tragedy and humour ; all her moods, thoughts, and instincts were vividly genuine and her own, and her daily talk, like her letters, was admirable both for play of character and feeling and for choice and colour of words. On those who knew the pair first after their marriage her personality impressed itself almost as vividly as his ; and in my own mind his image lives scarce more indelibly than that of the small, dark-complexioned, eager, devoted woman his mate. In spite of her squareish build she was supple and elastic in all her movements ; her hands and feet were small and beautifully modelled, though not meant for, or used to, idleness ; the head, under its crop of close-waving thick black hair, was of a build and character that somehow suggested Napoleon, by the firm setting of the jaw and the beautifully precise and delicate modelling of the nose and lips : the eyes were full of sex and mystery as they changed from fire or fun to gloom or tenderness ; and it was from between a fine pearly set of small teeth that there came the clear metallic accents of her intensely human and often quaintly individual speech.'

Mrs. Stevenson's first letter is from Davos in the winter of 1880 :—

' MY DEAR MR. COLVIN,—As Louis shows no disposition towards letter writing, dry rot having eaten deeply into his vitals, I feel that I must at least drop you a note to let you know that we are living, and in good hopes of more than that. Of course our arrival at once effected a change in the climate of Davos, so that we have been living in an atmosphere of fog and rain until to-day, which is clear and bright. Even at its worst, though, Davos seems to be the place for Louis ; I believe if anything will cure him it is this place, and we are greatly pleased with the doctor, in whom we feel confidence, and who is a very pleasant gentleman. He says that Louis has chronic pneumonia, with infiltration of the lungs, and enlargement of the spleen. Dry rot I believe to be consequent upon the state of Louis's spleen, and to have nothing to do with his mind, which is some consolation. We find many pleasant people here, and Louis and Mr. Symonds are, so to speak, Siamese twins.

' We nearly had a tragedy yesterday. Louis and I and Watty Woggs, the dog (his name has somehow become changed), were out for a walk, all in the highest spirits, Woggs especially, who somehow became entangled as to his hind legs in a bit of circular string, which so frightened him that he fell upon the ground in a violent fit. He seems pretty well this morning, but we were all very much upset by the mishap, as we have grown to love Woggs dearly. I think he was very proud of the sensation he created.

' I find that I am an invalid too, though I had not guessed it until the doctor told me. He says that I should not be so fat, and that it (the fatness) is caused by a disease of the stomach ; so I am put upon diet, and am going through a course of medicine. I was so strict with Louis about obeying the doctor's orders that I believe he is glad to be able to retaliate.

' We expect and look forward to the promised visit at Christmas as a certainty, so you cannot be so cruel as to disappoint two invalids, now can you ?

' Give my dearest love to my pretty friend, who really (but that you must know as well as I) grows more lovely as time passes by. I wish I knew how she did it. I should like to drink from the fount of perennial youth too. I will leave room for a line from Louis.'

MRS. ROBERT LOUIS STEVENSON
AT THE AGE OF 30

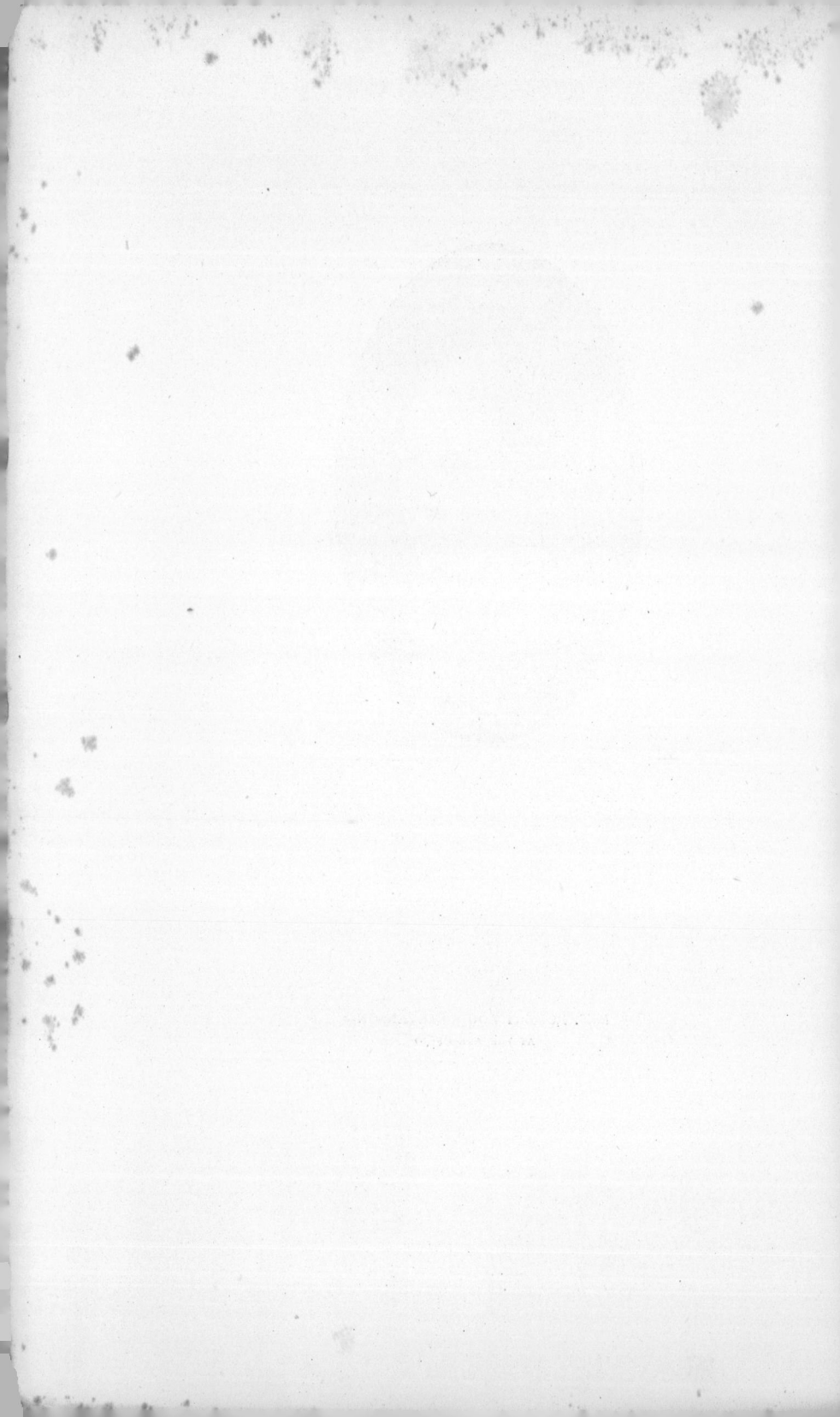

Mr. Symonds was John Addington Symonds.

The line from Louis is missing.

The pretty friend would be Mrs. Sitwell.

Watty Woggs was a black Scotch terrier given to Mrs. Stevenson by Sir Walter Simpson, R. L. S.'s companion in the *Inland Voyage*. It was first called Walter and then Wattie. Later, as we shall see, its name was modified. Colvin seems to have loathed it.

The year 1881 broke very sadly for Mrs. Sitwell.

A letter from Colvin to Henley on January 7 [1881] tells the story : ' If you don't hear anything of me for the next little while, know that it is because of a great anxiety which has come upon us. Bertie is ill—a threatening of lung disease— and is ordered at once to Davos with the hope (almost promise) that the taking of the trouble in time will cure it and set him up. His mother goes, and I take her (on Sunday) as far at any rate as Paris.'

Bertie Sitwell was then eighteen and had just left Marlborough. Later in January he died, in his mother's arms. Stevenson's beautiful consolatory poem is well known, but I quote it again :—

' IN MEMORIAM, F. A. S.

' Yet, O stricken heart, remember, O remember
    How of human days he lived the better part.
  April came to bloom and never dim December
    Breathed its killing chills upon the head or heart.

' Doomed to know not Winter, only Spring, a being
    Trod the flowery April blithely for a while,
  Took his fill of music, joy of thought and seeing,
    Came and stayed and went, nor ever ceased to smile.

' Came and stayed and went, and now when all is finished,
    You alone have crossed the melancholy stream,
  Yours the pang, but his, O his, the undiminished
    Undecaying gladness, undeparted dream.

'All that life contains of torture, toil, and treason,
Shame, dishonour, death, to him were but a name.
Here, a boy, he dwelt through all the singing season,
And ere the day of sorrow departed as he came.'

One more reference to young Sitwell I should like to give. It is in the letter from Philip Burne-Jones from which I quote—the nonsensical part—in an earlier chapter: 'You say you were glad to see me at Walton—What can I say? How can I tell you my delight if I thought my presence could ever bring you the least gladness! I may, because I am a young thing, remind you dimly of the life you loved best in the world—but this is all I could have in your heart, in common with that life—& for the rest how deep the chasm between me & him—how hopeless the intrusion of another—that gap how impossible to fill—But that you should in any way love me for being a young creature—for having known Bertie & been at school with him—is an honour which I should consider most sacred—& should try with all my might to make myself—the shadow of the reality that is gone—worthy of the affection I still marvel you can bestow.'

The first of the new Stevenson letters, to which we now come, is a joint letter from Braemar in the summer of 1881 :—

'MY DEAR MR. COLVIN,—Louis asked me to write, but for the life of me I cannot remember what he wanted me to say; he is in bed, asleep, I hope. I suppose the real thing is that he only wants to have the feeling that there are letters coming and going, and general friendliness. Let me know, please, just when you will arrive, and I will meet you. I don't doubt that it can be so arranged that a bed can be managed for you in the house, I can talk of that when I see you. In the meantime, come on, though I fear it will not be very pleasant for you, though your advice will be very profitable to me in many things. Louis can hardly talk to anyone without being very ill after it, or in fact do anything. I am quite disheartened, and in the lowest possible spirits, so pray excuse this letter if it is not all it should be. At any rate I mean well. I cannot even find the paper box to get a decent sheet to write upon. Love to all, and hoping to see you very soon,—Truly yours,

'FANNY V. DE G. STEVENSON'

Here R. L. S. has written : ' This was what was wanted : we have sent for an oil stove. When that comes, as it should soon, we can warm your room for you ; and then, maybe, we 'll have to ask you to buy the blankets. For at this rate there will never be any more money made by,— Yrs. ever, R. L. S.'

Mrs. Stevenson resumes : ' My dear friend, This letter has been lost and found again. Louis has taken cold, which is bad ; how bad one cannot tell for a day or two. Pray come. But there will, alas, be no " cracks " to speak of. A very little of that brings on either a hemorrhage or cold sweat. *Literally*, not figuratively, nothing is what Louis is able to do. It will be a disappointment to you, I know, but all the same, come.'

The next is also a double letter. The first part—to " My dear Maud "—is to Mrs. Churchill Babington. Mrs. Stevenson's letter is to Mrs. Sitwell. Though there is no address or date, the letters were written at Braemar, September 1881 :

' MY DEAR MAUD,—Many thanks indeed for the invitation. A dozen things make it impossible for us to come this time. First, Fanny has to stay some days in Edinburgh—Will not likely get away till Tuesday. Second, I myself can only get to Edin[b] by Thursday and have to travel slowly and take care of myself. I am some the worse for this abominable summer up here ; and I almost believe I had better not go visiting ; much talk being the mischief.

' I believe Fanny is as much disappointed as I can be ; for I am sure she would like you, and I know she thinks she would. As for the Professor, *cela va sans dire.*

' I shall be sure to get a sight of parties somehow in London ; but how, when or where I cannot yet foresee. I have a pig-snout naso-oral respirator on my face, and look the dismallest figure of fun. Love to all. Ever your afft. cousin,   R. L. Stevenson '

' To my dearest Frances,—We cannot come, which is a great disappointment to me ; and the cause, too, is a trouble. Louis is not so well as he should be : this place has been poison to us all. I have been seldom so wretched as I have been here, shut in by the hills, no doctor, and no one to whom I could speak without reserve. I have felt sometimes like the ancient mariner, that I must stop some one on the street and pour out my heart to him. Fortunately I have never met a wedding guest, or I should have at once fixed him with my eye. I believe from what I have been told that nature has given me the eye for that sort of demonstration, and it seems almost a pity to waste it. I am in rather better spirits just now, as to-morrow we shake the mud (not the dirt, it has been too wet for that) of Braemar from our feet, and leave it, I hope forever. I fancy that Davos will be our home—think of home at Davos—for a pretty long time now. I *do hope* I shall see you and dear [Colvin ?] in London, I do not feel as though I could go away and not see you. Louis is in front of the window as I write, throwing kisses from his " pig's face." The pig's face was telegraphed for immediately upon Dr. Balfour's arrival, and is a most appalling addition to the countenance. It is a respirator with tar oil in the snout, and I believe is a good thing. I think we will be in London on Saturday or thereabouts. [illegible] and I will stop with Bob's mother, but Louis will only see his doctor and then go on to some place in the country. I felt that I *must* see you. I do not see how I can go on with courage, unless I see one of my

real, dear friends before I start. I fear I have got morbid ;
I cling to the hope of seeing you more than I can tell. I
am so sorry that I could not see Maud. It made us both
quite unhappy to have to refuse her invitation. I wish
now, that I had not tried to write to you, for I meant to
write so cheerfully and gaily : but who can be cheerful or
gay in a wet gray pit of poison ? I can only pour out my
hateful rancour. Give my love to [illegible] and to Maud,
and my regards to the Professor [Colvin again]. Don't
trouble to write to me, dear.

' FANNY '

The following letter from Stevenson to Mrs. Sitwell is
undated, and although the heading of the notepaper might
lead one to range it with the letters from Davos in the
autumn of 1881 (compare with that to Sir Edmund Gosse
of November 9, 1881, from the ' Davos Printing Office '
in the complete correspondence) it is almost certain that
this belongs to a later period. Compare the letter to Mrs.
Sitwell written at Hyères in April 1883, where Stevenson
refers to the *Child's Garden of Verses*, then in course of
composition ; which, as in this new letter, shows that he
has asked for Mrs. Sitwell's criticisms and has profited
by them :

' Davos

'PRINTING OFFICE

' Managed by

' Samuel Lloyd Osbourne & Co.

' The Châlet

' My dear, Fanny would have written to you long ago
but she has been very far from well. Today she is up again ;
but still rather a wreck ; she has, it is thought, drain-
poisoning ; she had diarrhœa very bad, pain, great weakness, spotted throat, and I know not all what. I do hope
she will get over it soon.

' We are installed in the châlet, somewhat at the mercy
of a pretty (yes—that is so—contradiction though it seems)

pretty Swiss servant. It is very pleasant up here on the edge of the wood, with the valley right at our feet ; and the air is much clearer than below. But we can scarcely say it has yet begun to be good weather—the winter lingers ; it comes in whiffs and goes again, leaving behind a steaming, belated kind of summer. Not wholesome at all, by fire, nor quite agreeable. I hope it will soon pass.

' We have just had Oscar Wilde's incredible letter to Colvin and have roared over it, the bad child dancing to a T. I read his poems and found, with disappointment, they were not even improper. This letter is his liveliest work—what would not *Punch* give to publish it verbatim.

' Talking of Felix, do not let him work too much. I know he does ; he was quite overworked when he came to Scotland ; so that we were quite pained to see it. I hope that was only London ; but he must not go on with too much. He serves his friends too much as we all know ; but he would be even kinder to them if he husbanded his health.

' I am so glad you like the Children's Songs ; five more have been despatched, I do not know if they are so good.

' All that you wanted done has been done, I believe.

' Please believe me, with all love from me and Fanny,— Always your faithful friend,

' ROBERT LOUIS STEVENSON '

' I went at once and saw Miss von Glehn ; and I believe we shall see more of her. F. of course cannot go just now. She tires me with the G. G. — Grisly Goose — Gaping Goneral— ; but of course one smiles and feigns freely. But it is a G. G. I love not.'

I do not identify ' G. G.,' but Felix was one of Stevenson's names for Colvin, and the name by which Lady Colvin always called him. Wilde's letter seems to have perished.

After Davos, Stevenson was ordered to the south of France. Colvin writes to Henley, on May 20, 1882 : ' I am writing to Louis to-night,—but oh if he knew what a struggle I have had to keep decently abreast of my duties, he would not be vexed with me for not writing.   Besides, what could I write that would not have betrayed an anxiety which it was essential to hide from him ?   However, write I will : it is bad enough to think that I have given him any pain under any circumstances.

' I am in fear about this journey for him.   It seems so impossible that it should be made without something happening to excite him.   With no one knowing any French, or having any particular heads on their shoulders.   Oh if among all his friends there was only one both practical and with money and leisure to play Providence in the crises as they come, and to tip the railway guards and hotel people and generally pad and prepare the way for him on his travels.'

Henley and Stevenson seem to have had an idea of contributing to the *National Review*, a Conservative periodical started in 1883 with Alfred Austin as its editor. Here is Colvin at his most indignant and remonstrative : ' . . . And now look here ; I shall be really and seriously hurt if you do anything to make Louis contribute to this foolish Tory magazine, for which they have had to advertise, like gabies as they are, and go beating the bush for " latent and undeveloped Conservative talent."   In the first place, you are not politicians at all, you or he : *you* are Beaconsfieldian by a literary whim, and have never thought about politics at all : he is the son of his father, and that 's all. The game is too serious a one, I mean the government of men and orderings of societies, for this side or that to be taken up in a freak, and if your politics, such as they are, were anything *but* a freak,—well, I should think a good deal less of you than I do.'

And again :—

' Mr. Cecil Raikes advertising for latent and undeveloped Conservative talent, and fishing up you and Louis—I should like to see your faces when you found yourselves in the basket of those solemn and timorous High-Church gentlemen ; and I should like to see theirs still more.   Raikes and Louis, good Lord !   Lord Carnarvon and you, my golly ! Why, the very sight of such Tories as you could make good Radicals of them in two twos, and theirs of you ; and where would the magazine be then ?   No, the thing is a folly, and has been done in a peculiarly foolish way.—And that little whipper-snapping all-round failure of an Alfred Austin is the best kind of an editor they could get.—But enough ; I don't want you to be absurd, still less Louis.   So drop it. My dear old carping and rusty old fine-gentleman and Club-Whig of a Newton, I don't mind ; *he* may join them, and welcome, and has : but Louis and you, no never.—Muck !— Yours ever,   S. C.'

Deacon Brodie was produced in London in July 1884, and Colvin writes :

' MY DEAR HENLEY,—Thanks for your letter.   I think you are not at all right about the public and the Deacon. I thought I felt their pulse too, and that by the play as a whole they were disappointed, baffled, and thrown out, but much impressed by particular scenes, and quite awake to the power of particular passages both of acting and writing. The call was a mark of appreciation for these, and not of approval of the thing as a whole.   And in the main the critics seem to me to have been both just and generous. What one of them says is true, the Deacon *is*, as you have written him, morally unintelligible, unconvincing, and non-existent, neither can any amount of brilliant speeches or effective acting make him otherwise.   All of which you knew quite well yourself two or three years ago.   Another time it will be all right, no doubt : but don't make the mistake of despising your critics.

' I saw Louis to my great delight for half an hour last evening.   Thought him quite as well as I expected, and yet frail and frightening : and more loveable than ever.   He has brought rain with him as we foretold, but I am in great hopes it won't last.—Yours ever,   S. C.'

This is Colvin's next letter :

' MY DEAR HENLEY,—I was sorry indeed to have your news of Louis, and wish we had sent him off to the mountains a month ago.   You must, and I know will, be on your guard against letting him work too hard : I 'm *afraid* the brain exertion isn't good : and yet what is to be done ?

' £100 for three years of *Otto* don't sound bad I think, and I am very glad to hear there is so much to be had : it will be something to push Longman's with.[1]

' By to-night's post I send you the *Black Arrow* : if possible look at it yourself before taking it anywhere : I see it is rather *less* good than I thought and I 'm afraid might do him harm on the whole : clever as it struck, but dullish and put-up, and as unlike the reality of *Treasure Island* as possible.   I am no longer sure that I shall be able to get away before Monday (instead of Saturday as I intended)— but on or about that day I shall most likely turn up at Bournemouth.   Let me hear your plans, and if you have any further news.—Yours ever,   S. C.'

From Mrs. R. L. S. to Mrs. Sitwell late in 1884 : ' If you *could* come and stay with me a few days I cannot tell you what a comfort it would be to me.   Louis is ill again, *not* this time with hemorrhages, but a cold, a present from his mother, a parting gift, so to speak. . . .

' If you can't come, or if it would inconvenience you, especially on account of the weather, don't think of it, but please, my darling friend, do what is best for you.   It is more for the comfort of your presence that I wish you than anything else.'

From Mrs. R. L. S. to Colvin : ' I am grieved that you cannot come to us.   Louis is ill again, with a dreadful cold settled all over him, the very worst one he has ever had with the exception of the one at Nice.   I dare not dwell on the subject ; his mother gave it to him in spite of all my entreaties, and went off saying " now that Louis has entirely

---

[1] In the *Empire Review*.

recovered his health, we shall expect him to spend his
Summers in Scotland with us."

' I hear that Henley is not at all well. I write to say that
he might as well bring his influenza here, and join us, as he
can do no harm, and I long for some different events after
these three weeks of chilling selfishness. If Louis dies of
this it will be murder. You see that I am not in a fit state
to write to any one.'

Colvin to Henley on November 30, 1884 : ' I have very
disquieting accounts from Bournemouth. If ever I am
hung it will be for throttling Mrs. T. S., and I shall go smiling
and with a good conscience to the gallows. It appears that
after having crushed and exhausted him with three weeks
of their society (H. James was in high indignation after
having witnessed three days of it) she has left him the legacy
of an influenza cold, which has congested all his organs as in
the old Hyères time. Fanny, on her account, is evidently
nearly off her head also.—I wish I could go down but
cannot at this moment.'

Mrs. R. L. S. to Colvin. From the New London Hotel,
Exeter. [August or September 1885] : ' Louis has been
very ill indeed with a serious hemorrhage, the worst that
he has had except the one at Hyères. As usual, it was very
sudden, and in the night, but the people of this house had a
doctor, ice, and all that was needed in ten minutes. . . . The
people of the house had had the same thing, a hemorrhage
I mean, befall a daughter, so they knew how to be of efficient help. The next day Lady Shelley, who was at Torquay,
and Miss Taylor came and stayed till they were assured that
the worst was over.

' Lady Shelley has sent Louis all sorts of things for his
comfort, a bed rest and bed table upon which he is this
moment going to have his dinner. She also wanted to lend
me a nurse, but I refused. Dr. Scott wrote and offered to
come, " as a friend," he said in brackets, if it would be
any comfort to me. By that time Louis was better, so I
declined with a heart filled with gratitude. Such an offer

as that gives me a feeling of sincerity that nothing else could.

'We saw Hardy the novelist when we were there and liked him exceedingly.

'I have been reading the beginning of Henry James' new novel. Most excellent, I think it, and altogether a new departure,—not but that I have always liked his other work : but this is different, with the thrill of life, the beating of the pulse that you miss in the others.' [1]

Lady Shelley was the wife of Sir Percy Shelley, and Miss Taylor the daughter of Sir Henry Taylor, all resident in Bournemouth. Dr. Scott was one of the doctors to whom Stevenson dedicated *Underwoods*. Henry James's novel was *The Princess Casamassima*.

Mrs. R. L. S. to Mrs. Sitwell. From Bournemouth. ['Skerryvore,' 1885]: 'As to Louis, he is much better, though still bad enough : he has had the worst hemorrhage he has ever had in England accompanied by congestion of the brain. Henley must not come to him now with either work or business unless he wishes to kill him.

'My back is broken altogether, but not with moving. I had to lift Louis in and out of bed ten times in one night. He was quite off his head and could not be contradicted because he was bleeding at the lungs at the same time, and got into such furies when I wasn't quick enough.'

Mrs. R. L. S. to Colvin. No date : 'Of course you are more than welcome, you always are, as you know, and we are most anxious to talk to you about all kinds of things, besides. I am going to Bath for a day or two, but will be back to see you. The "family" are at Bath, and it seems the best place found as yet for the old gentleman, who is much better and more like himself. I have not been very well, though I have found the coca wine a blessing and a boon. Lady Taylor feels so well while taking it that she is convinced that it must be a most dangerous remedy. Isn't that like Louis ? '

---

[1] In the *Empire Review.*

Mrs. R. L. S. to Colvin. ' "Skerryvore," 1885 : To begin, Louis is the better for the moving, it having the same effect as a change of climate. The name of Sea View still remains, according to the gallant captain's taste, and Skerryvore is, as yet, but whispered between only our Scots and their relatives by marriage (that's me ; for if I am not Louis' relative by marriage, then, pray, what am I ?).

' H. J. [Henry James] did find us, Louis was well enough to see him, we are devoted to him, and he comes to us every evening after dinner. I think there is no question but that he likes Louis ; naturally, I have hardly been allowed to speak to him, though I fain would. He seems very gentle and comfortable, and I worship in silence,—enforced silence, —enforced by the elegant, though brutal Mr. Stevenson.

' The front door, by my exertions, and a charwoman's, is much improved, and more drawn into harmony with its surroundings.

' Louis did receive the stamped request, and did something vague. Pray remember me with many kind messages to the providential Hammond. I think you mean he is full of writing to Louis and not me ; as I said to Sargent, " I am but a cipher under the shadow," to which he too eagerly assented. It is only kind custodians who write to me : and now and then a lonely Symonds, or a savage Henley who attacks me.

' I am much taken up with the thought of the Spanish *Treasure Island*. Louis means to write to Mr. Hammond and find out how to get it. Having got it, he hopes to learn Spanish by its means. I am glad indeed that you like *Otto*. I have begged to have a few things marked out, not much. My hand has been laid upon him in no spirit but that of kindness,—upon Otto I mean, not Louis, to whom I am often unkind, though always, I hope unintentionally.' [1]

Mr. Hammond was Basil Hammond, a fellow of Trinity and lecturer on history.

Colvin writes to Henley about this time : ' Have you read

[1] In the *Empire Review*.

Otto ?—and do you agree with me as to its excellence— especially the beginning and end ? '

Mrs. R. L. S. to Mrs. Sitwell.   From Bournemouth. [Spring, 1885] :

' MY DEAREST FRIEND,—Many thanks for your kind and pleasant letter. It is very comfortable to know that we have a home really and truly, and will no more be like Noah's dove, flying about with an olive branch, and trying to pretend that we have found a bit of dry ground to perch upon. I do hope that you will be able to come and visit us in it, and dear Sooka too. I never saw a place that seemed arranged so exactly to suit our requirements as this place, which is to be called " Skerry Vore." There is even a little studio for me to dabble paints in, and the garden is delicious. When we are rich enough (if I am not too fat by that time) there is a stable all ready for my horse. A fine dog house also awaits my Bogue.

' We have just had a visit from Beerbohm Tree, whose name, I am sorry to say, is treated with shocking levity by Louis. He seems a very nice, modest, pleasant fellow, and we were much pleased with him. I see that the great Oscar is coming here in a fortnight. I rather wish he would come to see us ; I feel slightly curious to look upon the disciple of the aesthetic. A French paper that Louis got this morning describes his personal appearance as being like a " white malady." It sounds very dreadful indeed, and I hope is not absolutely correct. I read *Otto* to Mrs. Stevenson, and do you know she objected and applauded precisely when you did. I shall have to go to Hyères soon, now, to settle our affairs, but how to leave Louis, for I shall have to take Valentine with me, I do not know.

' What a dreadful thing these explosions have been. Our Arabian tales have been a good deal knocked over by them, but Louis is remodelling where it is necessary as hard as he can. It is a great advertisement if one may be allowed to say so. I cannot tell you how I admire the English police-

man.   I want Louis to write an article about them.   It is
lucky I am not a housemaid or a cook.   At the first sight
of a policeman I should be a lost woman.   They are expected
to be braver than generals, and wiser than Mr. Gladstone ;
and the expectation is verified.   I wonder if the dynamiters
will come blowing up Louis and me, and our Valentine and
our Bogue.   It wouldn't be so very surprising.   I feel no
vocation towards being made a martyr, but I do not believe
anything could happen more to the point than for them to
blow up a young French girl, an American woman, and a
romantic young author.

' *Couldn't* you just come down to me for a few days ?
It would be such a delight and joy.   In this request Louis
joins with all his heart.' [1]

Skerryvore was the name of one of the lighthouses built
by Stevenson's family of engineers.   Bogue was the name
by which Wattie was now called.   In the interim it had
been Woggie, and Woggs.

Beerbohm Tree was at Bournemouth to talk about the
plays that Stevenson had been writing with Henley.   The
Arabian Tales were the new series of *New Arabian Nights*
which Stevenson was planning with his wife, resulting in
The Dynamiter.   The explosions were those of the Fenian
outrages of that year.   Valentine was Mrs. Stevenson's
French maid.

Mrs. R. L. S. to Colvin.   From ' Skerryvore.'   [1885] :
' Mr. Sargent came last night to do the portrait.   It begins
well, and one hand that is finished expresses about all of
Louis.   God grant the head may follow suit.

' I have another play in my mind which I told to Archer,
who thinks it more to the point than anything else, and begs
to have it written.   He is a very nice fellow, indeed, and
I should write to him at this moment, only I have broken
my glasses and dare only to write to an indulgent Custodian.'

John Sargent painted Stevenson twice.

A letter from Colvin to Henley thus refers to the portrait :

[1] In the *Empire Review*.

' I was sorry not to be able to see anything of Fanny when she came—but she should have given a word of warning. I hope the cat will eat Woggs, and I hope Woggs will eat the cat.—These animals are always demons.—I have an idea of going down there for a few days the week after next. It is a great thing to be able to have some hopefulness about him again. Have you seen Sargent's picture ? It 's him to the life in gesture and expression—living life, with a touch of *charge*[1] : but somehow small and perky and peaky a little too : as clever as possible, but not satisfying.' A criticism which recalls Sargent's own remark, that a portrait is ' a picture of a man or woman, with something wrong with the mouth.'

The play was, I think, *The Hanging Judge*, which Mrs. Stevenson and her husband wrote later. Archer was the late William Archer.

Mrs. R. L. S. to Colvin. From ' Skerryvore.' [1885] : ' I am sure the money you sent was but a small item in the expense we brought upon the moment. I know your expenses. There are other things we owe, such as gratitude and the like, but we are proud of the debt, and it can hardly be spoken of.'

Mrs. R. L. S. to Colvin. From ' Skerryvore.' [1885] : ' Please don't be so stern with me. You don't know how frightening the thought of your displeasure is. I hardly dare raise my eyes to the photograph that guards our slumbers. Long ago you said you would lend Mr. Smith's. I have steadily begged for a sight of it, but I suppose you don't know that. Most humbly contrite for no fault of my own.'

Mrs. R. L. S. to Colvin. From ' Skerryvore.' [1885] : ' I am very fond of the father, but not so fond of him, after all, as I am of Louis, and the spirit of self-sacrifice is not strong in me. Except for this touch of hemorrhage, which began yesterday morning, and is now no better, no worse, Louis is remarkably well.

' I send with this a note to Mrs. Jenkin, which I beg you

---

[1] A French word signifying ' représentation exagérée d'une personne.'

to post for me, as I have entirely lost her address, and don't know what else to do.   Her son, Frewin, took some photographs of Louis, one of which is rather like, but over-beautiful, Christ walking on the waters, as Lady Shelley said.   Dear old Sir Percy took a number, one or two of which I think really very good.   As soon as I can get some I will send you the best of each.   It is very odd that while one represents an angel, the devil must have posed for another, so ghastly, impishly wicked, and malignant is it.   Plainly Jekyll and Hyde.

' Do you ever see our dear friend, Henry James ?   He was in this country when I last heard from him.   We think most highly of the new novel as it goes on.' [1]

Mrs. Fleeming Jenkin is referred to.   The James novel is still *The Princess Casamassima*.

Mrs. R. L. S. to Colvin.   From ' Skerryvore.'   [1885] : ' Smeuroch, Mr. Stevenson's dog, now lives with us.   She is a cat killer ;   imagine how I enjoy her society with my poor Ginger (who, by the way, is a dog killer), walking stiff legged and big tailed about the house ! ' [2]

Mr. Stevenson, who owned the dog, was R. L. S.'s father.

Mrs. R. L. S. to Colvin.   From ' Skerryvore.'   [1885] :

' BEST OF CUSTODIANS,—Our conduct, as usual, has been horrid :   but you, as usual, I trust, will prove forgiving.   I begin to believe that Louis and I are both suffering, not from softening of the brain, but ossification of the intellect. We are able to eat and sleep and behave rudely, that is all. I am glad you are having such a complete change, though it does seem to remove all chance of a visit here, which we would love.   However, I suppose we, or one of us, will go to the " mommy " as you say we may.   We have had a good deal of wearing company for some time :   our own house was full, and we had also a couple of dependencies in the neighbourhood.   Louis' mother and father were here.   Aunt Alan, and Miss Ferrier and Henley, we have also had Teddy Henley for a couple of nights.   Bob and

[1] In the *Empire Review*.   [2] In the *Empire Review*.

his family, and Katherine and hers are also in the neighbourhood,—and Sam 's here.   It has been such a difficult party that I quite broke down under the strain.

' Through it all the dear Henry James remained faithful, though he suffered bitterly and openly. He is gone now, and there is none to take his place. After ten weeks of Henry James the evenings seem very empty, though the room is always full of people. As the time passed we came to have a real affection for him, and parted from him with sincere regret.

' We have started more or less of an intimacy with the Taylors :—that is, the daughters, Sir Henry himself being almost too beautiful and refined and angelic for ordinary people like us. Also we are rather intimate with the Shelleys. Lady Shelley is delicious,—naturally no longer young, suffering from the effects of a terrible accident that has left her a hopeless invalid ; but with all the fire of youth, and as mad as some other people you know, and ready to plunge into any wild extravagance at a moment's notice.

' Sir Percy is an odd creature : Do you know him ? He is the poet's son only in being so exceedingly curious. I think we will come to be very fond of him. They have a lovely little theatre at their place here, and give very delightful entertainments, which will be pleasant for us. They have a bust of Mary Wollstonecraft done from a death mask, over which Louis raves : and justly, for it is the most interesting thing ever seen. I think we are very lucky to find two such pleasant families in Bournemouth. Other people pour in upon us in droves, but they are all alike, and I find none to interest or amuse. After speaking of the weather and kindred topics, they generally observe, " your husband is quite literary, I understand." Now what should one say ? I murmur vaguely, " I dunno, m'sure," at which they show faint surprise, and slightly bridle. But I can think of no other formula.' [1]

[1] In the *Empire Review.*

Colvin was, of course, the Custodian—a reference to his position at the British Museum. Being in residence he was not only Keeper of the Prints, but on certain nights confined to the precincts, responsible for the whole place. Bob was R. A. M. Stevenson. Katherine was Katherine de Mattos, Stevenson's cousin. Sam was Mrs. R. L. Stevenson's son, Samuel Lloyd Osbourne, soon to be promoted to the name of Lloyd. Mr. and Mrs. Thomas Stevenson, Colvin tells us, never quite seemed to realize how necessary it was for their delicate son to have quiet when he was suffering from one of his attacks of hemorrhage.

The first letter from Henry James that Colvin preserved has reference to this visit.

He writes : ' I have just (an hour ago) come back from three days at Bournemouth, whither I went to see Stevenson, about whom I should like to talk to you (they appear to be more or less expecting you). My visit had the gilt taken off by the somewhat ponderous presence of the parents—who sit on him much too long at once. (They are to remain apparently another week, and I cannot see why *they* don't see how they take it out of him.) He was bright and charming, but struck me as of a smaller vitality than when I saw him last,—a very frail and delicate thread of strength. If he could be quite alone on alternate or occasional weeks, it would be a blessing.' [1]

Mrs. R. L. S. to Colvin.   From ' Skerryvore.'   [1885-86] : ' Louis is most anxious to make a change, and the Highlands are suggested, but we are cut off from that refuge, as Louis' father would instantly join us, which would kill Louis. Indeed we can think of no place where he is not likely to be with us except the continent, and I recoil from the hot dreadful journey. Louis is thinking a little of going by sea to Bordeaux, thence to the Pyrenees. We had spoken eagerly of going North, to Norway, or somewhere, but then there is the voyage, and the uncertainty whether it could suit. Can you suggest any place ? Louis says it must be

[1] In the Fitzwilliam Museum.

where he will be amused, and as he can find no amusement in England, I don't know what to do. France is so hot and unhealthy in the Summer, but I rather think he has got his heart set upon it. From Bordeaux he would go to Paris, and then the mountains. He thinks it would be cheap, but I fear he is wrong, and I fancy, too, there would be diligences which he can't stand. I wish somebody could advise me.

' I almost incline to think the Monument as good a change as anything else. It cures seaside liver, and amuses, and is safe and not far. Please give me some really monumental advice.'

R. L. S. and his wife to Mrs. Sitwell. From ' Skerryvore.' [May 1886] :

' MY DEAR FRIEND,—I know I should have written, but I haven't been able to ; all day I read to Sam. Louis is much too tired through having like an idiot obeyed the doctor's orders to take exercise, and Sam takes one cold after another ; and odd times I fill up by coughing myself. What do you hear of C. S. ?   D—— shame she broke down, which is probably a good job for all concerned except me. I am not so bad as all that ; only idiotified and rheumatic and the like : but Sam's new cold is truly vexing. We hope for the best : no letters can flow from this place, till some one of us shakes off the cloud of impotent gloom which hangs (I speak for myself at least) like a dream mountain on my shoulders.—Ever your friend,

' R. L. S.'

C. S. probably S. C.

Mrs. R. L. S. to Colvin. From ' Skerryvore.' [September or October 1886] : ' We arrived very comfortably indeed, and the journey seemed to do Louis good, but I am afraid the piano is *not* good for him. In the morning he gets up feeling very well indeed, and at about ten sits to the piano where he stays till three or after, drinking his coffee, even, at the instrument. At three or thereabouts

he breaks down altogether, gets very white and is extremely
wretched with exhaustion until the next morning again.
I do not know what to do about it. He always says that
the first thing is to cut off his pleasures, which is pretty
true : and I haven't the heart to try and stop the piano.
It was that he wanted to come home for, and it is now
wearing him out entirely.' [1]

The Stevensons, says Colvin, ' had just gone to Bournemouth after a visit to me at the official house I inhabited
at the British Museum. Stevenson was an eager lover of
music and keenly interested in musical theory ; at various
times of his life he tried to learn the practice of this or that
instrument, but the frailty of his health prevented the
attempt ever being carried far.'

Mrs. R. L. S. to Colvin. From ' Skerryvore.' [1886] :

' FAITHLESS, BUT STILL DEAR CUSTODIAN,—Restore that
painting ! Instantly restore that picture so basely pur-
loined from the innocent and youthful Sargent ! To-morrow,
to-day, restore it. The parents are here and demand a
sight of it. This is only a note to say that I feel almost
positive that they will be gone before you come. If they
are still here, then I fear I can't offer a bed, but I feel positive they will be gone. I simply cannot write you, having
no news. This is just to assure you of the warmest welcome
when you do come, and to demand the picture. I will soon
really write. In the meantime, with much love from
Louis, who is better, am affectionately yours,   F.'

Mrs. R. L. S. to Mrs. Sitwell. From ' Skerryvore.'
[Early Spring, 1886] : ' I do hope there are some good
accounts of our dear S. C. : we are most anxious about him
until we hear that he is really better. Sam sends his love,
as do I. I have written to Mr. James, but cannot write
to any one else on account of every moment being devoted
to Sam. You, my poor dear, know as no one else can,
about that.'

[1] In the *Empire Review*.

Mrs. R. L. S. to Colvin. From 'Skerryvore.' [1886] :
'Louis fancies that he feels some stirring of the intellect.
I hope he does, for it was growing alarming. I began to
fear he would never work again. *Do please* send the photograph. It was not kind of the magician to give you one,
and not me. I will take the greatest care of it, and return
it at once. We have had such a kind letter from the dear
Henry James, whose new novel seems most excellent in
all ways.'

Henry James's new novel was probably *The Bostonians*.

Mrs. R. L. S. to Colvin. From 'Skerryvore.' [1886] :
'Speaking of demons, this morning Valentine [the French
maid] brought in a sheet of white paper with, apparently,
several bits of broken twig on it. She said, "Please don't
touch the paper, but look closely and see if you can see
anything curious about any of these bits of stem I have
been breaking off the ivy." "I can see nothing in any of
them different from other ivy twigs," said I. "Look
again," she persisted, and as she spoke touched one of them
with a leaf : imagine my horror when I saw the thing was
alive, and could hump up its back. Unless it is moving it
is absolutely impossible to tell it from the other twigs. I
was afraid after seeing it to strike a match lest it should
turn and upbraid me. Are these things common in
England ? If it isn't usual to meet them, I still possess the
beast, and could send it to any one who pines for society
of that description, we don't.

'*P.S.*—Lady Shelley tells me she has met you and found
you delightful.'

R. L. S. and his wife to Colvin and Mrs. Sitwell :

'*Skerryvore, Bournemouth, May* 25, '86.

'MY DEAR PEOPLE,—I almost never get a moment to
write, Sam not yet being able to go out to speak of, and
keeping me busy all the time. Louis cannot work, but I
am not distressed about that, as he is really wonderfully
well. I do not think his lungs have been in so good a

state for a long time. He is enjoying the piano immensely, and is learning to play in a way. I should like so much to hear you play your " piece." The Skerryvore lantern is being put up, and when next you come you shall [Here Stevenson begins to write.] In Bright's to-day, the man told me Jekyll had been preached about in St. Peter's, and next day a lady came into the shop and asked for " That book about *a medical man who lives here in Bournemouth*, who took something, and came to a bad end." He gave it up,—as he said, " having heard of no physician who had poisoned himself in Bournemouth." And by subsequent visitors found out at last what it was. The preacher must of course have said that the author lived in Bournemouth. I took up this sheet, while F. was in the middle of a sentence. The boy is coughing again ; I fear he shd not have been out. I went and saw Lady Taylor to-day ; she looks rather ill, I was sorry to see her. Sam and I are learning the piano at no end of a rate ; we now play the rottenest duet extant, but we shall do better next time for we come round [*sic*].—Yours ever affectionately, R. L. S.'

' I know nothing of Miss O'Whatshername but have seen her books well reviewed ; kiss her for her mother. I know nothing of the crow [?] excepting this, that I defy it. I am told it will defy me. We have a hedgehog : that is all right ; but we shall soon have no pigeons ; except vicariously in the form of a certain fluffy cat, who eats and indigests upon 'em daily. We play on him with a hose, and we have morbid recourse to mechanical arts so as to bar his passage : but it will not do ; pigeons and a cat are, I fear, incompatible : what would Captain Best say ? R. L. S.'

Mrs. R. L. S. to Colvin. From ' Skerryvore.' [1886] : ' If you prefer waiting to see Louis alone, Sunday week *may* not be the best time. It is needless to say that whenever you do come you will be received with joy and thanksgiving. Louis has a cold which has not affected him, at least as yet, as seriously as colds used to do.   The tale he has sent Longman I think a very good weird thing.

'The yellow cat Ginger is a great comfort to all but the Bogue [the dog], whose heart is torn with jealousy.

'I am most anxious to have Henley down here for a while, but I suppose it would be of no use while the parents are here.   They are coming for a change for the old gentleman, who is in an hypochondriacal state.'

Mrs. R. L. S. to Colvin.   From 'Skerryvore.'   [1886-87] : 'Louis had a bad night, through Charley Robertson's sending him the letter of some idiot who said "Mr. Stevenson is neither a gentleman nor respectfull."   I was angry with all of them for this general impertinence, and after removing Louis' answer, sent one of my own, less stilted in style, but likely to make people more uncomfortable.

'I hope you will soon see that old young lady—or young old lady, which is it ?—Mrs. Procter, and explain why I did not go to see her as I promised.   Please give my love to all monumental people, and all they love.'

Mrs. Procter—widow of 'Barry Cornwall,' born in 1799.

Mrs. R. L. S. to Mrs. Sitwell.   From 'Skerryvore.' [1886-87] : 'The Jenkin book moves on apace, and I think is good, very good.'

Stevenson's memoir of Fleeming Jenkin, who had died in 1885.

Mrs. R. L. S. to Mrs. Sitwell.   From Edinburgh.   [May 1887] : 'We have arrived to find our dear old man passing away painlessly.

'Would you believe it that the old man is up and dressed every day ?   Until yesterday he went down stairs for the day.   He has always said that no man who respected himself should die in a bed, and unless he passes off in the night he will die "as a gentleman should" according to his own creed.   Louis is taking it very well ; at least just now.   But really the bitterness of death was past long ago.' [1]

[1] In the *Empire Review.*

To Colvin after Mr. Stevenson's death. From 17 Heriot Row, Edinburgh. [Spring, 1887] :

' DEAR FRIEND,—Louis has a bad cold, the usual thing. Not quite such a double-barrelled one as the museum one, but bad enough, and increasing in the usual way. It is depressing. A poisonous sun is shining ; I believe they call it fair weather. . . . I wish you had been here this week, you might have saved Louis this. When *he* says that going out in the rain at night is good for him, instead of harmful, strangers believe him, and I am crowded back as a "meddlesome female," as I suppose I really do seem to be. I must say that Dr. Balfour has acted most kindly to Louis. He kept him out of Heriot Row even the night his father died, which is more than I could have done myself. He did all he could to keep Louis in check, and is watching him most carefully now. All this old pretending that Louis was only nerves and not ill is at an end. He, the doctor, is continually warning me to take care of Louis, as he is seriously ill. Much love to you all, dear friends,

' FANNY '

Mrs. R. L. S. to Colvin. A few days later, from 17 Heriot Row, Edinburgh. [Spring, 1887] :

' BEST FRIEND,—You have heard that Louis's cold is better, but I thought I should tell you more about it. Dr. Balfour, to our surprise, has become, apparently, a sort of second rate guardian angel, hovering over us with protecting wings until we are dying with bewilderment. He went so far as to keep Louis out of the house the night of his father's death, leaving Mrs. Stevenson alone with servants. He would have kept him away altogether if he could. When this cold came on, he (the doctor) said it *must* be stopped and he would stop it, it was going on just as at the Monument, but after three days inhaling through a machine like a table cruet, the symptoms began to change for the better, and I believe it has been kept off the lung

altogether.   Twice a day does the kindly physician call to
see us and no care and pains are spared.   In one way it is
depressing, as he says frankly that though Louis may have
ups and downs he can never really be better, and will
always have hemorrhages more or less bad according to the
care he takes of himself.   He says just what Ruedi always
said, that it is fibroidal disease of the lungs, for which there
is no cure, only palliation.

   ' Yesterday he took me in hand.   Of me, he said that I
had had wrong treatment from all the doctors but Dr.
Goring ; that if I had held to Goring's treatment steadily I
should now be much better.   As it is, he says the thing has
not progressed so far but that I may be quite cured in time,
though it may be several years.   He doesn't think Aix very
important for me, though it might do some good.   At the
same time it might do harm unless the doctor there understood the case thoroughly.   It is very strange, is it not ?   I
mean, this change of face.   Mrs. Stevenson seems very well,
and is looking much better again.   It is a dreadful day, and
Louis is staying in bed, though otherwise he would be
getting up.   I don't know when we shall get away.   Louis
has to see to all the business and settling up of things, and
that takes time and waiting, and much worry.   There were
a lot of trustees appointed, but Mrs. S. and Louis have shaken
themselves loose and are attending to affairs themselves.   I
have no time to write more.   Please give thanks for letters,
and much love to that dear lady, and to yourself, from us
both.—Ever yours affectly.,
                                   ' F. V. DE G. STEVENSON '

   Mrs. R. L. S. to Colvin.   ' Skerryvore.'   [Spring, 1887] :
' As to our going away : Mrs. Stevenson will this year get
some money from the business, so she proposes to stand all
the expense she can of a winter in Colorado : she, Louis,
Lloyd, and me, accompanied by Valentine and John.   We
should go in August.   Do you know a couple of elderly
quiet people who would like to take our house at a high

price while we are gone ? This couple must love cats
tenderly, and take Ginger to their bosoms. Also Agnes as
housemaid and attendant upon the cat. Does such a couple
as this exist ? If not, please have them prepared for us at
once, or no more call yourself guardian angel.

' I should be more glad than words can express if you
could see us for a day or two. If Louis is well enough we
want to come to you : but the weather must be good in
London, and the man must be reasonably good in health,
the man and poet, I mean ; for no such shabby trick is to
[be] played upon you again as was done last year. Let us
know how the weather goes, and whether you want us when
we can come. Our dear love to all and every one.

' We are just dying for the *Keats*, especially Lloyd, who
has heard so much of it, and yet knows so little.' [1]

Colvin's book on Keats in the ' English Men of Letters
Series ' was about to be published.

Mrs. R. L. S. to Colvin. From ' Skerryvore.' [1887] :
' Could a guardian angel give me some information in return
for the many uninteresting facts I have laid at his feet ? I
wish to see the Honolulu Queen or the Princess, preferably
the latter. Now how shall I direct a note to either or both
of them ? The princess is an intimate friend of Belle's, and
has been told by Belle that I will go to see her. But Belle
has no idea of the dignity that doth hedge a queen, in
England, at least. The princess is also called Mrs. Dominis,
though I don't know how to pronounce the name. Belle
gives a very amusing account of how she and the king
designed all the fine clothes the queen is to wear at the
jubilee, while she, poor soul, stood by weeping bitterly at
the idea of having to wear them, declaring that *nothing*
would induce her to go to any jubilee.

' You, who associate with duchesses and such like aristocracy, might also tell me how I should address the dusky
Princess. I suppose she knows no more than I do, but
that is no consolation to me. Please bring your birthday

---

[1] In the *Empire Review*.

ROBERT LOUIS STEVENSON IN THE MID EIGHTEEN-SEVENTIES
FROM THE DRAWING BY T. BLAKE WIRGMAN BASED ON THE ORIGINAL CHARCOAL DRAWING BY
MRS. OSBOURNE, AFTERWARDS MRS. R. L. STEVENSON

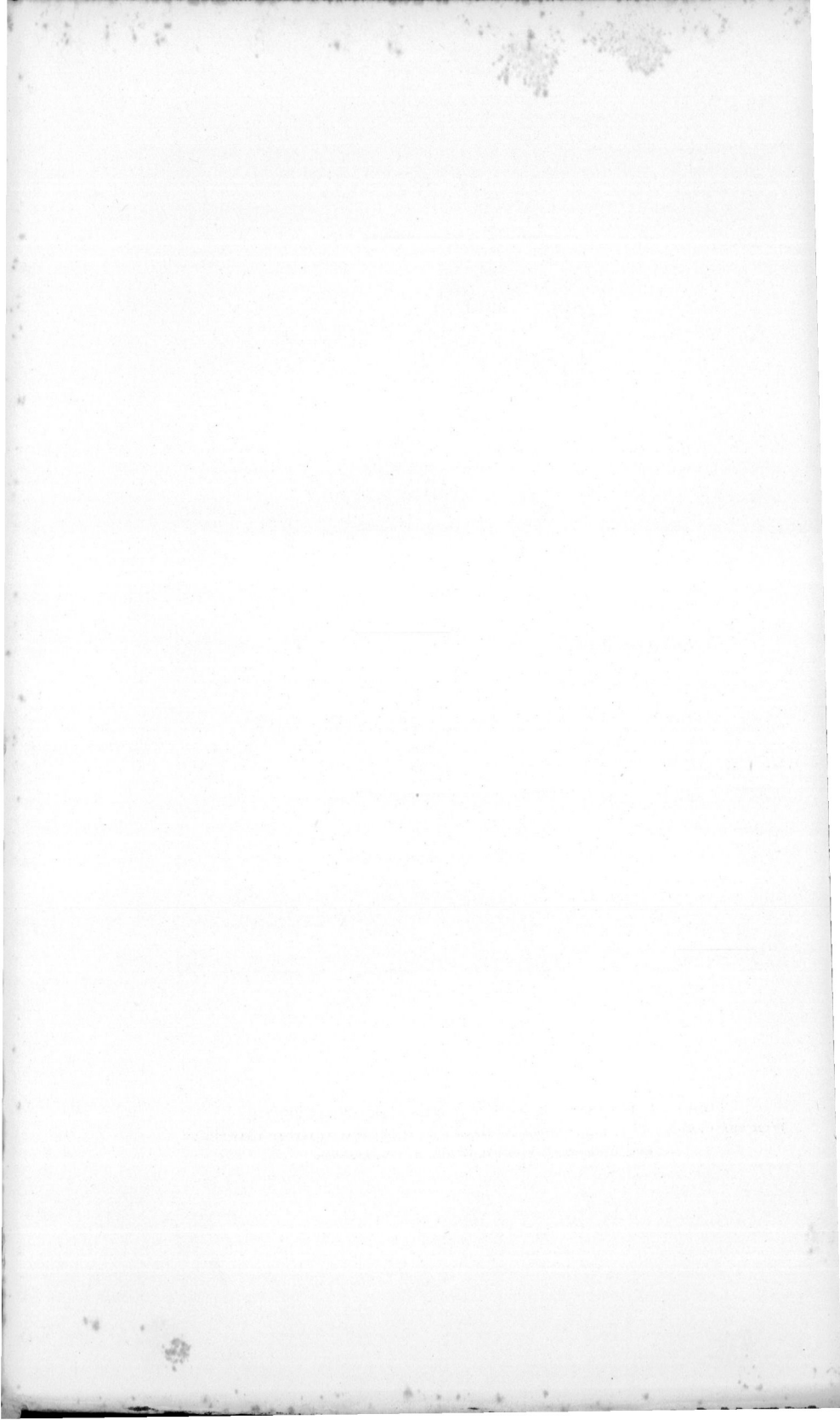

here.   The babe has arrived, but has been so closely clasped to Louis' bosom that I have not yet had more than a sight of its outer garments ; which are very becoming and well chosen.'

'The babe' was Colvin's monograph on Keats, which I imagine had been specially bound.

Writing of Stevenson in *Memories and Notes*, Colvin says, of the family's departure from England in August 1887 : ' My next vision of him is the last, and shows him as he stood with his family looking down upon me over the rail of the outward-bound steamship *Ludgate Hill* while I waved a parting hand to him from a boat in the Thames by Tilbury Dock.   From our first meeting in Suffolk until his return with his wife from California in 1880 had been one spell of seven years.   From that return until his fresh departure in 1887 had been another.   Now followed the winter spent at Saranac Lake in the Adirondack Mountains.'

A few days later came a letter from Mrs. Stevenson, written on the steamer :

' S.S. " *Ludgate Hill*,"
' *Sep.* 4*th* [1887].

' DEAR MONUMENT,—And that reminds me that I am sure you have not registered as *Monument*, and that I shall have to pay sundry extra sixpences for the address to which I shall send a telegram the moment we arrive in New York. My next telegram after that I shall send to *Monument* on the chances.   So far, with one exception, our journey has been a most prosperous one.   Louis has gained strength every day to such a degree that we have really made up our minds to a life on the ocean wave.   Unless something unforeseen happens to prevent we shall dash across the continent, take ship on the Pacific side, and head for Japan. Before I go any farther, I had better hark back, and tell you at once what the untoward event has been, lest you think it worse than it is, or concerning Louis ; he, I know, being your first thought.   Mrs. Stevenson has turned out a regular sea bird !   We call her Mother Carey's chicken,

M

the stormy petrel, and etc. We have had to watch her lest she should be washed overboard, or should take it into her head to mount the rigging ;—but we never thought of the dangers of a hammock. This morning one was swung for her ! Instantly any number of other giddy young things piled into it, she leaping on at the last ; the rope broke, and down came the whole of them, all upon her, except Lloyd, who managed to get a shake that sent him pale and dizzy. She got some jar to her spine, and has been lying where she fell, some [few] hours ago. She seems quite cheerful, and says the pain is less, but we cannot yet tell whether it is serious or only a passing thing. If I send my letter off with no further reference to the accident, you may be assured that it is because things are all right.

' The passage has been a very rough one ; equal, they say, to a January one, but nothing seems to have harmed Louis. We have been in gales and squalls and have had continual high seas. Also, the *Ludgate Hill* is a *roller*. To-day is one of our best days, and yet I write with difficulty. Of course we shall be very late in getting in. I hope you will not be alarmed at not hearing when you had a right to expect a telegram. I suppose there was never a worse ship than this ; and yet we have enjoyed every minute on board her, except when we (Valentine, Lloyd and I) were seasick. Rows of horses look through the windows and watch us [illegible] ! each port-hole frames a stallion's head ! We have cows, and there are thirty monkeys and a baboon on the lower deck. Our stallions are worth twenty thousand pounds, and pay first-class passage. One horse-owner physics his sick mare from his [illegible] bed through the port-hole. When it rolls heavily, the horses, who have their sea legs now, run forward, and then back, making a curious rhythmical trampling. There never was so strange a ship. All these extending erections on deck remain. Not a single passenger knew about the horses, nor understood that this was any different from an ordinary passenger ship ; not even the ship's doctor, nor many of the [sailors].

'Mackenzie the champion chess player is aboard. He objects to nothing in particular but the humiliation of being seen to land from a vessel like this. The second day out one of the stewards jumped overboard. It is believed that he was a gentleman gone a little mad. Except for him, there was but one other man who could be fairly called a gentleman aboard (barring our own party), and he is French, and only 19. All this is not complaints, only description, as both Louis and I can get on very well with any sort of people, and have been much amused by these. It was well that we had Mr. [illegible]'s champagne, as what we took ourselves would not have been enough for our necessities.—On board ship champagne is a necessity.

'Louis has just come to say that his mother seems much better, and has been able to move to a more comfortable place, so I trust it is not so bad. It is so very difficult to write in a ship that rolls so heavily, and as I know there will be a great scurry at the end, I shall beg you to pass the news (good news, I call it) on to our dear Henry James. I may not be able to make out another letter, and I should wish him to know as soon as possible all there is to tell, and our dear love. I wish I didn't hate your photograph. Valentine is sitting beside Mrs. Stevenson reading aloud *Daisy Miller*. Louis says it is very funny to hear it read in Valentine's accent. I have knitted one sock since we left, but as it seems to be nowhere like Lloyd's leg and foot I have misgivings as to whether he may not be deformed. Our kindest regards to your brother, and again our love to you.—Ever affectionately,

'F. V. DE G. STEVENSON'

CHAPTER XIII

THE PRINT ROOM AND THE FIRST BOOK ON KEATS

1884–1887

IN 1884 Colvin had been appointed to the post of Keeper of the Department of Prints and Drawings in the British Museum, and this he held until his retirement, under the age regulation, in 1912. He continued to hold the Slade professorship until 1885, but had of course to give up the Fitzwilliam. I take from *The Times* the following summary of his work as Keeper : ' Colvin's studies and experience at Cambridge proved of great value to his work as Keeper of the National Collection of Prints and Drawings. He reorganized the arrangement on more modern lines, undertook a critical revision of the drawings, and had the majority of them remounted on a system which has since been imitated in all the leading collections on the Continent. His relations with collectors and influential persons, whom he advised and guided in their studies, and his all-round knowledge of history, literature, and scholarship were invaluable to the Museum. During his Keepership there were acquired by purchase the Malcolm collection of drawings and prints, the Reeve collection of drawings and etchings of the Norwich School, the finest collection existing of drawings by Lucas van Leyden, a remarkable series of drawings by Tintoretto, a fine collection of Japanese woodcuts and drawings, and many other accessions, generally chosen with fine taste and judgment and bought for the most part at prices which were very low compared with those which have prevailed since 1910. The most notable gifts and bequests to his Department were the Mitchell German woodcuts, the

Cheylesmore mezzotints, and the Salting engravings and drawings. An important branch of his work was the arrangement of exhibitions, admirably chosen and catalogued, in the gallery of the department. The Guides to these exhibitions were excellent ; the Rembrandt catalogue especially is a document of great importance for the study of the master's work, which had never before been placed in chronological order. Towards the end of his Museum career he took a great interest in Japanese art, just before the great rise in prices which would have made it impossible for the Museum to compete with collectors of Japanese drawings and woodcuts.'

Mr. Laurence Binyon, who was one of Colvin's assistants in the Print Room for many years and is now Deputy Keeper in charge of the sub-department of Oriental Prints and Drawings, kindly sends me some notes on Colvin as Keeper : ' During his twenty-eight years' term of office he made the department much more important than it had been before. A fine scholar, with keen literary enthusiasms, and a social acquaintance both wide and distinguished, he brought a new atmosphere into the Print Room. He had had predecessors who knew their special subject extremely well and were regularly consulted by collectors for authoritative opinions : but I fancy that (with certain exceptions) they were apt to confine themselves to acquiring a first-hand acquaintance with engravings and drawings, especially the former. However this may be, it is certain that Colvin greatly raised the standard of scholarship expected in the staff. He brought to his special work all the interests of a wide culture ; and the Department, which had been obscurely lodged in makeshift fashion, first in one and then in another corner of the Museum, was, some years after he took it over, adequately installed on the two floors which it occupied till his retirement, when it was transferred to its present quarters in the new building.

' At Cambridge Colvin had lectured on various phases of art, on Greek sculpture, and on European painting of all

periods. As Director of the Fitzwilliam Museum, he was
well acquainted with all the schools of painting, but was not
a specialist. His knowledge of prints was equally wide, and
he was very thorough in all his studies. He was not, I
think, a born connoisseur, his judgment was not instinctive
enough for that. It was with his mind rather than through
his senses that he trained his faculties. But when he
applied himself to a subject, the patience and detailed
accuracy he brought to bear were astonishing. Also he had
the gift of lucid and concise exposition. The Guides he
wrote to the exhibitions he arranged were models of their
kind. Not till the Print Room was at last allotted a Gallery
of its own, could any adequate exhibitions be held : but the
series which Colvin organized in it rightly attracted much
attention. One of these especially is of some historic
importance. That is the exhibition of Rembrandt etchings
and drawings ; for this was the first attempt to arrange the
complete etched work of the master in chronological order.
On this exhibition is based the arrangement in Mr. Hind's
Catalogue of the Etchings, now the standard work in the
subject.

' Another memorable exhibition was that of the Malcolm
drawings. The acquisition of the Malcolm collection for the
Museum was, I suppose, the most notable achievement of
Colvin's Keepership. It was indeed a magnificent addition
to the treasures of the Department, and it was due to his
personal enterprise and exertions that the Government was
persuaded to give a special grant and thus secure the collection for the nation. When it is remembered that no one
had been able to persuade the Government of the day to
buy Sir Thomas Lawrence's collection—the most splendid
collection of Old Master drawings ever made—for a sum
much below its value, Colvin's achievement will be more
fully appreciated. Other splendid collections, such as the
Mitchell collection of German engravings and the Cheylesmore collection of mezzotints (to name but these), came to
the Department by gift or bequest during Colvin's time :

and he never spared efforts to persuade possible givers to enrich the nation in this way, often with success.

'Brought up under the influence of Ruskin, and sharing the tastes of his own generation, Colvin had a special fondness for the Italian Quattrocento, in which Burton made the National Gallery so rich. The Print Room has one of the finest collections of early Italian engravings in the world; and Colvin made it his business to study these, not merely in relation to other engravings but to the whole of early Italian art. The work on which as a student and historian of art he prided himself most was the big folio volume in which he had reproduced, complete in facsimile, the Florentine Picture-Chronicle once belonging to Ruskin and purchased from him by Colvin for the Museum. In this work Colvin set out to prove that the Chronicle drawings were by Maso Finiguerra, once reputed the inventor of engraving, and certainly an engraver, though as to what works should be attributed to him authorities were in debate. In its close texture, its reasoned exposition, its lucid marshalling of facts, its wealth of illustrative material, drawn from literary documents as well as from architecture, painting and sculpture, this study is a typical example of Colvin's method. He examines with great minuteness and patience the drawings and the engravings in question; and though in some quarters his theory was combated, it is, I believe, accepted by the most competent authorities on Florentine art. A similar large folio was devoted to the Early English Engravers; here the collection of the material was made by Mr. Arthur Hind, while Colvin arranged it and summarized the subject in an essay, written, like all his work in this kind, with admirable exactness and breadth. His collaborator remembers with gratitude the aid of his skilled and shaping hand. He liked to be workmanlike in his writing, and liked the same quality to be shown in any writing done under his direction. He had a care for good English, and set an example in his own terse and clear style.

'Like all of us, Colvin had his " imperfect sympathies " as

well as downright dislikes. For French art, especially of
the modern period, he had no great love, I think. And I
sometimes wished that he had been a little less fond of
early Italians and a little more intent on getting together a
full representation of the drawings of the English artists
who really count. However, when his interest was really
roused, he readily became enthusiastic ; and I was very
grateful for his sympathetic reception of the suggestion that
the Museum should acquire Mr. James Reeve's collection of
Norwich drawings, with its wonderful series of Cotmans.
At that time Cotman's name had no prestige, the market
value of his drawings was about a tenth that of David Cox's.
Again, during the latter years of his Keepership he grew to
take an ardent interest in the collections of Chinese and
Japanese art, and very greatly enriched them by his
purchases.

' This gift of enthusiasm, still more evident in his literary
preferences, he retained to the end with the keenness of
youth. And indeed under a manner that often seemed
stiff and shy he concealed an emotional and excitable
temperament, capable of occasional explosions. He had
deep feelings, strong affections and antipathies ; but as a
Museum official he rarely allowed his natural impulsive-
ness to appear. His presence carried authority, he presided with a due sense of his dignity. A Keeper of a Department needs not only to be a scholar, but an administrator :
and on the administrative side, though faults might perhaps
be found in details, Colvin maintained a high standard of
smooth and effective working. He did far more than any
of his predecessors, by arrangement and cataloguing, to
make the collections serviceable to students.'

The Keepership of the Prints carries with it a residence
within the Museum precincts, and it was therefore then
that Colvin's London life began. Never again did he leave
London except on brief holidays, and his house—at the
corner on the right as you enter the gates—gradually
became a literary and artistic centre, with Mrs. Sitwell as

a visiting hostess. Owing to Colvin's straitened circumstances, due to certain family claims which in his chivalry
he felt himself bound to honour, he could not, although
both of them were free, offer his hand to Mrs. Sitwell, until
nearly twenty years later. It was to this house that
Stevenson came, on his visits to London from Bournemouth
from 1884 to 1887.

'During his visits to my house at the British Museum—
"the many-pillared and the well-beloved," as he calls it
in the well-known set of verses, as though the keepers'
houses stood within the great front colonnade of the Museum,
which they do not, but project in advance of it on either
flank—during such visits,' says Colvin, 'he never showed
anything but the old charm and high courage and patience.
He was able to enjoy something of the company of famous
seniors who came seeking his acquaintance, as Browning,
Lowell, Burne-Jones. With such visitors I usually left
him alone, and have at any rate no detailed notes or
memories of conversations held by him with them in my
presence.'

These are the well-known verses :—

'TO S. C.

'I heard the pulse of the besieging sea
Throb far away all night.   I heard the wind
Fly crying and convulse tumultuous palms.
I rose and strolled.   The isle was all bright sand,
And flailing fans and shadows of the palm ;
The heaven all moon and wind and the blind vault
The keenest planet slain, for Venus slept.
    The king, my neighbour, with his host of wives,
Slept in the precinct of the palisade ;
Where single, in the wind, under the moon,
Among the slumbering cabins, blazed a fire,
Sole street-lamp and the only sentinel.

    ' To other lands and nights my fancy turned—
To London first, and chiefly to your house,

The many-pillared and the well-beloved.
There yearning fancy lighted ; there again
In the upper room I lay, and heard far off
The unsleeping city murmur like a shell ;
The muffled tramp of the Museum guard
Once more went by me ; I beheld again
Lamps vainly brighten the dispeopled street ;
Again I longed for the returning morn,
The awaking traffic, the bestirring birds,
The consentaneous trill of tiny song
That weaves round monumental cornices
A passing charm of beauty.   Most of all,
For your light foot I wearied, and your knock
That was the glad réveillé of my day.

' Lo, now, when to your task in the great house
At morning through the portico you pass,
One moment glance, where by the pillared wall
Far-voyaging island gods, begrimed with smoke,
Sit now unworshipped, the rude monument
Of faiths forgot and races undivined :
Sit now disconsolate, remembering well
The priest, the victim, and the songful crowd,
The blaze of the blue noon, and that huge voice,
Incessant, of the breakers on the shore.
As far as these from their ancestral shrine,
So far, so foreign, your divided friends
Wander, estranged in body, not in mind.'

Two or three letters from Laura Tennant belong to this
chapter : very slight, but full of a charming personality.
Miss Tennant was a daughter of Sir Charles Tennant.   One
of her sisters, Charlotte, had married Lord Ribblesdale,
and another, Margot, was one day to marry Mr. Asquith,
afterwards Lord Oxford.   This is the first letter :—

' *The Glen, Innerleithen.*   [1884.]

' DEAR MR. COLVIN,—My brother-in-law Lord Ribblesdale
is anxious to do some reading at the British Museum and
I feel sure you could be of great use to him—both as to his
writing and as to his reading.   He will give you this letter
wʰ I have made bold to write remembering yʳ kind words

to me at Mr. Earle's and at 35 Gros. Square when you promised to help me in any way you could. I am afraid my literary powers are likely to remain latent all my life but Ribblesdale I feel sure has a future before him and a gift of style very unusual. I sh^{ld} like you above all people to encourage him and to get to know him. He is besides being a brother to me, a great friend of mine—I am sure you will be interested in him. I am very anxious he sh^{ld} work : he has the power and the will ; a little success is the spur he needs. After all because a man is a good judge of a horse and rides well across a stiff country—and belongs to the tottering House of Lords it is no reason he sh^{ld} be debarred from all reasonable pursuits.

'I am going to Rome for two months the beginning of Feb. and will not be in London till after Easter. I hope to see you then—

'Let me hear from you about this if it does not bore you. —Yrs. always sincerely, 'LAURA TENNANT'

Again, soon afterwards, written in red ink :

'I won't start the male fashion of dating letters !—I *will* be feminine.

'*The Glen, Innerleithen, N.B.*

'DEAR MR. COLVIN,—Thank you very much for y^r kind letter. I am a good friend but certainly a casual correspondent—most unreasonably—because letters are my chiefest joy—and indeed I entirely sympathize with Eve— I sh^{ld} have done the same had I lived in a benighted garden where no postman's knock was ever heard to relieve the monotony of wild beasts' noises—A Parcel Post w^{ld} have prevented the Fall I am sure—

'As for what you so graciously say about me, I am sure I could do something if I had the talent of expression but I am dumb when I feel—and generally also incoherent. As long as I live I shall have keen literary instincts but whether they will develop remains to be proved.

'What do you mean about my *Being*. Every one *bes*. It's not greatly to *my credit* that my mother brought me into this muddled world.

'Oh ! dear, I daresay it's as good as the one I left—I am quite *alone*—here—with two infants and a dog. I read and write all day and revel in my own society. I quite agree with Alexandre Dumas who, when asked how he had enjoyed a fearfully dull party, said " I sh[ld] not have enjoyed it if *I* had not been there."

'How delightful one is to oneself.

'I have just finished the Carlyle. I always am behind the rest of the world.

'I delight in it, and think Carlyle comes out better than ever, tho' I regret his baldness in the artistic faculty—

'What shall I read ? I am not sure about Rome—probably it will never come off. D.V. never lets things come to pass except things one never wants.

'I shall be in London Sunday the 1st or 2nd is it. If you are in town will you call ? between three-thirty and four-thirty ? We have had a very family Xmas—and a happy-family New Year. I am glad you liked Ribblesdale. He is nicer than I am.

'I am going to stay with my—our—friend Mrs. Horner on the 28th. What message shall I give her ?

'With all the nicest from myself,—yrs.'

'LAURA TENNANT

'*P.S.*—Forgive my having written with my heart's blood ! I rather like it—I shall be here till the 22nd of Jan.'

Froude's *Carlyle's Life in London* was published at the end of 1884.

The next letter tells of the writer's engagement to Alfred Lyttelton, the barrister and cricketer.

'*Easton Grey, Malmesbury*, 27 *Jan.* '86.

'DEAR MR. COLVIN,—Lady Ribblesdale writes to me about yr. dinner and sayd she told you about my engagement w^h was v. hard lines as I wanted to announce it myself to the sound of trumpets.   Well don't you think I am very clever to have resisted to such purpose ?   I don't think you will denounce matrimony when you come to dine with us some future day and you see a woman not given over to jam pots and towels and yet perfectly happy and what's more making her husband happy for I promise you I shall do that.

'Of course I shall not change to any of my Friends and I hope you won't say what most people say, I mean—that I shall quite forget my old Friends in the Archipelago of new ones.

'I don't think it is at all ideal to lose one's individuality and to pick up scraps of one's husband's and I don't intend to change one inch of myself as far as my Friendships go— tho' I hope to develop all that lies fallow of good in me and to starve all that is rampant of bad and there is lots ! Wish me good, dear Mr. Colvin. Happiness cannot always be and I w^ld rather have what is Eternal wished me.—Yrs. in sincerity,   LAURA TENNANT

'This is the 85th sheet today, so forgive writing !
'I am so afraid I shan't be in London on Sunday ! Write to me to Wilbury House Salisbury please.'

Laura Tennant did not survive the birth of her first child, in 1886, to the grief of countless friends.

In 1885 I find this note from Whistler, expressing his willingness to give his ' Ten O'clock ' at Cambridge :—

'DEAR PROFESSOR,—I accept with pleasure the flattering invitation you have conveyed to me from the gentlemen at Cambridge.

'Therefore I will arrange to come to you on the 11. March— and deliver the address that I gave here in Prince's Hall.

'With many thanks for the courteous hospitality you offer me,—Very sincerely yours,
                                        ' J. McN. WHISTLER '

In 1886 Colvin was elected a member of the Literary Society, a company of authors, artists, statesmen, and men of intellectual activity, who met to dine together once a month, and still do so. The origin of the Literary Society is not too clear, the earliest information belonging to 1803, when there were four members. In 1804 there were twenty-seven, the President being the Dean of Westminster, Dr. Vincent. The first recorded dinner was April 3, 1807, when there were thirty-three members, and Sir James Bland Burges was President. Among the members were William Wordsworth, William Lisle Bowles, John Philip Kemble, William Gifford, Samuel Rogers, and 'Conversation' Sharp.

At the time Colvin joined the Literary Society it consisted of the following members, in their order of election : The Right Hon. Spencer H. Walpole (President), the Duke of Argyll, the Earl of Carnarvon, Gathorne Hardy, Sir Douglas Galton, Sir Charles Newton, John Anthony Froude, General E. B. Hamley, Matthew Arnold, Sir John Lubbock, Lord Chief-Justice Coleridge, Bishop Magee, the Earl of Selborne, Sir M. E. Grant-Duff, Sir James Paget, William E. H. Lecky, Sir Stafford Northcote, Vice-Admiral Astley, Cooper Key, Dean Church, Lord Carlingford, Sir Garnet Wolseley, Sir G. O. Trevelyan, Mr. Justice Denman, Sir Frederick Burton, Arthur J. Balfour, Sir James Fitzjames Stephen, Lord Walsingham, the Hon. Edward Stanhope, Frederick Locker-Lampson, J. E. Boehm, C. S. C. Bowen, Spencer Walpole, Professor Flower, Professor Huxley, Canon Liddon, Lord Lytton, Lord Aberdare, Henry James, the Earl of Dalhousie. There were also the following honorary members and supernumerary members : Sir Richard Owen, Sir Henry Wentworth Acland, Professor Jebb, Archbishop Thomson, Henry Reeve, George Richmond, R.A., and the Marquess of Dufferin and Ava.

In due time Colvin became Treasurer and then President. At his first dinner, on December 6, 1886, his fellow-diners were Lord Coleridge, Sir Edward Hamley, Charles Newton,

Dean Liddon, Douglas Galton, Henry Reeve, and Andrew Lang.

Colvin resigned from the Presidency after the dinner of March 7, 1921, and was succeeded by Mr. John Bailey. The company on Colvin's last evening as President consisted of John Bailey, Harold Baker, Maurice Baring, W. Bateson, Basil Champneys, Julian Corbett, Lord Crewe, Geoffrey Dawson, Edward Elgar, Arthur Elliot, Herbert Fisher, Captain Harry Graham, W. P. Ker, E. V. Lucas, John Murray, B. L. Richmond, John Sargeaunt, Lord Sumner, G. M. Trevelyan, Hugh Walpole.

Although no longer President, Colvin continued to attend the Literary Society's dinners until ill-health forced him reluctantly to cease. His last attendance was on March 2, 1925, when the company consisted of John Bailey, Harold Baker, Lord Balfour, Sir James Barrie, A. C. Benson, the Archbishop of Canterbury, the Hon. Evan Charteris, Geoffrey Dawson, Captain Harry Graham, Sir Edward Grigg, Sir Ian Hamilton, E. V. Lucas, John Murray, Sir Henry Newbolt, Sir James Rennell Rodd, J. St. Loe Strachey, Lord Sumner, G. M. Trevelyan, and Mr. Edward Wood (now Lord Irwin, Viceroy of India).

Colvin's first book on Keats, the monograph in the 'English Men of Letters Series,' was published in 1887, and it may be said to have crystallized his reputation as a critic of the finest discrimination, distinguished style, and scrupulous care. His every effort, even a brief review, had been of a piece; but in Keats he found a subject to kindle all his fires. Many of the letters bear upon this admirable work. A very great old lady, to whom Lowell paid in verse one of his golden compliments and to whom, in her way, Lady Colvin was a successor—Anne Procter, widow of 'Barry Cornwall,' friend and biographer of Lamb—wrote to Colvin in 1887, when she was nearly eighty-eight, to thank him for sending her his *Keats*.

'At present,' wrote Mrs. Procter, 'I have only cut the pages, admired the paper & printing—and read where you have done me the honour to mention me.　What a fortunate blunder that was of mine about the eyes—It has been the cause of handing me down to posterity !　I use the word blunder but I stick to blue.　As to the brother, I don't care for brothers.　If you have one, does he know the colour of your eyes ?　Think over your friends and see how seldom you know the colour of anyone's eyes. . . .

'There is a feeling of profound sadness comes over me when I see a work like yours, and think how little the man whom you have embalmed, ever hoped for fame.　How while he lived, he had so few admirers.'

The reference is to a passage in Colvin's monograph on Keats, where in collecting evidence as to the colour and quality of the poet's eyes, Colvin says : ' A shrewd and honoured survivor of those days, herself of many poets the frequent theme and valued friend,—need I name Mrs. Procter ?—has recorded the impression the same eyes have left upon her, as those of one who had been looking on some glorious sight.'　In a note in the appendix Colvin adds : ' Mrs. Procter's memory, however, betrayed her when she informed Lord Houghton that the colour of Keats's eyes was blue.　That they were pure hazel-brown is certain, from the evidence alike of C. C. Clarke, of George Keats and his wife (as transmitted by their daughter Mrs. Speed to her son), and from the various portraits painted from life and posthumously by Severn and Hilton.　Mrs. Procter calls his hair auburn : Mrs. Speed had heard from her father and mother that it was " golden red," which may mean nearly the same thing : I have seen a lock in the possession of Sir Charles Dilke, and should rather call it a warm brown, likely to have looked gold in the lights.'

Here are other letters.　From Matthew Arnold :

'*Pains Hill Cottage, Cobham, Surrey,*
'*June 26th,* 1887.

' MY DEAR COLVIN,—I finished your *Keats* yesterday on a journey from Westmorland to London.　I would not

thank you for it until I had read it. You have got the
Life rightly written at last—its story and personages made
clear. It is not much of a story, nor are the personages
great, but one is glad to have them right, for the sake of
Keats and of our conception of him. The criticism all
through the volume interested me extremely ; you never
gush, but the tone of admiration mounts in some instances
too high for me. What is good in *Endymion* is not, to my
mind, so good as you say, and the poem as a whole I could
wish to have been suppressed and lost. I really resent the
space it occupies in the volume of Keats's poetry. The
Hyperion is not a poetic success, a *work*, as Keats saw, and
it was well he did not make ten books of it ; but that, of
course, deserves nevertheless the strongest admiration, and
its loss would have been a signal loss to poetry ; not so as
regards the *Endymion*.

'But the value you assign to the "Belle Dame sans Merci"
is simply amazing to me.

' On the whole, however, it is a long time since I have read
any criticism with such cordial pleasure and agreement as
this volume. The remarks on Spenser are excellent ; my
high pleasure began there. How true it is that one's first
master, or the first work of him one apprehends, strikes the
note for us ; I feel this of the 4th Eclogue of Virgil, which I
took into my system at 9 years old, having been flogged
through the preceding Eclogues and learnt nothing from
them ; but " Ultima Cumaei," etc. has been a strong influence with me ever since. All the remarks on the diction
of Keats, and indeed of others too, are good ; it would be
hard to beat, for truth and utility, the three or four lines at
the bottom of page 146. Very good and just, also, is all
you say about the sense in which Keats is and is not Greek ;
in fact, as you truly say, he is on the whole not Greek.
" Loading every rift of a subject with ore " is not Greek ;
I had written *dangerous* against the phrase, and lower down
on the page I found you calling attention to the danger.
The extract from Landor's letter was new to me ; it sums

N

the matter up very well.   If Keats could have lived he
might have done anything ; but he *could not have lived*, his
not living, we must consider, was more than an accident.
Once more, I thank and congratulate you, and remain,—
Ever sincerely yours,   MATTHEW ARNOLD

' I should say most pressingly, Come down for a Sunday,
only we are crammed in this cottage at present by having
with us my American daughter and her nurse and baby.'[1]

The passage referred to by Arnold was either this, on
page 147 : ' In the execution, he had done injustice to the
power of poetry that was in him by letting both the exuber-
ance of fancy and invention, and the caprice of rhyme, run
away with him, and by substituting for the worn-out verbal
currency of the last century a semi-Elizabethan coinage of
his own, less acceptable by habit to the literary sense, and
often of not a whit greater real poetic value'; or this, on
page 151 : ' To imagine and to write like this is the privilege
of the best poets only, and even the best have not often combined such concentrated force and beauty of conception
with such a limpid and flowing ease of narrative.   Poetry
had always come to Keats, as he considered it ought to
come, as naturally as leaves to a tree ; and now that it came
of a quality like this, he had fairly earned the right, which
his rash youth had too soon arrogated, to look down on the
fine artificers of the school of Pope.'   There was nothing
applicable on page 146.

From Coventry Patmore :

' Hastings, June 16, 1887.

' MY DEAR COLVIN,—I have been reading your *Keats*
and find to my pleasure and relief that you have said everything about your subject that I meant to say.   I have
never read a piece of criticism so warmly appreciative and
yet so severely just.

' I forget whether I sent you my new 2 vol. edition published about a year ago.   If not I will send it to you.   In

---

[1] In the Fitzwilliam Museum.

it I have given all the little work of my life its final finish, and removed, I hope, all the flies that damaged the ointment, in the old edition.—Yours very truly,

'COVENTRY PATMORE '[1]

From Frederick Locker-Lampson :

' *Rowfant, Crawley, Sussex,*
' *22 June* 1887.

' MY DEAR COLVIN,—I do not know how many copies of *Keats* you have given away, but I am sure that none of the recipients have received and read with greater pleasure than myself—my sincere thanks for the beautiful large-paper copy.

' The book came on the 16th : I began it at once & finished it only yesterday.   There is a good deal of reading in it.

' You have given us *an admirable portrait of the poet*, formed out of fragments of earlier notices, & you have added a good portion of very valuable new matter.

' I once met Miss Reynolds who knew Keats, & whose recollections harmonized with your view, & I once had a talk with Haydon, who had a defiantly attractive manner, but Landseer, who knew him much better than I did, told me he was destitute of principle.   I saw Mme Llanos once or twice in Rome—and have somewhere written down my talk with Leigh Hunt and others.

' Old Severn gave me a photograph of his last sketch of Keats, and I have pasted it, & a fragment of Keats MS., in your volume, with a desire to do it honour !   I have two vols. *Annals of the Fine Arts* (1819-1820) in which the Sonnet to Haydon, to the G. Urn, & to the Nightingale are given.   Have these books any real interest ?   Among other MSS. of Keats I have Act V of his *Otho*.

' Shall you send me a reply to my circular about the Literary Society ?—Yours . . .

' F. L.-L.' [2]

1 and 2 In the Fitzwilliam Museum.

' 29 *De Vere Gardens, Kensington, W.,*
June 15, '87.

' MY DEAR COLVIN,—I have read with delight and thank-
fulness your precious book : Keats may stay there, just as
he was, and be loved and honoured accordingly. Every
touch, to the minutest, of your added knowledge is so far
pure gain to our appreciation of his character. There is
more of criticism than usually goes with biography—so
much the better, for yours is just as it should be. All
congratulations to you !—Yours sincerely,

' ROBERT BROWNING ' [1]

' 1 *Marloes Road, Kensington, W., May* 5.

' DEAR COLVIN,—In writing a brief pot-boiler on Keats
for an edition, I have of course used your book. I don't
see why you should add to it, it is about as good as it can
be already. However, you may have materials.

' The Dean of Salisbury tells me that Lockhart was art and
part in getting *Keats* republished by W. H. Smith (two
editions). I don't know the dates, but must look into it.
He says J. G. L. particularly admired the Odes, also that,
to please Sterling, who was dying, he offered to publish
anything he liked to send. He did send a review of Tennyson, which nearly gave Croker fits, he was in a great rage
(1842-43). Thus my poor old J. G. L. brought forth fruits
of repentance.—Yours very truly,   A. LANG

' Some one told me last night that J. G. L. and his wife
were wretched together ! Oh Lord, what liars we mortals
be.' [2]

In 1887 the *Papers of Fleeming Jenkin* appeared from
the house of Longman, under the editorship of Colvin and
J. A. Ewing, now Sir Alfred and Principal of Edinburgh
University. Jenkin's vigorous and versatile mind has great
attraction, but the special value of the book lay in the
biography of his friend which Stevenson had written for it.

---

[1] and [2] In the Fitzwilliam Museum.

Colvin's character sketch of Jenkin and of his wife (from which I have already quoted) is among the best things in his *Memories and Notes* : 'The variety and genuineness of Jenkin's intellectual interests proceeded in truth from the keenness and healthiness of his interest in life itself. Such keenness shone visibly from his looks, which were not handsome but in the highest degree animated, sparkling, and engaging, the very warts on his countenance seeming to heighten the vivacity of its expression. The amount of his vital energy was extraordinary, and no man ever took his own experience with more zest or entered with a readier sympathy into that of others. An honest blow he was always prepared to take, and every honest pleasure he relished with delight. He loved to do well all he did, and to take not only a part, but a lead, in bodily and other pastimes, as shooting, fishing, mountaineering, yachting, skating, dancing, acting and the rest. But in conversation and human intercourse lay perhaps his chief pleasure of all. His manly and loyal nature was at all times equally ready with a knock-down argument and a tear of sympathy. Chivalrous and tender-hearted in the extreme in all the real relations and probing circumstances of life, he was too free himself from small or morbid susceptibilities to be very sparing of them in others, and to those who met and talked with him for the first time might easily seem too trenchant in reply and too pertinacious in discussion. But you soon found out that if he was the most unflinching of critics and disputants, he was also the most unfailing and ever serviceable of friends. Moreover, to what pleased him in your company or conversation he was instantly and attractively responsive. He would eagerly watch for and pounce upon your remarks, and the futile or half-sincere among them he would toss aside with a prompt and wholesome contempt, his eye twinkling the while between humour, kindness, and annoyance ; while on others he would seize with gusto, and turn them appreciatively over and inside out until he had made the most of them. In my own intercourse with him, no subject was more frequently discussed between us than the social advantages and disadvantages of scientific and mechanical discovery. I used to speak with dislike of the " progress " and " prosperity " which cause multitudes to teem in grimy alleys where before a few had been scattered over wholesome fields, and with apprehension of the possible results of his own last invention on population and on scenery. He would thereupon assail me as a puling sentimentalist : I would retort on him as a materialist and Philistine.'

In 1891 Colvin issued through Messrs. Macmillan an edition of *The Letters of John Keats*.

Let me add to this chapter some letters from Andrew Lang. Colvin first met Andrew Lang at Mentone when he was staying with Stevenson in 1874, and he gives in *Memories and Notes* a piquant passage contrasting the two young Scotsmen. Andrew Lang died in 1912, and Colvin, writing in 1921, says : ' It seems indeed but the other day that we had to mourn the loss from among us of that kind, learned, whimsical, many-faceted character—scholar, critic, poet, journalist, folk-lorist, humanist, and humorist ; and in the mind's eye of many of us there still lives freshly the aspect of the half-silvered hair setting off the all but black eyebrows and gipsy eyes ; of the chiselled features, the smiling languid face and grace behind which there lurked intellectual energies so keen and varied, accomplishments so high, so insatiable a spirit of curiosity and research under a guise so airy and playful.'

The series of notes from Andrew Lang—very swift and practical—touch upon Scottish history in relation to Stevenson ; and the part played by John Gibson Lockhart, whose biography Lang was writing, in the tragedy of Keats. There are dates but no years. I make a few characteristic extracts, and take this opportunity of again expressing my regret, which hundreds of readers must share, that by his own wish no collection of Andrew Lang's letters may be made.

This is the first letter from which I quote :—

ANDREW LANG

FROM THE PAINTING BY SIR W. B. RICHMOND

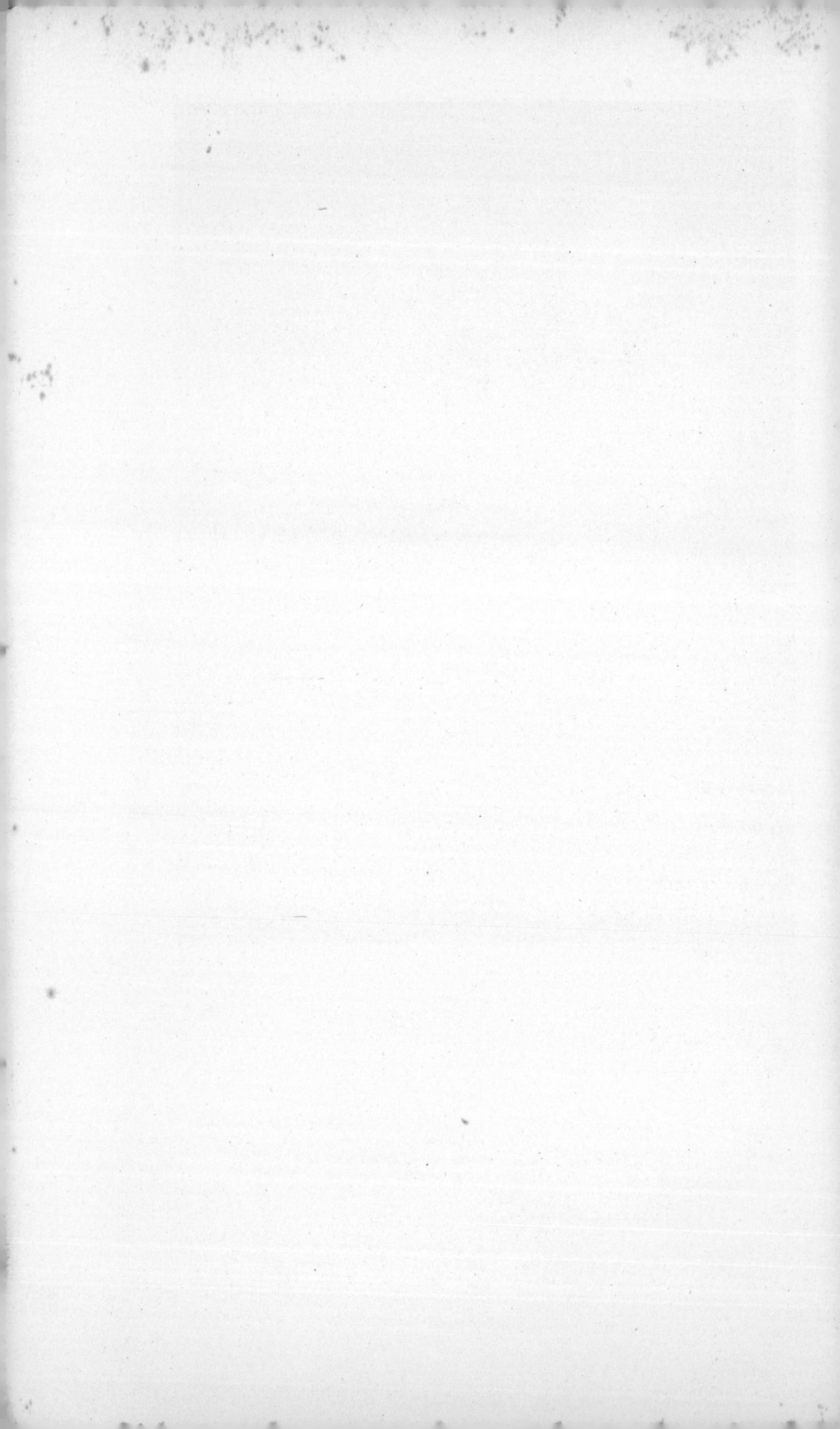

' I hope you *will* do a regular life of Keats. I don't believe anyone has a higher opinion of him than I have, as a man and a poet. The Highland tour really killed him, " not Launcelot or another." '

Some years later Colvin was to do what Lang required.

' The pamphlet is " A Supplement to the Trial of James Stewart, &c." by a Bystander, London 1753.

' James was hanged on November 8, 1752.

' R. L. S. took James Mohr, the meeting at Tyndrum, and a great deal more from this tract, which is in the Signet Library here.'

—The reference, of course, is to *Catriona.*

' Do you know whether he [R. L. S.] means to do my Prince Charlie tale ? If not, I 'd make a push at it, and introduce Alan Breck, who is a historical character, if I please. He was really a tall man, despite Stevenson.'

' Swinburne's efforts to make himself out an athlete who has breasted mountain slopes with the Master [Jowett] are very funny. At least, in my time the Master's efforts to cross a burn were plucky, but quavering.

' However he ends up all right. The Master never criticized bards to me, I think he only discovered Swinburne after the men had found him out.'

In an article in the *Nineteenth Century* for December 1893, Swinburne had written thus of Jowett : ' The physical energy with which he would press up a hill-side or mountain-side— Malvern or Schehallion—was very agreeable and admirable to witness : but twice at least during a week's winter excursion in Cornwall I knew, and had reason to know, what it was to feel nervous : for he would follow along the broken rampart of a ruined castle, and stand without any touch of support at the edge of a magnificent precipice, as though he had been a younger man bred up from boyhood to the scaling of cliffs and the breasting of breakers.'

The next extract refers to Lang's interest in occult matters and his inquiry into the famous Cock Lane ghost. Colvin,

I assume, had deprecated such studies, and had probably urged him to keep to solid ground : ' Israel is joined to his spooks, till he finishes a book called *Cock Lane*. There is so much Anthropology, Folk Lore, and Bibliography in my spooks, and so few people can, or do combine these topics, that I seem called into the field. As to weakening the mind, look at Wallace ! But I never go near mesmerists or mediums, never did, nor will. I don't think the matter important, but it does vex the scientific gents, a set of Philistines. Moreover, so please you, other studies weaken the mind, even ART has begotten a very sickly lot, not very moral neither, I need not mention names. Then think of Bimetallism, or any hobby. My mind to me a kingdom is, and when I have finished *Cock Lane*, I cast the dust of the dead off my feet. The dead might be better employed, and no decent " corp " ever walks. I keep an eye on my mental biceps, and I wish my physical one were in no worse condition.'

Finally, another word on spooks and their fascination to this fastidious inquirer : ' As for *Cock Lane*, I may never produce it, though it is nearly ready. It gets one into such bad intellectual society, with some exceptions. Yet when I think of S. Joseph of Capertino,—" why are their graces hid," in the Bollandists ? It is so funny. It was a toss up if he was a Saint or a Medium, and the Church gave the batsman the benefit of the doubt. I really think the S.P.R. [Society of Psychical Research], that is, F. W. H. M. [Myers], has shewn much pluck and perseverance. Yet the hero is not quite *à mon gré*. There is *something* at the bottom of it all, something uncomfortable, far from consolatory : rather low : I wish there wasn't. The cosmos is a rum place : she 's a rum one, is Nature.'

CHAPTER XIV

GEORGE MEREDITH

1885 AND ON

COLVIN tells us that he first met Meredith in 1878, ' and then only to shake hands on the introduction of Louis Stevenson. Stevenson was staying at the Burford Bridge Inn with his parents, busy upon the early part of his *New Arabian Nights* (the Suicide Club chapters), and finding himself thus almost at Meredith's door, had sought leave, sensitively and shyly, not without fear of a rebuff, to pay him the homage of a beginner to a master.'

Meredith was then fifty and was at work on *The Egoist*. ' As regards my own relations with Meredith,' Colvin continues, ' I have told how I shook hands with him across a stile in 1878. But my intimacy did not begin till after the death of his second wife in 1885 and my own removal from my previous headquarters at Cambridge to take up work at the British Museum. The days of his neglect were then passing away. . . . At the same time his bodily, though not his intellectual, vigour was beginning by gradual degrees to flag. The reddish brown had quite faded from his hair and given place to the shade between grizzled and silvery that went so well with his habitual, unvarying suit of warm light-grey set off by a bright scarlet tie. But both of hair and beard the crop was as rich and wavy as ever ; and the features retained unimpaired, alike their fine cutting and their firm resolute air. His voice had not at all lost—indeed it never lost—its strong virile *timbre*, nor his utterance its authoritative rotundity and fulness; for his speech was ever clear-cut and complete, and the fashion, growing, I fear, in our modern English conversation of lazily mumbling and muttering at one another from behind our teeth slurred, half-articulate sounds instead of formed words, had no countenance from him. . . .

'Divers common friends have assured me, and I can easily believe, that the master was never more himself than when he occasionally received on their Sunday afternoon peregrinations the company of walkers whom Leslie Stephen had organized under the name of the Sunday Tramps. None but the youngest of my readers will need telling how Stephen excelled no less as an athletic walker and mountaineer than as a masterly critic, editor, and biographer: "long Leslie Stephen," as we used commonly to call him, for long he was alike of back, leg, and stride, of nose and of beard (the fine forked and flowing auburn beard depicted in Watts's well-known portrait). He had no small talk, and to strangers or ordinary acquaintances was apt to seem a character even sardonically dry and shy. But no man had a greater power of winning the love of those to whom he felt himself drawn. He had for wife first one of the most delightful of women, and after her death another who was also one of the most beautiful, and for devoted men-friends a pick of the choicest spirits of his time, both English and American. Of these friends Meredith was one of the closest.

'A contrast,' says Colvin, 'marked Meredith's "show conversation" in mixed company and his intimate talk in the privacy of friendship. No man could be more gravely or more sagaciously sympathetic when the appeal for sympathy was made, or could put more of bracing life-wisdom into advice on matters of conduct when his advice was sought. To women (at least to the right kind of women, for with sentimentalists or self-flatterers of either sex he had small patience) he could be the most chivalrous-hearted and tenderly understanding and honourably helpful of men, as beseemed the creator of Lucy Feverel and Rose Jocelyn and Renée and Clara

Middleton, of Rhoda and Dahlia and Diana and the rest :
his temper and discourse in these respects being in life and
in literature entirely and admirably the same. In *tête-à-
tête* intercourse he rarely, in my experience, mounted the
high intellectual or fantastic stilts, but would enter simply,
with the power and incisiveness of a master but on perfectly
free and equal terms, on almost any subject of human or
historical or literary discussion.

' A very frequent subject of talk between us was the
duty and necessity for England of the obligation to national
service. He conceived military training to be a thing desirable in every state, desirable for the sake of the manhood,
the self-respect, the physical and moral health of its citizens,
and desirable for ourselves above all peoples. He held that
if our population would not shake off its carelessness and
sloth, born of plethora, and submit to that discipline, as
well as to other wholesome disciplines of mind and body,
our day was done. He believed that a more sternly trained
race like the Germans would surely win against us and
deserve to win. These convictions at the same time did
not shake his attachment to the Liberal party in the state,
which almost to a man was vehemently opposed to them.
When I urged that he should strive to convert his political
friends and should in writing declare his mind on the question in terms more calculated to strike home than the
cryptic utterances which he puts into the mouths of a
Colney Durance or a Simeon Fenellan, he was apt to answer
as though the matter were one which concerned him not
as one of ourselves, but only as a critic and onlooker.

' In discussions on England and her character and
destinies he would always separate himself from his countrymen and say " You English." This attitude seemed to
me to be due partly to a cherished consciousness of, or at
all events belief in, his own purely Celtic blood (his father
having been Welsh and his mother Irish), partly to the sense
of alienation from the sympathies of his countrymen which
had been forced on his proud and sensitive nature by their

long neglect of his work. Dearly as he loved, and deeply beyond all men as he knew, the English soil, he would sometimes inveigh against defects of the English mind and character in the tone not only of a detached stranger but almost of an enemy. This from such a man, by that time at any rate recognized as one of the glories of our age and country, was a thing that I used sometimes to find hard to bear. The true key to his mind in the matter is perhaps to be found in his words written in 1870 : " I am neither German nor French, nor, unless the nation is attacked, English. I am European and Cosmopolitan—for humanity ! The nation which shows most worth is the nation I love and reverence." Nearly thirty years later, in one of his very last letters, he writes : " As to our country, if the people were awake, they would submit to be drilled. . . . The fear of imposing drill for at least a year seems to me a forecast of the national tragedy." Conceive what would have been his scorn for those who shrieked against the duty of imposing national service even after the outbreak of the world war, during those months of deadly peril to all that England stands for and holds dear.'

After reading *Memories and Notes*, in 1921, Sir James Barrie wrote : ' Hearty thanks for sending me the Boxhill paper. I don't see how a thing of the kind could be more delightfully done, best of all I think is what you say of Meredith's talk—at all events, it seems to me that in those passages you place him as he really was, and I don't think it has been done before.'

' I think,' Colvin continues, ' one of the things which made Meredith tolerate my company was the interest, puzzled and fretted interest though it often was, which I took in his poetry. Very much of this had always repelled me by its obscurity : but among the rest, the things relatively clear, there were some that seemed to me in various kinds unsurpassed, as in the simple lyric kind *The Sweet o' the Year* and *Autumn Even Song* ; in more strenuous and ambitious kinds *Melampus* : *Earth and a Wedded Woman* ;

GEORGE MEREDITH

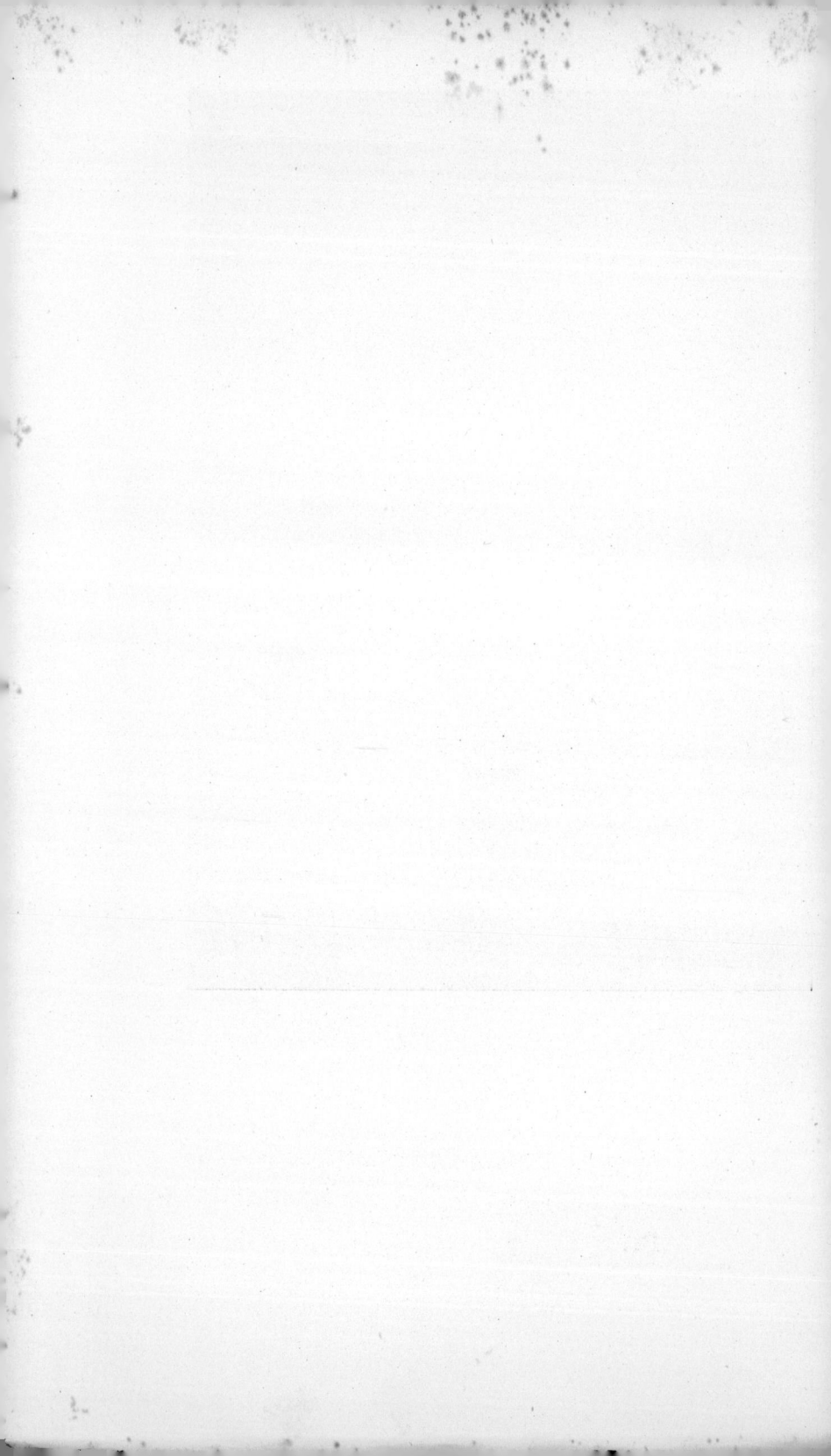

Love in the Valley, surely as rich and original a love-lyric, or lyric and idyll in one, as was ever written. Equally pre-eminent among lyrics political seemed to me the ode *On France* written after her overthrow in 1870 and foretelling for her much such a resurrection as we afterwards witnessed. I was proportionately disappointed at the difficulty with which I found myself trying to follow the odes *On Napoleon* and *On French History* when he read them to me, then fresh written, in 1898.'

In 1915, when Colvin was preparing his lecture on Con-centration in Poetry, he returned, as we shall see, to a remark made to him by Meredith, for his inspiration, and devoted much space to an analysis of his friend's Muse.

Among Meredith's letters is one to Mrs. Sitwell, who seems to have been trying to find a governess for Meredith's daugh-ter (now Mrs. Sturgis). The first to Colvin, in 1886, is a characteristic invitation : ' You will delight me by coming. But if it does not suit you to hit on Saturday for the Sunday, then decide to stay over Monday ; for you know this country, which is a home of woods, & London on a Monday, when pious Philistines & their other end, the ragtails, are but half emerged from the front & hind of a common drunkenness, is desolating to the soul. So give yourself to me & Grace for Monday.'

In the following note we have a reference either to rival governesses, or to alternative services rendered. Again Meredith is true to type : ' The difference between £70 & £100, gapes ogrely. I will draw it closer, if only for the sake of appearances. But, as I had to calculate, the girl will have to come to London weekly for certain lessons. You know her & can tell the lady of her that she is a friendly puss. There is not alive a more loyal little woman.'

In March 1892 we have this : ' The look out of window is as if one saw Nature's picked skull. But in an hour the S.W. can give it the face of youth & show how *ver egelidos refert tepores*. The sky winks for a genial Sunday—per-haps the Saturday. I dare not prognosticate to a Londoner,

who is unpardoning at a disappointment.   But this week
or next or anywhen, be bold, I say.'

In 1898, when Meredith was trying to make a play out
of *The Egoist*, he thus describes the task : ' While you inhale
it [the name of Gastein] I am dialoguing *The Egoist*—a
dreary walk backward.'   The last letter, dated November
24, 1901, has reference to Mr. Binyon's dramatic version,
never produced, of Meredith's novel *Vittoria* :

' MY DEAR COLVIN,—Mr. Binyon's Poems are known to
me, & I think hopefully of them.   I do not gape for work
of mine to be brought before the public, but if he has taken
heartily to the notion in this case—not merely following a
hint,—I shall not object.   As to the verse, supposing that
he chooses verse,—I would counsel him not to be guided by
his master, though, for me, I catch the dramatic accent
intended by Mr. Bridges in the run of his lines.   Reviewers
& the public are conservative in the matter of blank verse :
they take no account of spondees (got by proper names) &
the ducks & drakes of double pyrrhics to present emotion.
Perhaps they are right—when the iambic is not too stiff.—
Ever yours,   GEORGE MEREDITH '

Meredith died in 1909.

Before passing on to new names I should like to quote a
passage from an anonymous review of *One of Our Conquerors*
in the *National Review* written by Mrs. Sitwell.   So few
examples of her literary work are identifiable that I am glad
to print it both for its ability and its subject matter.   In
this book she says, ' Mr. Meredith is at once at his worst
and at his best ; more Meredithian than ever in language
and manner, but more than ever a searcher of the heart of
man, and especially of woman.   No one can number among
Mr. Meredith's shortcomings sentimentality, failure of
insight, or a hand that shrinks from using the scalpel.   The
more ought good women, and those who believe in them,
to be grateful to him for the treasures of love, loyalty, and

tenderness with which he endows the honourable maids and mothers of his creating. But in order to come at these treasures what a quickset hedge of thorns does this most perverse of gifted writers drag us through! For whole chapters we are made to wince and dance with impatience at his exasperating literary attitude, and then in the next we are brought to our knees with admiration. In dealing with the essential human emotions and relations of the mother and daughter, who are the heroines of his tale, he shows a strength and delicacy of handling that can hardly be overpraised, and from

> ' " The trembling living wire
> Of those unusual strings "

strikes harmonies as moving as they are fresh. In all that concerns these two lovely and lovable women, around whom the real interest of the book is centred, there is scarcely a false note.'

The following letter from Mr. Douglas Freshfield, the Alpine explorer, to Colvin after the publication of *Memories and Notes* may round off this chapter. It is dated January 19, 1922: 'I have been enjoying your reminiscences, and when I got to Meredith and your discussion with him as to Preservation of Natural Beauty and his contradictory attitude on it I was led to turn to a drawer where I have kept a few letters and find this wh. seems to the point :—

> ' " *Oct.* 16, 1908.

' " Those old days of the Tramps are lively in my mind. I know you 're a Keeper of Ashdown Forest. My own quarrel with present-day developments lies in the hectoring of lovely open country by hideous villas. I have been motoring over Surrey, Sussex, Hampshire, and feel what the old saying ' eyesore ' means. Yet it signifies increase of wealth and the absence of wealthy proprietors. So I am struck dumb.—Your faithful

> ' " GEORGE MEREDITH "

' I envy you,' Mr. Freshfield continues, ' your power of remembering conversations without notes.   Most people can only recollect what they said themselves !   I am glad you stand up for Rossetti's poetry.   He always has seemed to me one of the few masters of the sonnet—which A. T. [Tennyson] called " dancing in chains." '

CHAPTER XV

MRS. R. L. STEVENSON'S LETTERS: II
THE SOUTH SEAS

1887–1892

STEVENSON'S published correspondence tells much of what happened after he left Bournemouth and England for the South Seas; but even more can be learned from his wife's vivid pen.

I quote freely from her many letters, chiefly to her dear Custodian but also to Mrs. Sitwell, during this period of voyaging. Some of them have already appeared in the *Empire Review*. There are also three which, in order to complete the story of the South Seas adventure, Colvin included in the edition of Stevenson's correspondence. Naturally I do not reprint those here, but readers of these others may like to refer to them.

Mrs. R. L. S. to Colvin. From Saranac Lake, Adirondack Mts., December 6 [1887]: '*The Hanging Judge*, amid much dissension and general acrimony, has been finished. I want to go somewhere where people have not only no intellects, but no pretence to intellect. I had better return to Bournemouth for that. Louis is very well here, and no cold has fastened upon him, as yet, though he has had threatenings which have miraculously disappeared. I hardly dare write it with the fear of nemesis in my mind, but Louis has not, since he left England, brought up one drop of blood from his lungs. He looks extremely well, and works along at his magazine articles, which is next thing to resting, and plays much on a battered old piano we have hired from a livery stable man. We

o

have had several falls of snow, but just now the ground is quite black. I took Louis out twice in a sleigh and went quite a long way. Once when I was driving a pair, and they pulled too hard, he took hold of one bridle rein to pull back the liveliest horse, and he is the man who says a *horse* has no sense. I was so savage that he fortunately dropped it in time, or we should have had a fine spill.

' Does that most beautiful creature, Lady Colin Campbell, still remember me ? You spoke as though she did, and I hope it is true, for I should like to have her remember me. I so admired her. She seemed like a walk in the woods, and fine, supple, wild beasts, and all those things that I love, and a woman besides. Any of us can be a woman, and some of us are very nice ones, but it is only given to a few to be so much more of nature.

[*In the upper left-hand corner of the first page, in Robert Louis Stevenson's handwriting, there appears the following note :*]

' Passage at end marked out by R. L. S. F. says it was too warm an expression of affection. Well—I will tell you when we meet, but it will be cold porridge then.

' R. L. S.'

The Hanging Judge was a play written by Stevenson and his wife in collaboration. It was not played and has not been published.

Stevenson's home at Saranac Lake is now a permanent memorial of him, stocked with souvenirs. When I was there in 1920 I sent to Lady Colin some leaves from a tree in the garden.

The next letters, said Colvin, when preparing his article for the *Empire Review* in 1924, ends the period just before Stevenson's *Vailima Letters* began.

Mrs. R. L. S. to Colvin. From Taiohae, Hiva-oa, Marquesas Isl., August 18 [1888] :—

' DEAR AND NEVER FORGOTTEN CUSTODIAN,—Oh, that you and a few—a very few friends were with us in these enchanted Isles to stay for ever and ever, and live and die with these delightful miscalled savages. That they are cannibals may be true, but that is only a freak of fashion like the taste for decayed game, and not much more unpleasant. Last evening we had a savage queen to dine with us; I say savage, because her son, who came with her, continually referred to themselves as " we savages." The old lady has presided at many a sacrificial feast, and ordered many a poor witch to instant execution, and yet a more gracious affection-compelling person I do not expect to see until I again meet Lady Shelley, of whom she greatly reminded us. Not a word of any tongue could she speak but her own, and she was deaf besides, but we managed to pass more than three hours very pleasantly in her charming society. She wore a white dress made like a night-gown, of very fine material, no underclothes, and a white china crêpe shawl heavily embroidered and fringed. Her hands and what could be seen of her feet and legs were elaborately tattooed. Even Mrs. Stevenson has grown to dislike the look of un-tattooed hands. The queen, they say, is entirely covered with the most beautiful tattooing that has ever been done in the Islands. On Monday next, Stanilao, the heir appa-rent, has invited us to a picnic. We are to go on horses, natives having gone on ahead to prepare a meal. I am rather curious as to what will take place, as the point of interest, a balancing rock, has been tabooed for many years, though it stands in full sight of the village, and even Stanilao has never been near it. He made a little speech to us last evening thanking us formally for our sympathetic treatment of " his savages."

'It was a sad business when we left Anaho. We had eight particular friends there whom, I suppose, we shall never see again. When we first arrived there they swarmed over the vessel like flies, clothed in breech cloths and tattooing only. For their farewell visit the beachcomber had made them all white trousers and shirts. Every man was as clean as a new pin, and shining with cocoanut oil, their finger nails, even, as carefully looked after as our own. We gave them what keepsakes we could find among our things, and they presented us with tappa cloth beaten out of the bark, oranges, cocoanuts prepared for drinking, some rare shells, and to Lloyd one of them gave a carving done on the bone of one of his ancestors. We had gingerbread and a glass of rum all round, the whole party took a last walk through the vessel, we shook hands, and parted. Hoka, the beautiful dancer and the most graceful person I have ever seen, dropped all his usual airs and graces, and sat most of the time staring on the floor just as we do when we are very unhappy and distressed; sighing heavily, when he had shaken hands he turned his head away, and never once looked back. Typee, the chief, on the contrary, stood up in the midst of his men, waving his hand and making gestures of farewell as long as he could see us. As the canoe went off the captain saluted Typee, when all the men uncovered. Our cannibal friend, Koamoa, was, I am sorry to say, too drunk to come aboard, and was left on the beach hanging over the branch of a tree. It seems that a Corsican had come over in a boat with a demijohn of rum, which was more than the old chief could stand. Our own Hoka, I fear, believes in eating one's enemies. He had had a quarrel with the Corsican, who called him " cochon " and " sauvage." Hoka's reply was " you are more of a savage than I am," whereupon the man struck him a boxer's blow of which Hoka had no understanding. He said he was going to get a gun soon, and then he could go over to the Island where the Corsican lives and shoot him, after which he meant to cut off and eat one of his arms. In the next Island we are going to visit, a man whom the whole population hated was killed for vengeance. The question was how should every man have a taste of his enemy without the authorities finding it out. This was solved by filling matchboxes with the cooked flesh, and passing them about. I think the combination of the civilized matchbox and the " long pig " very interesting. Three months ago, a little boy was called for at the school by a couple of people who were decoying him into a quiet spot for the purpose of killing and eating him, but he discovered their evil intention in time to call for help.   Three of the townspeople have lately disappeared mysteriously : they are supposed to have fallen victims to private vengeance.   Lloyd has had given him by a native woman an ornament to wear in the war dance.   It is composed of locks of women's hair made into a sort of gigantic fringe.   As many as ten women were killed to make this ghastly ornament, their bodies being cooked for the dancers' feast.

' I am glad to tell you that quite suddenly Louis' health took a change for the better, and he is now almost as well as he ever was in his life.   It has been a mistake about the cold places, warmth and hot sun is what he needs.   Certainly we have found the right place for him : and we both love it.   It is hard that we should ever have to go away. Stanilao says that Dominique is still better, and if we conclude to come back here to stay that is the Island for us. I think it is very nice of Stanilao to praise another Island when he would so much like to have us here.   Our next point is Hiva-oa, for which we start in three days, taking with us a most delightful person called Frère Michel, who builds churches not to be conceived of.   I have made awful drawings of one which will delight your soul, and fill you with pleased laughter.   My dearest love to you all, best beloved friends.   Louis is away walking in the hills, Lloyd playing on the fiddle.—Ever yours affectionately,

' F. V. DE G. STEVENSON ' [1]

Mrs. R. L. S. to Sidney Colvin and Mrs. Sitwell.   From Honolulu, June 18, 1889 :—

' MY DEAR ONES,—This is about the last chance for a word of good-bye.   The seachests are all corded up, Mr. Strong is just finishing a last transparency for the magic lantern, Louis is resting prior to the fatigue of bidding

[1] In the *Empire Review*.

farewell to his gracious majesty [Kalakaua], and we are all in our travelling clothes, while Ah Foo scans the horizon for what he can clap his eyes on.   I wish you could see the preparations Ah Foo and Lloyd have made in case of ship-wreck.   Mysterious parcels of garden seeds and carpenter's tools are stowed away in all sorts of inaccessible places.   I am sure they will both be disappointed if we are not cast ashore on a dissolute island, though I believe Ah Foo would really prefer to trust to his own hands unaided by the arts of civilization : he can make fire by rubbing two sticks together ; he can catch fish without hook or line, and bring birds down with a stone, to say nothing of being able to use a bit of stone for a knife or hatchet, in the native fashion, or to walk up the stem of the tallest cocoa-nut tree.   In fact he is civilized just so much as we should like to have him, and a savage just as far as it is useful. He has fallen heir to rice lands, houses, and bullocks in China, and his presence is urgently demanded by his rela-tives.   After much weeping and tribulation and sleepless nights it was finally arranged that he would start on the cruise with us, remain so long as he was necessary to our comfort, and then branch off towards China.

' His is a sad case ; he has almost forgotten his own tongue, and has entirely fallen out of sympathy with his own countrymen : he is much more like an emotional pirate in manners and appearance than the suave, soft-speaking elegant gentleman that a man of property in China should be.   I am afraid his mother, who seems a stiffly conventional person, will loathe the very sight of him.   The second son is holding the property pending Ah Foo's return, and in the meantime is ill-treating and cheat-ing the family.   It is that, and not the money that is taking Ah Foo home.   He proposes to go home and " lick um my bludder " until he is brought to a proper sense of his duty, then turn over everything to his mother and come back to the white man's country again.   I hope he may come back to us, but where may such will-o'-the wisps be by that time ?

ROBERT LOUIS STEVENSON

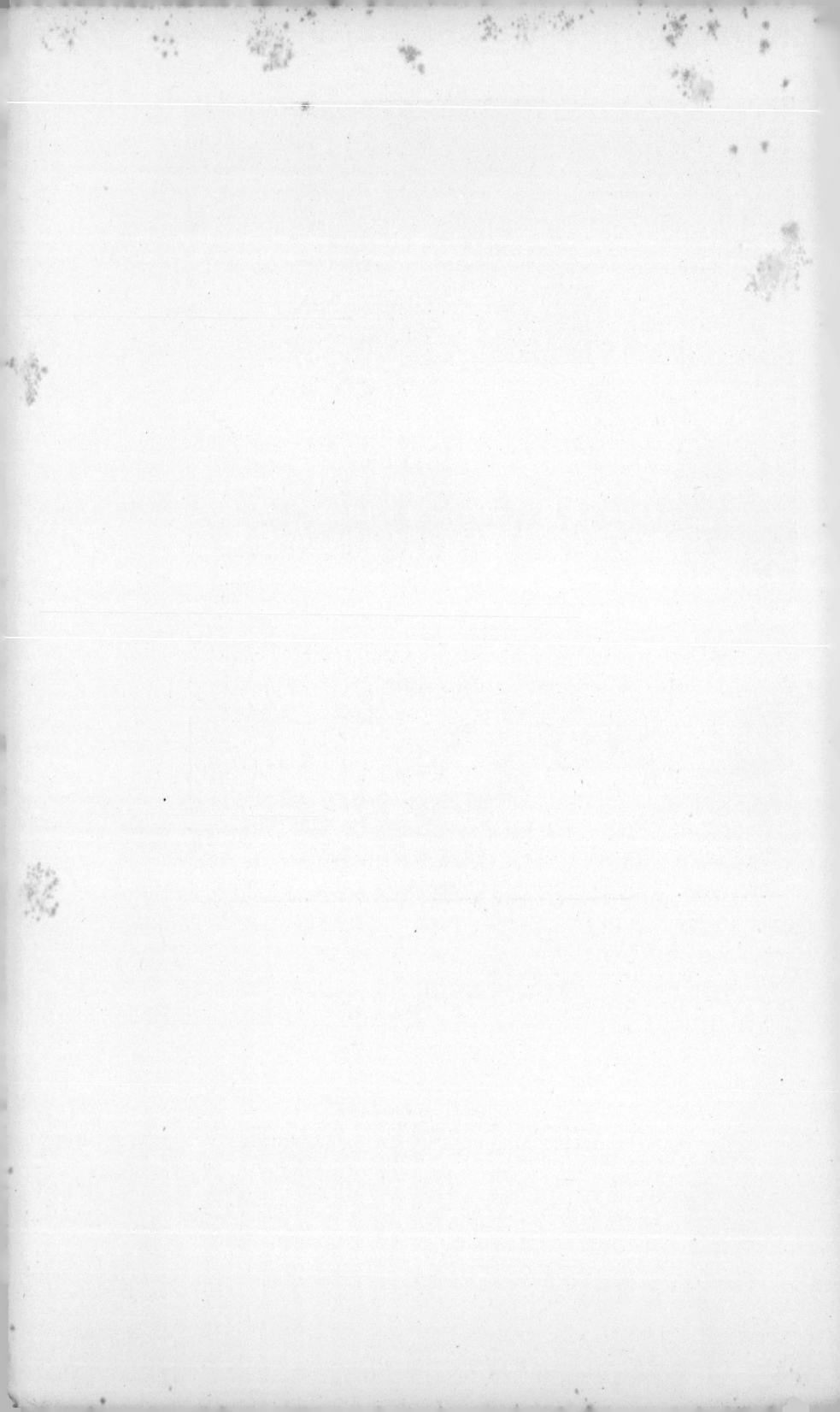

With you, I trust. Had we known the truth about our dear friend we should not now be here. We only learned it too late, after we were committed to the cruise. That is the only person in the world for whom I should be willing to have Louis sacrifice himself in any way. I do not mean to say that Louis is not continually offering himself up on unworthy altars ; but it is not with my consent. . . .

'Louis is coming round now to my view of his book of travels, and I think that by the time we arrive in Sydney he will have forgotten entirely that he ever held any other and will look as coldly upon the scientific aspect as ever I have done. It should be the most entrancing reading that man ever engaged in.

'And if you could only see him ! I do not think he is much below his old good average of health. It seems incredible, and like a dream. If I can only take him back to you like this ! But even if that is not to be, for a time he has lived the life of a free man, and that is something gained for him. It is a delight to me beyond words, as it would be to you, to see him, bare-footed, and half clothed, flying about with his usual impetuosity, accompanied by no fear of danger.

'I must stop now for other things. With dearest and best love to you all, including our dear Henry James to whom I hope to write yet this evening.' [1]

Mrs. R. L. S. to Mrs. Sitwell.   From Sydney, April 12 [1890] :—

'BEST OF FRIENDS,—I fear it will be a disappointment that we are not to be in England as soon as we expected. Louis has taken his first bad cold, most probably that dreadful influenza. He is better, though very weak, and the doctor said it would be suicide to start to England now, or to stay on here just as the bad season is coming on. At the critical moment I found a steamer of five hundred tons, the *Janet Nicoll*, which is about starting out on a cruise

---

[1] In the *Empire Review*.

in the South Seas of from two to four months' duration.   I
got our steamer tickets—already bought—advanced, and
took passage for our party for the South Seas.   I had only
thirty-six hours to arrange everything in ; I am more tired
than words can say, but very thankful of getting a change
for Louis so comfortably.   The vessel goes on a rather
mysterious cruise, and will give no information even to us,
of her business, nor of what Islands she will take us to with
the exception of Savage Island, the Tukelars, Penrhyn, and
Apemama.   We are not even allowed on board until two
hours before leaving lest we let some information leak out.
At the present moment the labour league is doing all it
can to prevent the *Janet Nicoll* leaving because of her
carrying Solomon Islanders as sailors.   There will be no
other passengers besides ourselves with the exception of
a young man in process of becoming a beachcomber, who is
to be dropped in the Gilberts.   We shall have nice large
cabins, and an awning is always kept up over the house.
There are also two bathrooms.   We have not been used to
such luxury.   Louis has been staying in the country, and
will not come to town till the steamer is about to start.   It
is odd that he had an attack of asthma the other night ; I
suppose only accidental.

' Of course this cruise will give additional interest to the
book. I am very glad you spoke of the historical and
scientific question.   It has been rather heavy on my mind.
If I were the public I shouldn't care a penny what Louis'
theories were as to the formation of the Islands, or their
scientific history, or where the people came from originally
—only what Louis' own experiences were.   And no one
has had such experiences.   All the South Sea books speak,
by hearsay only, of the terrible Tembinok', but we threw
ourselves into his arms, and went and lived with him for
months, and learned to love him almost as much as we
admired him.   I have sent him an ensign that I designed,
and we shall carry with us his palace flag.   What a surprise
it will be when we steam into Apemama and hoist his flag,

which we mean to do. Our photographs have all been
finished up, and we have really lovely and wildly interesting pictures. The camera goes with us this time. I feel
so ashamed to tell you that we are off again, for I know how
you were looking forward to meeting Louis: but then I
know, too, that you love him with a generous and not a
selfish love.' [1]

In February 1890, Colvin tells us, the Stevensons, intending to return to England, for a spell or for permanence, had
sailed to Sydney. But there Stevenson was again taken ill
and reluctantly came to the conclusion that the South Seas
must be his only home.

Mrs. R. L. S. to Mrs. Sitwell [1889] : ' Louis is gone up to
the colonies to get the sea air there and back. He still keeps
very well, but rather overworked his brain lately, so is
trying his remedy for everything, the sea. I was not well
enough to stand the knocking about of the ship, so perforce
had to stay at home. I have been very ill since Louis went,
but of course he doesn't know that. It was a little alarming
to find my head going wrong in the middle of the night, and
no one on the premises but an imbecile drunken German man,
and some fifty yards from the house, a young Samoan chief
about seventeen years of age.

' The chiefling is all that one could ask, and much more
than anyone could expect. I wish you could have seen the
wise youth the other day sitting in judgment to decide a
family quarrel. It came about in this way. My best working man who has long shown a burning desire to become what
Lloyd calls " an old and attached " threw himself on his
knees before me saying, " I belong you now." " No you
don't belong me," said I ; " you can't unless *I* say so."
" That 's all right," returned Sapelli ; " you no like me,
you kill him. You all the same my mother now. You
savee I no belong this Island. I Fatuna man. Long time
ago, I leetle young boy, one American whaler man he stealee
me ; long time I go catch whale. By and bye Captain he

---

[1] In the *Empire Review*.

go home, no want me any more ; he put me shore in Apia.
I no got father, I no got mother, I no got brother, I no got
mother, I no got brother, I no got sister, I no got friend
neither. My wife, she Samoa girl, she no good : she no
like me any more : she like Samoa man. I no got nobody :
I allee same one fellow." The latter expression means " I
am all alone."

' Fortunately, for my heart was melting toward Sapelli,
who had not, in his sorrows, forgotten to dye his hair rust
colour, and bedeck it with flowers, to say nothing of being
rubbed down from head to heel with scented oil (spots of
which he left on my floor), fortunately the young chief
(named Simele, possessing three titles, but called Henry for
short) came in at the critical moment. " I must look into
this thing probably " (properly) said he. The wife and her
family were sent for, and after they, and witnesses on both
sides had been examined, Henry came to the conclusion that
there had been a general family quarrel in which Sapelli was
more to blame than the others. It ended in everyone con-
fessing their misdeeds and a happy reconciliation all round.
So Sapelli is no more " allee same one fellow," and the
day of his attachment to Vailima is put off indefinitely.
Henry is civilized beyond oiling down, and yet, as I see him
just now, you would probably think he looked as much of a
savage as the rest. He is clad in a very small red and white
waist cloth, a necklace of red berries is round his neck,
hanging low upon his brown chest, and on his head he wears
a wreath of fine fern leaves. He has cut his hair close
everywhere except just over his forehead where a crescent
tuft is left. In this tuft he has stuck a large scarlet flower.
He stands on a stump directing his men with many gestures
and the loud imperative tones of his voice reach me here.
He speaks with less than usual of the rich thick sweetness of
the Samoans, and is altogether of a tougher fibre than ordinary. His ambition is to " learn to do all things in the manner
of high English chiefs." The most deadly reproof we have
at our command is " Henry, that is not Ali in England."

(Ali means literally princely.)   We are building part of our
house, the expense and difficulty being so great at this time
of the year of getting up the building material, that we
thought it better to make only a beginning at present. . . .
   ' I suppose Lloyd has described my desperate engagements
with the man of genius over the South Sea book.   Many
times I was almost in despair.   He had got Darwin on the
Coral Insect—no, Darwin was " Coral Reefs " : somebody
else on Melanesian languages, books on the origin of the
South Sea peoples, and all sorts of scientific pamphlets and
papers.   He has always had a weakness for teaching and
preaching, so here was his chance.   Instead of writing about
his adventures in these wild islands, he would ventilate his
own theories on the vexed questions of race and language.
He wasted much precious time over grammars and diction-
aries, with no results, for he was not able to get an insight
hardly into any native tongue.   Then he must study the
coral business.   That, I believe, would have ruined the
book but for my brutality.   We had stopped when cruising
in the *Janet Nicoll* at a most curious and interesting Island.
We were all going ashore together, but to my surprise Louis
refused to start with us, but said he would follow in a second
boat.   Lloyd and I spent several hours wandering over the
Island having some odd adventures, and seeing many
curious things.   But no Louis.   At last we gave him up and
went down to the beach to return to the ship.   There was
that gentleman on the reef, half way between the ship and
shore, knee deep in water, the tropical sun beating on his
unprotected head, hammering away at the reef with a big
hatchet.   His face was purple and his eyes injected with
blood.   " Louis, you will die ! " I cried ; " come away out of
the sun quickly."   " No," he answered.   " I must get
specimens from this extraordinary piece of coral.   I can't
take the whole of it, for it 's too heavy, but after two hours'
hard work I have got off bits showing the different sorts of
frankings.   I still haven't got all there is to be got, and the
work is so hard nobody will help me."   He then showed me

the fragments that he wished me to take to the ship, for dinner, fatigue, nothing should get him away from the important discoveries he was making. I looked at his specimens with contempt. " Louis," I cried, " how ignorant you are ! Why that is only the common brain coral. Any schoolboy in San Francisco will give you specimens if you really want them." It was horrid of me, but it was true, and it had the effect of stopping off the coral interest. I showed him on board the very *Janet Nicoll* a picture of brain coral, there called " the common brain coral." Always, please, fall upon me when his work goes wrong. He will stubbornly hold to his own position, but is apt to give way if he thinks I am getting the blame. . . .

' He holds a most vexing theory at present. I plunged into the work of the plantation with so much interest that he says I have the true peasant nature, and lack the artistic temperament ; thereupon my advice on artistic matters, such as a book on the South Seas, must be received with extreme caution. He says I do not take the broad view of an artist, but hold the cheap opinions of the general public that a book must be interesting. How I do long for a little wholesome monumental correction to be applied to the Scotch side of Louis's artistic temperament. Let us have, I pray you, all we can get, though it is so long on the way as to be almost too late. Never had any man such enchanting material for a book, and much of the best is to be left out. " Very well," I say, " if you will not, then I shall. I 'll gather together all my letters, and publish them." ' [1]

Mrs. R. L. S. to Mrs. Sitwell, referring to early days in Samoa [? 1890] :—

' DEAR FRIEND,—Because I make my sacrifice with flowers on my head and point out the fine views on the way, do not think that it is no sacrifice and only for my own pleasure. The Samoan people are picturesque, but I do not like them. I do not trust them. My time must be

---

[1] In the *Empire Review*.

so arranged as not to clash with them.   I shall be able to get no servants but cannibal black boys, runaways and discontents from the German plantations.   A great part of the housework I shall have to do myself, and most of the cooking.   The land *must* produce food enough for us all, or we shall have nothing to eat.   I must also manage that. Oh it makes me tired to speak of it ; and I never feel well, then.   I don't want to complain.   I am not complaining, really, only telling you.   There is one thing more.   If a letter should come saying that you were dead it would kill Louis on the spot.   If ever there is any danger of that (and I pray God not) tell us, for Louis might as well, then, go to you and die with you as away from you.   I am very tired—do you understand what I mean ?   When Louis proposed to stay a few days in Noumea and come up on a quick vessel some instinct moved me to agree, and it was well.   We were caught in a very terrible storm, our coal gave out, we could hoist no sail and for two days and nights we were lost on this dangerous coast drifting about perfectly helpless and almost swamped by the water that washed over us sometimes half up the masts.   The inability to rest was so dreadful : one could neither lie nor sit, but only hang on to some part of the ship that would not give way.   Our captain was dangerously ill with gastric fever and we did not know whether he was quite right in his head when he sent word to us that he had made out a light, on Sunday night, and thought he knew where we were. Neither Lloyd nor I have got over the fatigue of it yet, and Louis had a smooth beautiful passage all the way up. It is because I am tired that I cannot write more clearly. I am so confused, yet, in my head.   I do hope and trust you are all well.   I cannot ask you to forgive me, but—I do want Louis, and I do want everybody to think I like going to Samoa—and in some ways I do like it ; I don't want people to think I am making a sacrifice for Louis. I fact I *can't* make a sacrifice for him ; the very fact that I can do the thing in a way makes a pleasure to do it, and

it is no longer a sacrifice, though if I did it for another
person it would be. I can't write any more, though I know
there are a number of things I want to say. I send you my
love. I understand you better than you understand me.'

Mrs. R. L. S. to Colvin :—

'*Apia, Jan. 20th* [1890].

'DEAR CUSTODIAN,—I hardly dare use that word with
the knowledge in my heart that we intend to remove our
bodily selves from out your custody, but as you know it
will be our vile bodies only : spiritually we are yours and
always shall be. Neither time nor space can change us in
that. You told me when we left England that if we found
a place where Louis was really well, to stay there. It
really seems that anywhere in the South Seas will do. Ever
since we have been here we have been on the outlook for
a spot that combines the most advantages. In some ways
I preferred the Marquesas, the climate being perfect, and
the natives people that I admired and loved. The only
suitable place on the Sandwich Islands is at the foot of
a volcano where we should have to live upon black lava,
and trust to rain for water. Besides I could not bear the
white population. All things considered, Samoa took our
fancy the most : there are three opportunities each month
to communicate with England by telegraph from Auckland,
Auckland being from seven to eight days' steamer distance
from us. You would hardly believe your own eyes if you
could but see Louis in his present state of almost rude
health, no cough, no hemorrhage, no fever, no night sweats.
He rides and walks as much as he likes without over-
fatigue, and in fact lives the life of a man who is well. I
tremble when I think of our return to England. I doubt
if he will dare stay there for long.

'Well, just as we had made up our minds that Samoa
was our choice we discovered by accident the very piece
of land that seemed to have been made to order for us. It
is already difficult to buy land here, and the difficulties

will increase by the action of the new law forbidding natives
to sell their lands.   This tract consists of between three
and four hundred acres, part of it table land of the richest
deep virgin soil : more than enough for a large plantation.
The rest is wild and picturesque : great cliffs, deep ravines,
waterfalls, one some two hundred feet deep, and everywhere gigantic trees of different species.   The whole lying
some four hundred feet more or less above the sea level,
and commanding magnificent views of the harbour, the
sea outside, and the surrounding country.   We shall be
two miles and a quarter from the town, not too near, nor
yet too far.   For this we pay ten Chili dollars an acre.   I
cannot count it up, but seven Chili dollars go to the English
pound.   With the land goes a herd of cattle.   One of our
friends has just been in to speak about purchasing the
cattle, or at least entering into some sort of arrangement
concerning them.   He says there are between fifty and
sixty head, and they are worth between forty and fifty
dollars apiece.   The man who owned the property offered
Louis seventy-five dollars (dollars are always " Chili ")
for his choice amongst the cows.   At any rate here is a
good bit towards paying for the land.   A surveyor is now
at work searching the boundaries, a lawyer who is most
anxious to have us return, remaining on the spot to see
that all is done correctly.   Every few days the lawyer (a
Mr. Carruthers) comes down and tells us of some new and
delightful discovery he has made.   He says, though he
has lived here for a great many years he has never seen
such grand and beautiful scenery, nor better or more avail-
able land.   Think of having three beautiful rivers of one's
own, and a waterfall shaded by gnarled orange trees within
five minutes' walk of one's door,—not that we have a door
as yet, but we have chosen the site for our house.   This
waterfall is not the two hundred feet one, but a more
modest and restful little fellow with a large swimming pool
at his feet.

' As I am writing through continual interruptions Louis

will look over my letter and correct any mistakes I have made as to facts. My Chinaman has learned how to take photographs and in a few days will go out to our land and take photographs to send you. He is calling me now to pose for him, saying that the " camphor " is ready. He makes a very economical use of English, one sound serving for many purposes. He has learned camphor wood trunk, so camphor is naturally used for camera. " Cocolet " means either cocoanut, chocolate, or cockroach. Sometimes a little confusion arises, but we guess his meaning from the context.

' Here is another interruption ; a madman has come in, and as I cannot make Louis understand that he mustn't engage him in conversation I fear he will never leave. It is very difficult to write under disadvantages : and good heavens—Louis is arguing with him !

' The hardships of our last voyage were very great, and almost too much for me. In fact Louis was the only one who came out of it with any degree of health and strength. The schooner was loaded with coprah (shelled cocoanut) which fermented and filled the vessel with an acrid noisome steam. The floor of our cabin was so hot that I could hardly stand upon it with bare feet, and to sleep in it was impossible. In all, our accommodations consisted of two rooms some eight feet square, one had a counter across it, and the other was the room in which we dined—in relays. The captain, it is true, had a trig cabin opening into the dining-room, but it could hold but one sleeper. All the rest of us, then, had to dispose of ourselves as best we could in the rest of this limited space. In the trade room with the counter, Lloyd, Louis and Joe were supposed to sleep : Ah Foo on the counter, and I on the floor below Ah Foo in a little passage way. All the trunks and luggage, and most of the trade stuffs, were piled upon the floor behind the counter, and in one corner were a couple of shut bunks. I forgot that the steward, Murray, slept also in the trade room. I used to go to bed (dressed)

with an open umbrella ; when the rain came through the
skylight I held the umbrella over my head, and when it
blew in at the open door upon my feet I held the umbrella
with my monkey toes : but when the sea washed in I had
to close the door and then we all began to suffocate. In the
dining-room slept Mr. Rick the American consul for Butari-
tari, Mr. Paul something I have forgotten, and either the
mate or the captain. . . . It was odd that our mate was
in a quiver of fear all the time, and yet slept through all his
night watches. I am bound to say, however, that he
wakened quickly. The night we lost our foretopmast he
was lying in the captain's berth asleep. At the first crash
of the squall he leaped out of bed, and crying out " This is
no time for fooling " thrust the captain on one side and
bounded on deck. I was very glad that I had my China
boy with me that night : hearing great confusion on deck
I woke up Ah Foo saying, " I think him got trouble on deck ;
more better you go and help." Our ship was manned, if
manned you can call it, by boys, and when Ah Foo got
forward he found them clustered together doing nothing.
He asked what orders they had ; " then why don't you do
what captain tell you ? " When they answered that they
did not know how, " then," said Ah Foo, " I lose my head.
I say ' all right, we go to bottom now.' " Fortunately his
head was soon recovered, for he put a rope in a hand, and
telling them to pull way on that, he climbed on top of the
galley and did exactly the right thing for which the captain
afterwards presented him with a sovereign.

' Ah Foo is coming back to us after he arranges his affairs
in China. He says he wishes to attach himself to us for
life, which alarms us a good deal, for he has already shown
symptoms of becoming the old attached servant. At Apemama he was very ill once. Instead of telling us he went
on like a martyr, an extremely sullen martyr, and when
Louis finally spoke sharply to him he became rigid with
dignity, replying, " Yes, Mr. Stevenson, I heard you. I
very sick : more better you get a knife and come kill me

P

now. I no can work," after which he retired to the kitchen and wept miserably. The moment a servant begins martyrdom is the moment, I fear, to part. Very soon the martyr is an absolute monarch, and the family are his slaves. Ah Foo having learned English from people who issued orders knows nothing about making a request: the effect on strangers must be very extraordinary when he comes into the room where Louis is and abruptly orders him out. The stretch of politeness is " more better you go now." To this manner please add the appearance of an unusually stalwart pirate.

' I wish you could have seen the countenance of the captain of the schooner when Ah Foo issued orders to him ; between surprise, anger and bewilderment he was absolutely dumb, and to the last day on board he was still unprepared and at Ah Foo's mercy. At this moment Ah Foo is away developing a photograph of Louis' private secretary, his first attempt at photography alone. If we can get a print in time I will enclose one. The secretary who usually comes clad in an undershirt and a strip of curtain stuff is gorgeous in the photograph with all sorts of finery. The undershirt is cast aside, leaves are bound round his loins, beads and parti-coloured leaves are twisted through his hair, and round his neck he has a borrowed chief's necklace of large white teeth, to say nothing of a bead bracelet borrowed from a lady. He looks much better in these borrowed plumes than when dressed as the secretary. He is a full blooded native, and the stupidest I know. We have another acquaintance—I do not know whether to call him a friend or not, an exceedingly clever fellow named Sitione. Sitione is a redoubtable warrior, and is covered with scars and wounds, one very bad one in the shoulder still not out of the dangerous state. I would betray Sitione's confidence to no one but you. When he thought, and we thought we were about to leave Samoa for ever, while talking about the likelihood of more trouble with the Germans, he told me that at the very beginning the Samoans meant to fall upon the whites and massacre all, friends and foes alike, fire the town, and take to the bush where they would become wild people again. A few days ago Louis was speaking to him about our projected house and said that he meant to make it very strong in case of another war. Sitione was very much embarrassed and hardly knew where to look. I am trying to make a little portrait of him (he is a handsome fellow) but the difficulties are very great. In the first place the paints become liquid in the heat, and run like water. Then I have only two old brushes, little camel hair brushes in the last stage of moulting. I mean to try to learn something about water colours, but fear the difficulties may be insurmountable. I had a sort of hurdy gurdy hand organ which Sitione coveted and wished to buy from me. He first came with a present of a kava bowl that I know cost him fifteen dollars ; that was followed by a spear that cost five ; and still the music box remained under Ah Foo's bed. Apparently becoming alarmed lest he lose that and his costly presents too, he began to haunt the premises with little baskets. He was rapidly falling away and growing haggard with anxiety, so yesterday the music box was handed over to him ; and now I expect to see him no more, and my poor little portrait must remain as it is. Among other interesting offerings he brought a photograph of himself which he was careful to inform me cost a dollar. Unfortunately it does not look in the least like him, but his costume of leaves and flowers and his sister's silver necklace and locket is gorgeous in the extreme.

'Since the departure of the madman we have had two more visitors ; the resident missionary of the London Missionary Society, and a Catholic priest. In Honolulu there was a missionary whom we liked very much, and here is another, almost his twin, a very clever and interesting man —and—the odd thing is they look like you, have much of your manners and speak with your voice. This man is English, named Clarke, the other—the superior one, an

American named Damon. Perhaps you have missed your true *spear* and should by rights be building coral churches in cannibal Islands. Speaking of cannibalism reminds me of a gruesome thing told me by a native in the bush where I stayed for a couple of weeks. During the war whenever a German or a Tamesese man was killed his head was cut off and carried off as a trophy. If the man wasn't dead but only wounded, they killed him. The head, when cut off, was taken up by the teeth of the conqueror, and brought in as a dog fetches a bone.

' I have belied my Sitione, for this moment he sends in a lot of fresh fish, every colour of the rainbow. It must have been a savage sight when Sitione had a head in his teeth. We were alarmed the other day at the condition of his wound, and rather advised him to go to the German doctor who is an excellent surgeon. He explained that he was waiting for our English man-of-war to come in, intending to ask the ship's surgeon to perform the operation. He had the greatest confidence in the German's skill, but feared his vengeance. As Sitione said, when he was unconscious with chloroform, and the doctor stood over him knife in hand it was but natural that he should remember some of the incidents of the war, and very possible that the knife might be used at least roughly. Louis went round to the chemist who dresses Sitione's shoulder, and he assured them both that it was perfectly safe to wait yet longer. " How did you get that scar on your temple, Sitione ? " I asked. " I was drunk, and fight ; get cut with spear." " And those scars on your side ? " " Some man shoot me there." " And these ? " " Oh that some kind of sickness." The kava bowl is a really beautiful thing, carved with six legs, from a solid piece of wood, and coated over the inside with the kava—stain is hardly the word. *I* have drunk kava, but noticed no effect whatever, though I took at least a teacup full. If you know the taste of burgundy pitch that is its flavour exactly.

' More visitors : a young lady of ten or thereabouts (ten

here is equal to fourteen in England) at each door, singing, and twisting their pretty little hands about.   In the bush I used to have a little party every evening : three lovely little seraphs, and one grown girl of extraordinary beauty. They sat in a row on the floor, a fine little naked boy within reach in case they became embarrassed, when he received a sounding slap.   As long as I let them stay they sang and danced like little angels.   A handkerchief round the loins, and wreaths, was the evening dress, except for the young lady, who generally came in a cotton chemise.   Once or twice she made a morning call in a piece of gunny sack, but never without a handkerchief tied round her neck by the two side corners so that the square end covered her breast.   I am sorry to say that this lovely creature, Zosephina by name, caused me considerable annoyance.   Louis and Lloyd went off with a couple of missionaries to visit a school at least four hours' sail from Apia.   At the same time Miss Zosephina disappeared, whereupon her mother demanded compensation from me, declaring that Lloyd had levanted with her.   One morning almost before break of day a native policeman appeared at the kitchen door and demanded Ah Foo's body on a charge of conspiracy and abduction.   Ah Foo refused to move until I had my breakfast when he went down to Apia and appeared before the native magistrate.   The verdict was two dollars fine for Zosephina's mother, and Ah Foo was advised to kick any of the family who showed themselves.   Zosephina returned in a short time to the bosom of her family, looking haggard and battered, and as though she had drunk for a week, but resolutely refusing to give any account of her absence.   I am assured that I shall like the natives very much when I really know them : perhaps I may, but I have my doubts.   They are a very different people from the Marquesans, the Tahitians, or even the Low Islanders, all of whom I liked, and many of whom I loved.

' Would you could see the flag I designed (made on board an American man of war) for our admirable king Tembinok'.

It has three crosswise stripes, orange, red and green : (he is king of 3 Islands) across these is an immense black shark (the royal family claim to be descended from a shark) with open mouth, white teeth, and a white eye with a black pupil. I mean to make him also a palace flag, and a coat of arms with the motto " I bite triply." Of all the kings I have met, and funny as it sounds I have met a great many, he is the most kingly. . . .

' You must not think that life on board the *Equator* was unmitigated misery ; on the contrary there were many mitigations. We had two birthday celebrations, one Louis', for which we killed our pig, a present from a native missionary in Bartatui, drank champagne, toasting all our friends, and sang songs prepared for the occasions. Then we fished for sharks, a wildly exciting sport ; I felt no qualms about killing the shark ; I even caught one myself, and have his teeth as a trophy. There were times when large sharks were hanging all round the vessel. One day a big fellow that we thought was dead suddenly leaped upon the deck knocking Ah Foo down, and was very near going down the companion way. Every few days Ah Foo speared one or more albacores, or dolphins or porpoise amidst the wildest enthusiasm. Even the chance of ship- wreck was a stirring thing ; the captain declared that I was bitterly disappointed that it didn't come off, and I had to unmake my parcels of shawls and medicines. The night we were prepared to take to the boats I held the ship's cat in my arms all night lest she might be forgotten in the confusion. We played cards in the evening and gambled for cowrie shells, and I became quite an expert at a game with draughts. The captain and Lloyd sang, and Lloyd played upon his little Hawaiian guitar accompanied by Joe on a real guitar. Louis' pipe lost its voice which was a misfortune. Sometimes the consul and Mr. Seward sang, and often we could get much amusement from the singing of the crew. The captain was an excellent story teller, and the greatest fun when he did not mean to be ; so altogether, in spite of bad weather, cockroaches the size of toads, which gnawed our nails and noses, and pulled our eyelashes while we slept, and the ravages of another insect which shall be nameless (he necessitates the use of a fine toothed comb) we passed the time more agreeably than you would think. Still there were hardships that we could not have borne a great while longer.'

Mrs. R. L. S. to Mrs. Sitwell. From Samoa [? 1892] : 'Louis' cousin, Graham Balfour, is here still, to our great pleasure, for we like him extremely. He fits into the family as naturally as though he had been born there, and it will be a wrench when he goes. He says he will come back, but I know what will happen ; he will marry somebody, and we 'll hate his wife, and there 'll be the end of it ; for of course if we hate his wife he must hate us. When he gets back to London you must all see him. He is the most reticent person in the world, so please make him talk to you ; you can do that if anybody can. I wonder what the paragraph in all the papers means about Louis being made consul ? I wish it might be true, and so do most people.'

CHAPTER XVI

COLVIN AS STEVENSON'S LONDON REPRESENTATIVE

1887–1894

AFTER Tilbury, although Colvin was to see Stevenson no more, his association with him may be said in a way to have become closer; because it was upon Colvin that the onus of finding publishers and editors for the books and articles coming from the Pacific was to rest. Never can an unofficial and unpaid agent have shown more devotion or zeal. Colvin, I am convinced, was, for himself, a poor bargainer : he had no financial genius or even talent ; but when it was a case of making money for his R. L. S. he became almost Semitic.

The one whose real duty it was to carry on such negotiations was Charles Baxter, who was Stevenson's accredited man of affairs ; but Baxter was a cheerful delegator. Colvin, however, although thus given a free hand, felt it incumbent upon him to let Baxter know what was happening, and in a series of letters lasting from 1887 until 1894 he reported progress. After Baxter's death these came back into Colvin's possession, and it is through reading them that I have realized to the full how diligent was this self-sacrificing London representative of the exile author. Most of them are too technical and commercial to be worth quotation ; they are largely taken up with balancing the merits and demerits, cautiousness or gambling tendencies, of various London and New York publishers. One or two, however, must be mentioned. Here, for example, is Colvin's report on the first night of Stevenson and Henley's high comedy, so agreeable to read in the armchair, *Beau Austin*,

which Beerbohm Tree produced at the Haymarket Theatre
on November 3, 1890 :—

' British Museum, London, W.C., Nov. 4, 1890.

' MY DEAR BAXTER,—Here in as few words as possible
are my impressions of the Beau. Please hand them to
Henley if he cares to know them.—A packed and picked
audience of people, very favourable to the authors, and
miles above the average intelligence of the British public :
with this audience, the piece was a fair *succès d'estime* :
not more. During the first three acts it promised to become
more : people were thoroughly interested and attentive,
even moved and pleased, though there was very little
applause : but the fourth act was quite ineffective. This
was to my mind mainly due to bad stage management.
The Pantiles were far too much in the country : there was
no attempt at a crowd, or at getting any effect out of their
emotions as onlookers, on which of course the whole moral
force of the situation depends : not more than 8 or 10
people on the stage all told (and a ridiculous dummy Duke
of York), staring like stuck pigs.—Also Tree, though he
was well got up and not vulgar, and did the courtly cere-
monious part of the business well enough, had no ease, no
passion, no gallantry even : but played with immense study
in a monotonous solemn key : the broken spirit and contrite heart kind of business, without a break, from the
moment his deceased friend the Colonel is mentioned. One
simply sate longing for Delaunay.—Mrs. Tree very fair in
the quiet parts : quite screamily feeble and commonplace
in the more powerful. Young Terry acted much the best.
The greatest disappointment was Brookfield, whose Men-
teith (make-up and all) was a kind of heavy Sam Weller.—
In a word, the actors all except one, though evidently
trying hard to do their best, were totally inefficient : and
the stage management of the fourth act was ruinous.—
Nevertheless, with that audience, the play, until the fourth
act, gave a great deal of enjoyment, and was followed with

keen interest : if hardly with enthusiasm. My impression is that with the same audience and good actors it would be a very great success : but that with an average audience and those actors it can be no success at all. In haste,—Yours ever,   SIDNEY COLVIN '

Stevenson thought very little of *Deacon Brodie*, but, made enthusiastic by Henley, had settled down, in his early days at Bournemouth in 1884-5, to more dramatic work with the same collaborator. There is a list in his handwriting of no fewer than sixteen plays—historical plays, comedies and melodramas—of which only two, after *Deacon Brodie*, came to fruition : *Beau Austin* and *Admiral Guinea*. At either Irving's or Beerbohm Tree's suggestion they wrote also *Macaire*, although it was never produced.

I omit all the letters referring merely to business details or to news from Samoa, and come to the last of the series, which deal, in the spring of 1894, with the plans for the limited *de luxe* edition of Stevenson's writings known as the *Edinburgh*, which was to bring in enough money to allay for ever the anxiety as to ways and means that seems to have continually brooded over the Samoan household. The following letter is a good specimen of Colvin's practical clear-headedness :—

' *April* 20/94, *British Museum.*

' MY DEAR BAXTER,—Enclosures duly posted to the respective publishers this morning. The thing seems to have made a quite first-rate beginning ; and if L. is £4000 or £5000 the richer by this time two years, you will indeed have served him well.—I had sent off a list of a preliminary notice to the *Athenæum*, but wrote off at once to stop it on receipt of your telegram : am glad I thought of consulting you on the point.—

' As to embellishments,—initials & tail-pieces may be dropped without a pang : even about frontispieces I am not so keen, if the edition promises to go as well without them : but I think at the same time it *would* be a help (and

perhaps enable you to ask a higher price—or is the question
of price settled ?) if we could get a really good emblematic
& decorative frontispiece to each volume. — There are
several young designers who might turn out work of the
kind I have in mind : notably Anning Bell : but must it,
in accordance with your plan & prospectus, necessarily be
a Scotchman?   Anning Bell may be that for aught I
know : if not, I could enquire for one who is among the
½ dozen men who are doing good work in black & white of
the kind I want.—

'Please answer as to the question of nationality, also
whether you would authorize me to have a trial design
made for one of the books—to be paid for whether used or
not—but only to be used, and the rest gone on with, if we
are both fully agreed as to its fitness ?   Don't forget also
to answer about *Catriona* map.—Yours,   S. C.'

Six days later Colvin wrote : ' Nationality apart, this is
the man to whom on artistic grounds I should give first
trial.

' What do you say ?

The following letter from the ' man ' himself was
enclosed :—

' 98 *Warner Rd., Camberwell, April* 26, '94.

' DEAR MR. COLVIN,—Unfortunately I cannot claim any
Scottish blood to my knowledge, but my knowledge on the
subject is slight and is soon lost in the mystery which wraps
the clan of Cockaigne ; the name, of course, is Scotch or at
any rate north country.

' Your project seems a charming one and I should very
much like to have a share in it.   If your colleagues will pass
me as " presumably Scottish," and I am beginning to feel
sure that I am—I am sure you will give me early information as to the details of size and shape, etc. of the work you
want from me, as I should like plenty of time to consider
it, before I make the first drawing—a fortnight or three
weeks say ;—perhaps it would be better if I could meet

you so that we might discuss it.—Believe me—Very
sincerely yours,   ROBERT ANNING BELL.

'*P.S.*—I now feel quite convinced that I am of Scottish
origin—!'

'*British Museum, London, W.C., Oct.* 13, 1894.

'MY DEAR BAXTER,—I 've a letter from R. L. S. with a
message for you : doubtless by way of supplement to what
he has written you himself.—" I forgot to tell Baxter that
the dummy had turned up and is a fine personable looking
volume and very good reading. Please communicate this
to him."—

'He also says the following about his work : as to which
I want to consult you. " I have been trying hard to get
along with *St. Ives.*—I should now lay it aside for a year
& I daresay I should make something of it after all. Instead
of that I have to kick against the pricks, and break myself,
& spoil the book, if there was ever anything to spoil : which
I am far from saying. Let nobody pitch into me about
St. Ives, or the Lord have mercy on his soul. I 'm as sick
of the damned thing as ever you can be ; it 's a rudderless
hulk, it 's a pagoda, & you can just feel—or I can feel—
that it might have been a pleasant story, if it had only been
blessed at baptism."

'Now this seems to me very serious. He 's not likely
to be wrong.—It 's a thousand pities he couldn't be told
to lay it aside comfortably for the present : all his best
work has been done with these gaps.—And the present
is rather a turning-point in his career. A failure—which
should be *not* a collaboration, & on his old adventure lines
—would do him permanent harm ; and lower his prices
as well as his reputation for good.—In the long run it would
doubtless be much best, for his *fortune* as well as his fame,
if this thing could be kept till he can get into the vein again.
—Now, how does the £ s. d. question really stand ? I
know he makes you anxious by overdrawing : but with
this sum of £5000 actually certain by means of the Ed. ed.,

and with his mother's income of £1200 a year or whatever it is, is there any real cause for anxiety ?—When will the Ed. ed. money be beginning to roll in ?—and could not a publisher or someone be got to advance whatever is necessary to meet his wants, on such absolutely certain security as that is ?

' Do please turn the thing over most carefully in your mind. Publisher's disappointments in the present should count as nothing against the ulterior harm of bringing out work that would make people say he was played out. *The Ebb-Tide*, ugly as it may be, can't make them say *that*.—

' You of course, and you only, know how his business affairs stand, but from my point of view (and that is not the literary only but the mercantile one too) it would pay much better to be able to wire him, " Let *St. Ives* slide for the present "—even if it had to be done at the cost of mortgaging part of his reversion—than that he should have to wring it out of himself with the distress he is evidently now suffering,—and at the cost of its quality.'

Two months later Stevenson was dead.

The ' Edinburgh ' edition, one of the finest complete sets of his work that any author ever had, consisted of twenty-eight volumes, and steadily grew to be more and more desired by collectors. It was not so much illustrated as decorated, and Mr. Anning Bell was among the contributors.

CHAPTER XVII

STEVENSON'S DEATH; THE *VAILIMA LETTERS*, *WEIR OF HERMISTON*, AND THE *CORRESPONDENCE*

1894–1899

ROBERT LOUIS STEVENSON died suddenly, in Samoa, on October 3, 1894, aged forty-four. Although his life may be said to have hung always by a thread, the news of his death came as a shock, not less to his friends than to strangers. If it is no exaggeration to say that thousands upon thousands of English-speaking people had the sense of a personal bereavement, it may be imagined how lost were such intimates as Colvin and Mrs. Sitwell.

Among the letters I find one from Burne-Jones to Mrs. Sitwell: 'I fear it is too true that news from Samoa— & I am quite miserable to-day—I have sent a wretched little note to Sidney—& I send a howl to you—about your note. I will answer it—day or two—this news has sickened me—for I wanted him to live for ever.'

Mrs. Fleeming Jenkin wrote :—

'*Dec.* 18.

'MY DEAR MR. COLVIN,—You will—I am sure—forgive me for troubling you—even today—with a few lines. It seems that we must believe this terrible news—that it is really true—& in the midst of my own sorrow my thoughts turn constantly to you. To Louis & to you I owe so much —the memorial to my husband—the work of his faithful friendship & of yours—has been my great comfort in all these years—& thus I must always think of Louis and of you together.

' Then I have loved Louis so well for 26 years, that I seem to guess at your loss through my own—& more than that—I have heard him speak of you many, many times —& so I know something of the other side of that great loss—the loss of being loved—as well as of loving.

' Please let me offer you the sympathy of a very grateful —& of oh ! a very sad heart.

' Do not write—if you will pardon my writing, it is all I want.—Yours most sincerely,   ANNE JENKIN '

From S. R. Lysaght, the Irish poet :—

' *Walton Park Hotel, Clevedon, Somerset, Jan.* 7, 1895.

' MY DEAR MR. COLVIN,—So great was his power of winning love that though I knew him for less than a week I could have borne the loss of many a more intimate friend with less sorrow than Stevenson's. Except for a short note from San Francisco I did not write since I left Samoa, and it is now a weight on my mind that I might have appeared careless or neglectful. The truth was that I thought there was no hurry and was always waiting for some supreme happy mood before I wrote to him—I began once or twice and stopped, thinking " No—no ordinary humour will do for this letter " ; and now my only consolation is that he was a man of such discernment and generosity as to know that I loved him truly and not to interpret my silence for indifference. Coupled with the sorrow of such friends as yourself my own is almost an impertinence, and yet, though I was with him for less than a week, I know that I may be numbered among those who truly loved him and who truly sorrow.

' Of you he spoke to me with a glow—a joy in remembrance, an exhilaration in the thought of my telling you of his surroundings, a deep friendship touching to me at the time and tenfold so now.

' I suppose I am almost the last English friend who saw him—and when I saw him last Easter, there was no suggestion of failure of strength—After all I had heard of his delicacy I was astonished at his vigour—He was up at 5 and at work soon after, and at eleven o'clock at night he was dancing on the floor of the big room while I played Scotch and Irish reels on the rickety piano. He would talk to me for hours of home and old friends, but with a wonderful cheerfulness—knowing himself banished from them for life and yet brought close to them by love. I confidently counted on his living—he took a keen interest in my own poor work and it was one of my ambitions to send him a book some day which would better deserve his attention. But my own sorrow and regret I feel can be nothing in comparison with those who, like yourself, have been knitted to him by years of love. But as I have lost my chance of writing to him, it is some relief to write to you, his dearest friend, and say that I also am among those who mourn,—Believe me, dear Mr. Colvin,—Very sincerely yours, SIDNEY ROYSE LYSAGHT.'

And here is a letter from Stevenson's mother, who was staying at Vailima when the fatal hemorrhage occurred :—

'*Vailima, Apia, Samoa, Feb.* 4, 1895.

' MY DEAR MR. COLVIN,—I thank you with all my heart for your most kind & affectionate letter. We all knew how you would mourn with us as well as for us in our grievous & irreparable loss. It is just two months today since that sad procession up Vaea mountain took place & the blank seems as fresh as ever & as impossible to realise. My own life is plucked up by the roots a second time & I feel as if I could never take any further interest in anything except in the dear and precious memory. It is soothing to find how universally my beloved child was appreciated & how thoroughly his loving nature was understood & yet it accentuates our loss. I know that I have much to be thankful for but Oh ! I long for my boy. I can't be thankful enough that I returned when I did & brought him all that he wanted from the old home & had the privilege of spending the last six months in his loved society. They were very happy months, he was much pleased with his house & enjoyed the society of the officers of the *Curaçao* who were always coming & going & he was just like a boy among them. He used to say that the Captain treated him as if he were " a slightly superior middy." When I arrived I thought he was working too much & I tried hard to persuade him to take a complete rest for a year, quoting A. K. H. B. about the risks of 45—but he would not listen to me & said that he must work. I am afraid he did not quite understand the telegram, he rather feared that the bargain about *St. Ives* was off altogether & that made him plunge into *Hermiston* but he seemed at the last to be working easily & with keen enjoyment. We all did our best to spare him but God willed it otherwise & we must submit & try to be resigned.

' Dr. Funk told me that death was caused by apoplexy followed by paralysis of the lungs. Fanny thought that he had said paralysis of the brain which led to some confusion in the first reports.

' Mr. Baxter arrived on 31st Jany. What a different visit it is from what we had all anticipated ! He brought us our copies of the 2 first vols. of the Edinr. Edition with which we are all much pleased. It did seem hard that my dear Lou should not even see it & that he should lose Mr. Baxter's visit which he had looked forward to with so much pleasure. What a life of disappointments he had from his earliest years & how nobly he bore them ! Now he is reaping his reward. Many thanks for promising to send all the extracts from the papers about him. I have begun an *In Memoriam* volume—it is my 7th volume of Reviews.

' Feby 24th. mail time draws near & I must finish my letters. I have now made up my mind to return home. I think my sister needs me more than anybody else so I hope to leave Samoa a month hence & to sail from Sydney by the Orient steamer *Orizaba*. I shall be in London for a few

Q

days with Mr. & Mrs. Black, 7 Petersham Terrace & I hope I shall get a sight of you if you are in town. I am sorry to tell you that Lloyd has at last taken this dengue fever that has been prevalent in Samoa for about 4 months. We hoped that we were to escape but last Wednesday Loia was suddenly struck down & he is in a very weak state. We feel anxious about him as he really never has been quite himself since our great trouble which told very heavily on him poor boy. I shall leave a line to give you the latest news.

'Feby 26th mail day. I am very glad to tell you that Lloyd seems decidedly better, he asked for an egg for breakfast today, almost the first thing that he has eaten. Fanny & Belle are both pretty well worn out with nursing him so they may not be able to write to you but we all unite in kindest regards & best thanks for much appreciated sympathy,—I am ever yours truly & affecty

'M. I. STEVENSON'

Colvin's first task in 1895 was to prepare for publication the *Vailima Letters*, which had been exclusively addressed to him. In the current editions of the Correspondence they are sorted into their natural places, but for some years they stood alone, and indeed they should perhaps still stand alone, for they are often rather more like epistolary essays than the familiar pen gossip of the less self-conscious correspondence which was to be published later.

Colvin, who calls them 'journal-letters,' thus, in his editorial preface, explains the situation : ' They occupy a place quite apart in his correspondence, and in any general selection from his letters would fill a quite disproportionate space. Begun without a thought of publicity, and simply to maintain our intimacy undiminished, so far as might be, by separation, they assumed in the course of two or three years a bulk so considerable, and contained so much of the matter of his daily life and thoughts, that it by and by occurred to him that " some kind of a book " might be extracted out of them after his death. It is this passage which has given me my warrant for their publication, and at the same time has imposed on me no very easy editorial task.'

Colvin also says : ' It belonged to the richness of his nature to repay in all things much for little, ἑκατόμβοι' ἐννεαβοίων, and from these early relations sprang both the affection, to me inestimable, of which the following correspondence bears evidence, and the habit, which it pleased him to maintain after he had become one of the acknowledged masters of English letters, of confiding in and consulting me about his work in progress. It was my business to find fault ; to " damn " what I did not like ; a duty which, as will be inferred from the following pages, I was accustomed to discharge somewhat unsparingly. But he was too manly a spirit to desire or to relish flattery, and too true an artist to be content with doing less than his best : he knew, moreover, in what rank of English writers I put him, and for what audience, not of to-day, I would have him labour. *Tibi Palinure*—so, in the last weeks of his life, he proposed to inscribe to me a set of his collected works. Not Palinurus so much as Polonius may perhaps—or so I sometimes suspect—have been really the character ; but his own amiable view of the matter has to be mentioned in order to account for part of the tenor of the following correspondence.'

I find Andrew Lang writing thus, after he had read the book, probably in proof : ' Next to nothing to mark. It seems to me odd that while Thackeray's shortest note was written in his own manner, there is next to nothing of what R. L. S. calls " style " in his letters. It seems to have been hard work for him to write as he did in print, or else a wind that blew as it listed, not a kind of expression he could not express himself without. *This* remark is far from lucid or elegant. The Samoan politics, like all politics, are a bore, luckily there is not much of them. How could he teach decimals to a child of nature ! To myself they could not be taught, not with tears of blood. I find it very inter-

esting as to character and landscape—it was not all beer
and breadfruit ; as we fancied. The South Sea Letters
were very hard reading, as well as hard writing, obviously
because it was a commission. I daresay you have left out
the best bits.' [1]

Colvin's next task, concurrently with the amassing and
arranging of the correspondence, was the publication of
Stevenson's unfinished romance, *Weir of Hermiston*. *St.
Ives*, also unfinished, had been entrusted to Mr. (now Sir)
Arthur Quiller-Couch, for completion, and I find a number
of letters from ' Q ' to Colvin on various points of difficulty. *St. Ives* was in a different class from *Weir of Hermiston*, and there was a definite reason for finishing it,
because it was already running as a serial in a magazine.
Among those friends to whom Colvin showed *Weir of
Hermiston* were J. M. Barrie, Andrew Lang, Henry James,
and W. E. Henley.

Henley wrote :—

' 9 *The Terrace, Barnes, S.W.*, 4/11/95.

' DEAR COLVIN,—Herewith, by registered post, the type-
written copy of *Weir of Hermiston*. I knew not that it
was so immediately wanted, so, being very busy indeed with
Burns, I did not open the parcel till your letter came this
middle-day.

' I have read it all : in parts perfunctorily, I fear ; but
mostly with great admiration. When it comes off—as in
the scene between Hermiston & Archie, after the scandal ;
in the wonderful chapter of the falling in love ; & in that
meeting—the last—by the Covenanter's Stone : it seems
to me the best he did. The characters of the two Kirsties,
too, are admirable, in conception & in drawing alike ; &
old Hermiston is a most notable piece of ventriloquism. I
doubt not that I should find much else to praise in a less
hurried reading ; but for the present this may suffice to
show that I 've found my Lewis again, & in all his glory,
in this the last work of his hand.

[1] In the Fitzwilliam Museum.

' On the other hand, I am really distressed to find that the thing—which I 'd heard was a more or less complete work—is but the first, the opening, chapters of a book ; is, in fact, a fragment, which cannot, by any stretch of words known to me, be described as anything else.   The story, as sketched by Mrs. Strong, is all to come : As yet, we have but the preliminaries—the preliminaries just posited & no more ; with the characters deploying into line to meet the first big situation—which is, the killing of Innes—the pivot on which the whole tremendous business of the consummation is to turn.   How Lewis would have worked that out, it is not for any of us to guess ; & I shall only say that all that business of the rescue & the flight to foreign lands appears to me altogether unworthy of the admirable beginning : as if he had made up his mind to deal with a piece of tragedy—extremely well finished in the later relations between Hermiston & his son, as in Hermiston's nickname, reputation, character, everything ; & had then, in a mental funk, declined to face the consequences & bolted off down a high way of the romance of adventure ; where he was altogether at home, & by which, as he knew, he could take his public with him to an ending which, for all its decoration of unconventionality, is essentially as conventional as they 're made.

' For this reason—(you haven't asked my advice ; but I make bold to give it)—I should print the thing as *a fragment, et praeterea nil* : &—this especially—I should decline to add a word as to the probable course of the story, which I should leave exactly as Dickens left *Edwin Drood,* a delightful & absorbing exercise to the imagination of everybody that reads it.   This for reasons which you can gather from what I 've written above ; & for this other : which is a big one :—that the tremendous situation up to which the story 's made & the book written—which is, in fact, the sole *motif* of the *Weir of Hermiston*—is lifted, bodily, from *Paul Clifford.*   Lewis knew the book, & we 've often discussed the situation : as we 've often discussed its possibilities for the theatre. (He wrote a play called *The Hanging Judge* in collaboration with his wife : in which the Judge was called on to sentence his wife's first husband.) And in any case, you, as editor, will have to face the music, & acknowledge his indebtedness ; if but to stop the mouth & forestall the brag of the average Ass. Surely, it were a thousand times better to do as I say ; & leave him smiling from the grave (as it were) in the face of a delighted & wondering audience, in the contentment of one who has something to say that none else can grasp, & that will never be said by anyone, since he, the only one to know, is stricken dumb ?

' I hope this view of the matter may commend itself to you. In any case, if I can be of use to you in the matter of the dialect (I am rather good at Scotch just now), I shall be glad to do my best. I think Lewis mistaken in writing " *ci*veelity " " *po*alatics," & the like, for they are English words, & the accent should, as in *Kidnapped* & *Catriona*, be taken for granted. Indeed, I 'm pretty sure that had Lewis revised these pages, he 'd have reverted to the sounder method. For the rest, you 'll find that, here & there, I 've ventured on an emendation. There 's but one l in " bailie " (—a magistrate). If you write " nee*gh*bours " instead of " neebors " you make the " gh " a guttural : which is absurd. Kirstie Junior could never have been " Lady Harmiston " ; the Scots law lordships are for the wearers alone ; Hermiston's wife was Mrs. Weir, & Archie would have been plain Weir of Hermiston. There are other points, I think, to which I might take exception ; but these are all I can recall just now. Excepting this : that " tragic meanness " occurs in a book of poetry I know, & should either be set in quotation marks, or changed. It occurs in the account of the hanging. " Antient blackness," in the chapter where Kirstie goes into Archie's bedroom, sounds to my accustomed ear like a reminiscence of another book of poetry, the work of the same master. But I haven't time to verify the suspicion.—Sincerely yours,

'W. E. H.'

Henley on *Weir of Hermiston* again, the next day : ' We know how Lewis worked : we know that no story ever passed through his hands without a hundred changes. We know that this is practically a first draft, and, knowing this, we may fairly confess to knowing nothing of the final tenour & the final form. I am utterly convinced (for one thing) that he did not make the elder Kirsty the extraordinary piece of womanhood she is merely to tell stories & hunger for Archie. Even as I am utterly convinced that he would, in the end, have gone back on all that business of the Four Black Brothers & the rescue, & faced his problem like a man.

' I am not sure that even he would have succeeded in making out a plausible excuse for Hermiston's determination to preside at his son's trial. Whatever Hermiston might have resolved, he would have had the whole Bench against him ; and Scotland was not so Roman as to tolerate the spectacle of a father enforcing the law (with a rope's end) against his son. In Bulwer, if I remember aright, the situation is less violently approached : in fact, is possible. We shall never know if it would ever have been that in R. L. S. What we do know is that we know—nothing at all. Nothing, at any rate, except that at a given moment he had such & such designs ; & that he might have [? reversed] these designs (as he was in the habit of doing) at any other moment, if any other moment had ever come.'

And again :—

' 9 *The Terrace, Barnes, S.W.,* 10/11/95.

' DEAR COLVIN,—A last tip (I may have sent it but I forget) : *The Hanging Judge* idea was suggested by a story in Sheridan Lefanu's *Through a Glass Darkly* ; a book for which R. L. S. had a profound respect. *I* brought it on the cloth, as a *motif* for a play. One was written (as I said), & submitted to Beerbohm T. But it came to nothing ; & it wasn't for years that he (Lewis) took up the Hanging Judge thing, & incarnated it in McQueen of Braxfield, who is Weir of Hermiston.

' Note, too, that the name " Weir " had a special significance for Lewis : as being the name of one Major Weir, who was called a Warlock, & was burned (together with his sister : with whom he was accused of incest) under circumstances of peculiar atrocity ; & whose fame was long a dreadful yet an integral part of the romance of Edinburgh. —Yours sincerely, W. E. H.'

Sir (then Mr.) J. M. Barrie wrote thus : ' I have read it with a delight beyond words and with a growing pain such as I never felt when reading a book before. For it is incomparably the best thing he ever did, and it is but a noble fragment. I think of the preface to *Prince Otto*, and here it seems to me that he *has* done it, here is the big book. The Edin^h. life, the Black Brothers, these are on the " bow wow " scale of Scott that he never touched before, and yet it is the women that surprise me. The rest is what I always supposed he could do, but I never believed he could do the women. The mother is more surprising to me than Braxfield, and the two Kirsties also. He seemed hitherto to be afraid of himself when writing of women, to doubt his own sincerity, so to speak ; Catriona was an exquisite child and Barbara Grant a fine treatment from the outside ; but here he gets " into " the very heart of woman, best of all in the last paragraph. Was not that what he wrote last ? And is it not a pleasure to know that he knew how good it was and went to his wife to tell her ? All day I have been thinking over the amanuensis details, and seeing in a vague way what a magnificent story was under weigh.

' It is most disappointing to hear that the publication is delayed. I 'll send it to Lang. . . . Do come early this week and let us talk about it.—Yours ever,

' J. M. BARRIE ' [1]

And here is Henry James :—

' 34 *De Vere Gardens, W., July 5th*, 1895.

' MY DEAR COLVIN,—Now that you have been so good as to let me read *W. of H.* you must also let me add a word

[1] In the Fitzwilliam Museum.

to what I said to you a day or two since in sending you back the MS. It weighs on my spirit greatly that there should, as I gathered from what you said, be a danger that the publication of this magnificent thing may be postponed to treat of other things—may not take place until the "psychological moment" is passed. And you didn't even tell me *why*—I mean what will be *gained* by this dreadful delay. I can't tell you how I hope so grave a mistake won't be made. Surely Mrs. Stevenson doesn't desire it ? Has she expressed any such wish ? The moment for the book to appear seems to me, overwhelmingly, to be the moment at which the emotion caused by Louis's death, & by the general knowledge that he had left a great piece, a supreme piece, of work unfinished, keeps the imagination of the public still *warm* about him and makes the work count double as a contribution to his fame. For God's sake let us have in this year of his death the thing he was so splendidly doing when he died ! It will deepen immeasurably all our sense of loss—& that sense of loss will add to our tenderness for the other things. If those come first (did you tell me there are 2 of them ?) the sense of loss will —as they are inferior—be cruelly less, & the whole air cold for *Hermiston* when it does come. I must tell you frankly that I should regard that as a great calamity & a grave unkindness to his memory. I can't imagine any reason for our taking the other things first that is not a reason of an order altogether inferior to this consideration that touches so the very essence of Louis's *honour* ! Do let me say to you very positively that I hope you will do everything in your power to make it easy as possible that *Hermiston* shall come to us with all the sacred beauty of its *hour* : & do above all let me hear if Mrs. Louis *has* pronounced.-- Yours, my dear Colvin, ever,   HENRY JAMES '

And again : ' If his [Burlingame of *Scribner's*] contention is just that the publication of *Hermiston* (I mean the success of the same) can be helped by any reference to my high

opinion of the fragment, he is highly welcome to make that
reference in any way in which you may have assented, or be
disposed to assent, to any similar reference to your own
pronouncement.   I shall be comforted by the company
and the cause.   Will you kindly say this to him—in anything you may be saying on the matter ? '

Weir of Hermiston came out in 1896, with Colvin's admirable Epilogue summing up the probabilities as to its
ending.

The first edition of Stevenson's Letters, the full correspondence, under Colvin's editorship, appeared in 1899,
without the *Vailima Letters*, but in the editions that are
now accessible the *Vailima Letters* are included.

I select a few tributes.

This from J. M. Barrie : ' It is a very triumphant result
and no other man could have done it.   I am saddened to
read your announcement that the biography will not be by
you, but you know how I must feel that you have built a
noble memorial to your friend.   Never was a literary man
with a better friend, and to all who can read between the
lines this will remain your book as well as R. L. S.'s—and a
mighty credit to you both.'

From Andrew Lang : ' The R. L. S. Letters reached me,
for review, in such wise that I had only two hours for the
whole job.   Therefore it is Nothing.   However, I said your
part could not be better done by men or angels, and that
is true, if trite.'

From Lord Carlisle, in January 1900 : ' I left England
just when the Stevenson book came out and so it happened
that I have only just got hold of it and I have now finished
it, to my great regret.   Why were there not six vols. or
better eight ?   That seems to me the only error that you
have made.

' I do congratulate you very sincerely on the way in
which you have succeeded in this delightful work.   I feel
more than ever to love and be charmed by your friend, and
I wish that it had been my luck to know him myself—

though you will likely say, that I do not in these days find
time to see much of the friends that I have—of which I
am only too conscious. . . .

'But I am surprised at your critical inaccuracy. You
state that Sam Bough was a "Scottish" painter. He was
a Carlisle man, although a member of the *Scotch* academy.
This is really equivalent to saying that Leonardo was a
Milanese. And I grieve for the base concession to Scot*tish*.
I observe that when Stevenson was young Scotch was good
enough for him and the later sham-tartan phrase only came
in later.'

From Will H. Low, the American artist and friend of
Stevenson, with regard to his review, in *Scribner's Magazine*,
of Colvin's edition of Stevenson's Letters. After stating that
Colvin, in the Introduction, 'had said all,' he continues:
'and said it—hence this letter—in a way that Louis,
somewhere, must rise and call you blessed. I cannot begin
to tell you in my left-handed way what a deep debt of
gratitude I and all who love R. L. S. are under to you. I
take it that as a rule, though the finished work shows no
trace of it, your writing is more the child of reflection than
spontaneity, but in this case you were surely inspired beyond
yourself. I have read, and re-read within a few months,
your *Keats* with pleasure and profit ; but so lucid, so sym-
pathetically appreciative and so temperate a performance
as the Introduction is not often given as the fruit of any
man's life. And here falls, as R. L. S. would say, a con-
fession which I must make. I have felt, to some degree,
chiefly through the assuring protests in the *Vailima Letters*,
that you had exercised your rights of mentor somewhat
unsparingly at times. But in the light of this last leave-
taking of our much loved friend your attitude seems the
only one you could have taken ; and he from whom we
expected so much knew as well as you that danger muffled
itself in the guise of toleration of aught save his best.
This is an awkward thing to say and is perhaps awkwardly
expressed, but I venture to say it, for I too loved him, with

perhaps a touch of jealousy, but at any rate with a love which took much of the light of life from me when he died.

' I am sorry for the cause of your relinquishing the Life, the more sorry for this foretaste of what it might have been ; but no circumstance of health or engrossing labor can now rob us of this Introduction, which will surely remain as an adequate *résumé* of Stevenson's work.'

Apropos Mr. Low, I am just in time to make an extract or two from his very sympathetic article on Colvin in the *Saturday Review of Literature*, of New York, for June 9, 1928. After remarking that America does not produce the ' exact equivalent ' of a museum official like Colvin, Mr. Low says that, in his own house, he ' gave the impression, rare, I think, among those who follow the hazardous life of literature or the arts, of absolute security, of a life sheltered, protected, and consecrated to those useful adjuncts of civilization, the arts, by the wise beneficence of his people, in full appreciation of the value of the arts, as a part of their national patrimony. I had long been familiar with what I may call a like national attitude in the French social system in regard to arts and letters, but to find it in a nation speaking my own language (with a slightly different accent at times) I thought gratifying, and in Colvin's case I considered its benefits well bestowed.'

The article closes with these words : ' withal, he was, in regard to his own work, exceedingly critical, if not humble, as the extract with which I began would seem to prove, and I am tempted, in conclusion, to quote a passage from a private letter written only a year ago to an American admirer, who moreover did not care for Stevenson : " I am only sorry (Colvin wrote) you do not share my loving admiration of R. L. S., I mean, as a writer, apart from what he earned as a man. In my view all that I have ever written, or tried to write, is not worth as literature any half a dozen casual sentences of his." '

From Marcel Schwob, the French critic : ' Thank you with all my heart for the two beautiful volumes of the

Letters of Stevenson. They are delightful. I have just
finished the first, and it seems to me now that I have known
Stevenson all my life and talked with him. All those who
love Stevenson through his books ought to be very thankful
to you. What a pity you do not write his life! I am so
sorry. . . . I shall try and have articles written on the
' Letters ' in various places. You can rely on me for that.
They are a " Livre de chevet." Never was more delightful
correspondence published.'

From Mrs. Humphry Ward : ' I feel I must send you
a few words of warmest congratulation even before I have
properly read your triumphant & delightful book. Humphry
and I have been snatching it from each other, and I don't
feel that I have done more than nibble as yet. But I have
seen enough to know that it is the book of many years,
that you have done it beautifully, & that it is a lasting
monument first to the most delightful of geniuses, & next
to the kindest of friends. What a bubbling source of life
& joy & humour he was, through all the miseries of the
body !—how good he was to befriend, to have for a friend !
The irrepressible, inexhaustible power of brain that the
book shows, the perpetual inventiveness, fertility and
resource, are only matched by the never-failing charm of
the man, the sweetness of his sincerity and courage and
fun, the pathos of his struggle with weakness & death. I
envy everybody who had to do with him—you & Mrs. Sitwell
and Sir Henley & Sir Gosse—most of all. Well !—he is
indeed placed among the stars, and there is not a human
soul that will not rejoice to see him there, and will not be
grateful to you for your share in the happy indisputable fact.'

One of the most charming letters in the collection is
that which follows, from a young actress who afterwards
became famous as a mimic on both sides of the Atlantic :—

' c/o "Dramatic News," New York, Dec. '99.

' MY DEAR MR. SIDNEY COLVIN,—I doubt if this letter
will ever reach you for I haven't the faintest idea how to

find you but I shall address it to " c/o Scribners " & trust
that they may forward it to you—Not that it will be of
any importance if you ever do get it, for it is only an insignificant word of gratitude, which can mean nothing,
coming from me—but it is deep & sincere & I feel a strong
desire to express it—I have just finished the first volume—
& am well on with the second of *Stevenson's* letters, & they
have given me an aching sense of friendship for him—&
indeed for you to whom so many of them are addressed.
I dread getting to the end of the volume & having to realise
that Stevenson is dead—& there can be no more of them
nor him——I once played " Arethusa " in the production at the Avenue of *Admiral Guinea*—& I have written
some valueless music to a few of the verses from *The Child's
Garden*—and somehow or other—I can't explain why—I feel
as if I knew Stevenson. I don't know why I write to you
to thank you for his Letters—except that they have moved
me & made me ache—& want to speak to some one who was
close to him. I beg you, Sir, to forgive me.—I am sincerely
& honestly—yours, CECILIA LOFTUS '
('CISSIE LOFTUS ')

There are many letters from Sir Arthur Quiller-Couch,
better known as ' Q,' chiefly about little problems that
arose from time to time during his task of completing
Stevenson's unfinished romance *St. Ives*. Now and then
he touches upon more general matters, as, writing from
Fowey (or ' Troy Town ') just after the Diamond Jubilee :
' We performed great feats here on Jubilee Day. I worked
the people up & we lined the streets with trees from end
to end, & put up arches & criss-crossed all between with
lanterns & bunting until I had a mile of green bazaar. And
we fed 1850 handsomely by the waterside (let alone 350
sailors, British & foreign, Swedes, Russians, Italians,
infidels & hereticks), & marched & counter marched by
hundreds in fancy dress under the lanterns, and then danced
till the gunpowder ran out of the heels of our boots.

'The local band under our windows roused us out at 7 a.m. and we crept to bed at 3 a.m. In short, sir, the place went off its head—*and* we hadn't a man drunk: a few merry, but not what-you-may-call-drunk. The town has been shaking hands upon it ever since.'

From Henry Sidgwick, in 1897, on Stevenson's *Lay Morals*, which Colvin seems to have submitted to him in proof: 'I certainly am inclined to regard [it] as of great interest —but rather because it throws light on Stevenson than because it throws light on ethics! It seems to me that the reader of Stevenson's novels soon gets the idea that he has a certain kind of interest in morality, but it often seems to be an interest of a decidedly eccentric and even hostile kind. I think therefore that both the fact that he threw his mind into the subject with so much vigour and also the exact attitude of his mind as revealed by these essays are valuable as clearing up a kind of perplexity, and satisfying a kind of curiosity which the discerning reader of his other books is likely to feel. The fact that the student of ethics will find them often amateurish does not seem to me to weigh much on the other side : Even when the substance of the thought consists of what an instructed reader may regard as rather trite half-truths, the expression is always fresh and vigorous—indeed, to my taste, it is liable to err from excess of vigour—so that the whole result is not dull.'

The last letter from Henley that I can find is dated 1898. Colvin had asked for information on certain points concerning Stevenson, which Henley was unable to supply. He concludes : 'It is a pleasure to know that you can work at all. Come & see me when you can or will. And call upon me for memories or the like whenever you choose to do so. I am always glad to be of use—if I can.'

CHAPTER XVIII

MRS. R. L. STEVENSON'S LETTERS : III
AFTER HER HUSBAND'S DEATH

1894–1900

WHEN, after Stevenson's death, Mrs. Stevenson was alone, first in Samoa and afterwards in Honolulu and California, it was to Mrs. Sitwell that she poured out her heart with fullest frankness. The letters, which are numerous, are of the deepest interest. Two only were printed by Colvin in the *Empire Review* in 1924, and these I mark with a footnote. The remainder now see the light for the first time.

To Mrs. Sitwell [December 1894] : ' I can tell you very little of the awful catastrophe that has befallen us that you do not know. Lately he had been in excellent health and growing fat, but so full blooded that I was troubled about that. The former hemorrhages had been a safety valve, and for a long time they had ceased. . . .

' I did not tell you the doctors' words about Louis : it was, they said, apoplexy combined with paralysis of the lungs. There was no suffering : almost instant and complete unconsciousness. You have a great deal of influence when you like. Will you not, for Louis' sake, start a popular feeling that his grave, where he lies wrapped in the Union Jack, shall not be on alien soil ? . . . Only oh be quick. I cannot tell you of the true kindness of the Samoan people. That poor chiefs brought their fine mats —which are equivalent to title deeds of estates—to throw over him that he might lie royally, like a high chief, is little compared to other things that I have not the heart nor time to tell. . . . For three days I had known that something terrible was going to happen in the house. That last day I was almost insane with terror and Louis had just been laughing at my childishness and teasing me about it.

'P.S.—I have not made my meaning clear about " alien soil." Louis asked to lie where he is, but he did not expect to lie in German soil. In memory of Louis they should give his beloved island an English protectorate.'

To Mrs. Sitwell. From Vailima. [1895] : ' I am just worn out with writing letters that have to be done ; at the same time I have a visitor in the house to entertain ; two more coming tomorrow, and Tuesday I am going across the island, carried by men ; all the food, bedding, &c. must be prepared here, and carried over the mountains. The village that I am going to is one that particularly adored Louis and has overwhelmed me with presents. I feel bound, now, to accept their present invitation, though it makes me tired to even think of it.' [1]

To Colvin. From San Francisco. [1895] : ' I believe, for him, all is for the best ; he went as he wished to go, when he wished to go, leaping off from the highest pinnacle with the great drums beating behind him. Could he have arranged his own life and death how little things would have been changed. With such thoughts I try to console myself and pretend that I would not have had it different. It is hard to believe that I am to go on and on indefinitely and always alone ; it seems impossible. After all these years of preparation I was not ready when the time came. That very day I said to him, " I am not a coward ; for a woman, I am brave." Vain words ; where is my courage now ? I am not altogether selfish in my grief, for I do think of the others who loved him—more particularly of you.

' Graham Balfour, the true and steadfast, one among a thousand, will be with us in another month. I fear this climate for him, but he will probably go almost at once to

[1] Printed in the *Empire Review*.

R

England. I want to go also to be with you when you are writing the Life, but I am not well and the expense is prohibitive. I know I could be of use to you and I grudge your not having everything that you might need : but there is the stern fact, I cannot.'

To Colvin. From San Francisco. [1895] : ' I am glad, but not surprised that you felt as I did about *Hermiston*. I hope you did not object to my note to the *Times*. I could not bear that story of Louis being depressed about his waning popularity. I saw it everywhere.

' I have found a scratching on an old canvas that I did of Louis when I first knew him. I cannot remember much about it, except that I idly marked it with charcoal without any intention in particular. Bob somehow had it and sent it to me when Lloyd was last in England. The interesting thing is that the likeness is very strong and brings back Louis's face as I first saw it. I am going to send a photograph of it to you. It is not artistic—it is nothing but a good likeness ; but I think that is much.

' I agree entirely with you that *Hermiston* is to [be] published *first*. There is no doubt in my mind about that. I am going to write down notes concerning Louis to send you : just small things that I remember. They may be useless but they may not, at any rate no harm will be done.

' I feel that in writing to you I reach our dear friend Henry James, but no one else.'

To Colvin. From San Francisco. July 17, [1895] : ' Graham Balfour has started for England and will arrive not very long after this letter.

' In looking over further papers to give Mr. Balfour to carry to you, I found the dedication to me as Louis first [wrote] it for *Hermiston*. Please put it in as he meant it to be. He pinned it to my bed curtains when I was asleep, with other explanatory verses. Please do not leave it out. I send you the original, though I believe you have a copy already. I would like to have this back again when you have finished with it.   Mr. Balfour will soon be with you, and can tell you of us what little there is to tell.'

This was the dedication to *Weir of Hermiston* :—

> ' I saw rain falling and the rainbow drawn
>   On Lammermuir. Hearkening I heard again
> In my precipitous city beaten bells
> Winnow the keen sea wind. And here afar,
> Intent on my own race and place, I wrote.
>   Take thou the writing: thine it is. For who
> Burnished the sword, blew on the drowsy coal,
> Held still the target higher, chary of praise
> And prodigal of counsel—who but thou ?
> So now, in the end, if this the least be good,
> If any deed be done, if any fire
> Burns in the imperfect page, the praise be thine.'

To Colvin.   From San Francisco.   Aug. 15 [1895] : ' Did I ever tell you that a Swedenborgian Minister, truly " a man of culture," asked me whether Charles was Louis' literary executor.   I said no, that Mr. Colvin was.   " Sidney Colvin ? " asked he, " the former Cambridge professor ? " I said yes, on which he expressed his satisfaction, saying nearly what I have always said of you, " one can always trust to his honour and his good taste."   " How do you know ? " I could not help but ask.   " I have read all he has written," was the reply.   A good many other people have begged me to tell them all that was possible about you, excusing their curiosity by their admiration of your work.   You seem to be very well known amongst the better class of people here.'

August 19th [1895] : ' What you say of *Hermiston* is exactly what I have thought all along.   *I insist that it comes out as soon as possible.*   It may be that you are wrong and that I am wrong, but I must act according to what seems to me right.   I do not think that you and I have ever differed in a matter of this kind, and I am exceedingly glad that we do not differ now.

' I send with this the photograph of the sketch I told you

of. The photographer has marked it over to get out the breaks on the canvas, but has really not changed anything except in making the thing look like a photograph. On the lower lip there is a smudge that should be put right, but I am afraid to touch anything just now. . . . I do not know how it will strike you, but inartistic as it is, it recalls Louis in his youth as nothing else does.

'Louis left me something better than money; he left me true and steadfast friends.'

Mrs. Stevenson's portrait of her husband as she first knew him at Fontainebleau was redrawn by T. Blake Wirgman, and was reproduced for Sir Graham Balfour's *Life*. I use it again in this book.

To Mrs. Sitwell. From San Francisco. September 13, [1895]: 'I have seen your brother; a really delightful brother, in no way to be improved upon. Also a handsome and very refined high bred looking brother. We talked of you, naturally, and I told him all I could think of concerning you. It was very touching to see with what difficulty he restrained his tears when speaking of you. "Fanny was my favourite sister," he said. And "Fanny has always wanted to see Venice; and so she shall, yet. I am determined she shall." He wished to know if you were beautiful as you used to be. I could only say that you were very beautiful when I saw you first, and very beautiful when I saw you last. Indeed I wanted to kiss him, and I almost believe if no one else had been present I should have done so. It seems odd to suddenly feel the most tender affection for a stranger; but I think your brother must be used to inspiring such sentiment. But I suppose there is nothing I can say about him that you don't know already except that I have seen him and loved him on sight. I am expecting him to come in any moment. . . .

'Please tell S. C. that "The Great North Road" is undoubtedly early work, but no one can give the exact date. I suppose he can guess as nearly as any one. As he says, in the early Henley period. I waited to ask Lloyd. I am

glad S. C. liked the photograph of the old thing I did of
Louis in his youth. It is almost in rags, having kicked
about in Bob's studio for years. I will try to remove the
smudge on the lip. It is so rotten that I may not be able
to do much with it.' [1]

The brother was Cuthbert Fetherstonhaugh, from whose
reminiscences I have already quoted. He thus corrobo-
rates, in that earlier book, Mrs. Stevenson's account of the
interview : ' When I was in San Francisco in 1896 I called
on Mrs. Stevenson, and as soon as I told her who I was she
put both arms round me and gave me a hearty kiss.'

To Colvin. From San Francisco. [1895] : ' Mr. Fetherstonhaugh has been to see me ; a very handsome, refined,
high-bred person whom I loved at sight. He gave me, in
parting, a little book with " from Fanny Sitwell's brother "
on the fly leaf. When he spoke of his sister Fanny it was
with difficulty he restrained his tears. As he turned to go
away I called him back and kissed him. It was an impulse
that I could not resist, but I think we were both old enough
to make it perfectly a right and proper thing. I have not
often been more touched.'

To Colvin. From Honolulu. [1896] : ' We are much
more comfortable here than in San Francisco : there is no
prosperity in the islands, so everything is down, and we
board, of the best, at a very reasonable rate. The Sans
Souci used to be a fashionable sea side place, but it is now
almost deserted. We have a fine large cottage in the grounds
all to ourselves. A friend of mine has lent us a horse and
a little carriage, a very neat turnout, so we are quite aris-
tocrats. Lloyd and I went today to see the queen for the
first time. As I looked at her kind and dignified face, and
remembered this day a year ago, and the terrible change
since then, I nearly fainted. When I could hear what she
said, she was talking of Louis : " It was through this door
he came, and in this chair that my friend sat. I was very
sad when he came, for it was just after the overthrow, but

1 This portrait is reproduced opposite p. 176.

he left me almost cheerful." How many could say that of Louis—I was very sad when he came, but he left me almost cheerful!—Two years ago I came up from Samoa to nurse him here, in this very house. Everything speaks of him to me, almost as much as at home. I walk in the paths where he and I walked; I sit at the same window where every evening we watched the setting of the sun. It is all like yesterday.

'I have read over the letters [the *Vailima Letters*] again and again. I am glad they were published. There is so much of Louis in them. He said to me several times, " Colvin sees me in an atmosphere of his own : when I am dead don't let him make me out a damned angel." These are the exact words. Well, the letters show all there was of the worst of him ; and anyone worth caring for will love him the better for that worst. And he will not have appeared as " a damned angel."

'I have had a little worry with Aunt Maggie about the inscription on the tomb. I suppose Palema has told you what we propose—his own verses in English on the one side of a high chief tomb, and the verse from Ruth, " Thy country shall be my country," in Samoan on the other. Aunt Maggie wants the usual texts, " In my Father's house are many mansions," and several others of the same sort. It is very difficult not to offend her. But of all things in the world Louis' tomb must show no bad nor even doubtful taste. I know what she really wants, poor soul. She was always doubtful of Louis' belief in what are called the truths of religion, and being doubtful wishes to convince the world at the sacrifice of her own sincerity. I said to her that he had been in his life a true follower of Christ, and that should be enough. She knows that as well as we. How many of the rest of us can say half as much ? One of the missionaries said to me that he wished that he had been able to come as near. And this missionary knew as much of Louis' mind on such subjects as was possible for words to convey, but he wasn't

the usual narrow idiot that missionaries generally are.   We
are very fortunate to have the best in Samoa.   The best,
it seems to me, of all denominations.   There is a little wild
Baptist missionary that I love ; and there is another, some
sort of dissenter, that I love also.   And so would you if
you knew them.'

Palema would be Graham Balfour.   ' Aunt Maggie ' was
the family name for Stevenson's mother.

To Colvin.   From Honolulu.   March 20 [1896] : ' Your
letter has filled me with the desire to go to England that
I might be near you during the work on the Life.   If I
went, I could not stay long ; of course I am not sure that
I could go at all ; it would depend entirely on finances.

' I am—I can only say infuriated—when I think of those
damnable newspapers, that they should have caused you
annoyance.   I quite understand why no one was ever
punished in San Francisco for shooting the editor of a news-
paper.   I think there should be a club something on the
lines of the Suicide Club, each member bound over to kill
an editor when the lot fell to him.   I think I would join
that club if they would accept women members.   Speaking
of clubs : there is a large philanthropic boys' club in
America with many " Chapters " in different parts.   The
Robert Louis Stevenson Chapter of Cincinnati, who used
to correspond with Louis, have sent me their badge, a bit of
blue enamel with R. L. S. on it, was it not nice of them ?   I
see your difficulty about the Life.   I should say go ahead as
frankly as possible, and then, if necessary, we could tone
down.   I should like to be honest, but at the same time not
to hurt anyone's feelings.   That always troubled Louis.'

To Colvin.   From Honolulu.   April 24 [1896] : ' And
now I am terrified lest I have given the impression that I
am absolutely meaning to go to you.   The trouble is I am
wavering about without courage.   Of courage I used to have
enough for all that came, but I fear it has been used up
almost entirely.   The one thing always in my mind is the
Life.   It is all we can do for Louis now, and you are the only

one fit for the work ; and as you say it will be a great work. Aside from all else there have been so few lives of such absorbing interest as Louis'. Even leaving literature out of the question.

'I want to write a long letter and say many things. I can't because I am too tired. Still I know that you understand much of what I should like to say, without words. My trust in you, my belief in you, my deep affection for you : it is of these I should like to speak. I know I need not, but as I write, my heart is full.'

Mrs. Stevenson, as it happened, did go to London for a while to discuss her husband's Life, which at that time Colvin was considering. In the end he decided to confine himself to editing the correspondence, and the Life was written by Graham Balfour. Finally let me quote from a letter written by Mrs. Stevenson on her return from London to San Francisco. It begins by referring to a poem written to her by her husband : 'I have just received your letter asking about adding the poem addressed to me, " Dusky, trusty," etc., to the new edition. Do just what you think well to do. It is a very beautiful thing, and I do not think it would be bad taste to publish it. As to the other, " Oh, God, if that were all," I agree that this should be kept for the Life. But there was another that Louis rather liked—I *think* it was called " In praise of dark women " ; what do you think of adding that ? I only suggest the looking at it. I shall, as I have always done, feel sure that you have done right, whatever your views may be. . . .

'I am glad you like the photograph of the portrait. I think I can put the blurred place right. It can do no harm to try as it would not be spoiled ; charcoal rubs off at once. I think there are indications of the parts rubbed off. It is a great chance that I have it at all. If I had only known when I 'sat " idly scratching " that day. The canvas is much dilapidated, having been lying about in Bob's place all these years. . . .

'I hear of several others proposing to lecture on Louis'

life in Samoa, but in particular is a Mr. Chalmers, the head of the Mission, a fiery little man of real genius, whose lectures are said to be superb. . . . If you could meet him you would find him more interesting than almost anyone you ever met. He is more of an explorer than a missionary, and with absolutely none of the narrowness of the usual missionary. The missionary society in Apia was shaken to its foundations when he was there. The natives were forbidden to dance, and Chalmers danced the Highland fling on the missionary verandah before a great crowd of them. He also smoked a pipe in public when smoking was considered one of the seven deadly sins. If he lectures in England I am sure that his lecture will be worth hearing. . . .

'A curious incident took place a day or so ago. It seems that an Indian boy who had been brought to Samoa when a child, when he was adopted and reared by the natives, thought it a good scheme to stow away on a ship and come to America. Naturally he was thrown out on the wharf like spoiled fruit. The poor wretch wandered about shivering in the cold, sleeping in doorways, and eating what refuse he could pick up, until he was nearly dead. "It is a strange place this," he said; "why, in Samoa everybody loves me; but here not one man loves me! When I asked for some bread nobody said, 'Come in, poor boy, and eat and rest while I get you some clothes'; no; they all said, 'Go away.'" He looked all along the streets for a cocoanut tree or a breadfruit, but could find none. "I walked seven miles, one day, and there was not a cocoanut," he said. At last, when he had taken a cold and felt dreadfully ill, Belle passed him, and his quick eyes caught sight of the South Sea ear-rings. "There," he said, "I looked up to the old man (South Sea for God) and said, 'Now, God, help me,' and began to sing a Samoan song." Naturally, Belle turned at once; when he saw her face fully, he cried out her Samoan name "Teuila." Of course, he is with us, sleeping in a camp bed in the kitchen, and acting as our servant, until we can persuade some ship to

take him home.   It is a pretty story, is it not ?   You never
saw anything as like a lost dog as when he came, nor anything as like the dog found as he is now ; our clothes are
brushed threadbare, and our shoes are blacked until they
are stiff.   But he thinks this a wicked, hard-hearted country.
" I am only twenty-two," he said, " and I don't want to
die, but nobody cared.   The people can't love each other
as we do in Samoa.   It was so strange to find that no man
loved me.   It made me very much 'fraid."   At this moment
he is eating a huge watermelon, the first fruit that he had
seen that is the same in Samoa.' [1]

Mrs. Stevenson died in 1914, and her ashes were placed
in her husband's tomb in the following year.   Her life, by
her sister, Mrs. Nellie Van de Grift Sanchez, was published
in 1920.

This chapter may fittingly end by recalling to readers'
minds the ' dusky, trusty ' poem :—

' MY WIFE

' Trusty, dusky, vivid, true,
    With eyes of gold and bramble-dew,
    Steel-true and blade-straight,
    The great artificer
    Made my mate.

' Honour, anger, valour, fire ;
    A love that life could never tire,
    Death quench or evil stir,
    The mighty master
    Gave to her.

' Teacher, tender, comrade, wife,
    A fellow-farer true through life,
    Heart-whole and soul-free,
    The august father
    Gave to me.'

---

[1] In the *Empire Review*.

CHAPTER XIX

HENRY JAMES

1885–1911

I CANNOT discover when Colvin and Henry James first met ; but the earliest letter in the collection belongs to 1885, and is quoted on page 168. Henry James was then forty-two, exactly Colvin's age, and was living in East Bolton Street.

The intimacy between him and the Colvins, whenever it began, was close, and lasted until his death in 1916. It was at one of Lady Colvin's musical parties in Kensington Palace Gardens that I had my only conversation with—or shall I say audience of ?—the great cosmopolitan, soon—for this must have been just before the War—to become a British subject. In an article in the *Empire Review* in 1924, not reprinted, Colvin makes a very interesting analysis of James and Stevenson, so different yet so sympathetic to each other. 'I have called them,' Colvin says, 'two of the finest of all artists in English letters. They were at the same time two of the most contrasted and unlike. The contrast was not less in the tenor and conditions of their lives than in the choice and handling of their themes and the measure and history of the welcome their works severally encountered from the public,—the early tales and novels of James being received with keen appreciation by at least the critical portion of that public, and the work of his latter years with relative and at last almost complete neglect ; while of Stevenson's much briefer career the first products made their way slowly, but the acclamation which followed on the appearance first of *Treasure Island,* and then of *Jekyll and Hyde,* continued to greet almost all his so versa-

tile and various work until the end.   Time flies and memories
are short : will readers forgive me if by some prefatory
words of reminiscence and quotation I seek to make the
circumstances both of the friendship and the contrast
freshly present to their minds ?

'Two things about Stevenson that were innate, ingrained,
and ineradicable were his Scotchness and his passion for
outdoor life and activity.   He himself speaks somewhere
of his Scotchness as "tending to intermittency"; and
no doubt his adventurous readiness to adapt himself to
new environments and experiments, his frequentation of
France and America and absorbing pursuit of letters, not
merely as a vocation or means of self-expression or appeal,
but as a fine art deliberately practised in the spirit and
familiar company of artists, had done something to modify
it in unessentials,—had superficially tempered the Scot in
him with alien elements.   But elsewhere he writes of himself
as haunted about the heart all the while, even in the midst
of the distractions and delights of his new tropical home, by
yearnings after "that cauld, auld huddle of bare hills," his
true, stern and naked motherland.   And not only did he
remain frankly Scotch to the end in the accent of his speech
and the racy, full-blooded human quality of his humour :
in the vital depths of his being he was the true descendant
of his stern-conscienced, indomitably hardy and strenuous,
coast-haunting, lighthouse-building Northern forbears ; only
by a perversity of Fate a descendant physically incapable
of following their vocation. . . .

'When at intervals during his semi-invalid years he was
able to get out and about, the company he most cared for
was at no time that which was to be found in drawing-
rooms.   Charmer though he could be among his equals, he
as a rule only cared to mix with such among them as either
presented to his discernment experiences or faculties for
experience beyond the common, or such as followed pursuits
akin to his own, writers and artists or trained lovers of
books and of the arts. . . .   A chosen few of these he

attached warmly to himself; but he had no inclination
to follow them into the ordinary haunts of polite society,
and the average members of that society, those having
no special gift or attainment or experience to recommend
them, he let go by him, as he has somewhere said, " like
seaweed." Elemental and unsophisticated human nature,
the seaman and the husbandman and the shepherd and
the smith, and all such as feel the daily pinch and stress of
life, down to the cadger, the chimney-sweep, thief, vagrant,
and prostitute—these, and the variegated company with
which he peopled in imagination the historic past, were
all more real and more significant to him than were the
majority among the comfortable classes of his contemporaries. Neither by gift nor choice had he the makings
of an attentive student of these, with their uneventful ways
of life—uneventful at any rate on the surface—with their
passions and tragedies, supposing them to have any, decor-
ously cloaked and veiled, their niceties and *nuances* of
smooth everyday intercourse and incident, their pettinesses
of social competition and intrigue, their intricacies and
delicacies of reticent pathos and subdued romance and
emotion conventionally schooled and harnessed.

' To Henry James, on the other hand, it was just the
intense perception and assiduous study of these niceties
and *nuances*, these subtle emotional half-tones of polite
contemporary life, which gave the motive and inspiration
of his art, but for one or two experimental exceptions
(among which I should point to *The Princess Casamassima*
as at once the widest in range and most elaborate in handling). American by birth, European and predominatingly
French by early habit and training, and finally by choice
and domestication deliberately and determinedly English,
he had no deep-seated primary cast of mind and temperament corresponding to that Scottishness of Stevenson.
Neither had he, so far as was apparent from his course of
life, anything of Stevenson's instinctive craving for action
and zest for whatever consequences action might entail,

but was rather both congenitally and by choice a looker-on.
. . . He has conferred many of his own characteristics,
only as exercised in a more ideal and romantic *milieu,* on
the personage of Benvolio in his early story so named. That
story, as many of my readers will remember, narrates with
characteristic subtlety of analysis and charm of style the
" hesitancies " of one in whose nature the passion to observe
replaces the passion to possess, and who until almost too
late is content to watch and study, without claiming her
for his own, the woman in whom he discerns " a divine
embodiment of all the amenities, the refinements, the
complexities of life."

' It is recorded of James how in the pursuit of this branch
of human study he, in the earlier days of his London career,
dined out in the course of a single twelvemonth not less
than a hundred and eight times. Of Stevenson during
my intimacy with him I cannot remember that he ever
once made an appearance at a set dinner party or in dress
clothes, though there is evidence of his having in early
Edinburgh days occasionally made so much sacrifice of
his Bohemian habits in order to please his parents.

' With all these contrasts between them of origin, of experience, of temperament, of predilection, the two men had
nevertheless much in common. Both were spirits essentially loveable, affectionate and generous ; both, as the
admirably untouchy reception by each of the other's very
frankest criticisms stands to prove, were signally free from
all taint of jealousy and meanness : both—though in the
case of Henry James it needed intimate knowledge to realize
as much—were men of exceptionally intense feeling, of an
emotional nature doubly and trebly as strong as the common
run of mankind. But the main resemblance, and that
which probably first drew close the links which were to
bind them, was their common attachment to the same
pursuit, their studious and passionate devotion to the art
of letters as art. Even here a marked contrast is to be
noted between their several methods and ideals as artists,

Stevenson both by nature and choice aiming constantly at
compression and simplification, at getting the utmost out
of the single, the one revealing and vivifying word, and at
the ruthless cutting down of the non-essential ; James on
the other hand ever more and more inclined to yield to his
love of particularity both in analysis and description, and
to pursue every clue of thought and motive to its subtlest
involutions and most entangled ramifications. Their letters
to each other already printed illustrate vividly their consciousness of such contrast, and constitute one of the most
interesting examples extant of the critical appreciation of
two gifted artists by each other. . . .

'It is not on points of style as such that the debate
between Henry James and Stevenson mainly turns, but
rather on the degree to which written narrative should seek
after pictorial effect and try to make visible to the mind's
eye of the reader the material setting of the actions and
passions which it relates—should or should not, as Stevenson phrases it, appeal to the optic nerve. " Death to the
optic nerve," I find him crying once in reply to his correspondent's petition for its indulgence ; and again, " War
to the adjective " ; and again, " How to get over, how to
escape from, the besotting *particularity* of fiction. Roland
approached the house ; it had green doors and window
blinds ; and there was a scraper on the upper step. To
hell with Roland and the scraper ! " James on the other
hand pleads earnestly for that satisfaction of the visual
imagination which Stevenson would refuse it.'

The only letter from Colvin to myself that I can find
bears upon the passage just quoted. The date is October
21, 1923, and the reference at the beginning is to Dean
Hole's *Little Tour in Ireland*, 1859, which he had expressed
a wish to read again and which I was fortunate to be able
to find for him : ' When a packet came on Thursday
addressed in a well-known handwriting, I made several
guesses at what it was likely to contain, but never thought
of my old beloved book of John Leech's Irish pictures which

I used to pore and chuckle over sixty—yes, just fully sixty
—years ago. It is a real joy to possess it again, and a
double joy considering whence it comes. How on earth
did you manage to pick up a copy of the first edition—I
shouldn't have cared a quarter as much for the reprint—
in no time like that ? I can't say thank-you warmly
enough.

' We are both keeping up after a fashion, though something of wrecks through having gone yesterday to the
mildest of picture-shows—the O. W. S. [the Old Water-
Colour Society], on a public day, and on my part also
through having ground painfully (but I am hoping successfully) out of myself a comparison and contrast of R. L. S.
and Henry James, by way of introduction to the letters of
Mrs. R. L. S. in the *Empire Review* and *Scribner's*.'

Several of Henry James's letters to Colvin are printed in
the two volumes of his correspondence issued in 1920. Those
which follow are new.

The first, undated, belongs to 1887. It refers to the
Stevensons' South Sea plans : ' What good news (except
of poor Mrs. S.'s *secousse*) & how reassuring, every way,
about those dear people. What a gallant little letter she
writes—& what a gallant little woman ! They are a
romantic lot—& I feel delight in them : with their plans
for the Pacific & Japan ! May Louis carry them out &
bring back things that the world won't willingly let die ! '

In March 1889 when Colvin was ill in Paris : ' This is so
little a note of business, or of any practical commerce, that
I shall be distressed if you take the trouble even to answer
it. It is only a retarded expression of interest in the
circumstances of your too long absence, which I have had
it at heart, always ineffectually, a dozen times, to give. It
is only when I hear that you judge yourself better that I
face the very gratified satisfaction I should have had in
telling in how friendly & troubled a spirit I participated in
your illness. People suffer & struggle, & we don't say
things, & opportunities go, & sympathy is obscured—but

let me at least give you a cordial sign, from city to city, with every wish for the fullest success of your present business.

'Many thanks for Mrs. Fanny's very natural & interesting letter—doubly refreshing after her long silence. I wish however, she *generalised* more, that is would give fewer " nigger " details & more white ones. Yet those about Louis's wondrous lustiness are, after all, white enough. In the face of such facts how can one grudge his really *living* —with such an apparent plenitude of physical life, no matter how literature suffers ? Oh yes, I 'm afraid it *must* suffer, it can't help it. But we must change our point of view, to be thankful for what survives, what he can still give us. After all he has *bien de talent* ! I have a little note from him also—but very, very casual, & not worth passing on to you. I am much touched by Mrs. Fanny's good message.'

'*Tregenna Castle Hotel, St. Ives, Aug. 23rd,* 1894.

' MY DEAR COLVIN,—It is doubly pleasant to hear from you when you are accompanied by a letter from R. L. S.— or from R. L. S. when he is escorted by a letter from you. The Samoan epistle requires, I am sorry to say, as much salt as possible to give it savour of satisfactory good spirits. He writes mainly—indeed exclusively—of an excursion he had taken in an English war ship and of the pleasure he had had in her officers ; but literally not a word of anything else save that he was bad in the head and languid in the heart. This was a mood, I take it—he says himself it would probably lift at any hour ; but it effectually curtains off, in the letter, everything else one wanted to know. I shall be as communicate as possible in reply—to heap coals on his head. Meanwhile *any* direct word from him gives me joy, as hinting that he hasn't forgotten a fellow—or sacrificed one wholly to cannibal friendships. I take comfort in the glimpse you give me of your own recreations and refreshments : barring the gaudy duchess (whom I

S

don't know) they sound innocuous and natural. I don't know Lady Agnew either (save, I think, for a single meeting in Sargent's charming picture) : I " know " all the while fewer and fewer people. But I rejoice in all *you* know, especially when they help to see you through dull German moments. My own recollections of such moments go back to long past years, but with a very kind remembrance (as to the only 2 or 3 Bader I know) of something summery and woodsy and wholesome in the ordeal.

' I have been 10 days at this place—almost my first vision of Cornwall and its meagre but almost elegant charm —and have taken some long strolls over moors and cliffs and bogs and briars with my neighbour Leslie Stephen. The bathing and the gorse are quite royal, and when the day is decent the sea is chrysoprase—or something of that sort—and I presently depart for regions as yet un- determined. I haven't such sumptuous alternatives as you ; I only long to be warm—a luxury this season quite denies one. It 's called " relaxing "—but would that it were ! Alas, the English summer ! If you do come back to the New Forest, I pray it be weak and indulgent to you. I aspire to keep away from London till October 1st, but stress of temperature may easily chase me home ; in which case I shall knock at your door. I have seen no one for weeks (save my friends the Stephens here) in spite of some days lately passed at the sweet Torquay—where I did see my host, the gentle W. E. Norris. There is a blessed absence of news of anything having happened to anyone. Absit omen ! Stia bene.—Yours evermore,

' HENRY JAMES

' *P.S.*—Lest this should reach your hotel after your departure, I cautiously send it to the Museum.' [1]

' 2 *Wellington Crescent, Ramsgate. Thursday.*

' MY DEAR COLVIN,—I have my apparent bad manners to you much on my conscience, but please believe 1st that

[1] In the Fitzwilliam Museum.

HENRY JAMES
FROM THE PAINTING BY JOHN S. SARGENT, R.A., IN THE NATIONAL PORTRAIT GALLERY

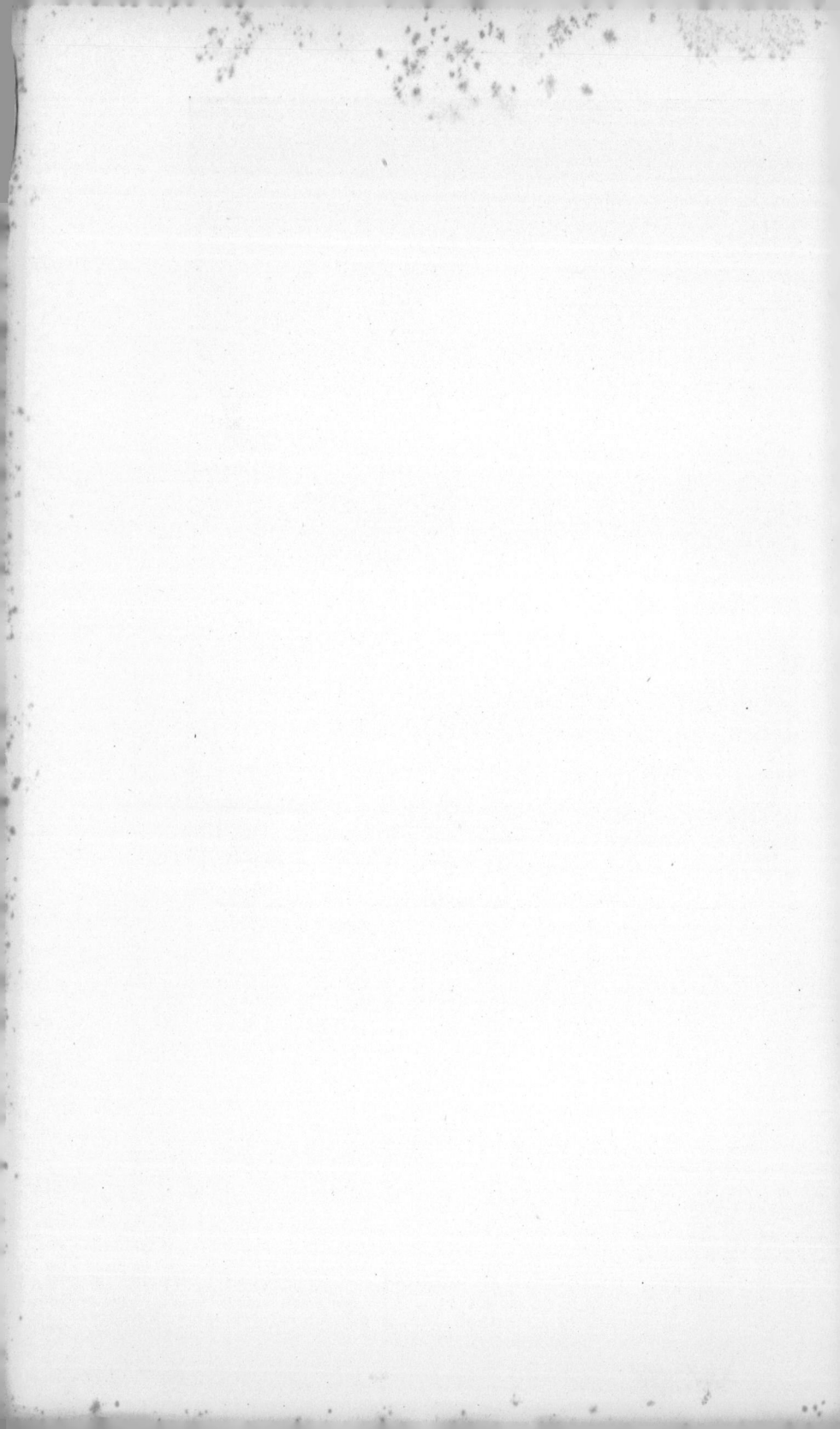

my motives have been pure and high in surrendering to
them when further struggle was hopeless, and 2nd that it
has been a part of the same unwilling servitude to have
been unable to address you an earlier explanation. The
last time I saw you (just after my return from abroad) you
kindly asked me to come and see you and listen to some
portions of the particularly interesting and intimate last
communications from R. L. S. I promised myself this
extreme luxury—but I reckoned without the deluge. The
deluge came in the form of an hourly more and more impossible London, from which after much vain floundering
I sought refuge in this ridiculous ark. Here I have been,
trying to do my work and mind my business ever since.
Therefore I have been particularly out of hail of Samoa.
Samoa and Ramsgate—what would the Islander think of
me ? Tell it not at Vailima ! *C'est pour vous dire* that
I shall knock at your door as soon as I return to London,
which, alas, won't happen till this month raves itself out.
Meanwhile I know that you stand as a rock in the uproar.
I hope the rock has human shape and satisfactions, however.
Will you commend me very kindly to Mrs. Sitwell, not
apropos of rocks ? I haven't, to my loss, seen her for ages.
Don't think of answering this, which is nothing but your
strict due ; and believe me,—yours always,

' HENRY JAMES ' [1]

Dated August 30, 1895 : ' I am touched by the liberality
of your letter, shamed by its humanity, charmed by its
contents, & altogether delighted to get news of you. I had
had a letter from Graham Balfour, but your own is considerably more vivid. It 's particularly delightful to hear
that Buxton heals & helevates you : I am reassured at
having so good a word for the place. A friend of mine
(W. E. Norris of Torquay—still there, I suppose, or at any
rate for the last month) wrote me *pis que pendre* of it. . . .
When *I* go (I shall end there, I feel), I shall leap from peak

[1] In the Fitzwilliam Museum.

to peak of the hills, even if the effort terminates my shrunken
existence. I wish we might leap together. But somehow
we never do. I return next week to Torquay, where before
my present incarceration, of too many days, in town, I spent
some time. I like the emptiness & prettiness, & soothing-
ness of it immensely, but I fear I have no present prospect
of becoming even a householder there. Even if I did, on
a tiny scale, I shouldn't give up my London quarters.
More before I arrive. London, thank God, a desert with
lovely days & lovelier nights. I may not return to it till
Nov. 1st.'

On December 26, 1895 : ' Don't think me a monster of
unsociability, of unfriendship, if I tell you the truth on
the question of accepting your hospitable invitation for
Monday. The great dining-out business has lately reached
a point with me at which I have felt that something must
be done—that I must in other words pull up. I have been
doing it nightly ever since Nov. 1st, & it has left me with
such arrears of occupation on my hands that it is imperative for me to try & use a few evenings to catch up. I am
therefore accepting no invitations for the present—having
got all the last but one well behind me. This is the plain
unvarnished tale that I let loose at you instead of gracefully romancing about another engagement. Alas, " Alas "
is hypocritical ! what I *really* mean is that I can never dine
out any more at all ! It has come to the question of that
or leaving London, & I must try that first. It is heroic &
really tests me, to have to take you so early in the period.'

To Mrs. Sitwell, after meeting Mrs. R. L. Stevenson in
London, May 28, 1898 : ' I want to talk with you of those
people—who are very touching & interesting to me : Fanny
S. so fine, in her way, & so almost putting—dimly—the
other there between. She is like an old grizzled lioness—
or resignedly captive South-sea Chieftainess.'

From Rome, June 4, 1899 : ' I have been away from
England (the country !) since the beginning of March & am
homesick now & eager to get back ; but circumstances here,

have still their hand upon me, & I am (ergo) going tomorrow, for 3 or 4 days to Marion Crawford at Sorrento. Then I push back to Florence for 10 days, Turin, Paris &c., & Rye—in which latter place I shall crouch so toilingly & workingly & unsociably that to leave it again soon will go hard with me—only I *must* go, on some business, up to town. I will then notify you promptly & we must indeed have the good talk you speak of. You can't desire it more than I—& you must have much to tell me. I 'm intensely void of any London or personal—other-personal news ; & there are things I do want so to know. I hope health, sleep, work, book, & everything in general are well with you. I find R. L. S. in *Scribner's* delightful, but can't forgive the beggarly brevity of their snippets. . . .

' Rome is hot & empty & pleasant—the emptiness peopled by a charming soft wind-stir & cool nights—a really happy time to be here. I 've been here a month—more—& was a month in Venice—besides other times elsewhere. The H[umphry] Wards have delightful Villa Barbni. at C. Gandolfo—& I just spent 4 or 5 picturesquissimo days there. She is writing an " Italian " novel—& A. Sterner is here for the pictorial embellishments. There are likewise just now thrillingnesses going on in the Forum—which I will tell you of—for I too shall have gossip. Heaven speed our exchange of it.'

The next letter followed upon Colvin's decision not to write the official Life of Stevenson.

To Colvin. From Rye, September 27, 1899 : ' I shall tell you better than I can do here, when we meet, that I really rejoice in your renouncement. . . . It was an impossible business to my sense, & an impossible relation, & if I had been nearer to you earlier in the whole history (the best years of it,) I should have taken the liberty of advising you in that sense. It is, roughly speaking, because I can't but consider that with your admirable *D.N.B.* article, the *Vailima Letters* and the so abundantly personal & autobiographic new volume (with all your notes) Louis (the

most *self-recording*, into the bargain, of all writers) has
been, with all respect, sufficiently biographised. Everything that *has* been done is a massive monument; the
Edinburgh edition is *itself* essentially that; & your hand
is, intensely, in all.   Requiescat ! There ! '

Colvin had written the article on Stevenson in the *Dictionary of National Biography*, to which he was a valued
contributor.

From Rye [1899], referring to the first edition of Stevenson's Letters, which Colvin edited—in proof.   To Colvin: ' I
got back here only Saturday night—kept in town by much
complication & anxiety ; & I find the two packets (volumes,)
of R. L. S. sheets very safe & sound for which many thanks.
I had to spend (sick with a vile cold) all yesterday, writing
accumulated letters ; & haven't yet had time to read your
introduction.—*Afternoon.*   I *have*, now, had time ; have
read it, & greatly congratulate you on it.   A very difficult
thing to do—I mean to foreshorten a figure of so many
attitudes & yet touch on all (represent all,) of them ; & you
have excellently done it, & been vivid & temperate at once.
I shall write my article on the book as soon as ever I can—
but don't quite know where it will appear : I shld. say in *N.
American Review* for sure, were it not that I think they
may there already have engaged for one.'

From Rye, November 18, 1899, on receipt of the edition
of Stevenson's Letters in book form.   To Colvin : ' I ought
already to have signified to you my pride & pleasure in
receiving the 2 vols. of the Letters.   What a beautiful &
lordly book !   It is precisely because I have been occupied
in *saying* that, these last 3 or 4 days, that I have left myself
time for nothing else.   I have done for the January no.
of the *North American Review* such an article as I *could*,
under pressure of some haste.'

To Colvin.   From Rye, January 26, 1900 : ' Please
don't consider my delay in thanking you for your letter
about my R. L. S. in the *N.A.R.* due to any failure of
extreme pleasure in receiving.   It has all been quite other

frustrations. I am infinitely gratified by what you say of it—all the more that I but very barely indeed contented myself. I don't know why I found him so difficult—but I did. Partly, doubtless, because he has been so much be-written—in an inferior way. And I left unsaid all the really critical (I mean closely analytic) things about his talent, manner, literary idiosyncrasies, views &c.—the things one would have liked most to say. But the condi-tions of space, attention, in which any literary criticism that is not the basest hand to mouth journalism can get itself uttered at all now, are too beggarly for one's courage. You are quite right—wholly—about my being in places too entortillé. I am *always* in places too entortillé—& the effort of my scant remaining years is to make the places fewer.'

To Colvin. From Rye, December 28, 1903 : ' I rejoice to hear of your betterment, and I hope Sandgate will polish you off to the brightest, bravest shine. Likewise I congratulate you on having found there quarters and conditions that make these dark midwinter days more bearable than your own monumental fireside, backgrounded by the rich dim tapestry of Bloomsbury. Likewise, further-more, there is a thrill in thinking of you both as so much more of neighbours—except that you aren't really—scarcely a wee bit. The Ashford station (of waits and draughts and glooms, in the gaping voids of the winter train service) too perversely and depressingly interposes. Let me declare that in spite of it, however, I would do everything possible toward coming over to luncheon with you—to sleep *wouldn't* at present be possible ; but the conditions, as they press upon me, show as but meagrely favourable.

' It seems sadly crooked, further, that H. G. W., who is really a dear, and who is certainly, at the least, the leading ornament of Sandgate, should be away just at this time. And I 'm sorry, though not surprised, to hear of his errand. He was here, for a day, with poor Gissing, a couple of years ago, and the latter struck me then as quite particularly marked out for what is called in his and my profession an unhappy ending. But what a brick is Wells to go to his aid. I doubt if he has another creature to look to—in the way at any rate of a sane and sturdy man.'

The H. G. Wells's then lived at Sandgate. George Gissing the novelist was ill at St. Jean de Luz, and Mr. Wells, one of his truest friends, had gone to be with him. As a matter of fact he died on the day on which Henry James wrote this letter.

'November 6th, Lamb House, Rye, Sussex.

'MY DEAR COLVIN,—There are stupid reasons—but I won't trouble you with them—why I have suffered two or three days to elapse since seeing in the *Times* that you had somehow met with (what sounds like) a rather grave accident. My immediate impulse was to write to you, but we live in a day in which one is *always* writing and in which immediacy therefore comes off as it can. The worst is that I have thus taken time to worry and imagine and think thoughts—one of which is that you are perhaps in dire discomfort and pain. And though this makes me say : " Ain't I now gladder than ever of that affair in the Marylebone Road last summer and above all won't *he* be ? " even this but makes me feel that there are two of you there to be concerned in the matter, and I think of you *both* as knocked down or run over, or whatever the horrid mischance may have been. You are neither of you to take any trouble to have me told, for I of course know that you will have been deluged with the letters which at present add a horror to misfortune. But you are to take this for a sign of tender interest, as sincere as it is, alas, helpless. I can't even come to see you—so far as you are accessible to such demonstrations. By the time I shall be able to you will be whole and happy again, for I remain here till after Christmas, and I hope with all my heart that your confinement will be a very short affair. I have thought of you both so often since Marylebone, and with so vivid a sense of what Marylebone had done for your happiness, that this in a manner but seems an intensification of that opportunity—that is of my opportunity to say to myself very grimly and blankly : " Who will be beautifully and exquisitely at *your* side when you break your leg, or worse ? " I turn from that grey picture to the majestic Monument and seem to see it turn ruddy and cosy in the November dusk, so that I can at last wonder if anything worse has happened to you than the fancy to refine a little upon your advantages—that is upon your sense of felicity. But don't refine all the rest of us wholly away, and don't be any the more interestingly the worse for your mishap than you can possibly help. Please think of me, both, as full of affectionate participation, and believe me,—Yours very constantly,   HENRY JAMES ' [1]

Colvin had had an accident in which his leg was broken ; and though it was soon mended, he always afterwards walked with a slight limp.

To Mrs. Sitwell, referring to an article on Stevenson, which he had written. From Rye, January 27, 1900 : " It gives me pleasure—much—that you who knew the dear being from so early & so well—should care for what so late a comer as I say—*could* say, about him. I did it in a hampered sort of way—but if I did it at all I feel a pious joy— only also a kind of sadness in having finished & put *from* me one's last utterance about him. I shan't ever make another—& it 's like leaving him & breaking off. Of such a texture is our life & our feelings. I am very homesick for town, & shall not again—between November & April— hibernate amid the pure elements. I pine for the sound of the busses and the colour of the jars at night in the chemists' windows.'

No date. Love of London again : ' I do wholly agree with you as to the preferability of London when nature is one waterspout that I quit it almost with tears even for so brief a period—it 's the Ark in the Deluge.'

[1] In the Fitzwilliam Museum.

No date.   A word for the country : ' Thanks for your good wishes in the matter of the ministrations of Pye Smith.   I *am* much better, mainly,—but really think it less Pye than Rye, than, in short, the absence of Pie : i.e. the innocent country life, the no Dinners, the plain living & high thinking.'

To Mrs. Sitwell.   From Rye, September 25, 1900 : ' Very remote & romantic you sound to me all, & rusticating in conditions of ideal irregularity : by which I mean nothing worse than that if one has a house, in a little south-coast prosy town, on one's back, a pang of envy seizes at the image of far-away nests in the northern heather, impro-vised haunts of the eagle & the grouse ! My ornithology may be wrong, but my vision I feel is roughly true.   I greet very cordially both your comrades & send them lively con-gratulations on each other & on you.   Tell Colvin from me, please, that I encountered him—his Doppelganger—to-day, as it oddly happened, at the good bicycle-man's of this place, in the shape of a gentleman so startlingly & utterly & completely resembling him in every particular of face & form that it constituted the strongest approach to identity (through similarity) that I 've *ever* encountered.   He was cycling through & having a repair done, & while he waited, & I waited, I couldn't help asking him if by chance there was any one he had ever been taken for.   He said No— with a good conscience apparently—& left me to marvel at the truth of my favourite theory—that nobody ever observes anything : nobody but me ! '

Finally there is this letter written to Colvin while he was at work preparing the four-volume edition of Stevenson's Letters, in which there were many new ones, and with which the *Vailima Letters* were merged.   James had been asked for permission to include some addressed to him.

' 25 *Irving St., Cambridge, Mass., U.S.A.,*
'*Jan : 5 :* 1911.

' MY DEAR COLVIN,—I am delighted exceedingly to find myself again in communication with you, however belatedly

—& I fear even this response to your so interesting letter with the R. L. S. question will seem to you tardy indeed. I have such arrears of information to make up in the way of reporting of myself that the mere vision frightens me off that ground—all the more that I *can't* report of myself now even if I would—I mean by reason of the fact that my long & difficult convalescence from a most damnable & distressful illness is in itself too subject to fluctuation—frustration, & that the slow, stiff, weary climb up-hill has slips & retrogressions that often belie my hopes, as well, I hasten to add, as advances or recuperations that frequently reassure my fears. I have had, alas, a hideous, a terrible, tragic fear—& have been in this appalling country (as my exasperated sensibility forces me to feel it) since August last. I have just taken my passage to England again—but only for June 14th, so that I have a terrible bit yet to wait. Meantime the sorest homesickness, the sharpest pangs of the exile, will be my daily portion—& yet I have reasons for remaining that make that anguish a matter of comparative indifference to me. I cling to this particular roof tree (my beloved brother's) in order to hold fast slightly the longer to his cherished shade, & to be with my admirable sister-in-law & my so interesting & delightful nephews and niece (4 in all & the youngest aetatis 19) ; they clinging also as closely to me & constituting almost the only society for which I am just now fit. The two Louis letters of which you send me copies come back to me from so far off like small pale fluttering ghosts & fill me with a thrill of tenderness. Use them by all means—they deserve immortalization, & oh do indeed let me have the originals & the other originals, as soon as I get home. *The Solution*, alluded to in one of the notes, is simply the title of a little old tale of mine, of years agone, published at that time in some periodical & reprinted in a Macmillan volume that had for its designation *The Lesson of the Master*—the 1st story of ½ a dozen. (It is not included in the quasi-collected editions of my products, but perhaps *will* be in some supplementary

volume.) Fanny S. will be a bigger fool than I ever took
her for if she resents the lively description of their domestic
broil.   It helps to commemorate her & makes her interesting—& just so, I feel sure, she will rejoice.

' By the same token don't hesitate to print the passage
about Meredith *tel quel*—leaving the " humbugging " un-
touched.   The word isn't invidiously but pictorially &
caressingly used—as with a rich, or vague, loose synthetic
suggestion.   Who in the world is there to-day to complain
of it ?   *Voilà !* '

' Here,' wrote Stevenson in the Union Club at Sydney
on February 19, 1890, ' in this excellent civilised, antipodal
club smoking-room, I have just read the first part of your
Solution.   Dear Henry James, it is an exquisite art ; do
not be troubled by the shadows of your French competitors :
not one, not de Maupassant, could have done a thing more
clean and fine ; dry in touch, but the atmosphere (as in a
fine summer sunset) rich with colour and with perfume. . . .'

The other reference is to the letter from Stevenson written
at Skerryvore on January 1887.   This is the passage : ' My
wife is peepy and dowie : two Scotch expressions with which
I will leave you to wrestle unaided, as a preparation for my
poetical works.   She is a woman (as you know) not without
art : the art of extracting the gloom of the eclipse from
sunshine ; and she has recently laboured in this field not
without success or (as we used to say) not without a blessing.
It is strange : " we fell out, my wife and I " the other night ;
she tackled me savagely for being a canary-bird ; I replied
(bleatingly) protesting that there was no use in turning life
into King Lear ; presently it was discovered that there were
two dead combatants upon the field, each slain by an arrow
of the truth, and we tenderly carried off each other's corpses.
Here is a little comedy for Henry James to write !   the
beauty was each thought the other quite unscathed at
first.   But we had dealt shrewd stabs. . . .'

This is the beginning of Stevenson's letter about Meredith :
Saranac Lake, March 1888.   ' My dear delightful James,

—To quote your heading to my wife, I think no man
writes so elegant a letter, I am sure none so kind, unless it
be Colvin, and there is more of the stern parent about him.
I was vexed at your account of my admired Meredith : I
wish I could go and see him ; as it is I will try to write ; and
yet (do you understand me ?) there is something in that
potent, *genialisch* affectation that puts one on the strain
even to address him in a letter. He is not an easy man
to be yourself with : there is so much of him, and the
veracity and the high athletic intellectual humbug are so
intermixed.'

CHAPTER XX

MARRIAGE AND RETIREMENT

1903-1912

ALL obstacles being cleared away, the Colvins announced, in 1903, their forthcoming wedding, and I find some letters bearing upon the news. Thus, Henry James wrote, in April :—

'The Reform Club, April 29th, 1903.

' DEAR MRS. SITWELL,—How charming & interesting your note, & how deeply touched I feel at having your news from you in this delightful way. It gives me the greatest pleasure & I very affectionately congratulate you both. Besides being good, your intention is beautiful, which good intentions *always* aren't. And it has a noble poetic justice, in which there is a dignity matching even with that of the Monument. You talk of the crown of your romance coming late, but what do you say to the total absence (at the same lateness) of all crowns whatever, whether of romance or of anything else ?—which is the chill grey solitary portion of your faithful old friend,   ' HENRY JAMES

' *P.S.*—Please give my particular love to S. C., as you will see him before I have the chance to give him the very consecrating handshake—as to my sympathy—that I am keeping for him.'

And again in July, to Colvin : ' I am venturing to send you, & to send Mrs. Sitwell as conjoined with you, & on the occasion of that conjunction, a very modest little token of old friendship & affectionate participation, in the form of a diminutive (*very*) silver salver, big enough to hold a glass of wine or a vase of flowers.   The packet goes to you with my name on it somewhere & carries you both the dearest benediction of yours very constantly,

'HENRY JAMES'

From George Meredith :—

'*June* 18, 1903, *Box Hill, Dorking.*

'MY DEAR SIDNEY COLVIN,—This is your birthday, & you are on the eve of a happier day.   It could not have been better determined by both parties for the satisfaction of their friends.   You seem to be sure of such happiness as the world can give—& that, as you have the wisdom to reflect, is as much as we have a right to claim.

'I have not touched my pen for weeks, & I write first to you.   Yours heartily,—With love to the lady,

'GEORGE MEREDITH'

Mrs. Richmond Ritchie, Thackeray's daughter, sent as a wedding present Cunningham's *Lives of the Painters*, and with it a note : 'There is something in a life-long romance which is so noble & beautiful that everyone must catch some light & inspiration from realising that such good things *are* in the world.   I hoped it might have been a prettier first Edition that I was sending you.   I am taking it to the post through the lanes full of birds & flowering bushes.'

From the late Edmund Gosse, to Mrs. Sitwell :—

'*May Day,*
'17 *Hanover Terrace, Regent's Park, N.W.*, 1903.

'MY DEAR FRIEND,—We are wondering and discussing whether we might be indiscreet, & dare to congratulate S. C., if not you,—when your most delightful letter arrived. For a Little White Bird that happened to have been hopping on the Archiepiscopal luncheon-table, and overheard an indiscretion, had twittered it to us several days ago in strictest confidence.   (I hope you admire my rococo style, the consequence of Emotion ?)

' You do not, I hope, need to be told how very, very glad we are that you both have been so natural and sensible and comfortable as to take this wise, graceful step.   Won't it be delightful never any more to have to say " good-bye " to another ?   " And they shall go no more out "—there is such a sense of eucharist in that.   I am writing you such a poor, incoherent note, because I want if possible to catch the post.   But why aren't you going to be married this very month of May ?   Why wait for July ?   I am all against useless waitings.—Yours most sincerely, and in great joy,

' EDMUND G.'

From the author of *Red Pottage* :—

' *Preshaw, Bishops-Waltham, Hampshire, May 2nd* [1903].

' MY DEAR DEAR MR. COLVIN,—I am so glad.   I have just heard from Mrs. Sitwell.

' I *forbid* you to answer this.   I shall have *two* friends at the Museum now instead of one.

' You once told me that I had a miserably small vocabulary, because I owned when I was ill I could only say Oh ! Oh ! all the time.   Now I can only say I am so glad, I am so glad.—Your friend,   ' MARY CHOLMONDELEY '

From G. K. C. :—

' 60 *Overstrand Mansions, Battersea Park* [1903].

' DEAR MR. COLVIN,—Things do sometimes occur in this world so beautiful and sensible that in thinking or speaking of them one forgets all about oneself.   In the reality induced by my genuine feeling I will not conceal from myself or you that I have long been afraid that I have from time to time distressed you, both by things due to my detestable negligence & by other things which I really could not have avoided.   But the news I have just heard about you is the kind of thing that in my eyes makes my short-comings quite as microscopic & irrelevant as my merits.   I have as much right to look on at your new arrangements with delight as a criminal has to admire a sunset.—

' I will not say anything more about yourself or Mrs. Sitwell, because congratulations upon these real things always seem to me to be quite unsuited to this nasty & elegant language in which we write letters. If we could write a page of very exquisite blank verse, it might be all right, or erect an altar and slaughter a thousand oxen. As a milder form of burnt-offering, the only thing that occurs to me is to send you the copy of the Browning I had long marked off for you. Of what I owe you in that connection I need not speak. You will, I think, find that in the later part your most generous suggestions have borne fruit : the earlier part, I am sorry to say, had gone to Macmillan's, just too soon to be recalled or revised.

' I think it must be something atmospheric connected with the news about you that has kept me reading *Across the Plains* for hours when I ought to have been working.— Yours always most gratefully,   ' G. K. CHESTERTON '

A third letter from Henry James brings us to the ceremony itself :—

Lamb House, Rye, Sussex. Sunday.

' MY DEAR COLVIN,—I am greatly touched by your letter. Most indubitably will I, & with joy, come up for 12.30, on Tuesday, at S. Marylebone Church, & for the G. Central Hotel afterward. I thank you much, both, for giving me this chance to testify to the faithful allegiance of yours always,   HENRY JAMES '

From an article by Mrs. W. K. Clifford in *The Bookman* for April 1928, I take, by permission, her description of the wedding and its preparation : ' The bleak house took on fresh life, new friends and old gathered round them and wedding presents poured in. The marriage itself was a very quiet almost secret affair ; only half a dozen people knew the exact time and day. It took place in Marylebone Church, where two other great lovers, the Brownings —they had both known Browning intimately—had been

T

married in the years long gone. It was a fine morning, but dull and grey with not a hint of sunshine. We were told to take ourselves at half-past twelve to the side door of the church. I met Henry James on the doorstep, for we were both invited ; we entered together to find beautiful floral decorations : " Are these for Mr. Colvin's wedding? " Henry James asked the verger. He was answered with a snort and—" No ; they are for a fashionable wedding at half-past two." The little group consisted of the Bishop who married them, bride and bridegroom of course, her greatest friend Mrs. Babington (who was appropriately Louis Stevenson's cousin), his greatest friend Basil Champneys, Henry James and myself. A favourite niece was the only other witness, but she sat far down in the church and did not in any way join the wedding party ; she had perhaps stolen in unawares, for she vanished quickly.

' When the ceremony was over we were asked to take ourselves to the Great Central Hotel, a quarter of a mile off, but not in a group lest anyone should wonder what it meant. So we walked there on different sides of the way, though no one would have suspected six sedate middle-agers, of course in everyday clothes, of anything unusual. We sauntered casually into the hotel, where a quiet little luncheon party had been arranged. It was very quiet indeed ; the Colvins were obviously full of happy embarrassment ; the guests were afraid to laugh and spoke only in low tones lest the waiter should suspect it was a marriage feast. We did not even drink their health till someone, Basil Champneys I think, suggested that it ought to be done ; then a bottle of still white wine was brought, our glasses were filled, and when the waiter was out of sight and hearing we drank to the bride and bridegroom with little nods and whispers.

' In the afternoon they were to start for Porlock on their honeymoon. Henry James and I went to see them off from Paddington. We were all standing by the carriage door, smiling and happy, but low-toned and discreet—for

BASIL CHAMPNEYS

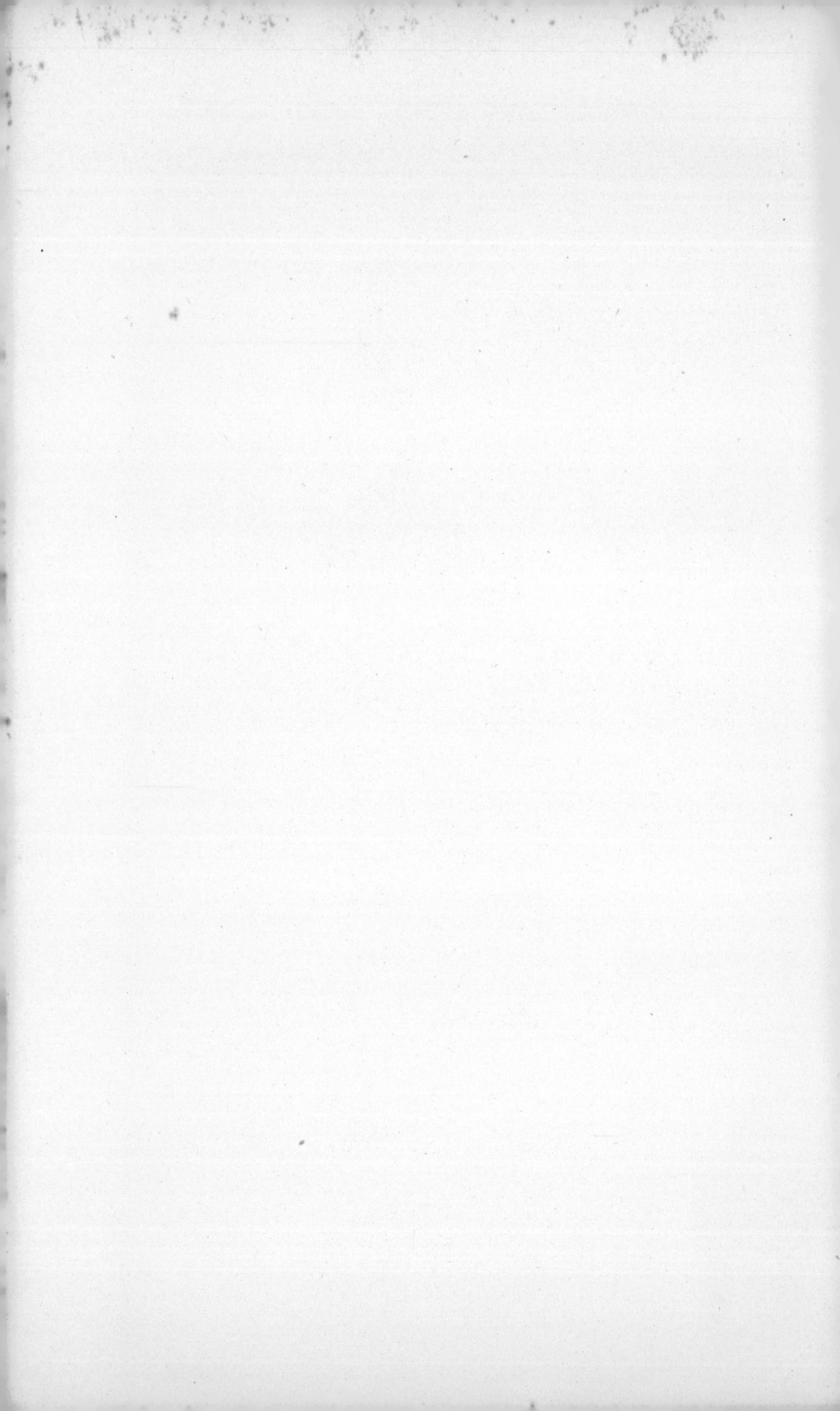

the newly-married still maintained their half-shy manner—
when suddenly along the platform came bounding a young
and beautiful figure in a red silk dress—one of the actresses
they had helped generously early in her career, who had
somehow heard of the affair just in time. She stood no
nonsense but flung her arms round their necks and kissed
them both joyously. They got into their train and went
off beaming with delight.'

A few days later Henry James wrote thus :—

'*Lamb House, Rye, Sussex, July* 14, 1903.

'DEAR MRS. COLVIN,—I am immensely touched by your
remembrance of a far-off friend in the midst of all the
isolating felicity that you describe, & that I can, through
all this last wondrous beauty of summer, easily constitute
for myself on your benignant shore. It gives me joy to
hear of your both being free of spirit and sense to grasp
at the happy days as they successively hover & as they (in
the manner of happy days) quite blandly melt. But draw
them out, & hold them tight, & keep in your hands as many
of the pieces as you can. I *am* preserving a good piece,
myself, as in lavender & tissue paper, of the—of our—
Marylebone Tuesday. Trust me for that. It has been hot
beastly summer here & propitious to garden life, but without
your woods, your immediate waters, your society (for each
of each) or, above all, your happy *interval* in the fray.
I am obliged to go to town tomorrow for 3 days, but don't
count it as an interval. My nearest approach to one has
been the presence down here for this past Sunday of your
delightful young Irish friend Jocelyn Persse. I feel as if
I ought to thank you for him. But the night wanes ; & I
am already thinking of the Bloomsbury sequel to the Marylebone morning. I in a manner await you both again & am
yours very constantly,   HENRY JAMES'

Among the letters is a considerable packet from Stephen
Phillips, in which, however, I find nothing that seems to
demand quotation. They are wholly concerned with the

work on which he was engaged, and are full of hopes and plans and frustrations. Although covering several years, they may fittingly be referred to at this point. Phillips, whom few now remember, first attracted the notice of readers of poetry with a slim paper-covered book entitled *Christ in Hades*, in Elkin Mathews' Shilling Series in 1897. In the following year he published *Poems*, in which was included ' Marpessa ' and ' The Wife,' the one charged with sweetness and tenderness, and the other a grimly realistic story of despair. Upon the Colvins these works wrought marvellously, and they entertained and made much of their young author, then in the thirties : a cousin of Colvin's friend and colleague Laurence Binyon. From lyrical and reflective moods Phillips passed on to dramatic, and gave the stage the splendour and terror of *Herod* and the wistful beauty of *Paolo and Francesca*. These both increased his fame and the Colvins' fervour. The intensity of the lovers' passion in *Paolo and Francesca* stirred Lady Colvin to her depths, while Colvin rejoiced in the good fortune that had brought poetry back to the stage.

There is no doubt that emotion got the better of judgment and that their praises of Phillips sounded extravagant ; none the less, the excess was a defect of a fine quality, and no one could have foreseen how unfit Phillips was to carry adulation and success, and how rapid would be his decline.

After Phillips's untimely death in 1915, aged fifty-one, Colvin wrote for Humphry Ward's *English Poets* his calm opinion. I quote the opening passage : ' In regard to this poet the critical pendulum had for some years before his death swung sharply from the side of over-praise to that of over-neglect. It will some day recover its equilibrium, and Phillips will then be recognized as having belonged, by the gift of passion (" the all-in-all in poetry," as Lamb has it), by natural largeness of style and pomp and melody of rhythm and diction, as well as by intensity of imaginative vision in those fields where his imagination was really awake, to the great lineage and high tradition of English poetry.'

And again of Phillips as a dramatist : ' It may justly be argued that Phillips's aim in drama was intended to be on Greek lines much rather than on Shakespearian : that the intense, the Shakespearian individualization of characters has been no part of the aim, still less of the achievement, of tragic drama in some of the great literatures of the world—it is not a capital element either in the Greek drama or the classical French : and again, that rhetoric in poetic drama there needs must be, and between the right and appropriate rhetoric of a situation, when it is touched with passion and imagination, as much of it in these plays truly is,—between such rhetoric and truly great dramatic poetry the line is difficult to draw, if it can be drawn at all.'

There is little of special interest to record at this time, but I may say that one of the most eventful moments in Colvin's life was when he received, in 1907, the following letter from Lord Curzon :—

' MY DEAR COLVIN,—As the new Chancellor of Oxford I have the privilege of drawing up the list of Hon. Degrees to be conferred at my Initiation on June 26. You are so eminent in so many branches of Arts & Letters that I feel that if I were fortunate enough to persuade you to come I should be conferring upon the University an honour greater than any it could bestow.

' Will you then accept the Hon. Degree of D.Litt. at my hands on that occasion ?—Yours sincerely,

' CURZON '

Colvin naturally accepted, the honour being one that he particularly valued, coming as it did from the other University. I find that he was also an Hon. LL.D. of St. Andrews and Corresponding Member of the Institute of France and the Royal Academy of Belgium. He was a member of the Council of the Hellenic Society, the School of Athens, the National Trust for Places of Historic Interest

294 THE COLVINS AND THEIR FRIENDS

or Natural Beauty, and the National Art Collections Fund,
to which he left a legacy.

There is in Lord Curzon's hand also this graceful invitation to Hackwood a few years later : ' I have a few
people staying here tomorrow till Monday, and the idea has
suddenly come into my head—what a charming thing it
would be for me, for us, if perchance you were free and
would like a little change to the country, and could be
persuaded to come down & join us.

' The suddenness and beauty of the idea must be held
to justify the extravagant shortness of the notice.' [1]

Two scraps from isolated letters may be inserted here.
This, from Mr. Rudyard Kipling : ' I shall be very happy
to come if I am alive, but I fancy I shall be frozen dead in
another 48 hours. Never again will I spend another winter
in this accursed bucket-shop of a refrigerator called England.'

And this from Lord Milner, about his portrait by Theodore
Roussel, the artist who painted Colvin's portrait for the
Savile Club : ' Personally I am quite unshaken about the
picture, only greatly disappointed for Roussel's sake that
it has been so badly received in some quarters. Some of
my personal friends have been the worst. They have not
even tried to understand what R. was trying to do. The
friend, who expects *one* portrait to represent you in *all* the
aspects agreeable to him, and in no other, may be a treasure
as a friend, but as a critic of a work of art he is hopeless.'

Colvin's name as a knight appeared in the New Year
Honours on January 1, 1911. From the letters of felici-
tation I choose one from J. M. Barrie : not then Sir James,
and not then a member of the Order of Merit, as he now is :—

'2 *Jan.* 1911.

' DEAR LADY COLVIN,—Another letter ! But you must
not trouble to answer it. I can't however resist writing to
congratulate you both, and to you in preference because I
can't to his face tell Colvin what I think of him. However,

---

[1] In the Fitzwilliam Museum.

to you! He is probably quite unaware that for many years he has added dignity to the calling of letters and that (as I believe) everyone who follows it holds him in honour. By his fellows he is most admired—it is what everyone would like best. It has certainly been many a time a pleasant thought to me that Sidney Colvin *is*.—Believe me always very sincerely,   J. M. BARRIE '

In 1911 Colvin brought out a new four-volume edition of Stevenson's correspondence under the title *The Letters of Robert Louis Stevenson*, in this work the *Vailima Letters* being sorted in in their chronological order. In 1912 came his retirement from the Museum, and this is the letter written by Sir Frederic Kenyon on behalf of the Trustees of the British Museum when that event occurred :—

'*British Museum, London, W.C., July 8th*, 1912.

' MY DEAR COLVIN,—The Trustees on Saturday desired me to convey to you an expression of their regret that your connection with the Museum has been terminated by your retirement, and of their cordial thanks to you for the services which you have rendered to them and to the Museum during the twenty-nine years that you have been Keeper of the Department of Prints and Drawings. The great advance made by the Department during that period is the best measure of the skill and judgment with which it has been administered ; and if the Print Room now stands, as they believe it does, at the head of all such institutions in the world, they recognise that this is largely due to the work of yourself and of those whom you have trained and directed. They are aware that the Department has owed many of its most important accessions to the liberality of private donors, and they know that the extent of these donations is due to the influence which you have personally exercised in the interests of the Museum.

' The Trustees regret that the regulations with regard to the age-limit should have necessitated your retirement before the transference of the Print Department to its new quarters ; but they hope that you may long have health and strength to enjoy your freedom from official labours. Believe me—Yours very sincerely,

'F. G. KENYON'

Colvin's retirement from the Museum was marked by a banquet to him by his friends on November 1, 1912, at which Lord Crewe took the chair and the company was representative of the literature, learning, and art of the day. The principal speeches were made by Lord Crewe, Sir (then Mr.) Austen Chamberlain, Sir Martin Conway, the late Lord Moulton, and Sir (then Mr.) Robert Witt. Colvin's own remarks, some of which, concerning Cambridge, I have already quoted, were perhaps a shade too literary for the best oratory, but they do not read the less pleasantly for that.

Much that is in the speech as privately printed was not spoken at all, owing to the passing of time ; and it was for this reason, since the speech enunciated the credo of a museum director and art critic, that Colvin circulated it afterwards. Of museums he spoke thus : ' The great problem of museum management is how to prevent the treasures so gathered and set out from being dead things ; how to arouse in those who come to see them a living sense of what they are and mean. What can one do to awaken the mind of the average man and woman to some dim perception even of their surface qualities and significance— let alone all that tremendous tale of skill and effort, of human self-protection, self-help, and self-expression, of the passion for perpetuity, of joy, devotion, and aspiration that lies behind the surface ? The problem is no easy one. One way at least is that we, their keepers and expounders, should keep our own interest in them ever alive and enkindled in ourselves, and never let the work lapse for us into a matter of flat drudgery and routine, like the drudgery and routine of commonplace and less privileged professions. Another way might be by greatly developing the system of

oral exposition lately begun in the British Museum : I remember Sir William Harcourt, when he was Chancellor of
the Exchequer and would have had to provide the funds,
saying, wisely as I think, that he would like to see a specially
qualified cicerone-assistant attached to the staff of every
department.'

To the new developments in painting he came, by way of
answering the question, Who, should museums be weeded
out, would do the weeding ? ' Think,' he said, ' of the
fluctuations of taste, and how one age despises the work of
one period of the past and the next age takes it into favour
again. The eighteenth century would cheerfully have
swept into the dust-bin most, if not all, of the paintings
of the fourteenth and fifteenth. The nineteenth century
came and turned round and cherished them perhaps almost
too exclusively. The twentieth—who knows ?—may turn
round and despise them again. Take the present hour—
what violent conflicts of opinion surround us as to what is
worth doing in art and what posterity will value. The art
discussion and chatter of the day run all on post-impression-
ism—cubism—futurism. To some the products of these
theories are objects of mere derision and disgust. To others
they are big with the promise of a new birth of art. I will
own frankly that I am of the former persuasion. I do not
believe—I do not find in other matters—that age has yet
fossilized my mind or ossified my sympathies. And for
some at least of the prophets of the new art-creeds—need
I name Mr. Roger Fry—I entertain such respect and affection as would make me try my very hardest to go along
with them. But I cannot. To me their doctrine seems
untenable in fact and logic, and their practice a *reductio ad
absurdum* of their doctrine. This violent, forced simplification, most remote from true simplicity ; this self-imposed
crudity and barbarity and puerility of pattern in line and
colour : this professed interpretation of natural appearances,
not in themselves but in their inner emotional significance,
by means of rude painted symbols which may be sincerely

meant, but have the misfortune to be indistinguishable
from the daubings of incompetence or imposture, or even,
in some cases, of insanity—I cannot persuade myself to
find in these things seeds of regeneration, or anything more
than fruits of the aberration of an hour.   As for those who
call themselves futurists, the arrogance of the name surely
tells us what to think of them.   The house of the future,
gentlemen, by which I mean the house of fame, to be built
by the memory and esteem of coming generations—that
mansion may be vast but will assuredly be crowded.   It
will not have room for many of us—even of so distinguished
a company as are here tonight assembled.   Those who
think to storm it by a name, calling themselves futurists,
stripping themselves of the past, disowning and dishonour-
ing the past, knocking naked and self-disinherited at the
doors of the future—they, be sure, will fling themselves
against those doors in vain and drop unregarded, poor
ephemera, into the void.'

The peroration ran thus :   ' I am what is called a free
man, and I hope to devote the rest of my days to the pursuit
of literature, from which destiny drew, or pushed, me away
nigh on forty years ago.   Not that I am satisfied that either
museum work or literature was my true vocation.   My
true vocation, I sometimes feel with conviction, was to be
a millionaire.   I daresay stirrings towards the same career
have been felt by many of you.   I feel convinced that none
of you would have adorned it as I should.   What I am
thinking of is not a commonplace great fortune, but one of
the colossal sort that would enable a man to do and see done
on a great scale the things he really cared for.   Had I such
a fortune, Sirs, you should see things hum along lines that
I believe most of you here present do care for as I care.   You
should see great pictures from our private collections stream-
ing into Trafalgar Square instead of away beyond the seas.
You should see the National Art Collections Fund gloriously
endowed, and the National Trust for the preservation of
places of national beauty and historic interest enabled to

secure for the community a number, ten times greater than they can deal with now, of precious buildings and tracts and breathing spaces of health and beauty. You should see sites of ancient civilization excavated by the dozen simultaneously, instead of slowly as now by ones and twos. . . .

' But these are day-dreams, inspired perhaps by the glowing atmosphere of this festivity. They will pass by to-morrow, and I shall go back to my books, in hopes of perhaps doing something yet, in my advancing years, that shall make me more worthy of the kind thoughts you have of me, and at any rate beyond measure touched and encouraged by those thoughts and by your expression of them.'

Since Colvin in his speech referred to a contribution of my own to the bill of fare, I reproduce it here. The lines were printed on the back of the card, and ran thus :—

> ' How unfamiliar Bloomsbury has grown
> Since Colvin left that corner house of stone
> To which so many, nigh on thirty years,
> Have carried manuscripts, and hopes, and fears,
> Finding a welcome and encouragement
> And faring forth divinely confident !
> How unfamiliar ! nor can aught occur
> To give us back its ancient character.

> ' One book, if any one, is still to write :
> The eulogy of critics who incite ;
> Who wait not till the enterprise is done,
> But seek young talent out and help it on ;
> Ranking above appraisement at the end
> The constant stimulus of friend to friend ;
> Whose banner is disinterestedness ;
> Whose chosen recompense, those friends' success.

> ' And chief of such in these our latter days
> Is he whom we are gathered here to praise.'

What I was trying to express in verse Mr. Christopher Morley has said in prose. Speaking of the ' Monument,' which he visited in 1911 at Colvin's invitation, several

times, he recalls how himself when young ' looked with awe
upon his sacred relics of so many who had been until then
only wizard names. Those were happy days : there were
no wars, all was fair that time could bring, and to sit and
talk with the gracious host and great gentleman who had
known Ruskin, Browning, Meredith, Stevenson, Hardy
. . . to hear first of all from him the name (even then, 1911,
not much known) of Joseph Conrad, this was the kind of
escapade into amazement that a young man does not forget.
Oh, a very sound thing for a very young acolyte is that
sentiment of awe. One knew when one was near the
vibration of greatness.'

Colvin, as I have said, printed his speech in full, for
private circulation, and sent copies not only to all his hosts
at the dinner but also to many absentees. Among these
were Dr. Butler, the Master of Trinity, and the Archbishop
of Canterbury, a very old friend of both Colvin and Lady
Colvin. The Master wrote thus :—

' *November* 23, 1912, *Trinity Lodge, Cambridge.*

' MY DEAR SIR SIDNEY,—It is only to-day that I have
succeeded in giving myself the great pleasure of reading
your singularly eloquent speech. I really cannot think of
any speech in which so many gifted minds have been so
happily sketched for us—each sketch a real recognizable
Portrait. Perhaps your long life among Portraits may have
given you help and light in this direction !

' Among the many that have most come home to myself,
helping me to " look at " them again, and watch smile or
gleam or stammer, are Ruskin and Mat. Arnold and Jebb
and Thatcher and dear Henry Sidgwick. " A balanced
Ruskin, an unsuperior Arnold " are delightful incarnations
of the Unthinkable !

' I wish I could have *heard* the Speech, but we had a great
day here on Nov. 1st, and I felt tied to my post. I think
no sentence would have made me both laugh and sympa-
thise more than the charming [illegible words] towards the

bottom of page 15, where you reveal your "true vocation."
I remember once when I went into solitude for a few days at
the Bristol Hotel, Brighton, to get rid of a voiceless throat,
I spent the greater part of a happy walk towards Rotters'
Dean in going through a little disinterested meditation,
and thinking what I would do on Two Millions a Year!
O the many grand schemes of Philanthropy that have been
rendered abortive because no Peabody or Carnegie was
telepathic enough to lay the first stone.

'We are expecting Lord Crewe here in about an hour. I
think I must question him about the Dinner and the Speech.
—Believe me to be very truly yours,
                              'H. MONTAGU BUTLER'

And this is from the Primate :—

'Dec. 18, 1912, Old Palace, Canterbury.

'MY DEAR COLVIN,—I have been disgracefully remiss in
not thanking you more speedily for your kindness in sending me the text of a speech marked by a range of knowledge,
a forcefulness of wit, and a power of literary expression
which few could rival. Would that I had been among
those who listened to it. By some accident for which I
cannot account I heard nothing of the occasion until it
was too late.

'Your words about museum matters are of permanent
value. And now we shall await fresh output from your
brain & pen for the common good.

'With every highest & deepest good will to you & Lady
Colvin for Christmastide, I am—Vy truly yours,
                              'RANDALL Cantuar'

The Colvins after much search found a home that pleased
them at No. 35 Palace Garden Terrace, and there the rest
of their lives was spent, with an interval in the country
each summer.

CHAPTER XXI

JOSEPH CONRAD

1904–1924

So far as I can ascertain, Colvin and Conrad first exchanged letters in 1904, but the earliest letter in the *Life and Letters*, edited by G. Jean Aubry, is dated April 28, 1905. Conrad was then forty-seven, and had just finished *Nostromo*. Colvin, for some months, had been urging the Stage Society to produce Conrad's play *One Day More*, and the following letter (I am quoting only from those not already published) refers to the cast. It is written from London : ' I remain here bound fast by the necessities of dictation, which is the only way, as I discover, to break the high wave of work which threatens to swallow me up altogether.

' Reverting to the play. I imagine that the provisional committee (including Miss Constance Collier) is much too indulgent. Mr. Tree no doubt will show himself more severe ; and I am willing (quite honestly) to admit the justness of all his remarks—beforehand. I do not, even in my thoughts, question your judgment and experience. The only questions that arise are : Is the thing (so slight) worth the labour—which is partly answered by the fact of your interest ; next : what of the Time (with a cap. T). I am by no means sure that there is a playwright (let alone a dramatist) in me.'

In another early letter, undated, Conrad expresses what he feels about play-writing : ' As a matter of fact I *feel* on the subject with you. And this is not because I 've no conception, no general *idée à moi*, of what I 'd like to do on the stage. I have that. But I have also a very clear perception of my innate clumsiness in carrying out anything, unless with much toil and trouble. Work has never been to me a feast of cakes and ale.

'In this case I 've been hampered also by the particular ignorance of the craft. Therefore I went straight ahead catching the inspiration of the moment as it came for fear that a more careful reflexion would bring me to absolute inaction. The only thing I 've consciously looked to was versimilitude of dialogue. And even there I 've an uneasy suspicion of having failed.

'Not altogether, however, I suppose, since you think the thing worth talking over. I assure you that if there were no such being in the world as a theatrical manager I would still be most eager to hear (and absorb) your criticism.'

In June 1905 we have this : 'I repeat once more—pray have no scruples in handling the play in the light of your judgment. I could of course argue for days in defence of everything I 've done, but I know also of what strange illusions as to the *portée* of his work every imaginative writer is the prey. I am quite aware that it is quite inpossible for me to look upon that one little act *intelligently* —I mean in a detached manner. There would be always the question (not of amour propre at all) but of *feeling*— the feeling in which the play was conceived—in the way. The *end* is altogether tentative as it stands now.'

One Day More was performed on June 25. In August 1912 : 'Yes. We have the little car. It 's a worthy and painstaking one-cylinder puffer which amuses us very much ; but a journey of 80 miles is not to be undertaken lightly on the back of that antiquity.

'I have been doing uncommonly badly since April last. A most beggarly tale of pages ! And just now I feel out of sorts—devil only knows why. However, one must go on. Do or die. But at present I have no taste for either alternative.'

On January 20, 1914 :—

' MY DEAR COLVIN,—I 've been celebrating the publication of *Chance* by a fit of gout which has kept me in bed for several days ; or I would have written long before this to tell you how much I appreciate your good letter and the review in the *Observer*.

' Indeed I can't say much even yet. I am still muddled and, frankly, unable to think from this horrible gout. But I can feel (if I can't express to any purpose) a profound gratitude for what you have done for the book, and for all the body of my work, by your most friendly and discriminating review. I won't say more just now but I hope before long to thank you, in words if I can only find them, for this fresh proof of your most prized good will.—Yours ever,   J. CONRAD '

' My warmest regards to Lady Colvin. That she should have been interested in the book gives me the greatest delight.'

The following passage is from Colvin's review : ' Criticism has long ago, but popular favour hardly yet, fully recognized the extraordinary power and value of the work in tale, romance and reminiscence which Mr. Conrad has been contributing to our literature in the last eighteen years ; work which sets before us the fruits of a remarkable experience enriched a hundredfold in the ripening light and heat of imagination ; work combining, as scarcely any other in our time combines, the threefold powers of enthralling narrative, magically vital description and an unflagging subtlety and sanity of analytic character study ; work, finally, distinguished by so resourceful a mastery of English speech and style that we very rarely find ourselves thinking, whether to admire or to condone, of the fact that the writer is not English-born.'

A year and a half later Conrad thanks Colvin for a review, also in the *Observer*, of *Victory* : ' You cannot doubt, my dear friend and generous critic, that I appreciate pro-

foundly every line, every intention of your review. Many
thanks for all you found to say—for the warmth of your
praise and the really tender delicacy of your reservations.
I am touched when I think of you laying aside your work
and giving up your time and thought to mine. That in
itself I consider a very high recognition of my endeavours.
'I won't fill the paper this time. It's time for the post.
I'll only mention that the book has made a good start,
11,000 copies having been sold in the first 3 days. A rather
extraordinary success for—Yours ever,

'JOSEPH CONRAD'

The following passage, in August 1917, refers to a eulogy
that I cannot identify : ' I see that it is to your friendship
and to your authority I owe the (lavish ?—magnificent ?—
gorgeous ?) tribute from over the sea. You may be sure it
is very welcome. Authors, as you cannot but know, can
stand a lot of jam on their bread. And apart from that
I prize particularly every word said in favour of my
reminiscences.

'I think I'll drop this enthusiastic young man a line.
But not yet, as I am in bed with some sort of internal disturbance—and writing in bed even on an invalid table
worries and exasperates me beyond reason. I am a
ridiculous person.'

After telling of the way in which his elder son Borys was
being entertained by Americans while on leave in Paris,
Conrad adds: 'It strikes me I'll have to be mighty civil to
a good many Americans after the War.'

In the following letter, also undated, we have, I think,
a foresight of Colvin's *Memories and Notes*, as first planned :
' My head is very full of the work we talked about the other
evening. My mind's eye sees it in three vols. beautifully
printed, the grace and the earnestness of the near past
presented for us and our children with your fascinating
serenity of expression.'

On January 20, 1920, just after Conrad's return from his

U

triumphant visit to America : ' My old friend the gout
has come along to keep me company. That devil took
lodgings in my wrist, has enlarged it considerably and is
making himself at home inside in a way that causes me to
gnash my teeth when I don't want to do it. I don't want
to do anything. If you were to peep magically into my
study you would see me sitting absolutely motionless like
a crabbed, unasiatic-looking Buddha—and not even twirling
my thumbs—all day long.

' However, the last 3 days I 've managed to put in about
an hour a day pruning the text of *The Rescue* with the
utmost severity. I don't know when that work will be
published, and I am not much interested in it generally.
What however does interest me no end is your statement
about a forthcoming vol. of yours. I am more than delighted
to know that those most distinguished *croquis des personnes*
out of your past are going to be collected. In that good
company you enumerate, there will also be another *homme
du monde* of the widest sympathies and beautifully controlled
expression, scholar, artist, observer, judge of character and
devoted friend. You don't name him ; but I think that
in that book where his name will only appear on the title-
page much will be revealed to us of Sidney Colvin with
son tour d'esprit très avisé et un peu mordant, and expressed with a sort of fascinating quietness I have never
met before in anybody. I am *so* pleased you have made
up your mind ! I do really think too that the book may
very well turn out a *succès de librairie*. I won't expound to
you my reasons for so thinking, here and now, because of
" lack of space." But they are good, very good.'

On April 21, 1920 : ' I may safely say that this is the first
moment of moral and physical relief I have tasted since
our return from Liverpool just before Christmas. Perhaps
we both have " turned the corner " now ! At any rate if
Jessie has done so I am likely to follow ;—longo intervallo—
but still I will get round too, I think. I may tell *you* that
I feel very much shaken physically. Mental effort costs

me more than it ought to, I fancy. I have done some work, however—not of a very profitable kind tho'—three prefaces for my collected Edition. I have also finished a play—I don't know why. I mean I don't know why I have done that thing at all. But it's done. I had also no end of a grind over the text of *The Rescue* to make it fit for book-form.

'Heavens! How I have slaved over that book! That prose!

'And in this connection: I hope, my dear Colvin, you have understood that it is only absolute impossibility which prevented me dedicating it to your wife. I had promised it (*that* particular book) to Penfield the last U.S. Ambassador to the late Empire of the East, in the year 1914, in commemoration of my gratitude for his kindness to us—a kindness which had every appearance of a *Rescue*.'

Jessie is Mrs. Conrad. The kindness of Mr. Penfield was exercised in getting the Conrads out of Poland, where they were bottled up at the outbreak of the War, and restoring them to England.

Two undated scraps: 'I have made an enthusiastic note of your promise to read a little poetry with me when you come to see us.

'I look upon the promise as no small favour, for you have the gift of uttering winged words admirably. Admirably! I've heard you quote a few lines and it was enough to make me, as it were, sit up inwardly at once.'

And: 'How extremely kind of you to think of sending me the books. You are indeed a true friend. And what an interesting selection.

'I do hope I will be able to put on if only a Jaeger boot on Thursday. I hate going out in a cloth gout-boot—it's too early-Victorian for a common mortal. It was well enough for Lord Palmerston.'

After the receipt of *Memories and Notes* (in, however, not three but a single volume) :—

'*1st Nov.* 1921.

'MY VERY DEAR COLVIN,—The reading of *Memories and Notes* has been one continuous delight. As you know, I have been privileged to see some of these papers even in typescript—and some in their serial form. But the quality of their interest and freshness is of the kind that does not perish in the reading and re-reading. I feel much honoured by my presentation copy bearing corrections in the text in your own handwriting.

' These detached pages have a singularly charming oneness of atmosphere—a touching serenity in their clear light, and a classical simplicity of suggestive lines in portraiture and landscape which is most satisfying to one's tastes and one's emotions. My warmest and most loving congratulations on the effectiveness of your memory and the sureness of every vital touch. Dearest love to Lady Colvin (who ought to be pleased with the marvellous glow of the dedicatory preface) and to you from us both.—Ever yours,   JOSEPH CONRAD '

Conrad returns to *Memories and Notes* in his next letter, with reference to the paper on Stevenson, which had originally been given as a lecture : ' I have been deeply moved in reading your lecture. If Stevenson was a lucky man to have such friends as you, I may count myself as lucky too—with less merit but the more gratitude for that unexpected, unhoped-for good fortune. Infinite thanks for the matter and the manner, for the honour of being placed, in such generous spirit, near Stevenson—and for the choice of the extract, which surely had been dictated by a most friendly care.'

This is the passage : ' Of those who had not begun to publish before he [R. L. S.] died, the man I imagine him calling for first of all is the above-mentioned Mr. Conrad. Some time about 1880-90 these two seafarers, the Polish gentleman turned British merchant-skipper and the ocean-loving author cruising far and wide in search of health, might quite well have met in life, only that the archipelago of Mr. Conrad's chief experiences was the Malay, that of Stevenson's the Polynesian. Could my dream be fulfilled,

JOSEPH CONRAD IN 1924
FROM A PHOTOGRAPH IN THE POSSESSION OF MRS. CONRAD, NOW FIRST PUBLISHED

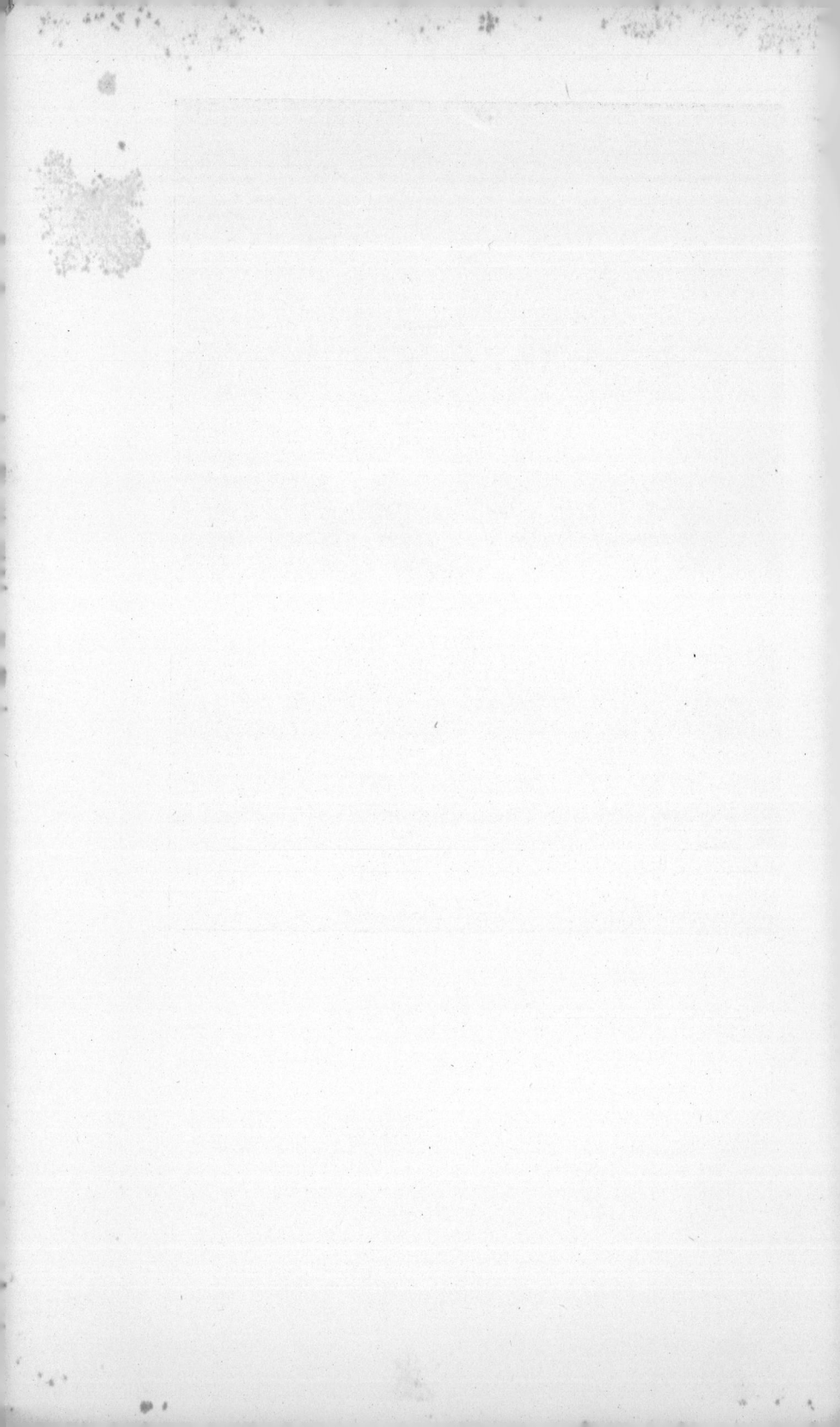

how they would delight in meeting now ! What endless ocean and island yarns the two would exchange ; how happily they would debate the methods and achievements of their common art ; and how difficult it would be to part them ! As I let myself imagine such meeting, I know not which of the two presences is the more real and near to me, yours, my good friend Conrad, whom I hope and mean to greet in the flesh to-morrow or the next day or the next, or that of Stevenson, since my last sight of whom, as he waved good-bye to me from the deck of the *Ludgate Hill*, I know as a fact of arithmetic, but can in no other sense realize, that there has passed a spell of no less than four-and-thirty years or the life-time of a whole generation.'

Conrad died in 1924, two days after Lady Colvin.

In the letters are constant references to Perceval Gibbon, the novelist, and to his two little girls : such as, for instance, this in 1918 : ' P. G. has seen me several times and asked me to send to Lady Colvin and yourself his affectionate regards. The poor man is not happy. He yearns for his girls, whom he has not seen for three years. He is now in the service of the Admiralty and has the rank of a Major of Marines. I think he is doing very good work. He is off to-morrow on a mission of 30 days to the French and Italian Navy. He has learned Italian and acquired an immense love for Italy, and he sleeps with the *Div. Com.* under his pillow.'

Here are passages from Gibbon's letters to Colvin. In August 1912: ' If I were to apologise for not writing sooner in answer to your letter of July 19, it might suggest that I had forgotten or neglected to do so. But it isn't so. Says I to myself, from time to time : " No need to send civil notes to a decent man like that. When it stops raining—if it ever does—something will happen and I 'll write and tell him about it." But, dash it, sir, it hasn't stopped raining, and the only thing that has happened is that I have bought a car—a real car—as the seller said, " a gentleman's car "—. Stop—I forgot. On the fourteenth of this month, my wife, who went to bathe while I was away for a walk, got out of her depth, caught cramp, and was narrowly saved from drowning by the only man within earshot who was willing to risk his life. It really was a near thing : I hate to think how near : and the rescue was well and gallantly done. When I went to the rescuer afterwards to thank him, he said : "Oh, please don't say anything. I 've always wanted a chance to do something like that."

' A Mr. Robert Ross has written to me and given me the privilege of putting my name on the general committee for a dinner to you in November—which I was delighted to do.'

Robert Ross, whose name will always be associated with that of Oscar Wilde for his chivalrous loyalty to that unfortunate man, had thrown himself into the project for the banquet to Colvin.

Gibbon's next letter, from Starasagora in Bulgaria, in December : ' It seems, after all, that I am going to miss your dinner ; I have no luck. I am here for the *Daily News* at my former trade of war correspondent, and at this moment am tied by the leg in this grievous Turkish town, 80 miles from the nearest fighting. It appears that Bulgaria means to win or lose her war without publicity, as far as she can ; at any rate, not one of us has yet heard a shot fired. We are walking about in our breeches and gaiters, slaving to get together items of news to supplement the silly official "bulletins," which never admit a defeat or even a large number of casualties. If I were you, I wouldn't believe too much of what I see in the newspapers from Starasagora ; " I works where it 's made."

' As to the dinner, I shan't be there. Probably, if I have luck, I shall be in the trenches before Adrianople. But though I shall not drink to you nor applaud the speech that praises you, my earnest friendship and sincere good wishes are not the less yours.'

Three more brief extracts from Gibbon's letters : ' We should have been in town with the babies, and rung you up to ask if we might bring them round, long before now, but for the " weeping weather." They came back from Christmas with a pair of colds ; my people, whom we had been visiting, have a house which is a powerfully conceived system of draughts ; and as the little devils take their time over colds and cling to them as if they were fond of them, their various engagements were called off. We were all to have gone to Conrad's for a sort of second Christmas festivity, but it proved impossible. But, if you will let us, we are coming just as soon as the weather eases off a trifle, and I know the babies will be glad to see you and Lady Colvin again.'

' Joan, having inspected the books, made a comment which would, I think, have pleased Caldecott himself. She had examined with particular care the one which illustrates the affair of the Knave of Hearts and had her finger upon the picture of the King chastising the Knave with his sceptre. " This," she said with emphasis,—" *this* is drawed proper ! " I am bidden by the pair of them to convey to you their love and to thank you in a variety of forms. Joyce says you are " something *like* a Sir " ; this is a comparison, strongly in your favour, with the only other person she knows who has a title.'

' I am trying to write short stories and, for the moment, failing dismally. I have a brain of dry pith and can't invent even anecdotes, much less imagine characters, situations and atmospheres. I suppose it will pass before we are forced into the workhouse. Thank God for the modern magazine, which will pay as much for an arbitrary sentimental invention as for a work of inspiration. As O. Henry said, whom should we do without it ? '

When the War broke out Gibbon was sent to Russia by the *Daily Chronicle,* and he wrote to Colvin no more, or no more of his letters were kept. He died in 1926.

CHAPTER XXII

THE *LIFE OF KEATS* AND *MEMORIES AND NOTES*

1917–1921

COLVIN'S principal work in the first years of his retirement was the completion of his large biography and critical estimate of Keats. The first book had been but an essay; the new one was to be definitive—if any author could bring himself to use such a word. Whether or no Colvin dared to, I cannot say, or whether the late Miss Amy Lowell also had enough temerity; but certain it is that, in America at any rate, her two great volumes effectively, on their appearance in 1925, eclipsed Colvin's single tome of 1917. While engaged upon the *Life of Keats*, Colvin brought out, in 1915, through Messrs. Chatto and Windus, a new edition of the Poems, chronologically arranged; while it was during his work on the poet that he set upon preparing his Presidential address for the English association, his theme being *Concentration in English Poetry*.

According to the lecturer, the subject was suggested to him by George Meredith; but let me give the story in his own words: ' Meredith was fond, especially in later years, of reading to any friend who might be with him the poetry he had last been writing. His tones in reading were impressively rotund, resonant, and masterful, but withal level and not much modulated. I have spent many hours with him listening to such reading, enjoying the rich roll of sound and the presence and atmosphere of his potent personality, but finding, as those familiar with his verse will easily imagine, the sense of what he read often hard to follow. As a rule he courted no criticism and allowed for

no difficulty ; but on the day of which I speak he was more
indulgent than usual. He paused to say that he knew
some people found his poetry obscure, and to ask whether
I did, and where, and why ? I tried to point out some
puzzles in his printed poems which I had failed to solve,
even with the page before me and full leisure to study it.
But he simply could not see that they were puzzles at all,
and closed the talk characteristically with a crow of exult-
ing laughter over the sluggishness of my Saxon wits. In
the course of it, defining his own aims and ideals in verse,
he repeated several times with insistence, " Concentration
and suggestion, Colvin, concentration and suggestion, those
are the things I care for and am always trying for in poetry." '

The lecture in its reprinted form makes excellent reading,
provocative at times and always alert and pointed. I remember the occasion well, and how Colvin's voice either
reverberated like an organ or shook with a deep tremolo
as the poets' periods moved him. He read poetry with a
kind of rapture that was capable of becoming almost a
Gregorian chant.

Looking now at the pamphlet I cannot believe that it
can all have been delivered orally on that afternoon, and I
cannot agree that extracts from Meredith are suitable for
public declamation. Colvin, however, was always critic
and writer rather than orator.

I quote a passage analysing and eulogizing Meredith as
a poet : ' I shall not take any of these [recent younger poets]
for my modern instances of the confirmed habit of concentration and condensation in poetry. More extreme and
conspicuous instances will at once occur to you. Browning
will most probably occur : Meredith, I should expect,
certainly. Between these two masters there was in fact
this in common, that each threw into his work an extraordinary amount of intellectual energy ; each crowded his
lines with meaning, and the result in both cases was frequent
obscurity, or at least a heavy strain on what Macaulay, in
that criticism of Dryden which Mr. Balfour quoted, calls

" the ductility of language." Or shall we fall back on a
more old-fashioned quotation, and say that each failed in
his degree to combine with his other excellences the particular excellence which Shenstone attributes to Pope, that
of " consolidating or condensing sentences, yet preserving
ease and perspicuity." Browning, as we all know, commonly uses a hurried elliptical style of great compression,
tacking clause on to clause in breathless, almost grammar-
less, apposition, throwing over the auxiliary parts of speech,
discarding relative pronouns, skipping here and hinting
there, and generally taking for granted that you follow the
connexions and understand the implied situations without
a word. In this characteristic manner he often keeps the
reader bewildered, but often also, especially in the lyric
form, achieves passages and phrases of true and admirable
poetic concentration. Nevertheless, if one had to name the
chief or dominating characteristic of Browning's work, it
would not, I think you will agree, be the habitual summari-
ness or capriciousness or compression of its poetic form, but
its unflagging, indefatigable elaboration and determined
elucidation of the matter whatever that may be. No poet
shows such prodigious activity and staunchness in pursuing
a subject to its last windings and recesses, and exhausting
its uttermost psychological possibilities. His uses of the
methods of concentration and suggestion are relatively but
incidental, are but tricks of style adopted for convenience
in the course of this inveterate pursuit. Therefore I shall
leave Browning out for the purpose of the present study,
and go straight to Meredith, with whom concentration and
suggestion were almost all in all. I have quoted his own
words spoken to myself as evidence that he aimed at these
effects consciously and of set purpose, though the purpose
was no doubt in the first instance prompted and directed
by natural instinct. We are too near as yet to be able to
take the measure of such a man. But I think there can
be no doubt that his mind and imagination were among the
richest and most resourceful, and above all the most rapid

JOURNAL VERSION

in working, that have ever expressed themselves in our literature. It interested me the other day to find a definition of genius in general quoted as thrown out by this man of genius in the course of conversation with a very straightforward and simple-minded witness, the American publisher Mr. S. S. McClure. " As nearly as I can remember," reports this gentleman, " Meredith said : ' genius is an extraordinary activity of mind in which all conscious and subconscious knowledge mass themselves without any effort of the will, and become effective. It manifests itself in three ways—in producing, in organizing, and in rapidity of thought.' "

' The actual words do not sound to my ear quite like Meredith's ; but the definition fits at least his own genius accurately, except that " extraordinary " is too weak a word to describe the activity of his mind. All its accumulated resources, conscious or subconscious, of human intuition, impassioned observation, and literary study ; all its fruits of meditation on the processes of nature and the issues of life ; all its unlimited energy in the clothing of intellectual ideas with figurative imagery, were spontaneously and instantly ready for use, nay, thrustingly and importunately ready, and by no means to be kept, supposing it had been in his nature to try and keep them, back. It may be regretted that his conscious artistic purpose was to encourage and spur rather than to bridle and restrain the exercise of all these faculties. He never fully realized the difference between his own mind and the minds of other people. He always seemed to me like one of those acrobats of the trapeze, less in vogue now than they were thirty years ago, whose gift and practice it was to hang by the hands and fling themselves through space, with what seemed the swiftness and certainty of actual flight, from one swinging bar suspended high overhead to another. To the spectator below, whose way of locomotion was by the humble means of his footsoles on the floor, the thing seemed a miracle. To similar half-miraculous and not wholly human faculties

are due the things that make Meredith's poetry so difficult
at first to follow : the way of never describing an object as
what it is but always by an image, or an action by its obvious
verb but always by some figurative substitute meant to
strike the mind more vividly ; the headlong leap from one
image to another, each separate image in itself often too
strained and too remote to be quickly apprehended : the
trick of letting syntax and construction trail after this race
of images as best it may or drop behind altogether ; the
habitual rejection, much more complete and scornful than
Browning's, of the auxiliary and explanatory parts of
speech ; the passion for packing and plugging into five
words the meaning and suggestive power of fifty.   You all,
I dare say, recognize the qualities in Meredith's works of
which I speak.'

Copies of the lecture were sent by Colvin to his friends.
I find Conrad thus replying :—

'Capel House, Orlestone, nr. Ashford, 19 *Aug.* '15.

' MY DEAR COLVIN,—It is a most delightful lecture and
most judiciously illustrated, if a mind so uncultivated as
mine dares express an opinion.

' You have said there any amount of just and penetrating
things.   I shall ask you when you come here to sign the
" opuscule " for me.

' I have felt suddenly that I would love to read poets with
you.   And not only those who need an interpreter—like
Meredith, for instance.   A poet who needs elucidation has
missed his mark, which is the centre of our emotions—and
that alone (and by the by your prose of this address is
full of illuminating phrases—of lines that both make clear
and suggest ; as for instance when you speak of Meredith :
" letting syntax and construction trail after this race of
images."   This is not the best instance, but that 's what I
mean.   It was real pleasure to read you on and on).   Tell
me please : did M.—in the example you give on p. 21—did
he really write *heeled*.   Dead leaves heeled !   In Wellington
boots I suppose.   Unless I don't know all the meanings of

the word heel. But otherwise the expression is grotesque enough for a printer's error for *heaped*—or any other word. There's no word that wouldn't do better than *heeled* there, because heeled is essentially false in suggestion.

' The indubitable misprint is in the quotation from Browning : groan for *grown*. But the whole passage is what you say—except for the last line, which sounds and looks strangely pretty-pretty after the quasi-Dantesque energy of the others.

' Strange notion of supreme beatitude !—eternal twilight and the Elect recumbent in bliss without any clothes, like gentlemen after a Turkish bath.

' Such then is, according to B., the reward of travail and sorrow, of sweat and tears for the faithful souls after the trials and temptations on this earth. Well : Maybe. But I think that he let the association of the grave creep into his conception of eternal life. A moment of weakness. But Keats, the wellbeloved, had never, never, such moments of " defaithance."

' I haven't left myself room to tell you (if it could be really told in cold ink) how much good our visit to you has done to us both. Jessie has come back rested and comforted by dear Lady Colvin's influence, and I made happy by her gracious words about my book—priceless indeed because one knows them to be sincere. Our run together that afternoon was like a draught of heartening elixir to me. You must both believe in our warm and grateful affection.—Yours ever. J. CONRAD '

One other letter on the lecture :—

'1 *Carlton House Terrace, S.W., Aug.* 6, '15.

' MY DEAR COLVIN,—1000 thanks for copy of your address. A most suggestive subject and worked out with your exceptional knowledge & skill.

' I think that the only poem of Meredith that I passionately care for is the only one that I thoroughly understand, viz. Love in the Valley.—Yours sincerely, CURZON '

The completion of the Keats book was made less easy by the War, which stirred the feelings both of Colvin and of his wife to the depths. All his resources of indignation, all her wells of pity, were excited day by day; and if he could have exchanged his pen for a sword I am sure he would have done so. It was no time, he was well aware, to be delving into the biographical details of a romantic neo-Greek poet. Still, it was as well that the task had to be performed; for it helped to quieten a very emotional nature.

In the course of working on the Keats biography, many points arose on which Colvin required assistance. Among his queries was the exact locality on the Dorsetshire coast explored by Keats and Severn when landing from the *Marie Crowther* on their way to Rome. The late Thomas Hardy, on being consulted on the subject, replied thus :—

'*Max Gate, Dorchester,* 14 *June* 1914.

' MY DEAR COLVIN,—We have been weighing probabilities in the question of the " splendid caverns and grottoes " of Severn, that you write about, and have come to the conclusion that he must mean " Durdle Door," close to Lulworth Cove. (You can get a postcard photograph of it— from Hills and Rowney, Dorchester : there is also an old engraving of it in Hutchins's *Dorset.*) Why we think it must have been Durdle Door is that it impressed my wife just in the same way when she first saw it as a girl.

' To see it from the inside (which would give the impression) they would have landed in the cave, & have walked over the cliff to the west, & down behind the " Door." The walk would have taken them only a few minutes.

' There is a smuggler's cave in Worbarrow Bay. But it is difficult to find, though in Keats's time it would most likely have been clearer. The only other cave I know about here is Cave Hole, Portland. But that is difficult of access except at low and quiet tides.

' I am sending some Keats names that I jotted down

when you wrote to the papers. They are useless, I fancy, which is why I did not send them earlier. However here they are. I knew personally all the persons mentioned, and used always to be struck by their resemblance to the poet.—Sincerely yours, THOMAS HARDY '

'*P.S.*—I assume that Swanage would be too far east. There are, of course, the Tilly-Whim Caves near that place.
' T. H.' [1]

Again, a little later :—

'*Max Gate, Dorchester*, 29: 7: 1914.

' MY DEAR COLVIN,—" Beautiful grottoes " is certainly rather an exaggerated description of what one finds at Durdle Door, and Stair Hole close by : yet an enthusiastic young Londoner *might* on a first impression use such words. Besides, if not Durdle Door, Stair Hole, &c., what place can it be that Severn meant ? The " Door " is an archway in the cliff, as you know : Stair Hole has caves & fissures into which the sea flows, & there is another cave at Bat's Corner, also close at hand.

' At any rate I cannot think of another point on the Dorset coast, easily accessible from a boat, which so well answers the description.

' The " cottages " would be those of the adjoining Lulworth Cove & village, but they do not, of course, *face* the " grottoes," as Severn seems to imply. I put that down to his fancy, as such a position would hardly be possible anywhere. With kind regards—Sincerely yours,
' THOMAS HARDY '

Here is a belated postscript : ' I forgot to say in my letter that some 40 years ago my father told me that the K——s of this neighbourhood came of a family of horse-dealers, who lived in the direction of Broadmayne. ' T. H.'

---

[1] In the Fitzwilliam Museum.

One more note from Hardy :—

' I just remember this trifle, & send it on for what it may be worth in your *Life*.

' Swinburne told me that Mrs. Procter (Barry Cornwall's widow) told him that one day when Leigh Hunt called on her father he brought with him an unknown youth who was casually mentioned as being a Mr. John Keats.

That learned Scot, the late W. P. Ker, with his accustomed readiness to help his friends, read the proofs of the *Life of Keats* while it was passing through the press. His letters are chiefly comments, but there is no harm in that when they come from so sure a hand. Thus, referring to the journal of Keats' and Brown's Highland walking tour :—

' Soon Ailsa Craig & presently Arran. Ailsa & Arran come together in the view—Arran rather sooner, if anything, I should say—as you cross the hill from the head of Glen App making for Ballantrae.'

' Where was it that they left Glen App ? I have had debates on this subject in Glen App itself, & I was hoping for news from your Plymouth Journal. Did they follow the present line of road up by Carlock ? Or did they turn off to the left (to the North) nearer the foot of the glen ?

' Cromarty never was the port of Inverness—Inverness is its own port.

' When were they at Beauly ? K. doesn't say they sailed from Inverness, & his taking " the smack from Cromarty " is ambiguous. It would be a natural obvious thing to go on from Beauly & get the boat at Cromarty. It would be much the same to come back & start from Inverness, and the " smack from Cromarty " would be likely to call at Inverness.

' Is it right to say " centre round " ? Can any movement centre round a centre ? I am not sure.

' Perhaps there is some room for misunderstanding about Keats's philosophy—not if the reader is careful—but a casual reader might mistake Keats's figurative language

W. P. KER

FROM THE BRONZE BUST BY JOHN TWEED AT UNIVERSITY COLLEGE, GOWER STREET,
LONDON

for defective thinking. Will you not add something to safeguard ?

' Keats's imaginative arguments are not mere picture thinking—jumping from one image to another.

' Have you ever observed that K. and Shelley about the same time are taken with the idea of the *Zeitgeist* as we used to call him ? Spiritual winds and waves are carrying all the minds of an age along with him—quite clearly explained or anyhow recognised by Shelley in Preface to *Revolt of Islam*—Compare the end of *Sleep and Poetry*.

' I am proud to think that I learned mythology out of Baldwin's *Pantocon*. It was a school prize of my Father's at the Glasgow Grammar School, & I have it now, though not at hand.

' I never knew till now that Baldwin was Godwin.

' I don't see anything wrong with the end of the poem. It has never sounded incomplete to me. Pæona is not bewildered. She has much to wonder at—like every reader of poetry who is not a poet. But she is not in distress or suspense. It is just the end of the story.

' Is not Leigh Hunt's sonnet one of the best in the language ? Hazlitt thought so, didn't he ? But then Hazlitt didn't think much of Astrophel, which proves that all knowledge is relative. I think it is a very fine poem. And it appears that L. H. had not got it in his fist ready made to slap on the table ; as critics have suspected.

' Even Scott did not know Galloway—*Guy Mannering* is written at a distance from the Object.

' Loch na Keal is better though not punctilious accurate Gaelic. You do not write " Mount ofolives," and Loch Nakeal is as bad as that.

' I don't like " bully " used of Christopher North.

' Rigby an *ignorant* caricature ! " teasing with obvious comment, and torturing with inevitable inference."

' Leese me on Rigby !

' Ben Johnson. Why sic ? It is a very good way to spell Johnson.

x

' Chatterton's fluent style would make a very good alternative after a surfeit of Milton.

' There are two " unrhymes " in *Lycidas*.

' Is it a hen nightingale ?

' He did not think of Saturn and his fellows as anything near to barbarians ; the tragedy is that their noble old order has got to be displaced & refuted. The speech of Oceanus would lose its meaning otherwise. And this I think explains the no ending of *Hyperion*. Keats had intentionally & with all his power—not out of innate gentleness but because it was his meaning—put all the dignity & majesty he could into Saturn. Then Oceanus Hyperion— He had then to go on to Apollo—but he had used up all his light already. Apollo could not be anything more than a variety of what had been already expressed—not without a miracle, like a picture breaking out suddenly with real sunlight on the landscape. The poem is really concluded, i.e. the speech of Oceanus explains everything, & you have just to believe that Apollo came and was very wonderful & glorious.

' These are of course not dogmatisms but considerations submitted for your judgment.

' Glasgow [the printing firm] has come back sober from the Fair [August Bank Holiday] and sends these three sheets which I have read with great pleasure & I am sorry the story is at an end.

' Consumption : why not combustion ?   " Consumption " is a word so often used in the story in another sense that it grates here like the name of someone we don't want to hear about.

' Is Lowell a chief poet ?   I hope not.

' What is something that will do as well as beauty ?   An excellent substitute for beauty ?   So I have seen in a Goodge Street grocer's window " Eggs equal to newlaid."

' I am not quite sure whether it is right to speak of the Desires & Aspirations & Dreams in *Adonais* as abstractions. But you leave no real doubt as to what they really are, though I think your idea of Shelley seems a little too near M. Arnold's ineffectual angel.'

In 1917 the *Life of Keats* came out. As to its merits there is a fine chorus of approval. I select a few letters from many. This from the Hon. Maurice Baring, whose elegiacs on Auberon Herbert were among the most beautiful poetry called forth by the War :—

> '*Head Quarters Royal Flying Corps,*
> '*B.E.F. France.* 2.12.17.

'DEAR SIR SIDNEY COLVIN,—I have been just spending some very enjoyable hours reading your *Life of Keats* ;—I will not be so impertinent as to say a word of praise—all I can say is that I wish there could be a companion life of Shelley of the same calibre, weight, understanding, sympathy & completeness. But unless you were willing to undertake the task I don't know who could. The fact that you point out & which I myself have often noticed that the Pro-Keats are seldom Pro-Shelley is very striking but not I think difficult to understand. My own experience is —Since writing these words a door has banged six times & a telephone has rung once, so that writing—consecutive writing, is difficult—I was going to try to say that my experience was among my contemporaries & people of the generation *after* me & that in my opinion from the point of view of one who fortunately admires & enjoys Shelley & Keats to the *n*th (Buxton Forman did—& you do I think !) it is Keats who on the whole has been by our generations— yours, mine & the one next to me—the more overrated of the two—Shelley the more underrated of the two—

' I always think that in Shelley's case two facts are overlooked, the rapidly arriving *maturity* coming after a hectic period of unripeness—(& everybody admits this in Keats' case—and Shelley seemingly was less immature in his early period than Keats) & the presence in Shelley of really astonishingly deep thought behind the rainbow veils—

' Another question which comes is this : a Russian once

said to me 4 years ago—the year before the War—" All you
literary people in England are so munched & drained by
the offsprings & tradition of the Sensuous school of delicious
language—Keats-Tennyson-Yeats tradition, that you are
quite incapable of doing justice to a poet such as Byron,
who whatever you say is grossly underrated, & who whatever you say is a great poet—"

' I repeat I should like 2 companion volumes : one on
Shelley & one on Byron by a critic as wide in sympathy,
as fine in discrimination, & as sure in scholarship, as yourself.
—Yours sincerely,   MAURICE BARING '

' *P.S.*—I am firmly convinced that we are no wiser than
Keats' generation & that even today we may be utterly
neglecting a possible Keats—I 'm not sure I don't know
a case which occurred in the last 10 years—a poet who
died anonymous & who is buried in the same cemetery
at Rome.'

A last letter from John, afterwards Lord, Morley :—

'*Aug.* 9. 18.
' *Flowermead, Princes Road, Wimbledon Park, S.W.*

' MY DEAR COLVIN,—It was a real pleasure to me to see
your hand again—so familiar and so uncommonly helpful
was it to me long years ago. It rejoices me to feel the
accents of good friendship in your letter, in spite of the
angry quarrels of the hour. . . .

' I have hunted bravely for the thing in V. H., but I 'll be
hanged if I can hit upon the guest minister. I envy your
evening with him. He was one of the giants, after all.

' Your Keats gave me lively satisfaction of the best sort,
and I understand that my satisfaction is shared by a good
public. I have a trifle of self-esteem in recalling—as you
also do—that it was I who started you on this subject—
so fruitful in your hand.

' All good wishes, my dear Colvin.—Yours ever,
' J. M.'

From Lord Tennyson : ' My Father said of Keats,
" Keats, with his high spiritual vision, would have been,
if he had lived, the greatest of us—There is something magic
and of the innermost soul of poetry in almost everything
which he wrote." Again, " Keats had a keen physical
imagination : if he had been here (at Murren), he would
in one line have given us a picture of that mountain." . . .
' Another saying of my Father's : " Keats promised
securely more than any English poet since Milton."
To *The Times*, after Colvin's death in 1926, Mr. John
Bailey sent the following letter : ' May I add one word of
supplement to the admirable notice of Sir Sidney Colvin
which I have just read in *The Times*? In it his *Life of
Keats* is barely mentioned, without comment. This seems
to me to do less than justice to what I venture to think is
the best critical biography we have of any of our greater
poets. If one takes the obvious names—Chaucer, Spenser,
Shakespeare, Milton, Dryden, Pope, Wordsworth, Coleridge,
Byron, Shelley—of which of these do we possess a life which
unites knowledge of the facts, emotional and aesthetic understanding, critical penetration, and certainty of judgment
as they are, I think, combined in Colvin's *Life of Keats*?
Of course it makes no pretence of competing with such lives
by contemporaries as Hogg's *Shelley*, Lockhart's *Scott*,
Moore's *Byron*, or with such a biographical and critical
essay as Johnson's *Pope*. But as a full-length biography,
critical and personal, written long after the death of the
subject and by a writer who never saw him, I cannot see
what rival it has in our language.'
Finally let me quote a rambling and very characteristic
letter from the late Oscar Browning :

' *Palazzo Simonetti, Via Pietro Cavallini, Roma,*
' *New Year's Day,* 1918.

' MY DEAR COLVIN,—I have just finished reading your
Life of Keats. I have read every word of it with the most
intense interest. I have no words sufficient to praise it.

It is a masterly work, and will be a standard book & place the fame of Keats on a permanent basis.

' I have had, for a good deal more than sixty years, very special relations with Keats. I went to Eton in 1851 at the age of fourteen, and I was in the division of William Johnson [author of *Ionica*], who was also my tutor, in my opinion the greatest genius who ever gave himself to the education of boys. We had to compose a copy of Latin verses every week, and one week he set us the speech of Clymene in "Hyperion" for a subject. I learnt it by heart and could repeat it now ; another time he gave us the "Pot of Basil," which I learnt in a similar manner. He often talked to us about Keats & offered a prize to any of his pupils who would learn "Hyperion" by heart. I began but did not get to the end. He also gave me a magnificently bound copy of Keats, I think Moxon's edition, which does not contain the "Belle Dame sans Merci," nor I think the "Ode to Melancholy"—which is of every thing that Keats has written the poem I most value. In your book you have not given much prominence either to Clymene's speech, which I consider a masterpiece, or to the melancholy ode, which is always with me. The consequence was that when I went up to Cambridge in 1856 I was *soaked* with Keats, & was always preaching him to the Apostles & other friends, & after I went as a master to Eton in 1860, to my boys. I don't think that he was much known at Cambridge in 1856, nor did Tennyson ever speak to me about him. My pagod at school was Byron, whom you detest, but I still think him the *second* highest poet, as all foreigners do. Tennyson had a great cult for him. You remember that the news of his death caused him a violent attack of illness.

' I was a great deal in Rome from 1863 to 1875—& Severn was consul here. I never met him. I once climbed up to his door in the Palazzo Pol with the intention of calling on him to talk about Keats, but I was afraid to go in. As [undecipherable word] once said to me, " *Autrefois j'étais timide, mais cela passe.*" It has been proved with me.

' I can't find any mistakes in your book except that you say that Leigh Hunt was present at the burning of Shelley. He certainly was not. I investigated the whole thing very carefully at Via Reggio some twenty years ago. The only people present were Byron, Trelawny & Mrs. Shelley, who carried the heart home in a pocket-handkerchief. It is a strange thing that Napoleon's heart also fell out, when he was being embalmed, & was nearly eaten by a rat. I used to stay a good deal at Fryston [Lord Houghton's house] & I remember that the book containing the Keats poems lay on the study table—but I never examined it, fool that I was! Do you know the story of " Keats, what's a Keat ? " One day at the Trinity High Table that was said. " O. B. is going to lecture this evening on Keats. ["] A science Fellow said " Keats ? what's a Keat ? ["] on which there was a great guffaw—Then Langley said, " It is all very well for you fellows to laugh, but I don't believe that any one of you could quote a single line of Keats." Of course there is one line which everyone knows, even science men. . . .

' You say nothing about the Keats-Shelley House here, of which I was one of the founders. I have a haunting suspicion that Keats really died, not in these hallowed rooms, but on the floor below. I believe that Severn said so, and it [seems] more likely that he lived on the ground floor instead of going up stairs—besides it would be cheaper—but hush ! hush !

' Nor have you said anything about our Keats-Shelley Association, which gives memorial lectures during the season. The High Priests are Nelson Page [the then American Ambassador] & Rome. All the aristocracy of Rome belong to it & no one else, except myself—I was once allowed to lecture, I suppose by mistake—a mistake never repeated. The subscription is £20 bis [?] a year— very dear.

' How many years have we known each other ? Did you or did you not on one occasion ask my advice about your course in life, when your relatives were urging you to embrace some lucrative occupation & I supported you in your determination to stick to art & literature ? Did it happen or did I dream it ?

' Rome has the best society in the world even in war time —but it *can* be cold.   Believe me—ever yours,

' OSCAR BROWNING '

In a letter in 1918, ' Q ' says : 'The Stevenson in "E. M. of L." begins to look as if it would never be written—that is, by me.   What with War and pressure of work I'm feeling like the West country lady who said that " in these days one cannot lie down at night & be sure of getting up in the same position next morning." '

As a matter of fact, the ' English Men of Letters ' volume on R. L. S. has not yet appeared.   It was subsequently given to Mr. Robert Lynd.

The Colvins during the summer of 1918 occupied my house at Tillington, close to Petworth, a circumstance which led to this postscript to ' Q's ' letter : ' It 's rather pleasant of you to be at Petworth.   I started my first book there—*Dead Man's Rock*, in Aug. or Sept. 1886—in a watchmaker's house by the Half Moon(?) just outside the big house.   I was tutoring young George Wyndham then : eldest son of the late Lᵈ. Leconfield, & brother of the present one.   He died young, poor boy !   We read the whole of the *Iliad* through together.

' Then I 'd go home & slug at the story.   Remember writing the first page and walking out along the road by the park wall, turning uphill by a pub. called the Light Horse-man, or some such name, & seating myself for a pipe on a hill that looked clear across to Tennyson's place [Aldworth]. I was back again next year (1887) when my copies of the book arrived from Cassell's.   Also I was just engaged to be married when I started the book—So you may give Petworth my love.'

In 1921 Colvin's last book was published : a collection of essays and character sketches entitled *Memories and Notes*

SIR SIDNEY COLVIN
FROM THE PENCIL DRAWING BY WILLIAM ROTHENSTEIN, NOVEMBER, 1897

of Persons and Places, 1852-1912, from which I have borrowed freely for these pages, but not so freely as to make that work a superfluity. The essay on Stevenson seems to have called forth some criticism from Maurice Hewlett, who was then writing a regular literary causerie in the *English Review.* Colvin must have remonstrated, for I find Hewlett writing, in April 1922 :—

' MY DEAR COLVIN,—I am sure that I shall take nothing that you say amiss. If I have been wrong in any matter of fact, which is perfectly possible, I shall not hesitate for a moment about withdrawing or correcting it. Opinions are another matter. What opinions I have about Stevenson's writing I have had for a long time. I should not have expressed them if Freeman's article had not brought them into my head again.

' The " friends " of whom I was thinking were you and Lang ; and what I meant was, obviously, that the sense of your loss moved you to instil in the general imagination what was so strongly in your own. The romantic and endearing figure was, in fact, a revelation to the public—of which, in my way, I was one. Until Stevenson was dead I had very little idea of him—though I had seen him once at the Savile. The idea which I then obtained was surely largely owing to the generous warmth with which you, Lang, and in a lesser degree Gosse and Mr. Graham Balfour, praised, and properly praised, your friend. I don't think Stevenson's novels so good as you think them ; but I accept every word you have to say of his charm, his high personal quality and power.—Yours sincerely,
' M. HEWLETT '

And again : ' I have never thought so highly of Stevenson's works as most people do—and soberly do consider the historical and descriptive things of his, his best work. I think he would have been a good historian. But these things could be better talked about over the round table at the club. I still wish you had not left Cambridge out of your book.'

And this was Hewlett's last word on the matter, in June 1922 : ' Please, my dear Colvin, don't be afflicted with what I, or Freeman, think proper to say about Stevenson. Neither of us can possibly matter, or can have any effect whatever upon S. or his memory. If " Lord, what is man ! " is a becoming reflection for me to make, it will be equally becoming for Stevenson. I had always thought him overpraised, and that such excess really obscured his excellence. When I found Freeman, unknown to me, saying so, I took up my own little parable. That 's really all. You mustn't look round and say, *Nous sommes trahis*, because two writers have the same idea.'

I find among the letters one from Hewlett to Lord Crewe, expressing regret that he could not be at the Colvin banquet in 1912, in which he says that it is for his work in connection with Landor that, as a literary man, he chiefly esteems him. Maurice Hewlett died in 1923.

The following enthusiastic letter crossed the Atlantic from Thomas Seccombe, who soon afterwards returned to England, only to die :—

'*Queen's University, Kingston, Ontario.*
'*27 Jan.* 1923.

' DEAR SIR SIDNEY COLVIN,—After anxious pursuit I have managed just to get your new book—they have a pernicious habit of getting printed tickets for all new books from Washington before issuing them here. I have been browsing over it all day and feel that I must write a word of cordial congratulation and thanks. The great old [Frederic] Harrison, the martinet, has passed away at last, it seems, and only yesterday I read in the *Times* of the decease of that good all-round Yorkshireman and my good old friend Armitage Smith : but all the same it is the day of *les vieux*. . . . Lytton Strachey is the only *jeune* and he looks about the oldest of the lot. I wish I could stand the treatment, but this place with all its sunshine is too much for me, and if I want to see my native land again I must seek a cottage in the south this summer. Our age will decline after the war. You were made of sterner stuff, you Victorians! Jenkin is the only one I could dispense with since Miss Masson's compilation. The other subjects are so delightful. I seem to be so dreadfully at home and homesick in Suffolk, riding from Ipswich to Aldeburgh through Woodbridge. How is Clodd and all his Meredithism ? Your Meredith is splendid. To my mind, between ourselves, he was not a patch on W. M. T., but it is no laughing matter, is it, to the nation that either should have been excluded from the Abbey at the expense of living ? How I rejoice in what you say about the Bride of L. and that puir thin fule T. F. H. I have still to read 6 and 7 but 12 and 14 are well within me and how I enjoyed the "Land's End of France." [1] Full of Loitz, Le Braz, and so many books that I cannot quite remember, yet quite like no other books. How I loved and remember wheeling about that Bodmin moor between Quimper and Carnac. How I envy writing that essay. Do hurry up with the next and do insert that Cambridge one. I am all agog now for R. L. S., Dobson, Long Leslie Stephen and your noble self. Swiftly may your year prosper and your luncheon table in the land of Croker where they still permit whisky on Burns Day.—Delightedly yours, THOMAS SECCOMBE '

[1] These were the chapters on George Eliot and J. F. Watts. Chapters xii. and xiv. dealt with Sir Charles Newton and Trelawny.

CHAPTER XXIII

'FAMOUS VOICES'

1923

ALTHOUGH he spent much time, without much method, in revising early essays—particularly one on the Centaurs— Colvin did almost no consecutive writing after the publication of *Memories and Notes* in 1921. His chief literary work at this time consisted chiefly in preparing the selections from Stevenson's letters to Mrs. Sitwell (from which I have quoted in earlier chapters) for the *Empire Review*. He had not enough strength for the necessary application, and he was harassed by Lady Colvin's failing health. One short paper he did, however, prepare : recollections of the manner and sound of the voices of some of his great contemporaries, and this little article I now reproduce from the pages of *John o' London's Weekly*, where it appeared :—

'FAMOUS VOICES I HAVE HEARD

' JOHN O' LONDON's editor having been interested, it seems, in the account of Rossetti's speaking voice which he found in my recent book of *Memories and Notes*, asks me for a column describing the voices of other famous men whom I have known.

' As a mere instrument the most musical and magical voice, the most caressing and conquering at once (I am talking of men only, not of women), was certainly that of Sir John Duke Coleridge, afterwards Lord Coleridge. I was not present at any of the great feats of forensic argument or persuasion which have made his name historical— the Tichborne case was, of course, the most famous of them

—and only knew him in private life, chiefly in his capacity as president of a certain ancient and distinguished dining society. An inexhaustible store of legal anecdotes used to furnish a larger proportion of his talk than some of us would have asked for, but the mere utterance had a charm which would have reconciled us to matter much less interesting. And one used to wonder whether this " silver-sounding instrument " was simply the fitting organ supplied by Nature to a temperament extraordinarily sympathetic and persuasive, or how much of it may have been a gift hereditary in his blood. Had the recorded irresistible charm in conversation of his grand-uncle, the poet Samuel Taylor Coleridge, over and above the genius and inspiration of his matter—had it been derived in part from the mere mellifiuousness of the accents which flowed from those loose, fleshy, irresolute, inspired lips of his ?

' The two great Victorian poets, Tennyson and Browning, had both of them voices which, heard whether habitually or occasionally, impressed the ear and still haunt the memory, but haunt it in very different modes. Both were essentially masculine ; Tennyson's a deep grand bass monotone, gruff without being harsh or grating ; his pronunciation of certain vowels had a provincial breadth derived, as I always understood, from his Lincolnshire origin, and he would pass from the most impressive recitation of poetry into ordinary colloquial talk with little or no change of key but still " rolling out his deep-mouthed a's and o's " with the same monotonous solemn sonority. I particularly remember how such transition to the trivial happened, almost without break or pause, on one occasion when, possibilities of imminent war being in the air, he had just thrilled his company to the very marrow with the closing words of the *Revenge* ballad :

' " And the whole sea plunged and fell on the shot-shatter'd navy
        of Spain,
And the little *Revenge* herself went down by the island crags
To be lost evermore in the main."

' Browning had no such impressive natural organ as his great contemporary. His ordinary speaking voice was extremely vigorous, somewhat louder—perhaps from his long custom of life in Italy—than is encouraged by social usage in England. But his utterance was much more flexible and dramatically varying with the theme than Tennyson's ; always virile, generally tending towards the harsh, but freely and expressively modulated for the different purposes of cordiality or admiration or sympathy or jest or narrative or argument. And sometimes it would be very moving to note how in the reading or recitation of poetry, whether his own or another's, his firmly modelled features would relax, his masterful accents break with emotion, and there would be unrepressed tears both on his face and in his utterance. I remember particularly how one day it was all he could do to master himself and get through the Pompilia section of *The Ring and the Book*, and how his hearers sat silently gulping down their tears in sympathy.

' George Meredith was another great Victorian whose genius made itself unmistakably felt in his voice and manner of speaking. If I were asked to define in one word the most notable quality of Meredith's utterance, whether in recitation or everyday talk, that one word would be " authority." Authority along with striking finish and fullness ; there was never in his manner of speaking, as there is in that of most of us, anything half-formed or slack or slurred ; it seemed as though such completeness, such decision and rotundity, were matters with him both of self-respect and respect for his company. Let no reader imagine that I am here describing that distressing thing, an underbred man's over-care and over-nicety in speech ; Meredith's high finish as a talker seemed to go congenitally with a like quality of finish in his whole make and being, his mind and even in his features. Some of his talk was in the vein of unsparing satire or *badinage*, such as was apt to search the conscience or try the vanity of his hearers. Much, on the other hand, was in that of sheer intellectual hilarity ; much, also, of sheer,

clear, and strenuous critical thinking. I never knew him
difficult or hard to follow in talk as we all know him to
have been often in writing. But authority, a masterful
completeness and exactness, were characteristic of him alike
with tongue and pen.

' Of Rossetti and his voice I have tried to tell elsewhere.
In reading or recitation, and not to a much less extent in
daily talk, he was the greatest magician of them all. To
hear him was to listen to a kind of chant, almost a monotone,
but one which managed to express with little variation of
pitch or inflection a surprising range and power of emotion.
A kind of sustained musical drone or hum, rich and mellow
and velvety, with which he used to dwell on and stress and
prolong the rhyme-words and sound-echoes had a profound
effect in stirring the senses and souls of his hearers. It is
close upon fifty years since I first heard him read his poems,
then newly recovered from his wife's grave, and the enchant-
ment of the experience was such that I have never to this
day been able to judge and criticize them as coolly as I
might have done had I read them for the first time to myself.

' An almost equal beauty and richness of the mere organ,
with a much greater art of variation and flexibility, belonged
to another poet of a generation nearer my own—namely,
Stephen Phillips. His place among the poets of the latter
years of the last century is not yet settled ; it was unfortunate for him that—although his life was not long—he
nevertheless outlived his own genius ; but the excessive
depreciation on the part of hack critics which followed his
perhaps excessive laudation seems now to be in its turn
exhausted. Whatever may be the ultimate verdict on his
original work, no one who in his good days ever heard him
read poetry will quarrel with the judgment that here was
almost an ideal accomplishment in the art—a combination
of physical gift with emotional and interpretative power,
with the expression of sensibilities alike metrical and
dramatic, which afforded his hearers an artistic experience
never to be forgotten.

' Lack of space debars me from any attempt to call up other voices which at various times have laid their spell upon and still haunt me.   Some foreign, as those of the illustrious poet Victor Hugo and the irresistible orator Gambetta ; some native, as those of Gladstone and of John Bright, each accustomed to dominate and persuade assemblies but both knowing well how to attune their accents pleasantly to private pitch ; or most rememberable of all, those of Shelley's friend Trelawny, who in his ninetieth year talked to me for nearly an hour in accents for the most part somewhat fatigued and muffled but for sudden brief bursts thunderingly rough, bluff, and impressive.   These among my seniors ; and to speak of only two among men contemporary with myself or a little junior, have I not as though fresh in my ears the voice of the great philosophical mathematician W. K. Clifford, haunting and captivating as it was by a kind of surprised and childlike innocence, at once rapt and placid, which went along with the weakness due to lung trouble ?—and last, shall I not have until the end that, vibrating with its Scottish accentuation and rich, in spite of his chest weakness, with power both from the inward spirit and from the habit of seafaring on storm-beaten coasts, of Robert Louis Stevenson ? '

CHAPTER XXIV

TRIBUTES TO LADY COLVIN

1924

LADY COLVIN became weaker and weaker as the year 1924 progressed, and after days of unconsciousness faded away on August 1st. Her friend Joseph Conrad died suddenly two days later, one of his last letters, when he knew that she could not recover, being to Colvin in these terms : ' With all my heart and soul, with all the strength of affection and admiration for her, who is about to leave this hard world, where all the happiness she could find was in your devotion, I am with you every moment of these black hours it is yours to live through.

' Pray kiss her hands for me in reverence and love. I hope she will give blessing thoughts to those who are dear to me, my wife and children, to whom she always was the embodiment of all that is kind and gracious and lovable on earth.'

Many tributes were written testifying to the constant rain of her sweet influence. Mr. Garvin, always a noble eulogist, wrote in the *Observer* : ' She can no more be forgotten than any of the greater Frenchwomen of the eighteenth century, for she matched the more famous of them all in mind, person, and influence. . . . Until lately she kept the quickest, freshest spirit of youth in everything. She encouraged the youngest talent. . . .

' She knew the latest thing of mark in books and reviews, in novels, poetry, criticism, the drama, music, politics. She caught the trifles light as air, and those who thought they

Y

brought her the secrets of the town often found that she was before them. Beauty like hers was genius. It was a sibylline beauty, over which time had no power, so austere and firm yet delicate was the architecture of her face, kindling with understanding and responsiveness. Divining intuition like hers was genius. Vitality like hers was genius. . . . For those who knew her best there is nothing in the world left to replace her. There is no one at all like her, nor is it easy to imagine that anyone else could ever have been like her. She was apart from all type, and you never thought of trying to describe by comparisons any feature or trait of hers. It is almost impossible to realize that she is dead, and hard to write about it. . . .

' The allegiance of women she knew how to win and keep, but it was delightfully like her humanity that, though her judgment of both sexes could be as severe on some occasions as her charities of understanding were boundless at other times, she was, on the whole, lenient towards that feebler and more perplexed species which is male.'

The anonymous writer in *English Life* whom I have already quoted supplemented Mr. Garvin's warmth : ' No woman was ever quite like her. Her beautiful face, so austere in structure, yet so richly illuminated by her wonderful smile, was a very exact reflection of her tender, profound, and noble character. How impossible it is to tell of her irradiating charm. Everyone in her presence was uplifted and comforted. She was the soul of honour, discretion and sympathy.

' Though she was the tenderest of beings it was not only upon this quality that people relied when seeking her counsel. They sought her help because of her rare insight into the developments of life's problems. She never tried to assuage for a passing hour the difficulties which confronted those who sought her advice. On the contrary she endeavoured to strengthen determination, to refresh hope, to enkindle a moral resolution capable of resisting the world's hardest buffetings.'

From the letters I choose two. From Sir Austen Chamberlain : ' I knew Lady Colvin so little except through R. L. S. that it is almost an impertinence to speak of her, but I have known you so long & like you so much, even though we have not very often met, that I must tell you of my sympathy for you & of my admiration for her. I suppose that few people have been able to do so much for a man of genius, who *needed* good friends, as Lady Colvin & you did for R. L. S. If that were all you had both done you might well feel that you had not lived in vain. You have much else to your credit in a public way, & she, I doubt not, in more private & womanly ways. But may I say without irreverence in touching holy things, that I think of you two always as a very perfect model of friendship to friends & of that something—that immeasurably more in your own lives which only those who have found the same complete unity & fulfilment in marriage can perhaps fully understand.

' When I think of your loss it sends a shiver through my soul. God strengthen & comfort you.'

From Lord Crewe : ' You must let me send you a word of affectionate sympathy. You know how much I have valued your friendship these many years ; and in later times Lady Colvin's welcome made visits to your house pleasanter still. The loss of Conrad, which must to you be a very real one, can only be merged in this deeper sorrow—I am indeed grieved for you.'

Colvin in course of time found some comfort in preparing a little memorial of his wife, in which he reprinted, with changes, the character sketch that he had written fourteen years before for an anthology of mine called *Her Infinite Variety*. I give it here in its latest form, as he amended it. The memorial also contained the photograph of Lady Colvin which is reproduced opposite the next page. The title was ' A Thorough-Bred ' :—

' Sprung from a famous north-country stock transplanted three centuries ago into Ireland, she is pure-bred through many generations, and shows it. Rather under than over the middle height, but perfectly shaped and proportioned, she bears herself so beautifully, and if need be so proudly, that showier women seem rustic or insignificant beside her. Her face is the transparent vesture of her spirit, and her looks a true mirror of the poignancy and integrity of her feelings. The features are large and noble, and modelled with the last subtlety of refinement ; at the same time they are tinted with the ebb and flow of so delicate a blood, and change so swiftly and harmoniously with the motions of her mind, that it is by play of expression even more than by purity of design that they charm and haunt you. Waiting for her smile is the happiest of anticipations, and when it comes it is always more enchanting than you remembered.

' Her voice adds to persuasion candour, and to candour kindness, in evidence which receives, although it needs not, a sure corroboration in her eyes. When she sings, the full richness of her spirit passes into her utterance, and those who hear her are transported. Such power upon others has not come to her without the discipline of extreme suffering. By nature sensitively impatient, swift, and proud, she has had to bear a double and treble share not only of life's cares but of its agonies. They have strained her strength but not her courage, and left their mark, but only in a beautiful underlying sadness which enriches and makes sacred all her mirth. For mirthful she can still be ; fun and mischief still lurk unquenchable in those faithful eyes ; the youngest has not so young a laugh as she, and she will still leap in her chair and clap hands with childish glee (and nothing becomes her better) at the anticipation of any simple gift or pleasure.

' As for the higher pleasures of art and nature, her presence enhances them inexpressibly. In the illumination of beautiful things, she seems to reflect and grow one with them ; without pretension or affectation of criticism, she takes into herself their very essence, which

MRS. SITWELL

AFTERWARDS LADY COLVIN

becomes part thenceforward of the affluence of her being.
Her friends not only learn in her company how to
enjoy, but in her absence no very choice experience can
befall them but of her they will be reminded, and to
her involuntarily give thanks for the best part of what
they feel.

'But life itself is most truly of all her sphere. She has
the genius of the heart, and in her own spirit a blend of
sensitiveness and high honour and fortitude which makes
of her a priceless counsellor. Comfort abounds when she
is by : something bids all who are not ungentle, men, women,
and children, turn to her and trust her. She cools and
soothes your secret smart before ever you can name it ;
she divines and shares your hidden joy, or shames your
fretfulness with loving laughter : she unravels the per-
plexities of your conscience, and teaches you that there is
something finer in you than you knew ; timorous or mean
or jealous thoughts cannot live in her company ; she fills
you not only with generous resolutions but with power to
persist in what you have resolved.

' In the fearlessness of her purity she can afford the frankness of her affections, and shows how every fascination of
her sex may in the most open freedom be the most honourably secure. Yet in a world of men and women, such an
one cannot walk without kindling once and again a dangerous flame before she is aware. As in her nature there is no
room for vanity, she never foresees these masculine com-
bustions, but has a wonderful tact and gentleness in allaying
them, and is accustomed to convert the claims and cravings
of passion into the lifelong loyalty of grateful and contented
friendship.

' With her own sex she is the soul of loyalty, and women
love and trust her not less devotedly than men. She loves
to be loved, and likes to be praised ; but no amount of love
or praise can make her believe that there is much remarkable about her. If she could read this testimony to her
worth she would be both pleased and moved, but between

smiles and tears, and somewhat of a loving shame, would remain unconvinced though the deposition should be borne by him who, owing her whatever he is worth, has the best right to speak, and witnessed by all the rest who, sharing the treasure of her friendship, surround her with their just allegiance in the next degree.'

CHAPTER XXV

THE END

1924-1927

THERE is little more to tell. Colvin's health steadily declined, and his loneliness was intensified by increasing deafness. He was also subject to sudden collapses which made it undesirable for him to go out alone. He insisted, however, as long as possible, on a daily walk to a neighbouring florist's, to buy flowers for the table beside Lady Colvin's chair, in which no one was allowed to sit. We did what we could to induce him to have a male attendant, but he refused ; he refused also to experiment with any device for the improvement of hearing.

His letters, which he continually rearranged, and his Will, which he frequently altered, were a source of consolation and employment, and he read the *Times* and the *Evening Standard* assiduously, as well as *Punch*, the *Times Literary Supplement*, and the *Graphic*. Disdaining circulating libraries, he bought from Mr. Bain such new books as he fancied, but was in the habit of laying them soon aside in favour of Wordsworth and Virgil.

For a few months he played with the idea of bringing out a new book of his own, mixed essays and criticism, but he lacked the power to concentrate on such revision and addition as would be necessary. The following is his list of contents of the proposed volume :—

Penthesilea (translation from the Posthomerica of Quintus Smyrnæus, with introduction about the Amazons in general).

343

Hymn to Demeter (translation of the Homeric hymn, with some comments).

Notes on the Centaur myth (a few points only relating to a huge subject).

Maso Finiguerra (boiled down from my big book establishing his identity for the first time).

Piero della Francesca and Luca Signorelli (reprints from old *Cornhill* articles, meant to be popular and knowledgeable at the same time).

On Concentration and Suggestion in Poetry (reprinted from a pamphlet of the English Association).

Keatsiana (or some better title, meaning points concerning K. which have come to light since my book).

Voices I Have Heard.

Robert Louis Stevenson and Henry James (meaning an article with many letters, to be reprinted from *Scribner's Magazine*).

Notes on Joseph Conrad (with extracts from unprinted letters).

Frederick Walker (essay written in *Cornhill* at the time of his death).

Of these articles, all had been printed before and were ready, short of final revision, except the notes on Keats and the notes on Conrad, which were never written. For the paper on the Centaurs, which had appeared in its original form many years before, Colvin assembled a mass of new material but did not arrange it.

His more intimate friends did what they could to cheer him, among regular visitors being Mrs. W. K. Clifford and her daughters, Miss Clifford and Lady Dilke, Mr. and Mrs. J. W. Mackail, Mrs. Madan, a near neighbour, Mrs. J. L. Garvin, Mr. Basil Champneys, Sir Eliot Colvin, Sir Edward Elgar, Mrs. Gaskell, Mrs. Ludo Foster, Mrs. Roscoe, Mr. and Mrs. Laurence Binyon, Mrs. Payne, Sir Robert Witt, Mr. John Bailey, Mrs. Theodore McKenna, and of course Dr. C. E. Wheeler, who was more than a physician both to Colvin and to Lady Colvin.

Colvin wrote many letters, always in his own careful
hand. One of these, never posted, which lies before me, has its
own story. Early in 1925 many, if not all, of the literary
men of England received a letter from an American school-
master, which most of them (as the adroit writer intended)
not unnaturally assumed to be addressed to themselves
only. It ran thus :—

January 29, 1925.

' DEAR SIR,—The five hundred and more young men and
young women training for business in the local Senior High
School are divided into little groups of eight each. Owing
to graduation the personnel of these " eights " changes
from year to year.

' For the past three years these groups of students have
each been selecting one well-known man or woman, whose
life has made an especial appeal to them, as a sort of
" guardian," believing that a little letter of kindly interest
from such a one would help them to do better work in
school and aid them in being better citizens in the business
world for which they are fitting themselves.

' One of these groups has taken the liberty of so choosing
you.

' I feel considerable hesitancy in troubling you for such
a letter, but I sincerely trust the time will present itself
and the inclination prompt you to send these friends of
yours a few words of greeting.'

On my next visit to Colvin I found him in a state of
delight at the honour thus paid him ; and handing me his
letter in answer, he asked if I thought that it would do.
When I said that I had received the same appeal he was
visibly depressed and withdrew his reply. I print it now as
an example of his punctiliousness and his attitude to life
and duty :—

' 35 *Palace Gardens Terrace, W. 8, 12.11.25.*

' DEAR SIR,—Writing in my 80th year and from a sick-
room, I cannot return much except bald thanks to you,

and to the young men and women students on whose behalf you write, for their wish that I should send some words of greeting in acknowledgment of their kind thoughts about me.

' The best advice I can give from my own experience is— In all your thoughts and actions accustom yourselves to be guided by any motive rather than the desire of your own success. To beat others in the competition of life is not half so interesting as to throw yourself into causes and interests which lie outside the question of your own success or failure : and of such the world is full. This is not to say, do not do anything short of your best in any department of life or work to which you may be called : but do it for the best's sake and not for the reward's sake nor for the sake of victory. My own life, so far as I am capable of judging it, has been instinctively lived on this principle : the source of the instinct having no doubt been my father, who was the most beautifully unselfish and kindhearted of men.

' To break for a moment the habit of privacy which I am accustomed to observe concerning my own affairs, I am going out of the world a poorer man in money than I came into it ; but may not that life count itself a rich one which won such a world's treasure as my wife for its own, and such a friendship—to name the foremost and most famous among many—as that of Louis Stevenson ?—Yours faithfully,   SIDNEY COLVIN '

Now and then he would hire a car for a country ride through districts round London which he had known in his youth ; but he always returned somewhat saddened by the changes that time had wrought : where he had known trees and meadows, finding nothing but bricks and mortar. On one of the last of such excursions I accompanied him— to Ken Wood, the preservation of which was the final enthusiasm of his life. To attain this end he worked hard, in public and private letters ; as I am sure Sir Arthur Crosfield, the prime mover, would testify.

I did what I could to teach him one or two simple forms of Patience ; but in vain. He would not learn : partly, I suspect, because his heart was with Backgammon, which he and Lady Colvin had played almost every evening of their married life and possibly longer.

As he grew feebler his memory became so bad that he often related the same incident or asked advice on the same point as many as three times during a single visit. One thing that he had much on his mind, which I am sure I heard in identical words thirty times, I take pleasure in recording, and that was his expression of gratitude to his servants—Edith Mattocks, Bessie Went (the daughter of his father's coachman), and Agatha Trist—for their care of him. No one, he used to say, ever could have had greater consideration or kindness.

To the last he wooed sleep by reciting passages from the poets, for his memory, although so unresponsive to what occurred yesterday, could reproduce with faithfulness all that he had seen or learned in the remote period of his youth : so much so that when he was in particularly low spirits I used to find that a few questions as to his Suffolk or Cambridge or early London days would quickly restore his serenity and even get him into a state of glow. He would describe Edward FitzGerald as he was accustomed to see him in his shawl about Woodbridge, a rather frightening figure to childish eyes ; oyster feasts at Ipswich when a shilling a hundred was the price and you washed them down with Felix Cobbold's stout ; or, passing to a later time, he would talk vividly about those strange creatures, Simeon Solomon and Charles Augustus Howell. As he returned more and more to the early times I noticed an increased old-fashionedness in his manner ; towards the end his ' thank-you ' was ' thankee ' unalloyed.

For the last two years he never took leave of me at the door—for it was his courteous custom, when well enough, to conduct me thither in person—without saying that I should not find him there next week ; and he was, I am

348 THE COLVINS AND THEIR FRIENDS

sure, disappointed as, morning after morning, the long
night over, he was conscious that he was still alive and
alone.

Sidney Colvin died, in his eighty-second year, on May 11,
1927. After cremation, his remains were laid beside those
of his wife and her younger son in the cemetery at the end
of Church Row, Hampstead. On the tombstone, which
was designed by Mr. Basil Champneys, was incised, by
Colvin's wish, the passage from Cicero's *De Senectute*
which runs thus in English : ' Whatever is natural must be
accounted good. When death comes to youth, Nature is
up in arms and revolts. Yet to old men, what is more
natural than dying ? '

At St. Martin-in-the-Fields a memorial service was held.
I quote the *Times* list of those who attended : ' Colonel and Mrs.
J. M. C. Colvin and Miss Camilla Colvin, Miss Brenda Colvin,
Mrs. Atwood Colvin, Miss Louise De V. Colvin, Miss Nella
Colvin, Sir Arthur Pinero, Sir Martin Conway, Lady Jekyll,
Lady Dilke, Sir Frederic Kenyon, Major-General Sir Louis
Jackson, Sir Charles Bayley, Sir Albert Gray, Sir Frederick
Macmillan, Mr. and Mrs. Laurence Binyon, Mr. Lionel Cust,
Professor A. R. Forsyth, Dr. and the Hon. Mrs. Dawtrey
Drewitt, Mrs. W. K. Clifford, Mrs. F. Payne, Miss Mary
Dunlop Smith, Mr. Selwyn Image, Mrs. W. B. Gladstone,
Mr. and Mrs. Frank Gibson, Mr. Percy Anderson, Mr. L. F.
Schuster, Sir Israel Gollancz, the Hon. Mrs. Taddeo Wiel,
Mr. and Mrs. Henry Sturgis, Mr. Geoffrey S. Williams, Mr.
A. R. Hogg, Lady (Edward) Bradford, Sir Charles Holmes
(representing the National Gallery), Mr. J. P. Heseltine,
Mrs. Theodore McKenna, Mr. H. W. Carrington (represent-
ing the Robert Louis Stevenson Club), Mr. Donald Macbeth,
Mr. Alec Martin (hon. secretary, representing the National
Art Collections Fund), Mr. Henry Oppenheimer, Mr. Alfred
Yockney, Mr. Arundell Esdaile, Mrs. Carslake Bovill, Mr.
Edmund Brocklebank, Professor A. M. Hind (representing
the British Museum), Mr. Campbell Dodgson, Mr. E. V.
Lucas, Mr. J. D. Gilson, Dr. D. S. MacColl, Mrs. Porter,

Mrs. J. L. Garvin, Mrs. Geoffrey Madan, and Mr. Arthur Yallop Wigg.'

Among the many testimonies to Colvin's sterling character and distinction as a scholar, critic, and administrator, which were printed in the papers, I quote only from one, with its more personal note, by his friend J. L. Garvin, in the *Observer*. Under the title ' A Perfect Friend,' Mr. Garvin wrote thus : ' At fourscore and two almost, Sidney Colvin, like Southey, has died amongst his books. Even the books, well-known and well-beloved, had become shadows in a world of shadows. His disappearance severs the personal link between this second quarter of the twentieth century and things so long ago that no man left living remembers them. Suppose we were talking of Mitford, the historian of Greece, who died in 1827 at nearly the same age. Mitford could recollect the heyday of Chatham and Washington and Pitt and Fox ; and of Johnson, Burke, Gibbon, Sheridan, Goldsmith, to name but a few. Colvin's memories were better, for his nature enriched them.

' His own work was good in several ways and part of it admirable. But his name will live longest for a different reason. He gave the best of his life to others, and his devotion was a legend. The record of " the irritable race of writers " is full of wounded vanities, real and imaginary offences, susceptible egotisms, feeling pin-pricks like poisoned stilettos ; spites and grudges ; grotesque misunderstandings and rancorous hallucinations. Literary history knows nothing to surpass Sidney Colvin's lifelong example of staunch and efficient unselfishness. As a boy he was steeped in Spenser, and that explained him. He meant to live for chivalry and the sense of beauty. As to ethics, though he was no orthodox believer, unselfishness was the essence of his code and the truth of his practice.

' To Stevenson he was the " perfect friend." Taking it for all and all, and reckoning a fine discipline of feeling that cannot be fully valued until things yet unpublished are revealed, no writer ever owed more to another man through

twenty years of life, and through more years after death,
than Stevenson owed to this elder brother in letters. Colvin's
other and greater distinction was that he married one of
the wonderful women of her time. His Spenserian dedication to her looked to the foolish like a rather old-fashioned,
square-toed attentiveness. It belonged in fact to the fibres
of his being and to his inmost notion of a gentleman. A
little exact and punctilious in his manners, the feelings
behind them were often Quixotic. His wife was no Dulcinea,
but as like Minerva with a heart as any mortal woman
may be.'

Mr. Hugh Walpole's tribute, written for this book, I
print in full at this point, not only for its fine quality and
summarizing value, but because it expresses what many
young men must have felt in their relation to these two
sympathetic elderly encouragers : ' It was one of the great
pieces of good fortune in my life that the Colvins were among
my first friends in London. The customary phrase to use
about people who during their lifetime were very popular
is that they had a genius for friendship ; it is a term more
misused than almost any other, but for once it must be said.
Friendship isn't an easy habit in these hurried noisy days ;
and to have many friends, to give each one an individual
colour so that not only do you seem to be dealing with them
as though they were unique in your life but you do actually
make them unique, this is a gift of the rarest and most
precious. It was the supreme gift that the Colvins possessed.

' They were fortunate, I think, in being perfect comple-
ments the one of the other ; they were alike in their enthusiasm and generosity of heart, and their passionate mutual
love gave them a beautiful unity, but they were quite
separate in their approach to life. Colvin was traditional ;
it is well known of course that he was always on the look-
out for new talent in art and letters ; but what he liked
was a new talent with old roots, and in the conduct of life
he was all for the traditions, perfect courtesy, an unflinching code of honour, decent manners and a certain avoidance

of the crudities that modern life seemed to him to be too fond of emphasizing.

' Lady Colvin was with him in her love for fine courtesies and honourable dealing, but beyond these she had a deep understanding of all the complexities of modern life ; you could not tell Colvin everything, because to shock him was to hurt him too deeply ; but there was nothing that you could not tell to her.

' She was not at all the sweet gentle white-haired old lady. With her passionate interest in everything, her fiery partisanship, as she sat there in her chair, the inevitable feather boa round her neck like a banner, the most exciting thing in life seemed always just to have happened to her. The astonishing thing was that the exciting event, when you came to hear of it, was something that had occurred to someone else rather than to herself. We all know that we spend most of our days in listening to the adventures of our friends and longing for the moment to arrive when we shall be able to slip in a word of our own affairs ; but in her case she joined so eagerly in the experiences of other people that you were amazed that she had time or energy left for her own. She was a terrible trap for egoists, and yet always after you had told her of your own adventures you caught from her a sense of the excitement of other people's and that did your egoism good.

' Because her own personal life had been in its early days a tragic one there was nothing in the life of another that she could not understand. Her curiosity was never greedy ; she loved to hear all the details but passed on from them always to give fully her pity, her admiration, her praise and her irony.

' This is certainly true of her : that beyond anyone else I have ever known she had the gift of telling you that you had been a fool without humiliating you. My own first meeting with them was in their house at the Museum ; a very remarkable evening for me because at that dinner-party I met for the first time two or three people who were to be among my best and most enduring friends. It was exciting for me too because only a short while before the Reading Room at the Museum had been my only place of resort ; there I used to sit the day long, knowing no one, wondering whether I ever would, and then only a few months later within the walls of the same building all doors were open to me.

' Colvin with his fine taste, and his bridging, as perhaps no one at that time save Sir Edmund Gosse did, the space between the old world of letters and the new, was an ideal friend for me ; and looking back now I wonder at the patience with which he listened to my infant prattle and accepted gravely my juvenile dogmatisms. It was very exciting to me also to have for a friend someone who had known Stevenson and Henley, Browning and George Eliot, Tennyson and Pater so intimately ; who, although he had known these men, yet felt that there was something in the new generation too.

' Robert Ross once said that Lady Colvin played the Cabot to Sidney Colvin's Columbus. They were teased sometimes, I think, about their eager quest for new talent, but it is a pity for the young generation to-day that there is nobody now, so honest and so generous, engaged on that same task.

' But Lady Colvin cared more for the person than for the talent. Without ever interfering, without ever demanding anything, without a reproach for neglect or a sign of personal hurt, she loved her friends always for what they were getting rather than for what they were giving her.

' When she was disappointed she found gallant reasons for defending the disappointer. She was by nature sharply perceptive ; no one ever had a quicker eye for little snobberies, falsehoods, disloyalties ; but by some especial gift of her own she converted these mean things, although she never denied that they were mean, into a general inevitable pattern of life.

' Colvin was more sentimental than she, and if something

looked ugly he would push it away and turn his back upon it, although his loyalty to his friends was quite as true and steadfast as hers ; but she shrank from nothing, and there never has been anyone who more truly, while she regretted the sin, loved the sinner.

' She had to the last that certain stamp of a great character, an eager acceptance of the whole of life. Every little pleasure was exciting to her ; she was like a child going to the world for the first time over a new play, a new book, a new picture. Great men like Henry James and Conrad found her the easiest companion because while she admired their genius she raised them as human beings on to no kind of pedestal. No one inspired her with awe, but no one rejoiced more completely in the fine things that her friends did.

' Lastly, to me her greatest quality of all was her tenderness. When you have been hurt or done something foolish or said some foolish word it is very hard to find a friend who will listen to the event without rising a little in his or her own estimation. The hardest things in the world are to give sympathy without mawkishness, to give advice without arrogance, but Lady Colvin in her concern over the event forgot herself and all personal reaction.

' She was a very great woman because she loved without selfishness, was intelligent without preciousness, laughed at life without cruelty and had great principles of conduct without priggishness.'

I am glad to be able to add to Mr. Walpole's tribute the words of an American writer whom I have already quoted in this book. Referring to the collection of letters to Colvin and his wife, recently sold, Mr. Christopher Morley wrote : ' Even if one had not already known it by personal memory and gratitude, one can divine what rare hospitality of spirit was in the two Colvins that caused so many to come to them with trust and homage. Sidney was always a knightly name.'

Mr. Walpole and Mr. Morley are among the Colvins'

Z

later friends.   Let me bring this volume to a close with the words of one who had known them nearly sixty years, Mr. Basil Champneys: 'I gratefully record that my friendship with the Colvins lasted and was strengthened to the very end ; that in retrospect the two are so closely united as to form one almost indistinguishable memory of what has counted among the special boons and privileges of a lifetime.'

INDEX

355

Printed in Great Britain by T. and A. Constable Ltd
at the University Press, Edinburgh